Books in the Security Series

Computer Security Fundamentals
ISBN: 0-13-171129-6

Information Security: Principles and Practices
ISBN: 0-13-154729-1

Firewalls and VPNs: Principles and Practices
ISBN: 0-13-154731-3

Security Policies and Procedures: Principles and Practices
ISBN: 0-13-186691-5

Network Defense and Countermeasures: Principles and Practices
ISBN: 0-13-171126-1

Intrusion Detection: Principles and Practices
ISBN: 0-13-154730-5

Disaster Recovery: Principles and Practices
ISBN: 0-13-171127-X

Computer Forensics: Principles and Practices
ISBN: 0-13-154727-5

Security Policies and Procedures

Principles and Practices

SARI STERN GREENE, CISSP

Upper Saddle River, New Jersey 07458

Library of Congress Cataloging-in-Publication Data

Greene, Sari Stern
  Security policies and procedures : principles and practices / Sari Stern Greene.
    p. cm. -- (Security series)
  Includes bibliographical references and index.
  ISBN 0-13-186691-5
  1. Industries--Security measures. 2. Computer networks--Security measures. I. Title. II. Security series (Upper Saddle River, N.J.)
  HV8290.G745 2006
  658.4'7--dc22
                    2005012527

Vice President and Publisher: Natalie E. Anderson
Executive Acquisitions Editor, Print: Stephanie Wall
Executive Acquisitions Editor, Media: Richard Keaveny
Product Development Manager: Eileen Bien Calabro
Editorial Project Manager: Emilie Herman
Editorial Assistants: Brian Hoehl, Alana Meyers, Sandra Bernales
Senior Media Project Managers: Cathi Profitko, Steve Gagliostro
Marketing Manager: Sarah Davis
Marketing Assistant: Lisa Taylor
Managing Editor: Lynda Castillo
Production Project Manager: Lynne Breitfeller
Manufacturing Buyer: Natacha Moore
Design Manager: Maria Lange
Art Director/Interior Design/Cover Design: Blair Brown
Cover Illustration/Photo: Gettyimages/Photodisc Blue
Composition/Full-Service Project Management: Custom Editorial Productions Inc.
Cover Printer: Courier/Stoughton
Printer/Binder: Courier/Stoughton

Credits and acknowledgments borrowed from other sources and reproduced, with permission, in this textbook appear on appropriate page within text.

Microsoft® and Windows® are registered trademarks of the Microsoft Corporation in the U.S.A. and other countries. Screen shots and icons reprinted with permission from the Microsoft Corporation. This book is not sponsored or endorsed by or affiliated with the Microsoft Corporation.

Pearson Education LTD.
Pearson Education Singapore, Pte. Ltd
Pearson Education, Canada, Ltd
Pearson Education–Japan

Pearson Education Australia PTY, Limited
Pearson Education North Asia Ltd
Pearson Educación de Mexico, S.A. de C.V.
Pearson Education Malaysia, Pte. Ltd

10 9 8 7 6 5 4 3
ISBN 0-13-186691-5

In loving memory of my parents, Edith and Irving Stern, and my mother-in-law, Patricia Boutiette.

Contents in Brief

Table of Contents

PART THREE Regulatory Compliance 387

Chapter 12 Regulatory Compliance for Financial Institutions 389

Security Series Walk-Through

The Prentice Hall Security Series prepares students for careers in IT security by providing practical advice and hands-on training from industry experts. All of the books in this series are filled with real-world examples to help readers apply what they learn to the workplace. This walk-through highlights the key elements in this book created to help students along the way.

Chapter Objectives. These short-term, attainable goals outline what will be covered in the chapter text.

Chapter Introduction. Each chapter begins with an explanation of why these topics are important and how the chapter fits into the overall organization of the book.

Chapter Objectives

After reading this chapter and completing the exercises, you will be able to do the following:

- Evaluate an organization's security policy.
- Create a basic security policy.
- Update a target system's patches.
- Shut down unnecessary ports.
- Scan a system for vulnerabilities.
- Activate port filtering in Windows 2000 or Windows XP.
- Use a port scanner.

Introduction

As you learn more about computer security you will learn new techniques for securing a particular system. However it is critical to be able to assess a system's security. This chapter discusses the essential steps in assessing a system for vulnerabilities. It is also important to assess a system's security level prior to implementing any security measures. Information about the current state of affairs will help you appropriately address any vulnerabilities.

IN PRACTICE: Using NetCop

Let us begin with NetCop, since it is one of the easiest to use port scanners available. IT can be obtained from many sites. You can download NetCop at http://www.cotse.com/pscan.htm.

When you download NetCop you get a simple self-extracting executable that will install the program on your machine and will even put a shortcut in your program menu. When you launch NetCop, it has a very simple and intuitive screen.

You can type in a single IP address, or a range of IP addresses. That makes this tool particularly useful for network administrators that wish to check for open ports on their entire network. Four our purposes we will begin by scanning a single IP address, our own machine. You can either type your machines actual IP address, or simply the loop back address (127.0.0.1). When you type in a single IP address and click on scan now, you can see it checking each and every port. This is very methodical but also a bit slow.

You can, of course, stop the scan at any time you desire. These results are from a machine the author used specifically for this book. You would, of course, get different results on different machines.

You can see that NetCop gives you useful information about open ports. Before you choose to close any port, you should make sure that the port is not one that you actually need for system operations. The following websites list all well-known ports.

In Practice. Takes concepts from the book and shows how they are applied in the workplace.

FYI. Additional information on topics that go beyond the scope of the book.

FYI: The Microsoft Patch

Go to http://www.microsoft.com and on the left hand side of the website you will find a link under the sub heading Resources, entitled Windows Update. If you select that option and follow the very clear instructions you will be able to correct any and all Windows patch issues on a target machine.

7

twork is to probe the network. This means using for vulnerabilities. These tools are often the same tempting to breach your security, so it is critical n this section we will use three separate analysis other tools freely available on the Internet, and ever these three are the most commonly used. We er, NetBrute, and NetCop. Also this section will ions in this book. We will conduct the exercise d of the chapter. The reason for this is simply that tical aspects of applying these tools Additional f the chapter.

Caution
Security Audit

When conducting a security audit, it's critical that you document the specific steps taken during the audit, any flaws found, and what corrective actions where taken.

1

Caution. Critical, not to be forgotten information that is directly relevant to the surrounding text.

Test Your Skills

Each chapter ends with exercises designed to reinforce the chapter objectives. Four types of evaluation follow each chapter.

Multiple Choice Questions. Test the reader's understanding of the text.

MULTIPLE CHOICE QUESTIONS

1. How does a JavaScript interpreter identify that a script is being used inside a web page?
   A. `<JavaScript>` tag
   B. `<SCRIPT>` tag
   C. `<JAVASCRIPT>` tag
   D. `<Script>` tag

2. Which of the following is NOT a valid language attribute for a web page script?
   A. JavaScript
   B. JavaScript1.2
   C. JavaScript1.3
   D. JavaScript1.4

3. Are JavaScripts and HTML tags case-sensitive?
   A. Both are case sensitive
   B. Both are case insensitive
   C. JavaScripts only are case sensitive
   D. HTML tags only are case sensitive

Exercises. Brief, guided projects designed around individual concepts found in the chapter.

EXERCISES

Exercise 4.1: Patching the System

1. Locate a system running Windows 2000 or later. Your own personal computer would be the preferred system. You may find that public computer labs not

Projects. Longer, guided projects that combine lessons from the chapter.

PROJECTS

Project 4.1: Personal Policy Password System

1. Analyze or develop a personal policy password system for your PC and online accounts.

```
"<P>Welcome to Internet Banking</P>"
"<P>Click NEXT to Continue...</P>"
```

2. Determine if your passwords are secure using the four basic password rules presented in this chapter. W

3. Write down if your passwords were secure and the steps that you will take to make them secure.

Case Study. A real-world scenario to resolve using lessons learned in the chapter.

Case Study

Now that you have learned how to insert simple JavaScripts into web pages, with calls to document.write Has the site used any of the features you have learned about in this Lesson?

1. Import the appropriate Namespaces

2. Execute the Query/Instruction

Using a web design package, or just notepad and your web browser, create a front page for an Internet banking that uses document.write to display text within the <BODY> section of the page. A link should be created to the login page, which will be examined in the next chapter.

- The Computer Security Institute: http://www.gocsi.com/
- The Computer Security Clearing House http://csrc.nist.gov/
- The Computer Emergency Response Team http://www.cert.org/

This icon appears in the margin wherever additional information or links to downloads can be found at the series companion Web site, **www.prenhall.com/security**

Preface

According to the Pew Internet and American Life Project, "on a typical day at the end of 2004, some 70 million American adults logged onto the Internet to use email, get news, access government information, check out health and medical information, participate in auctions, book travel reservations, research their genealogy, gamble, seek out romantic partners, and engage in countless other activities" (**www.pewinternet.org**).

We live in a truly amazing world where, with a click of a mouse, ideas can be shared across continents and cultures. From the fall of communism to delicate telesurgery, this ability to share information has profoundly and positively impacted our world. As wonderful as the interconnectivity is, however, there is a real and present danger. At risk is the confidentiality, integrity, and availability of the very information infrastructure that we have come to depend upon to run our lives, our economy, and our government.

Information security has taken on a new meaning in the twenty-first century. As security professionals, we have an obligation to design, adopt, influence, and implement environments that protect information and information systems from misuse. Information security is more than an activity and more than a profession—it is a civic duty. Each of us as individuals, organizations, institutions, and governments are entrusted with information. It is our job to honor that trust. This book focuses on achieving that goal.

Information security issues have been studied and deliberated worldwide. The International Organization for Standardization (ISO) has developed and published information security standards referred to as the ISO 17799:2000—Code of Practice for Information Security Management. This code of practice provides a framework for developing information security policies and understanding information security controls. Throughout this book, we reference the ISO 17799:2000 standard. It must be noted that we are using the standard as a framework and that this book is not to be construed as an official interpretation of the ISO 17799:2000. Organizations that choose to implement the standard should purchase the complete document from the ISO (**www.iso.ch**).

Audience

The responsibility for information security does not rest with a single role. This book is intended for anyone who is preparing for a leadership position in business, government, academia, or healthcare. Before embarking on a study of information security, students should have an understanding of the role of information systems in the business world, network infrastructure design, and fundamental security concepts. Mastering the information presented in this book is a must for future information security professionals.

Overview of the Book

Security Policies and Procedures: Principles and Practices is divided into three parts. Part One, Introduction to Policy, is designed to provide the foundation for developing, introducing, and implementing policies. Part Two, Information Security Policy Domains, explores information security policies and procedures across nine security domains. Part Three, Regulatory Compliance, is a practical application of policies and procedures in regard to compliance with federal regulations as well as industry best practices.

Part One: Introduction to Policy

The objective of a policy is to positively influence behavior. The goal of a procedure is to provide direction. Influencing behavior and providing direction are not unique to information security. Chapter 1, Policy Defined, begins by discussing policies and procedures throughout the ages. This historical approach allows us to understand the role that polices and procedures play in society, government, and religion. In Chapter 2, The Elements of a Policy, we will apply that knowledge to the development, introduction, adoption, implementation, and maintenance of security policies. Along the way, we will explore the significant elements and components of successful policies and procedures.

Part Two: Information Security Policy Domains

The goal of information security is to protect information assets and the systems that process, store, and transmit the information. This book focuses on developing policies and supporting activities to achieve this goal. However, before you can begin to write policies, you first must be able to answer the following questions: What are we protecting? Who (and what) are we protecting against? What are the areas of greatest risk and why? Information security is a very broad topic. Chapter 3, Information Security Framework, discusses these questions and introduces the ISO 17799:2000 Code of Practice for Information Security Management. The ISO 17799:2000 document, published by the International Organization for Standardization, has become a widely adopted framework for developing security policies and controls.

We will base our Part Two discussions on nine of the ISO 17799:2000 categories:

- Chapter 4: Security Policy Documents and Organizational Security Policies
- Chapter 5: Asset Classification
- Chapter 6: Personnel Security
- Chapter 7: Physical and Environmental Security
- Chapter 8: Communications and Operations Management
- Chapter 9: Access Control
- Chapter 10: Systems Devlopment and Maintenance
- Chapter 11: Business Continuity Management

Part Three: Regulatory Compliance

The need for and the importance of information security is rapidly increasing. The federal government has recognized this and has adopted a variety of regulations designed to safeguard the privacy of individuals and protect our nation's critical infrastructures. Part Three examines in-depth the impact of regulations as well as compliance requirements. Chapter 12, Regulatory Compliance for Financial Institutions, and Chapter 13, Regulatory Compliance for the Healthcare Sector, examine sector-specific information security requirements. Chapter 14, Regulatory Compliance for Critical Infrastructure, focuses on information security requirements in education, government, and publicly-traded corporations. The last chapter, Chapter 15, Security Policies and Procedures for Small Business, focuses on developing and successfully adopting information security policies and best practices for the small business environment.

Additional Information

Information security is a dynamic field. Throughout the book, you will find references to additional sources of information. We encourage you become familiar with these sources. This book also contains two useful appendices, Appendix A, Resources for Information Security Professionals, and Appendix B, Employee Information Security Policy Affirmation Agreement.

Conventions Used in This Book

To help you get the most from the text, we've used a few conventions throughout the book.

IN PRACTICE: About In Practice

These show readers how to take concepts from the book and apply them in the workplace.

FYI: About FYIs

These boxes offer additional information on topics that go beyond the scope of the book.

Caution

About Cautions

Cautions appear in the margins of the text. They flag critical, not-to-be forgotten information that is directly relevant to the surrounding text.

Snippets and blocks of code are boxed and numbered, and can be downloaded from the companion Web site (**www.prenhall.com/security**).

New key terms appear in **bold italics**.

 This icon appears in the margin wherever more information can be found at the series companion Web site, **www.prenhall.com/security**.

Instructor and Student Resources

Instructor's Resource Center on CD-ROM

The Instructor's Resource Center on CD-ROM (IRC on CD) is distributed to instructors only and is an interactive library of assets and links. It includes:

- Instructor's Manual. Provides instructional tips, an introduction to each chapter, teaching objectives, teaching suggestions, and answers to end-of-chapter questions and problems.

- PowerPoint Slide Presentations. Provides a chapter-by-chapter review of the book content for use in the classroom.

- Test Bank. This TestGen-compatible test bank file can be used with Prentice Hall's TestGen software (available as a free download at: **www.prenhall.com/testgen**). TestGen is a test generator that lets you view and easily edit test bank questions, transfer them to tests, and print in a variety of formats suitable to your teaching situation. The program also offers many options for organizing and displaying test banks and tests. A built-in random number and text generator makes it ideal for creating multiple versions of tests that involve calculations and provides more possible test items than test bank questions. Powerful search and sort functions let you easily locate questions and arrange them in the order you prefer.

Companion Web Site

The Companion Web site (**www.prenhall.com/security**) is a Pearson learning tool that provides students and instructors with online support. Here you will find:

- Interactive Study Guide, a Web-based interactive quiz designed to provide students with a convenient online mechanism for self-testing their comprehension of the book material.

- Additional Web projects and resources to put into practice the concepts taught in each chapter.

About the Author

Sari Stern Greene, CISSP, MCSE, MCT, MCNE, MCNI, CTT, NSA/IAM is President of Sage Data Security, Inc. At Sage, Sari leads a team of experienced security professionals. Sari specializes in providing information security services such as policy and procedure development, information security program development, risk and vulnerability assessments, and disaster recovery / business continuity planning to the financial, health care, and government sectors. Sari is actively involved in the technology and security community. She serves on the Board of Directors of MESDA and is a founding member of the Maine ISSA chapter. She also speaks at security conferences and workshops and has authored numerous information security articles, curriculum, and training materials. You can contact Sari at sari@sagedatasecurity.com.

Acknowledgments

This book was a team effort. Colleagues at and clients of Sage Data Security played an important role in its development. David Jacquet and John Hill Rogers both made significant contributions.

Our clients, who invite us to share their experiences, are a continual source of inspiration and knowledge. The majority of the policies presented in this book were developed for our clients. We are grateful to them for their feedback and their collaborative efforts through the years. Some early ISO policy development work was aided by ISO Security Solutions products. To find out more about their products, visit **www.isosecuritysolutions.com.**

Writing a book is a unique experience. Expertly and very patiently guiding us down this path were our development editors, Chris Katsaropolous and Emilie Herman. Tom Lewis, Ericka McIntyre, and Megan Smith-Creed from CEP turned our raw materials into finished copy. Steve Elliot brought us to Prentice Hall. To all, we say thank you.

This book has been quite an adventure. I am eternally grateful to my sons, Max and Ben, and to my husband, Eric, for their encouragement and devotion.

Quality Assurance

We would like to extend our thanks to the Quality Assurance team for their attention to detail and their efforts to make sure that we got it right.

Technical Editor

Michael L. Denn
Network Security Technology,
Texas State Technical College

Reviewers

Carol Buser
Information Technology
Owens Community College

Jeanne Nelson Furfari
Information Systems Technology
New Hampshire Community Technical College,
Pease Emerging Technologies Campus

Hermann Gruenwald, Ph.D.
University of Alaska, Anchorage

Charles D. Hamby
Computer Systems Technology
Matanuska-Sustina College

Part One

Introduction to Policy

Policy defines the rules, expectations and patterns of behavior. In Part One, we will be exploring policy from a historical, societal, and psychological perspective. Throughout the ages, policy has been used to define a course of action. We will begin with discussing the impact of policy on the development of humankind and how societies have evolved using policies as guides to chart a course through the rapidly changing world. We will apply that knowledge to the role of policy in corporate culture. We will explore in detail the significant elements and components of policy. We will relate the generic concept of policy to the specific requirements of information security. By the end of Part One, you will understand the process of successfully developing, introducing, and implementing information security policies.

- **Chapter 1:** Policy Defined
- **Chapter 2:** The Elements of a Policy

Chapter 1

Policy Defined

Chapter Objectives

After reading this chapter and completing the exercises, you will be able to do the following:

- Describe the cultural significance of policies.
- Recognize the role policy plays in government.
- Evaluate the role policy plays in corporate culture.
- Identify how federal regulations apply to corporations and other organizations.
- Apply the psychology of policy.
- Introduce a policy successfully.
- Achieve acceptance of a policy.
- Enforce a policy.

Introduction

When we hear the word *policy,* it seldom inspires great interest. What you might find interesting is the crucial role policies play in so many aspects of a corporation's operations, a society's rule of law, or a government's posture in the world. For those of you who may think that policies are nothing more than a collection of restrictive rules we are obliged to follow, we have some information to share that might change your mind. Without policies, people would live in a state of chaos, subject to the whim of anyone in power, and constantly having to re-invent the "wheel" of organizational behavior. Of course, since we ourselves create policies, they are never perfect. We might even say that bad policy has caused war, social unrest, corporate espionage, and myriad other problems throughout history. Though we are focused on information security policies in this book, it is important to gain an overall understanding of general concepts before we get specific.

In this chapter, we will explore policies from a historical perspective, talk about how humankind has been affected, and learn how societies have evolved using policies as guides to chart a course through the rapidly changing world. We will discuss the role of policy in the culture of a typical corporation, which is another way of relaying how people are impacted by corporate policies. We will also explore the role of policy in government. It is important that we have a clear understanding of the topics in this chapter before moving on. There are many avoidable pitfalls along the way to creating effective policies. Once confused, the effects can be disastrous. If treated properly as "living," dynamic documents meant to inform as well as direct people's behaviors and choices, policies are a critical component in the health of any organization.

Defining Policy

According to **www.merriamwebster.com**, *policy* is defined as:

1. prudence or wisdom in the management of affairs
2. management or procedure based primarily on material interest.
3. a definite course or method of action selected from among alternatives and in light of given conditions to guide and determine present and future decisions.

Information security policy can be defined as a document that states how an organization plans to protect the organization's tangible and intangible information assets. We also use these subdefinitions:

- Management instructions indicating a course of action, a guiding principle, or an appropriate procedure.

- High-level statements that provide guidance to workers who must make present and future decisions.

- Generalized requirements that must be written down and communicated to certain groups of people inside, and in some cases outside, the organization.

These definitions are very important, but what may be more important is to think of policies as "institutional memory." This means that policies transcend the current personnel within an organization and act as a sort of written memory for how things should operate, and how people within an organization, and in some cases outside of an organization, should behave. The goal of good information security policies is to require people to

FYI: What Are Tangible and Intangible Information Assets?

Let's start with the easy one: tangible information assets. Tangible assets include the facilities, hardware, software, media, supplies, documentation, and IT staff budget that support the processing, storage, and delivery of information.

Another way to think about tangible is physical, or touchable. Some examples of tangible information assets are computer systems and the data residing on them, including our customer data, employee data, and all other digital information; all of the paper and other hard copy information in existence; and, indirectly, all the people in our organization.

Intangible assets are both harder to define and to quantify. Intangible assets include the body of information an organization must have to conduct its mission of business. They include such things as our reputation, intellectual capital, intellectual property, and, indirectly, the people in our organization.

Note that an information asset may contain both tangible and intangible components.

protect information, which in turn protects the organization, its people, and its customers. Because information exists in many places, it is important to address more than computer systems in an information security policy. Our policy should seek to secure information that exists in three distinct states:

- Where and how it is **stored**
- Where and how it is **processed**
- Where and how it is **transmitted**

Given these three states, it is also important to identify where information resides, which again is in three general places:

- Information technology systems
- Paper
- Human brains

Table 1.1 illustrates the relationship between the three states of information and the places where information resides. When writing policies, we must first know what we are protecting and where it exists.

TABLE 1.1 The residences and states of information.

Information Residences	Information States		
	Stored	**Processed**	**Transmitted**
Information Systems	Hard drives; physical memory; backup tapes; all portable storage devices such as CD-ROMs, floppy disks, and thumb drives; cell phones; cameras	Server computers, mainframe computers, desktop computers, portable devices	Via Internet, Wide Area Network (WAN), Local Area Network (LAN), wired or wireless
Paper	Desks, file cabinets, pockets, briefcases, shredding rooms	Copy machines, fax machines, read by people	Fax, standard postal service, courier, pictures, read by people
Human Brain	Long- and short-term memory	All the synapses firing	Spoken and sign language

Looking at Policy through the Ages

Sometimes an idea seems more credible if we begin with an understanding that it has been around for a long time and has withstood the tests of time. Since the beginning of social structure, people have sought to form order out of perceived chaos and to find ways to sustain ideas that benefit the advancement and improvement of a social structure. The best way we have found yet is in recognizing our common problems and finding ways to avoid causing or experiencing them in our future endeavors. Policies, laws, codes of justice, and other such documents came into existence almost as soon as alphabets and the written word allowed them. This doesn't mean that before the written word there were no policies or laws. It does mean that we have no reference to spoken policy and law, so we will confine our discussion to written documents we know existed, and still exist.

We are going to look back through time at some examples of written policies that had and still have a profound effect on societies across the globe, including our own. We are not going to concern ourselves with the function of these documents. Rather, we will begin by noting the basic commonality we can see in the why and how they were created to serve a larger social order. Some are called laws, some codes, and some policies, and what they all have in common is that they were created out of a perceived

FYI: Myriad of Policy

If you "google" (**www.google.com**) the word *policy,* no less than 400,000 page hits will be offered to you, some historical and some current in-use policies. What you will find browsing through these many different page links is that there are too many kinds of policy to mention in just one book. There is foreign policy, privacy policy, environmental policy, drug control policy, education policy, trade policy, and of course information security policy, to name just a few. In addition to policy there is law, which can be thought of as policy adopted by a society through various legislative means to govern its people.

need to guide human behavior in foreseeable circumstances, and even to guide human behavior when circumstances could not be or were not foreseen. Equal to the goal of policy to sustain order and protection is the absolute requirement that our policy be changeable in response to dynamic conditions, which we call *change drivers*. We will cover change drivers more completely in later chapters.

The Bible as Ancient Policy

Let's start by going back in time 3,000 years and take a look at one of the earliest examples of written policy still in existence, the Torah. For those of the Jewish faith, the Torah is the Five Books of Moses. Christians refer to the Torah as the Old Testament of the Bible. If we put aside the religious aspects of this work, we can examine the Torah's importance from a social perspective and its lasting impact on the entire world. It was not called a policy, but we ask you to decide if the content of the Torah has similar intent and flavor to the policies we will learn about in this course.

Regardless of your familiarity with the Torah, it has profoundly impacted you and the society you live in. The Torah may have been the very beginning of a codified social order. It contains rules for living as a member of a social structure. These rules were and are intended to provide guidance for behavior, the choices people make, and their interaction with each other and society as a whole. Some of the business rules of the Torah include:

- Not to use false weights and measures.

- Not to charge interest.

- To be honest in all dealings.

- To pay wages promptly.

FYI: Life in Ancient Times

It might be helpful to first understand what life was like around 1000 B.C.E. Picture yourself in a world with rampant and uncontrolled disease, crime, social unrest, poverty, and superstition. A world where the rules people lived by were arbitrary, decided in the moment, driven by reactionary instinct or dictated by some mystical superstition without any basis in fact.

Now consider our own society. Disease is largely controlled, or at least treated with medicine. Crime is controlled through a justice system, including written law enforced by police and upheld and adjudicated by a judicial system, and in which convicted offenders are punished in a penitentiary system. In further contrast, social unrest is built into our system of free speech, poverty is managed with varying degrees of success by a social welfare system, and superstition has largely given way to science as we understand more and more of our world. No one would argue that our society is perfect, of course. But let's focus for now on the progress we have made.

- To allow a worker in the field to eat the produce he is harvesting, and for the employee not to take more than he can eat from his employer.

- To allow fields to lie fallow every seven years.

- To help those in physical or financial need.

- To give to the poor and not turn them away empty-handed.

- To fulfill promises to others.

Are these rules beginning to look familiar? These are policies! We can clearly see similarities between these ancient social rules and our modern social standards. Information security policies have the same goal: to secure our organizational information and protect it from all foreseeable harm while also leaving flexibility for the unforeseen.

As mentioned earlier, we are not concerned with the content of these ancient documents as much as the reason for their creation. The various common experiences of all peoples led to common behaviors and choices, which all too often led to the ills plaguing their social systems. With careful thought, clearly stated and communicated in written form, many of these social problems could be avoided by giving people rules to guide them through their daily lives. Any person who could follow these rules would certainly find life easier to navigate. And if *everyone* followed the rules, the entire community would become more stable. Time previously spent avoiding problems could instead be spent improving the community.

The U.S. Constitution as a Policy Revolution

Let's look at a document with which you may be a little more familiar: the Constitution of the United States of America. Our Constitution is the oldest written national constitution still in effect in the world. Again, it is important to understand the importance of this revolutionary document from a historical perspective.

The Constitution is a collection of articles and amendments codifying all aspects of American government and citizen's rights. The articles themselves are very broad principles that recognize that the world will change. This is where the amendments play their role as additions to the original document. Through time, these amendments have extended rights to more and more Americans and have allowed for circumstances our founders could not have foreseen. The founders wisely built into the framework of the document a process for changing it while still adhering to its fundamental tenets. Though it takes great effort to amend the Constitution, the process begins with an idea, informed by people's experience, when they see a need for change. We learn some valuable lessons from the Constitution, most importantly that our policies need to be dynamic enough to adjust to changing environments.

The Constitution and the Torah were created from distinct environments, but they both had a similar goal: To serve as rules, to guide our behavior and the behavior of those in power. Though our information security policies may not be used for such lofty purposes as the documents we have reviewed so far, you will see that the culture of every organization supports the greater society of which it is a part, and the need for guidance, direction, and roles remains the same.

Defining the Role of Policy in Government

Now that we have a perspective on how policies have shaped civilizations and their general characteristics, we can narrow our focus to the role that policies play in government. Again, governments use an endless variety of policies to dictate specific actions, decisions, and responses to circumstances that fall under the rules of each policy area. A policy area can be thought of as a general topic relating specific behavior and expectations. For instance, in the area of foreign policy you would find language related to a government's dealings with other sovereign nations; in the area of education policy you would find language related to federal standards for public and private education. It will be helpful to think of government as the elected and appointed officials charged with providing the direction and supervision of public affairs. In addition to policy there is law, which can be thought of as policy adopted by a society through various legislative means to govern its people. Laws have specific civil and criminal penalties that can be imposed for violations.

FYI: Foreign Policy 101

The first official U.S. documented foreign policy came from President James Monroe in 1823, known as the Monroe Doctrine. This was the first policy to not only assert our independence from European powers, but also to relay our interest in protecting the whole of the American continent, including South America, from invasion or colonization by any European power. In the Monroe Doctrine, we agreed to stay out of European affairs and all internal struggles unless our own interests were threatened, but we made it clear that any attempt at colonization in any part of the American continent would be considered a threat to our interests. This marks the official beginning of United States foreign policy.

To this day, the Monroe Doctrine is a part of our foreign policy. Foreign policy is defined as the ways and means used by a nation in its affairs with other nations. The policies must support the nation's goals and provide guidance to those who govern in dealing with any eventuality we may encounter in our relations with other nations.

Public affairs include every aspect of governing over a society, from providing defense, social services, law enforcement and judicial systems, postal service, public education, and others. Our federal government's policies apply to individual citizens and almost every kind of group to which individual citizens belong, including businesses, social and civic organizations, and state/local governments. The challenge for policy makers in the United States has been greater than for any other national government in history. The nature of our free society, the individual states each with their own individual policies, and the wide diversity of cultures in America makes the task of creating governing policies especially challenging

If we think of a government as one very large organization, we can apply the same reasoning and see the same needs as in any organization. Organizations and government alike need structure, consistency, and fairness to be successful.

Defining the Role of Policy in Corporate Culture

We began this chapter with broad examples of the impact of policy throughout history, and then narrowed our focus to the role of policy in government. Now we can concentrate on the organizations for which we will be writing our information security policies, namely businesses. So far we have explored the reasons why policies are so important to any group of people. The same circumstances that lead us to create policies for social culture and government culture exist for our corporate culture as well. *Corporate culture* can be defined as the shared attitudes, values, goals, and practices that characterize a company or corporation. So how does a corporation communicate its attitudes, values, goals, and practices to all of its employees, vendors, partners, and customers? You guessed it: With policies!

Policies contribute to the material success of any corporation by supporting the organizational goals and by providing expectations that help sustain consistency in the services, products, and culture within a corporation.

Consistency in Services, Products, and Corporate Culture

Consistency is fundamentally important from many different perspectives. As customers, we all want to be able to rely on a consistent experience in every product we buy. If we like a specific brand of dishwashing soap for instance, we would be very dissatisfied if it was different every time we bought it. As employees, we all want to be able to rely on the rules at our job remaining the same day to day. If the rules should change, we want some notice so we can prepare for the changes. How does a company create consistency for it customers and employees? The answer, of course, is effective policies. Of course, policies alone guarantee absolutely nothing as they require diligence, communication, training, and enforcement by people to make them truly effective and beneficial.

There is one sure way to destroy morale within an organization, and that is to be inconsistent regarding disciplinary actions or rewards. If two people violate the same rule in the same way, their punishment should be equal. Likewise, if two people excel in the same task the same way, their reward should also be equal. Taking the time and effort to prepare careful and clearly written policies will ensure that when similar problems occur, or similar excellence should be rewarded, the punishment or reward remains consistent no matter who is in charge. Remember the concept of "institutional memory" and how important it is that a corporation's expectations don't change with every change in personnel. The last thing any company wants is for two people, who have been treated differently regarding the same situation, to meet one day and exchange their stories. Many court cases owe their existence to a lack of consistency. From this perspective,

IN PRACTICE: Supporting Organizational Goals

Let's take the example of a large fast-food restaurant chain. One of the organizational goals of the restaurant chain is to consistently serve fresh, hot food to its customers no matter which of the locations a customer visits, in order to build customer loyalty and create repeat business. How can a policy support this organizational goal? It will be helpful first to try to think of a way to support this goal without *any* policy. What would happen if every location's operations were based on each restaurant manager's preferences or if individual employees decided for themselves? Without policy, this restaurant chain would never have grown past its first location.

Let's take another look at that organizational goal, and how policies can support its realization.

Consistently serve fresh, hot food: It is not enough to have a recipe, we must have a policy for our managers instructing them how to train cooks to prepare our food according to this recipe. We must have a policy for how the quality of the food will be measured. We must have a policy for how long a customer can expect to wait before being served, and another policy requiring a certain procedure be followed by the person serving the food to the customer. We must have policies dealing with sanitation, the purchasing of ingredients, and the rotation of those ingredients to ensure freshness. Lastly, we must have a process to ensure that our policies and procedures are being followed by all employees. In order to reach our goals of quality and consistency, we need a policy that is followed at every location and that dictates what will happen when our food preparation policy is violated. Without appropriate consequences, policies can be ignored, thus rendering them ineffective.

Employees can be trained to meet expectations. Since this chain of restaurants may have locations across the nation, their written policies are not subject to cultural differences, differences of opinion, or differences in judgment. Their policies support the goals of the organization by extending oversight of their operations to fulfill the mission of those individuals who created the corporation without having to clone themselves.

policies also protect the organization from lawsuits due to a lack of fair treatment of employees.

We mentioned previously the consistency we expect from the products we buy, but what about the services we buy? People get very nervous when their experience changes for the same service from instance to instance. For example, think about getting your car washed. Every time you have been to your favorite car wash, things proceed in the same manner. First you drive around and get in line, then an attendant asks you to roll down your window, then the attendant asks which service you would like. He then hands you a ticket and instructs you to approach the cashier, while your car moves through the automatic wash. The first attendant always sprays your wheels with a special cleaner. Your car comes out the other side and two more attendants dry it with towels, and then alert you that your service is complete, and you drive off happily comfortable in your consistent experience. How would you respond if the first attendant approached your car, opened the door and told you to go inside without asking which service you would like, and then drove your car into the automated washer without spraying your wheels?

The fact is, most people would feel extremely uncomfortable. More disturbing for the owner of that business, most people would not complain but would simply go to a different car wash next time around. This is why the smart business person trains her employees according to a process designed to give the customer a consistent experience every time. As a control against the inevitable lapse in consistency, many service businesses make comment cards available to their customers.

It seems that policies have a bit more to do with operating a successful organization than simply annoying the employees who must follow them. In fact, without policies it would be almost impossible to organize any group for any reason and for any length of time. In this Internet age, well-written information security policies are just as important to an organization that hopes to achieve its goals as our Constitution is to our nation.

Complying with Government Policies

Many specific government regulations apply to certain sectors of the business community. For example, the Gramm-Leach Bliley Act (GLBA), also known as the Financial Modernization Act of 1999, requires banks and other financial institutions to protect private financial information from damage, misuse, or disclosure. The act came about because the information banks possess can be identifiable and "whole" in regard to any customer. GLBA requires financial institutions to develop and adhere to an information security policy that protects customer information. Security policies must be reviewed at least annually and signed by the board of directors of the institution.

The Health Insurance Portability and Accountability Act of 1996 (HIPAA) requires much the same of health care organizations that GLBA does of financial organizations. Since private health care information is critical and must remain protected from damage, misuse, and disclosure, the government has written law that requires health care organizations to safeguard it with measurable steps. Health care organizations must create comprehensive information security policies that communicate in detail how information is protected.

Both of these acts illustrate how government policy can, in turn, require businesses to create their own policy. Much of the work in the field of information security comes from this relationship. Businesses need expert advice to achieve and sustain compliance.

FYI: GLBA and HIPAA Information You May Want to Know

For more information about the GLBA and other federal financial regulations, visit these Web sites:

- The Federal Trade Commission (FTC): **www.ftc.gov/privacy/glbact**
- The Federal Register: **www.gpoaccess.gov/fr**
- The Federal Financial Institutions Examination Council (FFIEC): **www.ffiec.gov**
- The Federal Deposit Insurance Company (FDIC): **www. fdic.gov**

For more information about HIPAA, visit these Web sites:

- The Department of Health and Human Services: **www.hhs. gov/ocr/hipaa/**
- The Centers for Medicare and Medicaid Services: **www. cms.hhs.gov/hipaa/**

Understanding the Psychology of Policy

Psychology is the study of mind and behavior. Because policy is meant to guide behavior, the way you implement it is critical to its acceptance within an organization. You must have a good understanding of the emotional impact policies will have on those who must follow them.

All any of us must do is think back to our childhood to a time we were forced to follow a rule we didn't think was fair. The most famous defense most of us were given by our parents in response to our protests regarding the reasons we must follow such a rule was, "Because I said so!" Though it is necessary for our parents to teach us that life is not always fair, we could not easily get away with using such a statement as a way to get people within an organization to follow our policies. We can all remember how infuriated we became whenever we heard that statement, and how it seemed unjust. We may also remember our desire to deliberately disobey our parents, to rebel against this perceived tyranny. In very much the same way, if our policies are not developed, introduced, and enforced with clear communication at every stage, they will probably not be widely accepted within our organizations. If our policies are not accepted, we cannot fulfill the objectives with which we set the course of our organization's development, which, in the case of information security policy, is to protect our vital information.

If you seek input from members of the organization when developing policies, introduce policies through organizational training programs, and consistently enforce policies, employees will be more likely to accept and follow them.

Involving Those Who Know What Is Possible

In many organizations, policies are written for people in specific roles by people who have never worked in those roles, or spent any time researching the demands and conditions of those roles. This is an all too common mistake, which will certainly have serious consequences to the organization. One of the easiest mistakes to avoid is introducing a policy to a group of people who find nothing recognizable in the document in relation to their everyday experience. Policies must relate closely to actual day-to-day behavior.

In addition to involving key people, we need to involve managers, directors, administrators, and anyone in a significant organizational role. The best way to involve people in our policy development is by conducting interviews. Asking the right questions will give us a solid idea of the current state of the organization with regard to the policies we wish to implement.

Identifying Key People in an Organization   As described previously, key people are those who have proven reliable and perform above the expectations of their job descriptions. They are the "go to" people in any department who become recognized as resources for all other people in that department. It is easy to locate them; all we must do is follow the trail of institutional knowledge to their door. Key people are the ones about who we often say, "If we lose her, we are in trouble!" Indeed, a current trend in business is to acquire insurance policies on key employees to protect the organization should it lose a key person for any reason.

Key people understand their job function, as well as the functioning of the organization. They can "cut through" the vision an organization may have of itself and get to what is truly possible. Through interviews with key people, we can learn where we must change the underlying culture in our organization to achieve our policy objectives. If we ask the right questions, the answers may either affirm that our policy is realistic in our current culture, or we may find gaps between the behavior we want to require, and the

IN PRACTICE: The Importance of Knowing What Is Possible

Managers at XYZ, Inc., require by policy that data processors meet a daily production quota. Data processors at XYZ, Inc., produce customer data sheets, which are in turn used to bill customers. The more data sheets produced, the more XYZ, Inc., can bill each day. Managers derive the number for their quota from a mathematical equation based on an acceptable profit margin. The quota is that processors produce 250 data sheets on a daily basis. When managers distributed this policy and the quota requirements, there was companywide rebellion, as the fastest computer at XYZ, Inc., was capable of producing only 175 data sheets per day.

We can learn two very important lessons from this simple example:

Policies and standards should require what is possible. If unattainable objectives are required, people are set up to fail. This will have a profound effect on morale, which in this case will affect productivity. Know what is possible. Policy objectives should be driven by realistic organizational goals. A dream of who we want to be is called a *vision statement,* and has no place in a policy. If managers at XYZ, Inc., truly want to realize their goal of 250 data sheets per day/per data processor, they will first have to invest in equipment that makes this goal possible.

If you want to know what is possible, ask someone who already knows. One interview with someone who knew the limits of XYZ's computer systems would have been enough to avoid the rebellion.

Lesson number 2 above, is the primary lesson we must learn in order to realize a successful implementation of our policies. When developing policies, we must seek the advice and input from key people in every job role to which our policies apply. Two very important benefits come from this involvement:

Key people are those who display greater skill, understanding, and performance than most others in any job role. By involving key people, we not only get an idea of what is possible, but we set the bar of what is possible to its highest attainable level.

Another reason key people are key people is that other employees seek them out for advice, assistance, and/or guidance. Key people are therefore a natural vehicle to spread information through an organization. They have the respect of their peer group, and people are used to receiving direction and guidance from them already.

1

behavior that is standard in our current culture. The difference between these two conditions is called a *gap*. When we take the time to identify all the gaps, then we can realistically find ways to close them through training and awareness programs meant to aid us in meeting our policy objectives. If we simply ignore the gaps, or don't discover them at all, we will find that we cannot comply with our own policy objectives.

An easy example would be to look at how our employees are protecting their passwords. Suppose we want to implement a policy that prohibits writing passwords anywhere in readable form. In an interview we would ask if people are writing their passwords anywhere, and find that they were writing them on "sticky notes" and affixing them to their computer monitors. With this simple question and answer, we have identified a "gap" between the behavior we want and the behavior that is standard in our current culture. To change this behavior will take more than writing a policy prohibiting it; we will have to train people and make them aware of the dangers of writing their passwords in readable form, and also teach alternative ways to remember their passwords.

What Are the Significant Roles? Like key people, people in *significant roles* have knowledge we must consider when developing our policies. Luckily, those in significant roles are very easy to find, and we know in advance the information we wish to gather from them. Some significant roles include:

- Department directors and managers, such as Human Resources Director, Director of Physical Security, Information Technology Director/Manager, Help Desk Manager, Sales Director/Manager, etc. These can vary greatly from industry to industry.

- Any supervisor or manager working for any of our vendors or outsourced service providers.

- Senior managers, executive managers, and all C-Level positions such as Chief Executive Officer (CEO), Chief Financial Officer (CFO), and Chief Operating Officer (COO).

In some cases, people in significant roles will do more than answer questions to guide us in policy development. Some will make decisions on what will be written in our policies, the controls we will choose to protect our information, and how we will structure our training/awareness programs.

Another aspect of significant roles is the different responsibilities pertaining to roles in the policy process from development to enforcement. In Table 1.2 you will see a chart of roles and responsibilities in regard to this process: who is who and who is responsible for what.

Changes in the Environment

Information security is not a static, point-in-time endeavor but rather it is an ongoing process. Change drivers are built in to our information security program. *Change drivers* are events that cause us to revisit our policies, procedures, standards, and guidelines. Some change drivers include:

- Changes in technology
- Changes in senior level personnel
- Acquisition of other companies and other significant changes to our organization
- New products, services, or business lines

TABLE 1.2 The roles and responsibilities relating to information security policies and programs.

Role	Who is in the role? Who do they report to?	What are the responsibilities of this role?
Board of Directors	If a publicly traded company: Persons elected by the stockholders of a corporation to manage and direct the affairs of the corporation. If a private company: Persons chosen by owners to manage and direct the affairs of the corporation. Reports to: n/a	To approve written information security policies. To provide oversight for the information security program. In some regulated industries, the Board of Directors can be held personally financially responsible if the company is not in compliance with federal laws. This is true of the financial services industry regulated by the Gramm-Leach Bliley Act.
Information/Data Owner	The manager or agent responsible for the function that is supported by the resource, the individual upon whom responsibility rests for carrying out the program that uses the resources. The owner of a collection of information is the person responsible for the business results of that system or the business use of the information. Owners include: C-level management, senior management, business line managers. Report to: Board of Directors	The owner is responsible for establishing the controls that provide the security. Where appropriate, ownership may be shared by managers of different departments. Data Owners make decisions on where to spend money and time securing organizational information. They should seek expert advice. Owners are also responsible and liable for the protection of their data/information, and they are the people from who policies are get their authority. They enforce policies as well.

Information/Data Custodian	Guardian or caretaker; the holder of data, the agent charged with implementing the controls specified by the owner. Custodians include: IT/IS staff and managers, computer technicians, file clerks. Report to: Managers, senior/ executive management, C-Level management	The custodian is responsible for the processing and storage of information. Custodians keep the technology running, and they are implementers of policies.
Users	The user is any person who has been authorized to read, enter, or update information by the owner of the information. The user is the single most effective control for providing adequate security. Report to: Supervisors, managers	Has the responsibility to (1) use the resource only for the purpose specified by the owner, (2) comply with controls established by the owner, and (3) prevent disclosure of confidential or sensitive information.
Information Security Officer	Depending on the size of the organization, there may be a dedicated Information Security Officer, or the responsibilities may be delegated to any senior manager or officer. Report to: Senior/executive management, C-Level management, Board of Directors	Responsible for administering the information security function within the company. The ISO is the company's internal and external point of contact for all information security matters. The ISO may be the central author of information security policies.
Internal Auditor	Accountant with specific knowledge of information systems. Report to: C-Level management, Board of Directors	Ensures that the company's information resources are being adequately secured, and that controls are functioning as intended.

When we encounter *change drivers,* we must reassess our policies, controls, and procedures. This requires the involvement and expertise of key people who have the knowledge and foresight to understand change as well as the real and perceived impact upon the organization.

Introducing a Policy

There are two action items in this phase of the policy life cycle. The first is to get approval from the powers that be, such as the board of directors and/or senior/executive level management. The second is introducing our policies to the rest of the organization. That's where the real challenge lies.

Getting Approval

Depending on the industry, your policies will be subject to approval from those in the organization who have authority, which in turn means they are likely to be directly responsible and liable for the protection of the information policies are written to protect.

In regulated industries, such as financial services or health care, information security policies must be approved by a board of directors. Both GLBA and HIPAA require written information security policies that are board approved and subject to at least annual board-level review. You may have to gain board approval before a year passes if you have had to change your policies in response to any one of the change drivers we mentioned earlier in this chapter.

It will be helpful to know who the typical board member is, how her time is best used, and the manner of reporting that will be most effective and efficient. Generally speaking, boards of directors are made up of nontechnical, very experienced business people from a spectrum of business sectors. Their time is a valuable commodity both as a cost to the organization and because many are active executives in other companies.

If your organization has existing information security policies, then it would be wise to highlight changes to already-approved policies to save time. You must remember to keep your policy document separate from companion documents such as standards, procedures, and guidelines. The board may request these documents as references, but keeping them separate will allow you to change them periodically without the need for the board-level approval policies require.

Once you have the "green light" from the authority, it's time to introduce the policies to the organization as a whole. This introduction will require careful planning and execution as it will set the stage for how well the policies are accepted and followed.

Introducing Policies to the Organization

We mentioned earlier in this chapter that policies should explain to affected employees *why* they must adhere. Introducing information security policies should be thought of as an opportunity to raise awareness throughout the organization, and to give each person a tangible connection to the information security program. We should also consider the medium in which we introduce our policies. Since we have already illustrated the importance of keeping policies separate from policy companion documents, we can use available technology to let employees use these documents all together while maintaining them separately.

The Means and Method of Introducing a Policy Question: What better way to introduce educational documents than through awareness training programs?

Answer: There is no better way!

There are many benefits to companywide awareness training programs aside from their natural benefit as a policy introduction tool. Companywide training builds culture. When people share experiences, they are drawn together; they can reinforce one another's understanding of the subject matter and therefore support whatever initiative the training was intended to introduce.

In the case of information security policy, there is a great amount of information of which the average person is not aware. We like to call this the *two wall challenge.* The first wall is a lack of awareness; the second, much higher, wall is the lack of awareness of the lack of awareness. When members of an organization don't know what they don't know, the organization is in a very dangerous position. This is especially true in relation to information security. Many people are completely unaware of what the Internet environment is like, or even how their computers communicate on the Internet. Information security has a direct relationship to our knowledge and acceptance of reality. If an employee doesn't know the reality, how can she participate in a program to protect information from that reality?

In order to tear down common misconceptions about what computers are and how they communicate on private and public networks, we must gather people together and demonstrate the reality. Talk is cheap, but a more appropriate truth might be that talk is cheap unless it is substantiated by experience. When you show people how fast a password-cracking utility discovers user passwords, the effect is immediate and discomforting. Likewise, when you show someone the complete text of his e-mail captured by a "packet-sniffer" application, he gains a full understanding of the meaning of "clear text." Most people become invested in the information security program once they understand what the Internet is really like. In fact, most of them want to rush home to secure their own personal computers. The "don't try this at home" adage applies here. Running tools that expose security weaknesses without explicit permission from management is a direct path to the unemployment line or—even worse—jail.

When we take the time to show people how easy a weak password is to compromise, their next question is, "How do I create a strong password?" Now that we have climbed over wall number two, the lack of awareness of a lack of awareness, we can start our conversation at a higher level: "I know that I don't know, so tell me what I need to know." A group training environment also has the effect of relaxing anxiety associated with feeling uninformed. Most of the people in the room have the same level of awareness, and are made comfortable when they realize they are not the only ones who don't know.

Only after we raise the level of awareness do we begin to introduce the policy. The policy was, of course, developed to protect the organization's information from all the threats we have just thoroughly demonstrated to the computer user community. Now they understand the reasons behind all the rules to which they were previously resistant. Now they can participate in the program with an awareness of the importance of the policy's dictates.

Achieving Acceptance of the Policy

Now that we have discussed the best ways to introduce our policy, we need to concentrate on the most important aspect of our process: acceptance of our policies by all members of the organization. Just like our information security program, acceptance is not a one-and-done undertaking. Acceptance can be like the stock market, where the markets move up and down in response to various input from outside and inside forces.

Some of these forces include executive level participation or "buy-in," proper communication, response to a changing environment, and fair, consistent enforcement of our policy. Enforcement will be discussed in the next section, so we can focus on the other forces here.

Organizational Culture Comes from the Top

There are two very distinct varieties of leaders in the world: those who see leadership as a responsibility and those who see it as a privilege. From these two varieties come equally distinct organizational cultures. In both varieties, the example is set at the top—in the executive management level—and it is the example itself that will be distinctly different.

Leaders who see their role as a responsibility adhere to all the same rules they ask others to follow. There is no more powerful motivation for people in any group than to see their leadership subject to the same restrictions imposed upon subordinate personnel. "Do as I do." This is the most effective leadership style, especially in relation to information security. Security is not convenient for anyone, and it is crucial for leadership to participate in the information security program by adhering to its policies and setting the example. Executive "buy-in" not only impacts the approval process, but the introduction, acceptance, and maintenance phases of the information security policy life cycle.

Leaders who see their role as a privilege have a powerful impact as well. "Do as I say, not as I do." This leadership style will do more to undermine an information security program than any other single force. As soon as people learn that their leadership isn't subject to the same rules and restrictions, compliance with and acceptance of our policies will begin to erode. As far as computers are concerned, there is no difference between the CEO and the administrative assistant. The same risks exist, the same threats and the same vulnerabilities; so there is no justification for leadership avoiding the necessary mandates of an information security policy.

In working with many different kinds of organization, we have seen both extremes. Invariably, the organizations in which leadership sets the example by accepting and complying with their own policy have the least frequent occurrence of information security related incidents. When incidents do occur, they are far less likely to cause substantial damage. When the leadership sets a tone of compliance, the rest of the organization feels better about following the rules, and they are more active in participating. We call this the ***culture of continuity***.

Reinforcement Through Good Communication

People forget things, especially when the concept is new. The complexities of computers and the Internet require more than one introduction before they can be understood by many people. For this reason, it is important to ongoing acceptance of an information security policy to implement a program to reinforce the knowledge that guides people to conduct themselves in such a way as to protect organizational information. In short, people need reminders!

There are many methods available to keep best practice security behaviors in the minds of organizational members. Some of the most effective include:

- Intranet home pages

- Paycheck envelope "fillers"

- On-line security awareness technologies

- Screen savers

- E-mail or discussion post distribution

- Permanent agenda item at all department meetings

Responding to Environmental Changes

Continuing acceptance of information security policies also hinges on making sure the policies keep up with significant changes in the organization or the technology infrastructure. If your policies are written to address technologies no longer used within the organization, people will soon begin to dismiss them. As they encounter outdated, non-applicable policy statements, the whole document will be degraded.

The same is true for changes in personnel, new products and services, or significant changes to the organization itself. We must create a mechanism to respond to change drivers so that when things change, our policy and policy companions change as well to remain pertinent.

Enforcing Information Security Policies

Though it is certainly the least enjoyable aspect of any policy life cycle, enforcement is among the most important. Depending on the nature of the information we are trying to protect in our policy, there are many methods we can use for enforcement. For behavioral policies, we can monitor people's behavior. For policies that we can enforce through technology using software, such as Group Policy in Microsoft Windows 2000/2003 servers, we can configure and audit use of the technology. For policies that address technologies we cannot enforce by software policy, we will have to get a bit more creative and/or employ the use of third-party monitoring and audit tools.

Enforcing Behavioral Policies

If we look back at any group to which we belonged, including our families, we can easily identify rules by which the group sought to maintain order. In the case of family rules, which can vary greatly from family to family, we all know a simple truth. If we broke a rule, and no punishment was forthcoming, we understood this to mean that the rule wasn't really a rule at all, but more a suggestion. Sometimes we were mistaken, and the rule *was* a rule, but our parents simply didn't want to enforce it vigorously. It's not easy to punish people, no matter what the relationship.

Though we are not children in our professional lives, the very same operating standard applies. If you don't punish those who break rules, then the rules themselves will soon become meaningless. Enforcing policies that dictate human behavior requires consistently applied consequences of violation to make the policies credible.

Consistency is the key. If we enforce our policy only in certain circumstances and for certain people, or if enforcement depends upon which supervisor or manager is in charge, eventually there will be adverse consequences. Once there is talk within an organization that there are different standards for enforcement, the organization is open to many cultural problems, the most severe of which involve discrimination lawsuits.

Few people enjoy punishing others, but leadership is a responsibility to the organization, and also to each person in the organization. Leaders must get beyond the unpleasantness of punishing people to serve the greater good. If our information security policies are "paper only" policies, then our organization is at great risk. Remember, we write policies to address our risk after we have identified threats and vulnerabilities. If our policies, meant to give clear direction, are not followed, then we are subject to the inherent risk we identified when writing the policies.

Since any compromise of our information could lead to severe financial losses, then it follows that enforcing policies is important to keep the organization alive, which means people keep their jobs. When a leader decides to "go easy" on someone, what she is really deciding to do is putting the organization in jeopardy for the sake of one person.

Consequences for policy violation should be commensurate with the criticality of information the policy was written to protect. A clear and consistent process should be in place so that all similar violations are treated in the same manner.

Enforcing Technological Policies

Enforcing technological policies presents new challenges, which are often added to those of behavioral policies. In some cases, we can require certain behavior through software. For instance, we can use group policy to mandate a password standard that requires a certain number of characters and a certain complexity. This makes enforcement easy as users cannot create a password that violates our policy. Other situations are not so clear.

Let's say we had a policy requiring people in our organization to use only a specific brand and model of PDA. How would we enforce this policy? It would be similar if we had a policy that prohibited the installation of software not appearing on an approved software list. Enforcing this policy would either require constant, time-consuming checking by dedicated personnel, or we could use auditing software to perform periodic checks on installed software.

There are many software auditing tools available. Some will inventory all installed software on a given machine of network, and others are designed to find specific file extensions such as MP3 files or other peer-to-peer application files.

It is important for an organization to audit software installations as a user may inadvertently expose the organization to copyright violations. It is also important as most people are not informed enough to know what any given application is really doing. Considering the ever-increasing threat posed by Trojan horse programs, no organization can afford to risk not knowing about all of the applications in use.

Summary

In this chapter we have discussed the various roles policies play, and have played, in many forms of social structures, from entire cultures to corporations. We learned that policies are not new in the world. When its religious intent is laid aside, the Torah reads like any other secular code of law, or policy. The people of that time were in desperate need of guidance in their everyday existence to bring order to their society. We learned that policies give us a way to address common foreseeable situations and guide us to make decisions when faced with them. Similar to the circumstances that brought forth the Torah 3,000 years ago, our country found itself in need of a definite structure to bring to life the ideals of our founders, and to make sure those ideals remained intact. The U.S. Constitution was written to fulfill that purpose and serves as an excellent example of a strong, flexible, and resilient policy document.

The function of well-written information security policies is to protect the organization, its employees, its customers, and also vendors and partners from harm resulting from intentional or accidental damage, misuse, or disclosure of information. We illustrated the importance of involving key people from each department of the organization as policy is developed, as well as those who occupy significant roles, especially in directorial or executive roles.

We learned that once we have gained approval from the authority that gives our policy its power, we must then introduce the policy to the individuals who must follow the policies. We discussed training programs as the best method to introduce a policy.

During the acceptance phase, we drew a clear distinction between leaders who follow their own rules and those who feel they are above them. We discussed the implications of both postures. We also discussed methods of maintaining acceptance through continuing awareness programs, and updating policies in response to change drivers and changes in an organizational environment.

Finally, we described the challenges associated with enforcing our policies. We discussed the value of consistency and fairness and the fact that dealing out punishment, though not pleasant, may save the organization from grave consequences and unnecessary risks.

Test Your Skills

MULTIPLE CHOICE QUESTIONS

1. The purpose of a policy is:
   A. to define the easiest course of action
   B. to define the most profitable course of action
   C. to define the least restrictive course of action
   D. to define expectations of how people and organizations will act

2. Without policy, human beings would live in a state of:
   A. chaos
   B. bliss
   C. harmony
   D. laziness

3. Approximately how long has written policy existed?

    A. 3 years

    B. 30 years

    C. 300 years

    D. 3,000 years

4. The earliest written policies included:

    A. how to treat people

    B. how to treat the environment

    C. how to conduct business

    D. all of the above

5. Policies are designed to be:

    A. static

    B. dynamic

    C. confusing

    D. hard to abide by

6. An information security policy is a document that states:

    A. procedures to implement a firewall

    B. an organizational plan to safeguard information assets

    C. suggestions on how to create a strong password

    D. guidelines on how to write a letter

7. A well-written information security policy includes:

    A. management instructions indicating a course of action

    B. high-level statements that provide guidance to workers

    C. generalized requirements for use both internal and external to the organization

    D. All of the above statements are true.

8. The difference between policy and law is:

    A. law is (policy) rules enforced by the government

    B. law is (policy) rules that have may have civil penalties

    C. law is (policy) rules that may have criminal penalties

    D. All of the above statements are true.

9. The U.S. Constitution was designed to be:

   A. guiding policy

   B. enforceable laws

   C. both guiding policy and enforceable law

   D. neither guiding policy nor enforceable law

10. Information security policies are designed to safeguard information stored, processed, and transmitted by:

    A. authorized users

    B. unauthorized users

    C. children of employees

    D. janitorial staff

11. Which is *not* a goal of an information security policy?

    A. to influence behavior

    B. to protect employees and customers

    C. to make it difficult to be productive

    D. to provide a decision-making framework

12. Information assets can be:

    A. tangible

    B. intangible

    C. both tangible and intangible

    D. neither tangible nor intangible

13. Which of the following would be considered an intangible information asset?

    A. computer

    B. backup tape

    C. institutional knowledge

    D. printed manual

14. Which of the following would be considered a tangible information asset?

    A. virus

    B. institutional knowledge

    C. wireless transmission signals

    D. laptop

1

15. The three "states" of information are:
    A. storage, processing, transmission
    B. storage, disposal, processing
    C. processing, transmission, reviewing
    D. reviewing, revising, printing

16. The Internet has added significance to the creation of information security policies because:
    A. information can easily be shared outside of the organization
    B. outsiders have a new way to access internal information
    C. transmission is fast and fairly anonymous
    D. All of the above are true.

17. Downloading and saving music on an iPod would be considered:
    A. information storage
    B. information transmission
    C. both A and B
    D. neither A nor B

18. Listening to music on an iPod would be considered:
    A. information processing and storage
    B. information transmission and processing
    C. information reviewing and listening
    D. information listening and transmission

19. HIPAA information security regulations apply to:
    A. transportation organizations
    B. financial organizations
    C. educational institutions
    D. health care organizations

20. GLBA information security regulations apply to:
    A. transportation organizations
    B. financial organizations
    C. military installations
    D. health care organizations

21. A good information security policy has the following characteristics:

    A. relevant, static, enforceable
    B. relevant, understandable, enforceable
    C. relevant, complex, enforceable
    D. relevant, dynamic, unenforceable

22. What is an efficient way to create valid policies that will be accepted by the target audience?

    A. involve only upper-management level executives
    B. involve only low-level employees
    C. involve employees at all levels of the company
    D. involve only outside, third-party consultants

23. What is the best way to introduce a new policy?

    A. e-mail it to the whole company on Monday morning
    B. have the President/CEO/Board e-mail it to the company on Monday morning
    C. set up awareness training programs that relate to the new policy
    D. warn the users two weeks prior to release that a new policy will soon be in effect

EXERCISES

Exercise 1.1: E-mail and its Relationship to the States and Residences of Information

1. Using Table 1.1 as a template, fit all the ways you use e-mail into each of the nine spaces.

2. Keep in mind how e-mail travels on the Internet, how you may use it, talk about it, share it, etc.

Exercise 1.2: Find a Policy that Affects You

1. Either at your job or at school; find a policy used for any purpose.

2. Describe how you are affected by this policy.

3. Describe ways in which this policy benefits you.

4. Describe ways in which this policy is administered and enforced.

Exercise 1.3: Find a Policy Reminder

1. Reminders of policies are all around you; find one at your school.

2. Reminders of law are all around you; find at least three in the next 24 hours.

Exercise 1.4: Downloading Music

1. Is it illegal to download music from the Internet? See if you can find a policy relating to this subject.

2. Do you think this policy will change over time?

PROJECTS

Project 1.1: Leadership Analysis

1. Think of two examples of places you have worked.

2. Considering our ideas about the two different kinds of leadership, place the owners or managers from your two examples into the category to which they best fit.

3. Write a paragraph for each owner/manager on how their different styles influenced how well most employees followed the rules set forth by leadership.

4. Cite any examples of how the leadership in these two organizations implemented and enforced policies.

Project 1.2: Training Development

1. You have been tasked with introducing a new security policy to your organization. The new policy requires all employees to wear identification badges. All visitors will be required to sign in and to wear visitor badges. Why would an organization introduce this type of policy?

2. You need to develop a strategy to introduce this policy companywide.

3. You need to develop a 10-minute training session on why this policy is important and how it will be implemented. Your session must include participant participation.

4. Design a 5-question quiz to ensure that your training program was effective.

Project 1.3: **Research the Constitution of the United States**

1. Find out what year the U.S. Constitution was written.

2. Find out what year the U.S. Constitution was ratified.

3. Find out what the first ten amendments are called.

4. Find out how many amendments are there in total.

5. Identify the last amendment and the year it was ratified.

BONUS: See if you can find out what the last amendment was that did not get ratified.

▶ Case Study

You have been called in by a large community bank, CommBank, to write an information security policy and to design and conduct the introduction of the new policy to all employees. CommBank is the best-managed bank in your state, and its management is known for their security awareness. CommBank has just acquired a small bank, TinyBank, and must integrate its operations into the larger framework existing at CommBank. TinyBank has no existing information security policy and the employees of TinyBank are not happy about the new culture with its new rules to which they are now subjected.

TinyBank has never conducted any information security training and it had no restrictions on the use of the Internet or e-mail at work. It also had no restrictions on employees installing software on their work computers. Employees have never been told the risks associated with free use of the Internet or e-mail.

CommBank has held annual information security training for all employees and executives; even board members are trained to understand the risks posed by the Internet.

Your task is to do the following:

1. With Table 1.2 as a reference, use the personnel resources from both companies to create a chart of roles and responsibilities regarding the creation and introduction of new information security policies. You must decide who will be interviewed, what tasks they will perform during the writing and introduction phases of the policy, and how the results will

▶▶ CONTINUED ON NEXT PAGE

▶▶ CONTINUED

be both measured and reported. You will have to guess responsibilities and reporting structure for positions that are not included in Table 1.2

2. Design a training program in which users are informed about the realities of Internet use, and are asked to sign an agreement stating that they understand and accept the rules set forth in the policy. You do not need to be specific, but rather simply outline what kind of training you will provide. For example; will you choose instructor-led sessions, online training, one-on-one training, or a combination of any or all of the three? Hint: Consider using some of the already-informed employees of CommBank to reinforce your training program.

3. Determine the best method to test employees on the information presented at the training sessions. For example, will you choose written tests, oral tests, or another method?

4. Document the challenges faced by integrating these two banks in relation to their current cultures. What possible problems might you encounter in creating an effective policy?

CommBank has the following human resources:

- A board of directors
- A Chief Executive Officer (CEO)
- An Information Security Officer (ISO)
- An Information Technology Manager with a staff of five technicians and two systems engineers
- A Human Resources Director
- Each branch has a branch manager
- Each branch has a head teller
- The bank outsources information security training to DataSafe, Inc., an independent information security firm

TinyBank has the following human resources:

- A Compliance Officer
- An IT manager and three technicians; the IT manager is also a systems engineer
- An internal auditor
- Each branch has a branch manager

Chapter | 2

The Elements of a Policy

Chapter Objectives

After reading this chapter and completing the exercises, you will be able to do the following:

- Create a policy with the appropriate standards, guidelines, and procedures.
- Develop a policy with the appropriate elements.
- Include the proper information in each element of a policy.
- Distinguish the difference between a policy objective and a policy purpose.
- Define a policy audience clearly.

Introduction

In Chapter 1, we learned that policies have played a significant role in helping us form and sustain our social, governmental, and corporate organizations. In this chapter, we will begin by defining the role of policy companions, including standards, guidelines, and procedures and the role they play in supporting, implementing, and maintaining policy. We will then break policy down into its essential components and focus on the elements that are required to make the document usable in the most effective and efficient way possible.

Some of the necessary elements of information security policies are mandated by regulatory requirements such as the two we discussed in Chapter 1, the Gramm-Leach Bliley Act and the Health Insurance Portability and Accountability Act. These federal laws require specific information be contained in an organization's information security policy, such as the date the policy was written and revised, a schedule for future review and revision, and a statement with consequences of violation.

Other elements that make a security policy document usable in the most effective and efficient way possible include the objectives of the policy, a statement of purpose, a statement of exceptions, and the policy statements themselves.

This chapter provides a detailed explanation of each of the recommended elements of an information security policy, though you should find these same elements in any policy document used for any purpose. We will also explore how these elements fit together and how they depend on and support each other while supporting the document as a whole.

Defining Policy Companions: Standards, Guidelines, and Procedures

Policies are important, but alone they do not accomplish very much. Policies need supporting documents to give them meaningful applications, a foundation from which they are conceived, and suggestions for how to best accomplish tasks associated with meeting their expectations.

Three kinds of documents are considered "policy implementation" documents or companion documents to policy. In this section, we will explore the uses of these three kinds of documents: standards, guidelines, and procedures. Each plays a significant role in turning policies into repeatable actions that are based on sound ideas and judgment.

Earlier we mentioned the many pitfalls we can encounter when creating information security policies. Here we warn you about the most troublesome of these pitfalls. Many organizations make the mistake of combining policies with the three companion documents into one big, unruly document. Many problems arise from this mistake, including:

- Difficulty of implementation: With all of these documents combined into one massive document, how do I communicate to each different department just what it needs to know to implement the policy?

- Difficulty of management: How do I maintain control over such a large document?

- Difficulty of updating: Since standards, guidelines, and procedures change far more often than policies, updating this whale of a document will be far more difficult than if these elements were properly treated as separate. Also, since Boards of Directors in many business sectors must approve policies, if we combine all of these documents into one place, every change to a procedure, guideline, or standard will require Board review for approval. This will become very costly and cumbersome for everyone involved.

2

Standards

Standards dictate specific minimum requirements in our policies. The most easily understood standard, for our time and purpose, is the password standard. A password standard dictates how an acceptable password is constructed. It might read like this:

Passwords must meet the following standard:

- Minimum of 8 upper- and lowercase alphanumeric characters.

- Must include at least one special character (example: *&$#!@).

- Must be changed every 30 days.

- Password history of 24 previous passwords will be used to ensure passwords aren't reused.

Our password policy, on the other hand, will read like this:

- All users must have a unique user ID and password that conforms to the company password standard.

- Users must not share their password with anyone regardless of title or position.

- Passwords must not be stored in written or any readable form.

- If a password is suspected compromised, it must be reported immediately to the help desk and a new password must be requested.

From this example, which do you think might change more often, the standard or the policy? Which is more general? Clearly, the policy represents expectations that are not subject to changes in technology, management, or foreseeable circumstances. The standard, however, is very specific to the current industry best practice and the technology platform in use.

Guidelines

While standards are very definite and required, *guidelines* are best thought of as suggestions for the best way to accomplish a certain task. In addition to using softer language, guidelines are likely to change more often than any other element in this family of documents. While our password standard is very specific, we can create a guideline to help people conform to our standard. It might read like this:

A good way to create a strong password is to think of a phrase, song title, or other group of words that is easy to remember and convert it like this:

- The phrase *Up and At 'em at 7!* can be converted into a strong password appearing like this: up&atm@7!

- You can create many passwords from this one phrase by changing the number, moving the symbols or changing the punctuation mark.

Guidelines offer suggestions for the best way to accomplish a task, as this helpful hint on strong password creation helps computer users to create easy-to-remember, yet strong passwords.

Procedures

A *procedure* provides a method by which a policy is accomplished; the instructions necessary to carry out a policy statement. Procedures focus on actions or steps and there is usually a starting point and an ending point to that action. In keeping with our other examples, let's demonstrate a procedure for changing a user password:

1. Press the Control, Alt, and Delete keys to bring up the log in dialog box.
2. Click the "change password" button.
3. Enter your current password in the top box.
4. Enter your new password in both the second and third boxes to ensure that you typed it correctly.
5. Click "OK" and log in with your new password.

There isn't much grey area in explaining a procedure. Just remember it as a series of steps to complete a task.

Developing a Policy Style and Format

Make sure you carefully consider the style and organization of your information security policies and companion documents. Style is critical. How the document flows and the words you use will make all the difference as to how the policy is interpreted. You need to know your intended audience and write in a way that is relevant and understandable. For example, consider the difference in the vocabulary you would use if you were writing a policy to be read by employees of a multinational organization for whom English may be a second language versus a policy for high school and college students working as summer camp counselors.

Plan Before You Write

Organize before you begin writing! It is important to decide how many sections and subsections you will require before you put pen to paper. By designing a template that allows you the flexibility of changing your policy without having to revisit the template, you will save yourself considerable time and aggravation.

There are two schools of thought in regard to policy format. The first is to write each policy as a discrete document. The second is to write one large policy document with multiple sections. We prefer to write our policies as individual documents. We like this approach for two reasons: (1) each policy document can be short, clean, and crisp and (2) each policy can be targeted to its intended audience. Of course, for purposes of accessibility, policy documents need to be stored together. This can be done either in a binder, a shared folder, or on a company intranet.

Let's start by looking at an example of a completed policy. Table 2.1 is a policy requiring confidentiality agreements. As much as possible, our goal is to keep policy documents short, generally fewer than two pages. We begin each policy with a heading that includes the name of the policy, the security domain it belongs to (we'll discuss domains in Chapter 3), and housekeeping items such as date, version, and approval. The body of the policy includes the key elements: Objectives, Purpose, Audience, Policy, Exceptions, and Disciplinary Actions. What are missing from our individual policy document are definitions. If you have multiple policies, definitions become redundant. Rather than overwhelm the reader, we incorporate definitions into a separate document. Let's continue examining each of these elements in more depth.

TABLE 2.1 A complete policy.

Subsection	6.1 PERSONNEL SECURITY	Change Control #: 1.0
Policy	6.1.3 Confidentiality Agreements	Approved By: SSG
Objectives	Confidentiality of organizational data is a key tenet of our information security program. In support of this goal, the [COMPANY] will require signed confidentiality agreements of all authorized users of information systems. This agreement shall confirm to all federal, state, regulatory, and union requirements.	
Purpose	The purpose of this policy is to protect the assets of the organization by clearly informing staff of their roles and responsibilities for keeping the organization's information confidential.	
Audience	The [COMPANY] confidentiality agreement policy applies equally to all individuals granted access privileges to any [COMPANY] information resources.	
Policy	This policy requires that staff sign a confidentiality policy agreement prior to being granted access to any sensitive information or systems. Agreements will be reviewed with the staff member when there is any change to the employment or contract, or prior to leaving the organization. The agreements will be provided to the employee by the Human Resources Dept.	
Exceptions	At the discretion of the Information Security Officer, third parties whose contracts include a confidentiality clause may be exempted from signing individual confidentiality agreements.	
Disciplinary Actions	Violation of this policy may result in disciplinary action, which may include termination for employees and temporaries; a termination of employment relations in the case of contractors or consultants; or dismissal for interns and volunteers. Additionally, individuals are subject to civil and criminal prosecution.	

IN PRACTICE: Using Tables to Publish Policies

The most professional (and efficient) format to use in writing policies is a table.

A table is made up of rows and columns of cells that you can fill with text and graphics.

Never created a table before? Microsoft Word makes the process easy.

1. Click where you want to create a table.
2. On the **Table** menu, point to **Insert**, and then click **Table**.
3. Under **Table size**, select the number of columns and rows.
4. Under **AutoFit behavior**, choose options to adjust table size.
5. To use a built-in table format, click **AutoFormat**.

FIGURE 2.1 The Table dialog box in Microsoft Word.

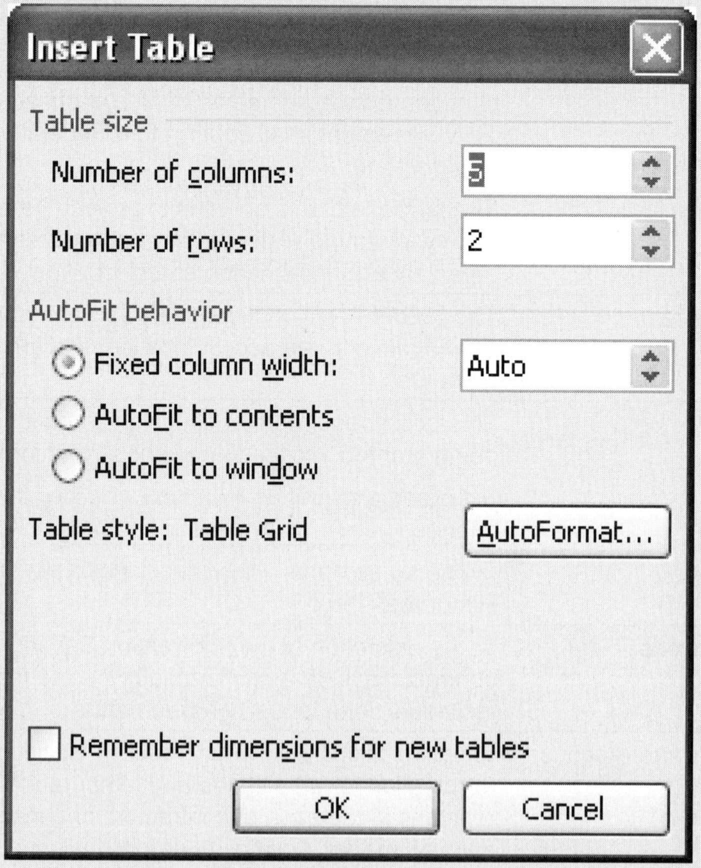

Defining Policy Elements

The policy document itself comprises multiple sections: Statement of Authority, Policy Headings, Objectives, Purpose, Audience, Exceptions, Enforcement, and Definitions. Each section has a specific purpose. The key to successful policy writing is to understand the goal of each section and to be consistent in how you write.

Statement of Authority

The *statement of authority* is *not* found in each individual policy document but rather serves as a preface to a group of policies and to your information security program. The statement of authority functions as an introduction to the information security policies, where the thought process behind the actual policies is presented to the reader. It explains what motivated the company to draft these documents. It often sets forth the regulatory compliance responsibilities that the company has—often by listing which federal regulations such as GLBA, HIPAA, or Sarbanes-Oxley pertain to the organization.

More than that, it is also a statement of culture, one that attempts to define for the reader the core values the company believes in and promotes, and what needs to be done from a security policy standpoint to ensure that these values can coexist with a realistic and strong security strategy.

The statement of authority also usually attempts to "recruit" readers and show them what is expected of them as employees.

To achieve this, the statement of authority typically uses such language as "the company has identified the rules set forth in this document as a requirement for all employees to conform to in order to defend both the company and the confidential data with which it is entrusted against hacking attacks" and "this document was crafted to provide assistance, guidance, and protection to our employees as it pertains to their professional responsibilities to both use and safeguard the company's confidential data." These statements are juxtaposed to both include the employees in a caring, supportive, and responsible professional structure and to explicitly outline for the employees' sake that, as members of this professional entity, they are unequivocally and directly responsible for the safeguarding of the confidential data that crosses their desks in the course of their normal employment by the company.

IN PRACTICE: Example of a Statement of Authority

Here's an example of a Statement of Authority that presents users of the policy with an introduction to the policy as well as a statement of the organization's core values. This SOA was developed

▸▸ CONTINUED ON NEXT PAGE

by a State Agency with a specific goal in mind. For many years, the organization did not have any formal security policies. In 2003, a State regulation was enacted that required the Agency to introduce formal policies based upon the ISO 17799 standard. Senior management felt that the best way to introduce the policies was to precede them by a SOA that demonstrated in gentle but definitive language the commitment of the Commissioner and the expectation of compliance.

"The [COMPANY] is committed to protecting the Public, our customers, our employees, partners, and the [COMPANY] itself from illegal or damaging actions by individuals, either knowingly or unknowingly.

The 21st century environment of connected technologies offers many opportunities to malicious or unknowing people from all over the world to anonymously attack, damage, and corrupt vital information; and to disrupt our ability to communicate effectively and accomplish the mission of our organization. Effective security is a civic responsibility, and a team effort involving the participation and support of every [COMPANY] employee and affiliate who deals with information and/or information systems. It is the responsibility of every [COMPANY] employee and affiliate to know, understand, and adhere to these policies, procedures, standards, and guidelines, and to conduct their activities accordingly. This policy statement has been adopted in order to provide guidance and protection to [COMPANY] employees and to safeguard the information resources entrusted to [COMPANY] employees."

Policy Headings

A *policy heading* contains all of the logistical information regarding a specific policy area. Information in the heading can vary as to content depending on how the organization has chosen to organize the document, but style differences aside, the information contained in the heading may include:

- Security domain (section), subsection, and policy number.

- The name of the organization and the name of the document.

- The effective date of the policy and the name of the author or authors responsible for writing the policy.

- Change control documentation or number (used for tracking revisions).

- Any relevant cross-references regarding other standards or regulatory acts.

- Name(s) of authority (approval) under which policy is written.

One of the central challenges in writing effective policies is found in organizing the document so that it can be used without confusing those who must use it. Finding the appropriate structure is important. The proper framework should be scalable without the need to revisit the structure. In other words, it should be able to accommodate additions and subtractions without losing organization.

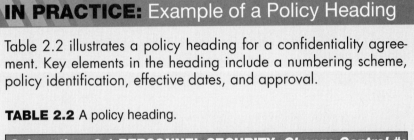

IN PRACTICE: Example of a Policy Heading

Table 2.2 illustrates a policy heading for a confidentiality agreement. Key elements in the heading include a numbering scheme, policy identification, effective dates, and approval.

TABLE 2.2 A policy heading.

Subsection	6.1 PERSONNEL SECURITY	*Change Control #:*
Policy	6.1.3 Confidentiality Agreements	*Approved By:*

Policy Objectives

What is the goal of our policy? This is the question we must answer to communicate our ***policy objective.*** The policy objective states *what* we are trying to achieve by implementing the policy. Policy objectives help focus the reader on the very subject they will encounter in the document.

The policy objectives act as an introduction to the content to come and the security principle that they address. It is a global objective, an all-encompassing statement that details the *what*—not the *why* or *how*. It is not an in-depth look at the situation or issue. It is not an enumeration of all measures that need to be implemented or standardized. Instead, it defines a generic need for the company, and the company's aim as it pertains to the topic highlighted in this policy.

Note that one policy can certainly feature multiple objectives. We clearly live in a world where business matters are more and more complex and interconnected, which means that a policy with a single objective might risk not covering all aspects of a particular situation. It is therefore important, during the planning phase, to pay appropriate attention to the different objectives that the security policy should seek to achieve.

IN PRACTICE: Example of a Policy Objective in Reference to Confidentiality Agreements

This example of a policy objective states one of the goals the organization hopes to achieve:

"Confidentiality of organizational data is a key tenet of our information security program. In support of this goal, the [COMPANY] will require signed confidentiality agreements of all authorized users of information systems. This agreement shall confirm to all federal, state, regulatory, and union requirements."

Remember that the policy objective section defines the "what."

What: Require a signed confidentiality agreement of all authorized users.

Policy Statement of Purpose

Now that we have defined what a policy objective is, let's focus on what is meant by *policy statement of purpose.*

Why does the policy exist? A statement of purpose is designed to give specific guidance to the reader regarding achieving a policy objective. The purpose begins with an explanation as to *why* the policy was adopted. It is important that the reader understand the reason the policy was adopted and in what context. The purpose then defines in broad terms *how* the policy will be implemented. The mistake that is often made in this section is to get too detailed. The specific detail belongs in the policy section.

IN PRACTICE: Example of a Statement of Purpose

This example of a policy statement of purpose gives the reasons for the policy's existence and how the policy will be implemented:

"The purpose of this policy is to protect the assets of the organization by clearly informing staff of their roles and responsibilities for keeping the organization's information confidential."

Remember that the purpose section defines the "why" and the "how."

Why: To protect the assets of the organization.

How: By clearly informing staff of their roles and responsibilities.

Policy Audience

Who is the policy intend for? The *who* is referred to as the policy audience. The ***policy audience*** element of a security policy needs to be clearly defined to reduce the chance of an ambiguity. An information security policy is a communication from the company's management. Some policies may be intended for a particular group of employees based upon job function. For example, an application development policy is targeted to developers. Other policies may be intended for a particular group based upon the roles within the organization. An example of this would be a policy requiring the Information Security Officer to report annually to the Board of Directors. Unless a policy specifies otherwise, it is generally safe to assume that the policy audience is all information system owners, custodians, and users.

The policy, or portions of it, can also sometimes apply to people outside of the company, such as business partners, governmental organizations, vendors, or clients. Entities that interact with an aspect of an organization or its information should probably appear in the policy in one way or another, though they probably will not be privy to the entire policy.

It is imperative, during the planning portion of the security policy project, to clearly define the audience for which the document is being drafted in the first place. This will ensure that the proper information is disseminated to the right people, and that all the people who should receive a copy of the policy have indeed been accounted for.

As an aside, and as an introduction to a notion that we will further investigate in the next chapter, it is important to not only see the audience as the target group of people for whom the policy is created, but also as a potential resource during the policy creation phase. Indeed, who better to help create a policy than the very people whose job it is to use those policies in the context of their everyday work? Who will have more insight on the actual, business-critical tasks being performed?

IN PRACTICE: Example of Policy Audience

This example of a policy audience clearly defines the target group of people for whom the policy is created.

"The [COMPANY] confidentiality agreement policy applies equally to all individuals granted access privileges to any [COMPANY] information resources."

Remember that the policy audience section defines the "who."
Who: All individuals granted access.

Policy Statement

Up to this point in the document, we have defined the goal (*what*), the purpose (*why*), and the audience (*who*). The **policy statement** focuses on the specifics of how the policy will be implemented; in other words, the rules.

This is the section where we will list all the rules that need to be followed, reference the location of the documents that explain the reasoning behind the rules, and, in some cases, reference the step-by-step procedures required to carry on the business tasks defined in the policy.

This part of the document is traditionally the one that constitutes the bulk of the final document known as the policy. It is a systematic list of all the rules and actions to be taken to control the risks associated with an organization's identified threats and vulnerabilities. A well-written policy will contain areas that address every aspect of operations and information, including physical security, business continuity, disaster recovery, personnel security, software development, access control, and any other applicable area affecting the organization's information assets.

The policy will also reference the standards, procedures, and guidelines that have been created by the company to support all the rules that make up the policy. Note that these policy companion documents are not written out and explained in the policy. Instead, they are used as a reference tool in correlation with the rules that are presented in the policy itself to support the implementation of the policy.

IN PRACTICE: Example of Policy Statements

The bulk of the final policy document is composed of policy statements. Here are some examples of an organization's policy statements:

- This policy requires that staff sign a confidentiality policy agreement prior to being granted access to any sensitive information or systems.

- Agreements will be reviewed with the staff member when there is any change to the employment or contract, or prior to leaving the organization.

- The agreements will be provided to the employee by the Human Resources Dept.

Policy Exceptions

It would be a perfect world if all policies were applicable 100 percent of the time. Unfortunately, we don't live in a perfect world, which means that from time to time, it is possible that our all-inclusive rules may not apply to all situations.

This does not in any way invalidate the purpose or quality of the rules present in the security policy. It just means that some special situations will call for special ***policy exceptions*** to the normal and accepted rules.

A simple example of this may be that a company, in order to protect its confidential data and its perimeter defense, would ban digital cameras from all company premises. Some of those cameras are very small, yet very powerful, and could be used to take snapshots of computer screens displaying confidential data or even as a simple USB removable hard drive to which to download confidential data. Banning cameras altogether means that we have identified a threat, and mitigated that threat down to 0 by simply banning the source of the threat.

However, a case could be made that the HR department should be equipped with a digital camera to take pictures of new employees to paste them on their ID badges. Or maybe the Security Officer should have a digital camera to document the proceedings of evidence-gathering after a security breach has been detected. Both examples are valid reasons why the company might need a camera. In these cases, an exception to the policy could be added to the document. If no exceptions are allowed, this should be clearly stated in the policy statement section as well.

The language used when creating the exception must be clear, concise, and indicate a process by which exceptions may be granted. The criteria or conditions for exceptions should not be detailed in the policy, only the method or process for requesting an exception. If we try to list all the conditions to which exceptions apply, we risk creating a loophole in the exception itself. It is also important that the process follow specific criteria under which exceptions are finally granted or rejected. Whether granted or rejected, the requesting party should be given a written report with clear reasons either way. Indeed, some employees may be upset that they cannot use a specific device while others can. In order to make sure that such a feeling does not fester into a negative situation, a rational explanation of the reason that motivated the exception should be added.

Finally, it is recommended to keep the number of exceptions low, for several reasons:

- Too many exceptions may mean that the rule is not appropriate in the first place. Should it be rethought or rewritten?

- Too many exceptions to a valid rule may lead employees to perceive the rule as unimportant, since so many exceptions can be made.

- Too many exceptions to a valid rule may be seen by some employees as a situation where favoritism is extended to some, but not all, employees.

- Too many exceptions are difficult to keep a track of and audit successfully.

IN PRACTICE: Example of Exception to Policy

This example of exceptions to a policy tells the reader who is not required to obey the rules as written in the policy. It also notes under what circumstances:

"At the discretion of the Information Security Officer, third parties whose contracts include a confidentiality clause may be exempted from signing individual confidentiality agreements."

Policy Enforcement Clause

The *policy enforcement clause* is where management gets to flex some muscle. This is where you get to add some bite to your bark. Choose your cliché, it all applies. Listing rules for the sake of listing rules does not ensure that those rules will be respected and adhered to. It would be nice to think that all employees understand and agree that company rules are created for the well-being of all, but the truth of the matter is that it is in human nature to reject what is inconvenient—and let's face it: many rules are inherently inconvenient.

We all know that convenience and security are mutually exclusive. Locking your front door in the morning adds to the security of your property against burglary, but it also adds to your inconvenience in that you have to take the time to lock the door in the first place, not to mention unlock it when you come back home! Most people never really think of locking a door as being all that inconvenient—yet they are most definitely distressed and/or annoyed when it comes time to perform the computer world equivalent: use—and remember!—a network password to log on to the corporate network.

The only way to try to enforce those rules is to include the penalty for ignoring the rules in the same document that lists them. That's where the organization can assert the seriousness of a policy. This can be called the "policy enforcement" clause, the "consequences for violation" clause, or simply the "disciplinary action" clause.

As with other elements, we do not list every possible punishment for every possible violation. It is best to indicate a disciplinary process and list the most severe punishment, which usually includes dismissal or criminal prosecution. Of course, the process must be developed and a schedule of applicable disciplinary actions for corresponding violations must be included. We must also have a contingency for repeat offenses.

Obviously, you must be careful with the nature of the penalty. Quite clearly, it should be proportional to the rule that was broken and the level of

risk the company incurred. For example, it would be extremely counterproductive to tell someone who forwarded a joke e-mail that she will be fired if
she were to do it again. Someone who willingly divulges his user ID and
password to someone over the phone just because he was asked, however,
has certainly put the organization—and therefore all employees, from the
C-Level executives on down—at a significant risk. Clearly, the level of
penalty needs to match the nature of the infraction.

However, it is not enough simply to set up a rule and a proper penalty
for breaking it. The company needs to address the third part of this situation: employee training. All employees should be trained in the acceptable
practices that are presented in the security policy. Without training, it is
hard to fault employees for not knowing that they were supposed to act in a
certain fashion, if that little detail was never explained to them in the first
place! Imposing disciplinary actions in this case would not only be an exercise in futility, but it would also contribute to an overall negative atmos-
phere that would adversely affect the corporate culture. We will cover these
training concepts fully in Chapters 3 and 10.

IN PRACTICE: Example of Policy
Enforcement Clause

This example of a policy enforcement clause advises the reader, in
no uncertain terms, what will happen if they do not obey the rules.
    "Violation of this policy may result in disciplinary action,
which may include termination for employees and temporaries; a
termination of employment relations in the case of contractors or
consultants; or dismissal for interns and volunteers. Additionally,
individuals are subject to civil and criminal prosecution."

Policy Definitions

Policy definitions can be seen as a sort of glossary that becomes a part of
the security policy. Because the security policy can include detailed, technical information, adding definitions to the overall document will enable the
target audience to understand the policy—and therefore makes the policy a
much more efficient document.

The rule of thumb is to include definitions for any instance of nonstandard language. Without implying that the reader is equipped with an IQ
that even Forrest Gump could surpass, it makes sense to err on the side of
caution and add definitions for terms that may not be especially well-
known. The purpose of the security policy as a document is *communication*

and education. The target audience for this document usually encompasses all employees of the company, and also at times outside personnel. Even if some technical topics are well-known to all in-house employees, some of those outside individuals who come in contact with the company—and therefore are governed by the security policy—may not be as well-versed in the policy's technical aspects.

Simply put, before writing down definitions, it is recommended to first define the target audience for whom the document is crafted, and cater to the lowest common denominator to ensure optimum communication efficiency.

Another reason why definitions should not be ignored is for the legal ramification that they represent. An employee cannot pretend to have thought that a certain term used in the policy meant one thing when it is clearly defined in the policy itself. When choosing which words will be defined, therefore, it is important not only to look at those that could clearly be unknown, but also those that should be defined to remove any and all ambiguity. Nobody enjoys legal proceedings, but a security policy could be an instrumental part of legal proceedings and should therefore be viewed as a legal document, and crafted as such.

IN PRACTICE: Example of a Definition

Any term that may not be familiar to the reader or is open to interpretation should be defined. In this case, the term Information Resources (IR) is probably much broader than most readers would expect and needs to be clarified.

"Information Resources (IR): Any and all computer printouts, online display devices, magnetic storage media, and all computer-related activities involving any device capable of receiving e-mail, browsing Web sites, or otherwise capable of receiving, storing, managing, or transmitting electronic data including, but not limited to, mainframes, servers, personal computers, notebook computers, handheld computers, personal digital assistants (PDAs), pagers, distributed processing systems, network attached and computer controlled medical and laboratory equipment (i.e., embedded technology), telecommunication resources, network environments, telephones, fax machines, printers, and service bureaus. Additionally, it is the procedures, equipment, facilities, software, and data that are designed, built, operated, and maintained to create, collect, record, process, store, retrieve, display, and transmit information."

> **FYI: Policy Resource**
>
> The SANS (SysAdmin, Audit, Network, Security) Institute was established in 1989 as a cooperative research and education organization. The SANS Institute develops, maintains, and makes available at no cost, the largest collection of research documents about various aspects of information security, and it operates the Internet's early warning system—Internet Storm Center. There is an entire section of the SANS web site devoted to information security policies. You can find this information at **http://www.sans.org/resources/policies/**.

Summary

We now know that our policy companion documents allow for changes to our organization's operations without necessarily changing our policies. Standards, guidelines, and procedures provide a means to communicate specific ways to implement our policies. We create our organizational standards, which specify our requirement for each policy area; we offer guidelines to help people to comply with our policies; and we design easily understood procedures so the people in our organization can consistently perform the tasks called for in our policies, without having to apply subjective judgment to what should be institutionally answered questions about what to do.

In this chapter, we focused on the different elements of a security policy. We saw that there should be an authority statement to reinforce company values and correlate them with the new rules introduced in the security policy. We then looked at the policy headings, where all the technical details relevant to the policy can be found, such as version number, identity of the author(s), date of creation, and more.

We highlighted the difference between a policy objective and a policy purpose. The objective of the security policy is to achieve a broad goal to more efficiently protect the company. The policy purpose explains how the company will protect itself from those threats using the actual rules of the policy.

We illustrated that the policy audience needs to be clearly defined in the document to avoid leaving any loopholes in the policy. This also makes all employees and other audience members realize that this policy is a set of rules and regulations that apply to them, and that they will have to follow. It focuses the audience on the ways they are responsible for protecting the company.

We defined the policy statement as being that element of the policy where all the rules are listed. We mentioned that the policy statement usually constitutes the bulk of the policy.

The policy enforcement clause is where we explain that there will be consequences for violating our policy. The audience needs to know there is a price to pay for breaking rules intended to protect the organization, its customers, and employees by safeguarding critical information. The policy enforcement clause needs to be spelled out accurately and fairly, and it needs to be consistently applied to all members of the defined audience.

Policy definitions add to making the document more accessible to the audience, and therefore are extremely important to the value of the policy. Indeed, it is quite difficult to follow a rule that contains language you don't understand, while it is very easy to break a rule you don't understand— without even knowing you were breaking the rule. Definitions should be accurate, concise, and precise. While we don't want to insult the reader, it is better to have more definitions than needed than the other way around.

Test Your Skills

MULTIPLE CHOICE QUESTIONS

1. The purpose of policy companions such as standards, guidelines, and procedures is to:

    A. provide the framework for policy implementation

    B. make the author feel important

    C. make the document look official

    D. conform to government regulations

2. The policy audience includes:

    A. only company full-time employees

    B. only a subset of the company's employees

    C. whomever the policy is applicable to

    D. all the employees of the company

3. What element of a security policy does the following phrase belong to? "This e-mail policy applies equally to all individuals granted access privileges to any of the company's information resource with the capacity to send, receive, or store electronic mail."

   A. the statement of authority

   B. the policy statement

   C. the policy headings

   D. the policy audience

4. The _____ is also a statement of culture, the aim of which is to "recruit" the reader and outline the core values of the company.

   A. policy statement of purpose

   B. policy statement

   C. policy enforcement clause

   D. policy statement of authority

5. A standard can best be defined as a:

   A. requirement

   B. suggestion

   C. guide

   D. law

6. What element of a security policy does the following phrase belong to? "This policy is established to achieve compliance with applicable statutes, regulations, and mandates regarding the management of information resources."

   A. the statement of authority

   B. the policy statement

   C. the policy objectives

   D. the policy audience

7. The _____ explains what motivated the company to draft the security policy.

   A. policy statement of purpose

   B. policy headings

   C. policy enforcement clause

   D. policy statement of authority

8. A guideline can best be defined as a:

    A. requirement

    B. suggestion

    C. series of directions

    D. law

9. The _____ contains all of the logistical information regarding a specific policy area.

    A. policy statement of purpose

    B. policy headings

    C. policy enforcement clause

    D. policy statement of authority

10. Which of the following statements is true?

    A. A security policy should only include one objective.

    B. A security policy should not include any exceptions.

    C. A security policy should not include a glossary.

    D. A security policy should not list all step-by-step measures that need to be taken.

11. Policy definitions are:

    A. a glossary of terms that should be explained

    B. a detailed list of the possible penalties associated with breaking rules set forth in the policy

    C. a list of all the members of the security policy creation team

    D. none of the above

12. The _____ contains the penalties that would apply if a portion of the security policy were to be ignored by an employee.

    A. policy statement of purpose

    B. policy statement

    C. policy enforcement clause

    D. policy statement of authority

13. Which section of the security policy includes the date the policy was written, adopted, and/or approved?

    A. the policy statement of purpose

    B. the policy statement

    C. the policy enforcement clause

    D. the policy headings

14. The _____ contains the actual rules and regulations that make up the security policy.

    A. policy statement of purpose

    B. policy statement

    C. policy enforcement clause

    D. policy statement of authority

15. What element of a security policy does the following phrase belong to? "Users must not download or install any software from the Internet."

    A. the statement of authority

    B. the policy statement

    C. the policy headings

    D. the policy audience

16. A procedure can best be defined as a:

    A. requirement

    B. series of directions

    C. suggestion

    D. policy

17. While the rules that are introduced in the security policy are meant to apply to all employees, there can exist some special circumstances where they should be ignored. Where are those circumstances defined?

    A. the policy statement of purpose

    B. the policy statement

    C. the policy enforcement clause

    D. the policy exceptions

18. What element of a security policy does the following phrase belong to? "Electronic mail system: Any computer software application that allows electronic mail to be communicated from one computing system to another."

    A. the statement of authority

    B. the policy definitions

    C. the policy objectives

    D. the policy statement

19. A security policy should include:

    A. absolutely no exceptions at all

    B. as many exceptions as can be thought of

    C. as few exceptions as possible

    D. at least one exception per rule

20. What element of a security policy does the following phrase belong to? "This e-mail policy was created to establish the rules for the use of corporate e-mail for the sending, receiving, or storing of electronic mail."

    A. the statement of authority

    B. the policy statement of purpose

    C. the policy objectives

    D. the policy statement

21. The statement of authority identifies:

    A. who has the authority to enforce the policy

    B. who has the authority to author the policy

    C. who has the authority to edit the policy

    D. the authority of the governing body

22. The name of the person/group (e.g., Executive Committee) who authorized the policy should be included in:

    A. the statement of authority

    B. the statement of authorship

    C. the policy headings

    D. the policy audience

23. When drafting a list of exceptions for a security policy, the language should:

    A. be as accurate as possible

    B. be as vague as possible

    C. reference another, dedicated document

    D. none of the above

24. What element of a security policy does the following phrase belong to? "The Company's goals for publishing our new Employee Information Security Policies are not to impose restrictions that are contrary to our established culture of openness."

    A. the statement of authority

    B. the statement of authorship

    C. the policy headings

    D. the policy audience

EXERCISES

Exercise 2.1: Standards, Guidelines, and Procedures

1. Create a one-sentence class attendance standard that supports the following policy: All students will comply with the schoolwide attendance standard.

2. Create a one-sentence guideline to help students adhere to the policy.

3. Create a three-step procedure for requesting exceptions to the policy.

Exercise 2.2: "Using My Car" Policy

1. Compose a policy that defines who can borrow your car, under what circumstances, and how they must treat the car. If you don't own a car, pretend that you do.

2. Your policy should be less than one page long.

3. Your policy should include all the essential elements.

4. You may use traffic laws, personal preference, mechanical knowledge, or a blend of all three as the basis of your policy. For example, your policy could prohibit the use of alcohol because it is against the law to drink and drive; or your policy could prohibit using the transmission for braking as this will cause undue wear on the transmission.

As a companion to your policy, you must create at least one guideline and one procedure. A guideline might be suggesting a certain brand of fuel. A procedure might be the proper way to start the car.

Exercise 2.3: Cohabitation Policy: Housemates

1. Create a housecleaning policy with specific duties for each member or roommate.

2. Address daily, weekly, bi-weekly, and monthly chores to be performed.

3. Decide what is policy and what is best separated into standards, guidelines, and procedures.

Exercise 2.4: Policy Exceptions

1. You live at home with your parents and younger siblings. The policy of the house is that all occupants are assigned housekeeping chores. Your elderly grandparents are planning to move in with your family. Should the policy be reviewed? Why?

2. Based upon your review, write an exception clause that explains what exceptions may be allowed and under what circumstances.

Exercise 2.5: Policy Definitions

1. The purpose of policy definitions is to clarify any ambiguous term. Assuming that you were authoring the policy, what criteria would you use to determine which terms should have definitions?

2. The challenge in writing policy is using language that your intended audience will understand. Assuming you had to write a policy that will be used for a multi-national organization with offices world-wide. What language challenges would you face? How would you address these challenges?

PROJECTS

Project 2.1: Categorizing a Real Security Policy

1. Go to **www.google.com** and locate the Tufts University Information Technology Resources Security Policy. Download the Microsoft Word or the Adobe Acrobat version, depending on the software you have available on your computer. Note that Acrobat Reader is a free download from the **www.adobe.com** Web site.

2. Read the whole document, and then break it down into elements such as those that were covered in this chapter. Write down all the elements that were used in this particular policy.

3. Equipped with the list of elements that appear in that policy, look back at this chapter and determine which elements do not appear in this policy. Create a list of those missing elements.

4. Focus on the policy definitions section. Do you think that it is extensive enough? Do you think that it is precise enough? Would you say that it is a high-quality document? Write a paragraph to substantiate your opinion.

5. Choose a couple of terms in the policy that are not defined in the policy definitions section and write a quick definition for each.

Project 2.2: A Study of the Enterprise Security Policy for the State of Mississippi

1. Go to **www.google.com** and locate the Enterprise Security Policy for the State of Mississippi. The first sentence in that policy, on page 2, is "The purpose of the Information Technology Security Policy is to create an environment within State of Mississippi agencies that maintains system security, data integrity and privacy by preventing unauthorized access to data [...]". This first sentence falls under a heading title of "Introduction." The next heading is called "Purpose of Security Policy." Do you think that this sentence was located in the right element? If yes, please explain your answer by writing a brief paragraph. If not, in which element do you think it should have appeared?

2. Read the policy. Which segment is used to list policy exceptions? Do you think that the language used in that segment is all-inclusive enough, or do you think that it leaves loopholes and errors of interpretation? Write a paragraph defending your opinion.

3. Where in the policy is the Enforcement Clause located (page number)? What is it called? How detailed is it? What is the maximum penalty according to this document? Do you think that the Enforcement Clause is a well-drafted document? Explain your answer by writing at least one paragraph.

4. Is a specific section of the policy dedicated to defining the policy audience? Where in the policy do you find a definition of the audience? How long is it? Do you think that it is an appropriate definition?

5. Based on the information you accumulated from reading this policy, and on your findings from point #4, write a policy audience section to replace what currently appears in this policy.

Project 2.3: Testing the language and clarity of a policy document

The following is an excerpt from the University of Florida's Information Technology Security policy. The full policy can be found at: **http://www.it.ufl.edu/policies/security/**

"General Rules

All IT security measures must comply with federal and state laws, university rules and policies, and the terms of applicable contracts including software licenses. Examples of applicable laws, rules and policies include the laws of libel, privacy, copyright, trademark, obscenity and child pornography; the Florida Computer Crimes Act, the Electronic Communications Privacy Act and the Computer Fraud and Abuse Act, which prohibit "hacking," "cracking" and similar activities; the university's Student Code of Conduct; the university's Sexual Harassment Policy. IT staff with questions as to how the various laws, rules and resolutions may apply to a particular use of university computing resources should contact the Office of the General Counsel or their appropriate legal services for more information.

Requests for exceptions to this policy must be submitted in writing by the Unit ISM to the OIT Security Committee for review. The UF ISM will respond to all requests for exceptions in writing.

This policy will be reviewed and updated by OIT Security Committee as needed, but at a minimum annually."

1. Make a list of all of the terms listed that you feel require definitions.

2. Ask one other student and one faculty member to read the excerpt and identify the terms that they are unfamiliar with. Are these lists different?

3. Combine the two lists. Write clear definitions for each term.

4. Request that the student and faculty member review the definitions and critique for clarity.

5. Create a quiz based upon the definitions. The quiz should have two columns. Column A should list the terms. Column B should list (in random order) the definitions. Ask someone who has not been involved in this project to study your definitions developed in step 3 and then take the quiz. Based upon the quiz results, determine if your definitions served their purpose.

Case Study

The purpose of this case study is to highlight the material covered in Chapter 2. To achieve this goal, let us focus on a scenario where a company that handles medical information had to create a new security policy from the ground up.

After determining who the security policy creation team members were going to be, the tasks were divided between the different members based on their respective roles in the company. The main issue with which this company was faced revolved around the fact that no one in the company, and therefore no one in the creation team, had ever written a security policy. Still, they decided to forge ahead without involving any experienced talent from outside the company.

One of the first actions they took was to scour the Internet in search of published policies that pertained to companies that happened to be in the same industry as they were. The consensus was that they could base their creative effort on what policies they found online, using this existing material as guidance. Specifically, they were interested in the tables of content of these different policies, since they offered a "creation roadmap" of sorts.

The most glaring defect with their strategy was that they had no control over the quality of the policies they found. Basing their creative effort on a bad template could only result in a flawed policy for their company. This issue became clearer as they gathered and compared the different policies that they had selected. The fact that no two policies contained the same list of elements became an apparent flaw in their strategy. Still, they forged ahead, their logic being that they could look at all the different elements present in all those policies, and decide which applied to their needs, thereby creating their own list of elements for their own policy. In essence, they were creating their own policy template.

The template they decided to use included the following elements: a statement of objectives, a loosely defined audience, the actual policy statement, and a policy enforcement clause. There were no policy headings, no statement of purpose, no statement of authority, no statement of exceptions, and no definitions.

▶▶ CONTINUED ON NEXT PAGE

>> CONTINUED

The quality of the policy could be found in the policy statement itself, because the information contained within was mostly content with which they were very familiar, since they were involved in the creation of their own company.

The flaws were multiple, however. For example, the lack of a statement of authority wasted an opportunity to reinforce the core values of the company, and therefore could not equate the policy with the very identity of the company. Furthermore, because the policy audience was badly defined, employees could not—or would not?—necessarily believe that the policy directly applied to them. The lack of a statement of purpose also had a negative impact on the adoption of the policy by employees. It was seen, by some employees at least, as a major inconvenience for no other apparent purpose than to create rules for the sake of it. Last, but not least, failing to include a definition section also meant that some of the material covered in the policy was not understood by all employees, further negatively impacting the value of the policy as a tool to help run the company.

In other words, the lack of an appropriate structure for the creation of the policy resulted in a document that was largely rejected by the target audience.

This failure cost the company in more ways than one: There was the loss of productivity for all the time spent crafting a flawed policy that had to be retired. There was the threat of damaging the corporate culture and the relationship between management and the rest of the employees. And finally, there was the threat of running a business according to a policy that did not adequately reflect the company's security needs.

1. You have been asked to evaluate this situation and meet with the policy committee to explain to them why a consistent format is important and the critical role each element plays in policy development. Your task is to develop a persuasive oral presentation.

2. You have also been tasked with hiring a consultant to help with the process of policy development. You need to develop a list of questions that you would ask a consultant about her policy writing skills.

Part **Two**

Information Security Policy Domains

Part Two focuses on answering four key questions. What are we trying to achieve in pursuit of information security? What is the ultimate goal of writing information security policies? How do we develop policy in an organized and methodical manner? Lastly, how do we integrate policy into everyday practice?

Protecting the confidentiality, integrity, and availability of information and information assets is the unifying goal of an information security program. In pursuit of that goal, we will be using the Organization for International Standardization (ISO) 17799 standard as a conceptual framework. Each chapter concentrates on the unique aspects of a specific security domain.

- **Chapter 3:** Information Security Framework
- **Chapter 4:** Organizational Security Policies and Procedures
- **Chapter 5:** Asset Classification Policies and Procedures
- **Chapter 6:** Personnel Policies and Procedures
- **Chapter 7:** Physical and Environmental Security Policies and Procedures
- **Chapter 8:** Communications and Operations Management Policies and Procedures
- **Chapter 9:** Access Control Policies and Procedures
- **Chapter 10:** Systems Development and Maintenance Policies and Procedures
- **Chapter 11:** Disaster Recovery and Business Continuity Policies and Procedures

Chapter | 3

Information Security Framework

Chapter Objectives

After reading this chapter and completing the exercises, you will be able to do the following:

- Plan the three main goals of an information security program: confidentiality, integrity, and availability—the CIA Triad.
- Classify data and information.
- Identify information ownership roles.
- Apply the ISO 17799/BS 7799 Code of Practice for Information Security Management.
- Understand the intent of the ten security domains of the ISO 17799:2000 Code of Practice.

Introduction

What are we trying to achieve in pursuit of information security? What is the ultimate goal of writing information security policies? What tangible benefit will come to our customers, our employees, our partners, and our organizations from our Herculean effort? Our focus in this chapter on information security framework will answer these and many other questions.

Framework lends itself to many easily related metaphors. The most obvious is that of any building: No foundation, no building. More specifically, the better the framing of any building, the longer it will last, the more it can hold, and the more functional it becomes. Of course, with any building there must first be a plan. We hire architects and engineers to design our buildings, to think about what is possible and relay the best way to achieve those possibilities.

In the same way, we need a framework for our information security program, which includes standards to act as our foundation. Additionally, like the many rooms of any building, each with its own functions, we must also classify our needs for the program into logical and manageable "domains," which lead us into subdomains that seem naturally subordinate to their parent domains. For example, under the parent domain Personnel Security we would expect to find things related to personnel, such as terms and condition of employment, employee screening, and so forth.

In addition to classifying our needs for the overall program, we must have a system to classify the information itself. If we don't distinguish sensitive information from public information, how can we effectively implement controls? We might spend too much money trying to protect public information, and not enough on the private and sensitive information.

Another issue we must keep in mind is information ownership. Who owns the data? Who is ultimately responsible for an organization's information?

If we create the framework correctly, any issue or concern we encounter will already have a logical place within. Without the framework, every new situation will see us repeating, redesigning, and reacting, which all together can be referred to as "unplanned" or spending time in crisis. Given all the years people have been doing business, and considering all the experience we have to draw upon, there is absolutely no reason to choose crisis over well-planned framework. In the case of information security, failing to plan and structure an organizational environment will eventually be rewarded with certain failure.

The one thing we need before we create a framework, however, is some kind of unifying principle to give us a goal to achieve. This is where we will begin this chapter.

Planning the Goals of an Information Security Program

CIA. It's easy to guess that the first thing that popped into your mind when you read those three letters was the Central Intelligence Agency. To those of us engaged in information security, however, these three letters stand for something we strive to attain rather than an agency of the United States government. Confidentiality, integrity, and availability—CIA—are the unifying principles or the goals of an information security program. They are commonly referred to as the *CIA Triad* of information security. Since they are interrelated and interdependent, we can also think of them as the unifying principal of any information security program. To understand their relationship to each other, it will be helpful to first explore each one separately. After exploring each, it should become clear how they depend on each other, and how the program depends on each goal being met consistently.

"C" Is for Confidentiality

When you tell a friend something "in confidence," what do you mean? You have relayed or disclosed a piece of information that should not be relayed or disclosed to anyone else. The goal of *confidentiality* is to prevent the unauthorized disclosure of sensitive information.

The information exchanged between doctors and patients or lawyers and clients is protected by confidentiality laws called the doctor-patient privilege and the attorney-client privilege, respectively. We place a very high value on this quality in people and express it in many ways, referring to those who keep our confidences as trustworthy, dependable, or loyal. The confidentiality of information is certainly not a new idea, so what's all the fuss about? Going back to Table 1.1 on the states and residences of information, we can find the answer to that question.

Computer systems and computer networks, including most importantly the Internet, are the main reasons why that dusty old idea, confidentiality, has taken on a new luster. What we take for granted in the year 2005 would have been considered magic just 20 years ago. The amazing speed at which we arrived here from there is also the reason we have such a gap in security, especially when viewed through the CIA lens.

The pace of the market doesn't slow to accommodate or even to take a passing glance at the problems to which it will give rise. So while it may seem that information security is a bit extreme sometimes, it is really a long overdue reaction to the explosion of information happening all around us since the birth of the public Internet.

As it pertains to information security, confidentiality is the protection of information from unauthorized people, resources, and processes. None of us likes the thought of our private health information or financial information falling into some stranger's hands. No business owner likes the thought of her proprietary business information being disclosed to competitors. If you need a very extreme example of how we prize our confidentiality, take a look at the punishments given to those who commit treason by disclosing state secrets to foreign governments.

Consider the three states of information again: Where and how information is stored, processed, and transmitted. Also reconsider the three residences: information systems, paper, and in every human being. Now consider all the ways in which information can be accessed and disclosed against the wishes of its owners, and you have identified the threats to confidentiality. These include:

- Hackers

- Password-cracking applications

- Unauthorized user activity

- Unauthorized transmission of information

- Improper access controls

- Shoulder surfing, or the act of looking over someone's shoulder at his computer monitor

- Improper disposal of paper and digital media

- Social engineering, or the use of trickery and deception to gain access to information by taking advantage of people's natural inclination to trust and be helpful

- Malicious code, including viruses, worms, and Trojan horse programs

In addition to threats, we must also consider carefully why we are vulnerable to these threats. For example, we may be vulnerable to shoulder surfing because we did not think about it when we designed our interior space, and so our monitors face in such a way that anyone walking by can see what we are working on. Another example of vulnerability would be the simple fact that we are connected to the Internet, which makes us vulnerable to just about everything on the preceding list of threats.

Before we jump into writing an information security policy for any organization, we must first consider the threats we face, our vulnerabilities to those threats, and the risks we face if any of the myriad threats were to exploit any of the myriad vulnerabilities. This process is called a *risk assessment,* and it is the foundation of a successful information security program. We must understand the risks we face to make decisions about how to control those risks to protect our information.

Some of the ways an organization can control risks to confidentiality include virus protection, firewalls, encryption for files and e-mail use, and, most important of all, end-user security training.

A well-planned and well-executed risk management methodology will help us to achieve our goal of confidentiality as well as the next two aspects of the CIA, integrity and availability.

"I" Is for Integrity

Whenever the word *integrity* comes to mind, so does the film "The Un-touchables," starring Kevin Costner and Sean Connery. The film is about a group of police officers who could not be "bought off" by organized crime. They were incorruptible. Integrity is certainly one of the highest ideals of personal character. When we say someone has integrity, we mean she lives her life according to a code of ethics; she can be trusted to behave in certain ways in certain situations. It is interesting to note that those to whom we ascribe the quality of integrity can be trusted with our confidential information.

As for information security, integrity has a very similar meaning. *Integrity* is the protection of system information or processes from intentional or accidental unauthorized modification. In the same way we count on people of integrity to behave a certain way, we rely on our information to be a certain way. In other words, is the information the same as it was intended to be? For example, if you save a file with important information that must be relayed to members of your organization, but someone opens the file and changes some or all of the information, the file has lost its integrity. The consequences could be anything from coworkers missing a meeting you planned for a specific date and time, to 50,000 machine parts being produced with the wrong dimensions. Another example is of a computer virus that corrupts some of the system files required to "boot" the computer. If the integrity of your operating system's boot files is corrupted, the computer is unusable.

To make this a bit more personal, let's talk about medical and financial information. What if you are injured and unconscious and taken to the emergency room of a hospital, and the doctors must look up your health information. You would want it to be correct, wouldn't you? Consider what might happen if you had an allergy to some very common treatment and this critical information had been deleted from your medical records. Or think of your dismay as you are visiting England on vacation and you confidently put your ATM card into the machine, only to receive a "no available funds" message. You know very well that the last time you checked your account balance, it showed thousands of dollars available. How do you think you would feel?

These are issues concerning the integrity of information.

Some threats to integrity include:

- Hackers

- Unauthorized user activity

- Interception and alteration of data transmission such as e-mail

- Improper access controls

■ Malicious code, including viruses, worms, and Trojan horse programs

Many of the vulnerabilities that threaten integrity are the same as those that threaten confidentiality. Most notable, though, is the threat of interception and alteration of data in transmission. Most people use e-mail and the Internet completely unaware that both transmit data in *clear text,* which is easily intercepted with any number of free software utilities called "network sniffers" or "packet capture" utilities.

In most cases, there is an ***inherent vulnerability*** to using technology. For instance, we are inherently vulnerable to Internet worms simply because we are connected to the Internet. We are inherently vulnerable to accidental modification of data because we are human, and humans make mistakes.

Some controls against the loss of integrity include digital signatures for e-mail, file hashing utilities that create mathematical algorithms out of digital files and alert us if anything about the file is changed, and behavioral controls such as separation of duties, rotation of duties, and end-user security training.

Integrity and confidentiality are very closely related. If a user password is disclosed to the wrong person, they could in turn manipulate, delete, or destroy data after gaining access to the system with the password they obtained. This is a clear example of a confidentiality threat exploited and leading directly to a loss of integrity.

"A" Is for Availability

The final component of the CIA Triad is also most often left out of consideration when one thinks about security. But, what is it to be secure? Would you feel secure if your car failed to start? Would you feel secure if you were very sick and your doctor could not be found? Whether or not systems and data are available for use is just as crucial as the confidentiality and integrity of the data itself. *Availability* is the assurance that systems and data are accessible by authorized users when needed. If we can't access the data we need, when we need it, we are not secure.

We must broaden our understanding of what information security means in several ways. For one, which we demonstrated earlier, information security is not just about computers, it is about information. For another, security does not pertain only to crime, malicious acts, or those who perpetrate them. It also pertains to feeling secure that the information can be used when needed, in the way needed.

As a matter of fact, availability is generally one of the first security issues addressed by Internet Service Providers. You may have heard the expressions "uptime" and "5-9s" (99.999% uptime), which means the systems that serve Internet connections, Web pages, and other such services will be available to users who need them when they need them. The ***Service Level Agreement*** is a type of agreement between a service provider and a customer that specifically addresses availability of services.

Just like confidentiality and integrity, we as humans prize availability. We want our friends and family to "be there when we need them," we want food and drink available, we want our money available, and so forth. In some cases, our lives depend on the availability of these things, including information. Ask yourself how you would feel if you needed immediate medical care and your physician could not access your medical records.

Some threats to availability include:

- loss of processing ability due to natural disasters

- loss of processing ability due to hardware failure

- loss of processing ability due to human error or malicious acts

- power failure

- Denial of Service attacks

- injury, sickness, or death of key personnel

- malicious code, including viruses, worms, and Trojan horse programs.

We are more vulnerable to availability threats than to the other components of the CIA Triad. We are absolutely certain to face some of them. For example, all computer hardware WILL fail in time; of this we can be sure. For this reason, there are many standard controls to address availability, and we have been employing methods of controlling availability issues longer than the other two in our CIA Triad with respect to information technology. We have tape backups, redundant controllers and drives in our servers, Uninterruptible Power Supplies (UPS) devices, power generators with automatic fail-over protection, environmental controls like air conditioning in our data centers, server clustering, and so forth. One might say that if it's not available, who cares if it's confidential or has integrity?

This brings us to the big question: Which is most important, confidentiality, integrity, or availability? Don't think for a second that you can just jump to an answer and be done with this one. In fact, this is the question that will inevitably cause the fiercest debates. The answer requires an organization to assess its mission, evaluate its services, and consider regulations and contractual agreements. Organizations frequently consider all three components of the CIA Triad equally important, in which case resources must be allocated proportionately.

Another question to answer is: How is availability related to the other two components of the CIA Triad? The easiest example is physical theft. If a criminal steals a server, the chance of the information residing on that server remaining confidential are slim-to-none. Another example would be power failure. If an organization must resort to emergency procedures that include paper and other nontechnological means, it is more likely that mistakes will be made and that information will be more readily disclosed to unauthorized parties.

So with the CIA Triad as the guiding principle of our ultimate information security goal, we know that each piece of our program must work toward achieving a state where data is confidential, has integrity, and is available.

The "Five A's" of Information Security: Some Other Meaningful Letters and What They Stand For

Now that we know about the CIA Triad of information security, we can also take a look at the "supporting cast" of information security principles, which are commonly known as the *Five A's.* Here is a quick explanation of each:

1. *Accountability:* the process of tracing actions to their source. Nonrepudiation techniques, intrusion detection systems (IDS), and forensics all support accountability.

2. *Assurance:* the processes, policies, and controls used to develop confidence that security measures are working as intended. Auditing, monitoring, testing, and reporting are the foundations of assurance.

3. *Authentication:* the positive identification of the person or system seeking access to secured information or systems. Passwords, Kerberos, Token, and Biometric are forms of authentication.

4. *Authorization:* granting users and systems a predetermined level of access to information resources.

5. *Accounting:* the logging of access and usage of information resources.

These principles of information security can be thought of as the mission of our information security program. If an organization can create a comprehensive information security program that consistently serves all of the preceding principles, it will have met the highest goals. It is important to remember that information security is not a "point-in-time" measurement but rather an ongoing process requiring vigilance and sustained effort. This is also why it is important to write policies that facilitate consistency and sustainability.

Now that we have identified the goals, we have to build a foundation capable of supporting the mission to achieve those goals. The rest of this chapter will focus on that foundation and framework.

Classifying Data and Information

Classifying information is a critical foundational component in a risk management program, and ultimately a comprehensive information security program. Different kinds of information have inherently different levels of importance to any organization. The challenges of information classification lay in the way most organizations store, process, and transmit their information. Any single system may contain information of every level of importance, creating complexities that are almost impossible to avoid. For this reason, we do not stop at classifying information, we also develop labeling and handling criteria that always default to the most important or sensitive information present. In other words, if we have a server with just one critically important directory, then the server must be treated according to the standards we have developed for critical information.

To begin, we have to design the classifications themselves. Once created, we will decide how information in each classification will be handled, and then we will decide into which category our information fits.

A common classification system would include the following categories:

- *Confidential:* Confidential information is meant to be kept secret and restricted to only a small circle of authorized individuals. Unauthorized disclosure would result in harm to the organization. Examples would be financial positions, laboratory research, and patent applications.

- *Sensitive:* Sensitive information is generally available internally on a "need-to-know basis." Unauthorized disclosure may result in harm to reputation, credibility, privacy, or regulatory compliance.

- *Public:* This information could be made public without any implications for the company (i.e., the data is not confidential).

IN PRACTICE: Classifying Your Telecommunications Information

To understand the importance of any concept, it is always helpful to draw a personal connection to the concept. You probably already have one or more classification systems in use without having formally decided to use one. Your own system might depend on who you are talking to as well as the type of information being exchanged. You have likely made many decisions about how each type of information should be treated, and which people and organizations with whom you will share each type of information.

Let's use as an example the information regarding your telecommunications use. You have a phone of a certain brand and model; you have a phone number and you also have any number of contacts in your personal phone book. Of these three types of information, can you identify any differences in their level of sensitivity? In other words, is one type more valuable than the others? The answer to these questions is the primary reason we need to classify information.

Considering the preceding classifications, where might you place each of the three types of information we have identified?

Would any serious implications arise if the brand and model of phone you use became public knowledge? What about your phone number? Finally, what about your personal phone book?

It would seem our three types of information fit into our three classifications quite well, with the possibility of exceptions. You may be happy to tell anyone who asks what brand and model of phone you use, while you may give your phone number only to friends and business associates. Your phone book, on the other hand, contains other people's information, which requires a greater level of care. After all, I may have given you my phone number, but not permission to give it to others.

Data classification is an important foundation for the information security program. Once we have classified information, we can pinpoint exactly where our energies and budget are best spent. We can also decide who in our organization will have access to each data classification and how we will handle each type of information. Perhaps most importantly, we can write policies that guide people to use and handle our information according to our rules.

3

FYI: There's More than One Way to Classify Information

Though we have focused on one type of information classification system, it is important to remember that there is no one standard that will fit every organization or every type of information. Additionally, we may have more than one classification system in place affecting certain kinds of information. For example, if we have one classification relating to the sensitivity information might have to disclosure, as cited in the preceding example, we might also have a classification regarding the need for availability for different kinds of information.

Some systems may require, based on a risk analysis, that they be available more than others. So we might have classifications that specify "uptime" requirements for any given system. If a Web hosting company has Service Level Agreements guaranteeing a certain percentage of "uptime," the risk is severe if one of the systems that serves customers under this agreement becomes unavailable. Remember, availability is one of the CIA Triad, and a critical aspect of information security.

The federal government uses a classification system that also corresponds to the authorization levels assigned to individuals. Most of us are already familiar with these criteria: Top Secret, Secret, Classified, and so on. To gain access to a top secret document, a person must have top secret authorization. This structure is referred to as **Mandatory Access Control (MAC).** MAC combines information classification with personnel clearance levels.

There are two other types of authorization systems: **Discretionary Access Control (DAC)** and **Role-Based Access Control (RBAC).** Discretionary Access Control works on the owner-user model. If I own the information, I grant you authorization to use it, at my discretion. Role-Based Access Control uses roles to grant authorization. For instance, bank tellers have access to certain information and loan officers have access to different information based on their job roles in the bank.

Identifying Information Ownership Roles

Who owns the information, and what does it mean to be an information owner? Good question. Though it may seem an easy concept, you might be surprised how often organizations get the answer wrong. It is often those in Information Technology (IT) or Information Systems (IS) departments who are widely perceived as owning the information. Perhaps this is due to the word *information* being part of the department title. For whatever the reason, IT and IS departments are rarely owners of organizational information. Rather, they are the people charged with maintaining the systems that store, process, and transmit the information and are known as ***information custodians.*** Information custodians are responsible for taking care of the information and the information systems. Information custodians are better known as system administrators, webmasters, and network engineers.

Information ownership is charged to those liable and responsible for protecting the information and the business results derived from using that information. ***Information owners*** are those authorities or individuals with original responsibility for the policies and practices of information. For example, a bank's senior loan officer might be the owner of information pertaining to customer loans. The senior loan officer has responsibility to decide who has access to customer loan information, the policies for using this information, and the controls to be established to protect this information.

Again, it will be helpful to draw a personal connection to the concept of information/data ownership. Even though a car isn't really information, the concept is analogous and a useful example. You own your car, and therefore you are responsible for many aspects of the car. In a previous exercise, we wrote a policy for the acceptable use of our car. As the owners of our cars, we must make the rules as to their use. We are liable for damage to our car and also if our car in any way damages other cars, property, or people. We also decide what kind of—and how much—auto insurance coverage we will need to protect us in case of an accident. Information ownership operates on the very same principles.

The ISO 17799/BS 7799 Code of Practice for Information Security Management

Securing information systems can be a daunting task. While organizations may have unique situations, they all have a common need to implement information security fundamentals in their quest to attain confidentiality, integrity, and availability (CIA). The ISO 17799:2000 Code of Practice for Information Security Management is a framework of information security recommendations applicable to public and private organizations of all sizes. According to the ISO Web site, "the ISO 17799 standard gives recommendations for information security management for use by those who are responsible for initiating, implementing or maintaining security in their organization. It is intended to provide a common basis for developing organizational security standards and effective security management practice and to provide confidence in inter-organizational dealings."

The ISO 17799:2000 Code of Practice for Information Security Management has its origins in Great Britain. In 1989, the UK Department of Trade and Industry's (DTI) Commercial Computer Security Centre (CCSC) developed the "Users Code of Practice" designed to help computer users employ sound security practices and assure the confidentiality, integrity, and availability of information systems. Further development came from the National Computing Centre (NCC), and later a group formed from British industry, to ensure that the Code was applicable and practical from a user's point of view. The document was originally published as British Standards guidance document PD 0003, *A code of practice for information security management.* After more input was received from private sector organizations, the document was reintroduced as British Standard BS7799:1995.

After two revisions in 1997 and 1999, the BS7799 was proposed as an International Standards Organization (ISO) standard. Though the first revisions were defeated, it was eventually adopted by the ISO after an international ballot closed in August 2000 and published with minor amendments as ISO/IEC 17799:2000 on December 1, 2000. Unlike other ISO standards, such as ISO 9000 used in manufacturing, there is currently not a certification process for ISO 17799. Lack of a certification process has not deterred organizations and governments worldwide from adopting ISO 17799 as their standard code of practice.

FYI: Who Is the ISO?

The International Organization for Standardization (ISO) is a network of the national standards institutes of 146 countries. Each member country is allowed one delegate, and a Central Secretariat in Geneva, Switzerland, coordinates the system. In 1946, delegates from 25 countries met in London and decided to create a new international organization, of which the object would be "to facilitate the international coordination and unification of industrial standards." The new organization, ISO, officially began operations on February 23, 1947.

ISO is a nongovernmental organization: Unlike the United Nations, its members are not delegations of national governments. Nevertheless, ISO occupies a special position between the public and private sectors. This is because, on the one hand, many of its member institutes are part of the governmental structure of their countries, or are mandated by their government. On

▸▸ CONTINUED ON NEXT PAGE

▶▶ CONTINUED

the other hand, other members have their roots uniquely in the private sector, having been set up by national partnerships of industry associations. ISO has developed over 13,000 International Standards on a variety of subjects ranging from country codes to passenger safety. More information about the ISO can be found at **www.iso.ch**.

Using the Ten Security Domains of the ISO 17799:2000

The ISO 17799:2000 standard is a comprehensive set of information security recommendations comprising best practices in information security. It is intended to serve as a single reference point for identifying the range of controls needed for most situations where information systems are used in industry and commerce, and to be used by large, medium, and small organizations. The term *organization* is used throughout this standard to mean both commercial and nonprofit organizations such as public sector and government agencies. The recommended practices are organized into ten "domains," or categories. Based upon these recommended best practices, organizations develop controls. The focus of the controls is the maintenance of confidentiality, integrity, and availability of information.

We will be using the ISO 17799:2000 standard as a framework for developing procedures and polices. Using this framework will allow us to organize our approach to developing policies; it provides a structure for development and a method of grouping similar policies. The first step is to become familiar with the goals and intent of each of the ISO 17799:2000 domains (categories). In subsequent chapters, we will examine each domain in depth; evaluate controls, policies, and procedures; and determine for which type/size organization the control and policy is appropriate.

Security Policy

The first domain focuses on providing direction and support for the information security program. This section stresses the importance of management involvement in establishing policy, the direction of the information security program, and a commitment to protecting both physical and logical information resources. This domain emphasizes the need for visible leadership and involvement of senior management.

Organizational Security

The Organization Security domain focuses on establishing and supporting a management framework to implement and manage information security within, across, and outside the organization. Security infrastructure controls should be both inward and outward facing. Inward facing controls and policies concentrate on employees' and stakeholders' relationships to information systems. Outward facing controls and policies concentrate on third-party access to information systems. Third parties include vendors, trading partners, customers, and service providers. This domain provides the structure for your information security program.

Asset Classification and Control

Information security assets include raw data, mined information, intellectual property, software, hardware, physical devices, and security equipment. It is essential to maintain an accurate inventory of information security assets. These information assets need to be classified to indicate the degree of protection. The classification should result in appropriate information labeling to indicate whether it is sensitive or critical and what procedures are appropriate for access, use, storage, transmission, or destruction of the asset. Earlier in this chapter, we discussed the importance of classifications; that's what this domain is all about.

Personnel Security

Human errors, negligence, and greed are responsible for most thefts, frauds, or misuse of facilities. Organizations need to implement controls for security in the hiring, employing, and termination of staff, management, and directors. Controls include personnel screening, acceptable use, confidentiality agreements, and terms and conditions of employment. This domain also addresses training employees in the correct (secure) use of information systems and how they can minimize the likelihood of security breaches. Lastly, the domain addresses the way an organization should respond to incidents affecting security and incident reporting mechanisms. Human nature is to be trusting. This domain reminds us that there are both good and bad people and that we need to keep our eyes wide open. The Human Resources Department should be involved in this area.

Physical and Environmental Security

The Physical and Environmental Security domain focuses on designing and maintaining a secure physical environment to prevent unauthorized access, damage, and interference to business premises. This involves controlling the physical security perimeter and physical entry; creating secure offices, rooms, and facilities; providing physical access controls; providing protection devices to minimize risks ranging from fire to electromagnetic radiation; and providing adequate protection to power supplies and data cables. To be successful in this area, you must involve multiple departments such as physical plant, maintenance, and physical security.

Communications and Operations Management

The Communications and Operations Management Security domain focuses on the requirements to ensure the correct and secure operation of information processing facilities such as data centers. The controls outline the responsibilities and procedures for the management and operations of information processing facilities and information systems. This includes detailed operating instructions and incident response procedures.

Network management requires a range of controls to achieve and maintain security in computer networks. "Housekeeping" measures include antivirus software, anti-spyware software, intrusion prevention and detection devices, backups, logging, and system monitoring. Special controls such as encryption or virtual private network (VPN) should be established to safeguard the confidentiality and integrity of data passing over public networks. Controls are required to ensure that the network is not attacked or compromised and also to maintain the availability of the network services.

Communications security addresses external exchanges of information. Recommendations include the consideration of strategies such as encryption to safeguard the confidentiality and integrity of data passing over public networks.

Access Control

The goal of the Access Control domain is to prevent unauthorized access to information systems. If this sounds familiar, it is because this is the goal of confidentiality. This includes defining access control policy and rules, user authentication and access management, (including password and access rights management), network access controls, operating system access control, use of system utilities, monitoring system access and use, and ensuring information security when using mobile computing and teleworking facilities.

System Development and Maintenance

In a perfect world, where companies are not subject to competitive and financial pressures, security would be built at the time of inception of a system. While this sounds like a dream, the reality is that identifying and defining security requirements at the seminal point in product development is cost effective and does lead to a better overall product. This begins with security requirements analysis and specification and providing controls at every stage, i.e., data input, data processing, data storage and retrieval, and data output. It may be necessary to build applications with cryptographic controls. There should be a defined policy on the use of such controls, which may involve encryption, digital signature, use of digital certificates, protection of cryptographic keys, and standards to be used for cryptography.

A strict change control procedure should be in place to facilitate tracking of changes. Any changes to operating systems or applications should be strictly controlled. Special precaution must be taken to ensure that no covert channels, back doors, or Trojans are introduced into the system for later exploitation.

Business Continuity Management

Protecting critical business processes from the effects of major failures or disasters and to minimize interruptions to business activities is the objective of the Business Continuity Management domain. A synonym for business continuity is *availability.* A business continuity management process begins by identifying the impact of events that cause interruptions to critical business processes and designing response, recovery, and continuity plans. The plan needs to be periodically tested, maintained, and reassessed based on changing circumstances.

Compliance

The objective of the Compliance Security domain is to ensure that the organization's information systems conform to local, national, and international criminal and civil laws, regulatory or contractual obligations, intellectual property rights (IPR), and copyrights. This domain requires input from the organization's legal advisors.

Is It Possible to Have Too Many Policies?

The answer is YES! For policies to be effective, they must be meaningful and relevant as well as appropriate to the size and complexity of the organization. Not all organizations will need all the policies referenced in the ISO 17799 standard. The key is to understand what policy and control may be needed in any given environment and then develop, adopt, and implement the controls and polices that make sense for the organization.

If you try to implement too many policies, you will overwhelm your intended audience. The same goes for polices that don't make sense or are too burdensome. All too often, users spend a ridiculous amount of time and energy avoiding or circumventing policies that were counterproductive to begin with. We can't say it enough: For policies to be effective, they must be relevant, understandable, and attainable. Policies must support, not hinder, the mission and goals of an organization.

Summary

Ensuring confidentiality, integrity, and availability as appropriate to the classification and criticality of information is the unifying principle of every information security program. In this chapter, we examined the CIA Triad and the threats to and inherent vulnerabilities that stand in the way of achieving our goals. We introduced the supporting cast of the Five A's and their relationship to CIA. To secure information appropriately, we must know how critical and/or how sensitive the information is. This is referred to as the *information classification process*. Once we have classified information, we can pinpoint exactly where our energies and budget are best spent. We can also decide who in our organization will have access to each data classification and how we will handle each type of information. Perhaps most importantly, we can write policies that guide people to use and handle our information according to our rules.

Writing policies without guidance or structure is an overwhelming task. The International Standards Organization (ISO) has published a technology neutral Code of Standards for Information Security known as the ISO 17799:2000. This standard has been internationally adopted by both private and public organizations of all sizes. The ISO 17799:2000 is divided into ten domains or categories. Each of these categories has a control objective, compliance requirements, and recommended policy components. The ISO 17799:2000 is very comprehensive and is intended to provide a framework for developing, adopting, and maintaining information security policies and controls.

Test Your Skills

MULTIPLE CHOICE QUESTIONS

1. The three principles in the CIA Triad are:

    A. confidence, integration, availability

    B. consistency, integrity, authentication

    C. confidentiality, integrity, availability

    D. confidentiality, integrity, awareness

2. A threat _____ a vulnerability.

    A. exposes

    B. exploits

    C. exacerbates

    D. extricates

3. Some threats to confidentiality include:
   A. hackers
   B. unauthorized disclosure of information
   C. improper access controls
   D. all of the above

4. Three controls to protect confidentiality include:
   A. firewalls, virus protection, and checksum utilities
   B. firewalls, virus protection, and digital signatures
   C. firewalls, intrusion detection, and e-mail encryption
   D. virus protection, digital signatures, and user training

5. As it pertains to information security, integrity is:
   A. the protection of organizational reputation
   B. the protection of system resources from accidental damage
   C. the protection of system information or processes from intentional or accidental unauthorized modification
   D. the successful secure combination of two or more information systems

6. We are inherently vulnerable to Internet worms because:
   A. worms are a dangerous kind of malicious code
   B. operating systems are known to be vulnerable when not patched properly
   C. we are connected to the Internet
   D. we use e-mail more than the phone

7. The most commonly overlooked security principle is:
   A. integrity
   B. integration
   C. availability
   D. acceptability

8. Some threats to availability include: (choose two)
   A. loss of processing capabilities due to natural disaster
   B. loss of processing capabilities due to human error
   C. loss of personnel due to accident
   D. loss of reputation from unauthorized event

9. The process of tracking actions to their source is called:
   A. accounting
   B. acceptance
   C. accountability
   D. actuality

10. The processes, policies, and controls used to develop confidence that security measures are working as intended is the definition of:
    A. insurance
    B. accounting
    C. assurance
    D. availability

11. The five A's of information security are:
    A. awareness, acceptance, availability, accountability, authentication
    B. awareness, acceptance, authority, authentication, availability
    C. accountability, assurance, authorization, authentication, accounting
    D. acceptance, authentication, availability, assurance, accounting

12. As it pertains to information security, MAC stands for:
    A. Media Access Calculation
    B. Mandatory Access Compatibility
    C. Mandatory Access Control
    D. Malicious Access Controlled

13. As it pertains to information security, RBAC stands for:
    A. Rules-Based Authentication Control
    B. Role-Based Authorization Control
    C. Role-Based Access Control
    D. Rules-Based Access Control

14. An information owner is responsible for:
    A. maintaining the systems that store, process, and transmit information
    B. protecting the information and the business results derived from use of that information
    C. protecting the people and processes used to access digital information
    D. none of the above

15. ISO stands for:

    A. Internal Standards Organization

    B. International Organization for Standardization

    C. International Standards Organization

    D. Internal Organization of Systemization

16. *Establishing and supporting a security management framework* is the objective of which ISO 17799:2000 security domain?

    A. Organizational Security

    B. Asset Classification and Control

    C. Security Policy

    D. Access Control

17. ISO 17799:2000 Code of Information Security Management was adopted from:

    A. BS 7799

    B. BS 7979

    C. BC 7799

    D. IE 17799

18. *User management and training* is found in which ISO 17799:2000 security domain?

    A. Compliance   *NO*

    B. Personnel Security *NO*

    C. Operations and Communications Management

    D. Systems Development and Maintenance

19. How many security domains are in the ISO 17799:2000?

    A. 10

    B. 100

    C. 12

    D. 20

20. *System audit controls* is part of which ISO 17799:2000 security domain?

    A. Compliance

    B. Access Control

    C. Audit Control —

    D. Organizational Security

EXERCISES

Exercise 3.1: Conducting a Security Survey

1. Pick four classmates to participate in a survey regarding information on their home computers.

2. Ask them which is the most important: That the information on their computer be confidential, have integrity, or be available.

3. Compile the answers in a table.

4. Use the same four people to conduct another survey. This time specify e-mail as the type of information. Compile the answers in a second table.

Exercise 3.2: Conducting a Survey of Other Students

1. Pick four people who are not in your class, but who attend your school.

2. Give them the same two survey questions as in Exercise 1.

3. Compile the answers in two tables.

Exercise 3.3: Comparing Answers from Each Survey

1. Compare the answers to both surveys for each group.

2. Compare the answers given by both groups with each other.

3. Write two paragraphs about the differences between responses to each question for both groups, and the differences in answers between groups.

Exercise 3.4: Identifying Information Ownership

1. Choose an organization such as your school or a company you work for.

2. Identify the various types and classifications of information the organization uses.

3. Identify who are the owners and custodians of the various types of information. State the reasoning behind these classifications of information and data ownership.

Exercise 3.5: Your Policy and the ISO 17799:2000

1. Using the car policy you developed in the Chapter 2 exercises, assign each of your policy statements to one of the ten security domains.

2. Write one more statement for your policy that fits into a security domain for which you have not yet accounted.

PROJECTS

Project 3.1: Classifying Your Personal Information

1. Create an information classification system for your own personal use.

2. Spend at least one half day paying attention to all the information you use by any means. Include conversations, paperwork you have to complete, homework assignments, e-mail, and Internet chat content.

3. Keep a record of all the types of information you used in one half day.

4. Assign each type of information a classification.

5. Did your classification system account for all the types of information you use? Write a paragraph explaining the reasons for your classifications.

Project 3.2: Protecting Your Personal Information

1. Using the information classification system and the types of information you used in Project 3.1, create appropriate labeling and handling procedures. For instance: How will you store bills, receipts from purchases, and bank statements? How will you label the storage media such as folders, file cabinets, and so forth? How will you handle disposal of items containing personal information? Write two paragraphs explaining your procedures.

2. Decide which type of access control you will use to protect your information. Will you use DAC, MAC, or RBAC? If using RBAC, you would have to place the people in your life into roles such as parent, sibling, friend, acquaintance, etc.; and then decide which information will be available to whom, based on his or her role. Make a chart with columns representing each role, who is in each role, and which information they have access to.

3. Create a system to control access to your information. For instance: You may have used academic grades as a type of information. Who will have access to your academic records? How will you know when this information has been accessed? How will you control access to this information? Write two paragraphs, one to answer each of the above questions.

4. What are the risks that the controls you created in Step 3 will not work as intended? For instance: What if you have decided that your sibling has no access to your academic information? What possible ways could your sibling gain access either intentionally or accidentally? Write a paragraph describing your findings.

5. Once you have identified the risk of your personal academic information being disclosed to an unauthorized party, you must create a control. Does this control have any impact on the system of controls you created in Step 3? Does this control introduce any new risks to your information security? Remember the CIA Triad. Write a paragraph explaining your findings.

Project 3.3: You and the ISO 17799:2000

You will now write a policy to protect your personal information using the ISO 17799 as your framework.

1. Using the preceding exercises and projects, create a short policy using the ten ISO 17799 security domains.

2. Use at least one supporting policy component from each of the ten domains and create a policy to address that section for each type of information you identified during your half day.

3. First, choose the sections from each of the ten domains you will be using and write a paragraph title for each.

4. Under each title, write a sentence or two describing the objective of the section and the purpose of your policy.

5. Under the objective and purpose, write down the intended audience for your policy.

6. Under the audience statement, begin writing your policy statements. Each should be one or two sentences long. For instance, if you chose the *confidentiality agreements section* under the Personnel Security domain, your policy statement might read: Siblings requesting access to my academic information must sign my special

confidentiality agreement prior to being granted access to my records.

7. You may use ideas and statements from any previous project or policy you have read so far.

Case Study

You have been contracted by a regional bank to rewrite its information security policies. The bank currently has an information security policy, but it is confusing, lacking in structure, and filled with discrepancies. The bank has recently acquired other banks and is preparing for a public offering.

The bank has heard of the ISO 17799 and would like to use it as the framework for the revised policies.

Where do you begin this project? Would you want to interview the author of the original policy? Would you prepare a list of questions based on the ISO 17799 to guide you in understanding what this bank can adhere to as policy? Which ISO domains and sections would you include, and why? Would you use any material from the original document in your new document?

Write a one-page explanation of how you would approach this project. Keep in mind, all domains and sections of the ISO 17799 are not automatically appropriate for every organization.

Chapter | 4

Security Policy Documents and Organizational Security Policies

Chapter Objectives

After reading this chapter and completing the exercises, you will be able to do the following:

- Compose a statement of authority.
- Develop and evaluate policies related to the information security policies document objectives and ownership.
- Create and assess policies associated with the management of security-related activities.
- Assess and manage the risks inherent in working with third parties.

Introduction

In Chapter 3, you were introduced to the ten ISO 17799 security domains. Starting with this chapter and continuing through the next seven, we begin the process of mapping the security objectives of each domain to realistic and usable policies. In this chapter, we have combined the first two domains—Security Policy (17799-3) and Organizational Security (17799-4)—because of their closely related goals and purposes.

Section 1 of the ISO 17799 is simply a paragraph describing the scope of the document. Section 2 defines the CIA Triad, risk assessment, and risk management. The actual security domains begin with ISO Section 3—Security Policy.

All eight chapters in this section of the book will follow the same format. We will begin with a description of the goals and objectives of the particular security domain. We will then discuss what should be covered in the policy, followed by a sample policy. All of these examples are pulled from real-world information security policies used in various organizational sectors, both public and private. We have chosen not to create policies that are as granular in nature as suggested by the ISO. Instead, to avoid redundancy, we are have grouped like goals and objectives together.

For security policies to be effective there must be commitment from leadership. This commitment needs to be communicated throughout the organization to vendors and business partners and the community at large. This commitment can best be expressed through a corporate policy statement known as a statement of authority. We will begin this chapter with a discussion of statements of authority. Once commitment from leadership has been established, "security champions" are needed to reinforce the message. We define a *security champion* as one who is willing to carry the banner of security often in the face of criticism, resistance, and ridicule. To effectively make their case, the security champions need the weight of written and adopted policies.

Composing a Statement of Authority

Imagine traveling to the fictional island nation of Sunshine. Before arriving, you spend time researching the local culture, language, currency, traffic laws, and customs. Why? Because you want to know how to behave, how to make friends, and how to stay out of trouble. For an organization, security policies are the mechanism used to communicate expectations of behavior. As with your research on Sunshine, though, you want assurance that the policies are correct and current. A statement of authority conveys to the reader the organization's intention, objective, and commitment. It is very important that the statement is issued by an authority figure, such as the Chairman of the Board, the Chief Executive Officer (CEO), the President, the Owner, or a Senior Manager. We have confidence in our currency because it is said to have the "full faith and credit of the United States of America." Information system users need to have same faith in the security policy. They need to know for sure that these are the directions and rules they should follow.

Who Should Sign the Statement of Authority?

In Chapter 2, we defined the statement of authority as an introduction to the policy, where the thought process behind the actual policy is presented to readers. It explains what motivated the company to draft this document. More than that, it is also a statement of culture, one that attempts to define what core values the company believes in and promotes, and what needs to be done from a security policy standpoint to ensure that these values can coexist with a realistic and strong security strategy. The statement of authority also usually attempts to "recruit" readers and show them what is expected of them as employees of the company or members of the organization.

Influencing and defining culture is the role of leadership. The signer should be seen as both a leader and a decision maker. The signer should be close enough to the organization that the members feel that they are in touch with the day-to-day operations. The catch is that the signer must also have the authority to enforce the policy.

Consider, for example, a large multinational corporation; the Chairman of the Board may be far removed from the operations and the employees. The employees might not even recognize his name. In this case, the regional or divisional president may be a much more appropriate signer. We can apply this concept to a smaller environment as well. Suppose a public high school decides to introduce new security policies that affect the students. Who do the students relate to more as an in-touch authority figure—the school board president or the school principal? For most students, the answer is the principal.

What Message Should the Statement of Authority Convey?

The goal of the statement of authority (SOA) is to deliver a clear message about the importance of information security to everyone who reads the policy. The SOA should be thought of as a teaching tool sprinkled with motivational "pep talk." In developing the SOA, you must remember that your audience may be varied in terms of their background, education, experience, age, and even native language. The SOA should reflect your organizational culture. If your culture is formal, then the SOA should be as well. However, if your culture is laid-back, then your SOA should be more relaxed. As a matter of fact, many organizations have discarded the term *statement of authority* with more friendly alternatives such as a "Message from the Chairman" or "Corporate Commitment."

The Role of the Security Champion

Creating a culture of security requires positive influences at multiple levels within an organization. The role of the security champion is critical. Security champions reinforce by example the message that security practices are important to the organization. A visible champion should be the Information Security Officer. In supporting roles, many organizations have information security committees or information security task forces. Generally, the members represent a cross-section of business lines or departments. In addition to providing advice and counsel to the ISO, their mission is to spread the gospel of security to their colleagues, coworkers, subordinates, and business partners.

IN PRACTICE: Sample Statement of Authority

This is a statement of authority from a state agency. When this statement was developed, the agency was introducing security policies for the first time. It was important to the agency's leadership that employees reacted positively and didn't feel like the policies were yet another layer of bureaucratic rules. The agency chose to begin its SOA with a personal note from the Commissioner.

A Message from the Commissioner:

"In conjunction with the Office of the CIO, and based on the International Standards Organization's (ISO) 17799 Standards for Information Security; we have endeavored to create policies which are clear, concise and easy to understand. We have also taken into consideration the ease of use and accessibility of these documents. It is so very important that these policies do more than dictate another layer of rules and regulations that we all must follow. Our hope is that they are educational, and that they speak the most important aspects of our existence, which are the public good, and our employees. I would like to thank you in advance for your support as we do our best to create a secure environment for public information, and fulfill our mission."

—Sincerely LJF, Commissioner

The Policy Statement:

The Department's intentions for publishing our new Employee Information Security Policies are not to impose restrictions that are contrary to our established culture of openness, trust and integrity. The Department is committed to protecting the Public, our employees, partners and the agency itself from illegal or damaging actions by individuals, either knowingly or unknowingly.

The 21st Century environment of connected technologies offers many opportunities to malicious or unknowing people from all over the world to anonymously attack, damage and corrupt vital public information; and to disrupt our ability to communicate effectively and accomplish the mission of our organization. Effective security is a civic responsibility, and a team effort involving the participation and support of every employee and affiliate who deals with information and/or information systems. It is the responsibility of every agency employee and affiliate to know, understand and adhere to these policies, procedures, standards and guidelines, and to conduct their activities accordingly.

This policy statement has been adopted in order to provide guidance and protection to agency employees and to safeguard the information resources of the State entrusted to agency employees.

Security Policy Document Policy–A Policy About a Policy

As you know by now, the essential foundation of a successful information security program is having *written* security policies that have been authorized and adopted by management and accepted by the user community. We can't stress enough the need for policies to be written. Spoken communication can easily become confused or misunderstood. Did you ever play "Telephone" as a child? In the game of Telephone, one child whispers a message to the child sitting next to her, who in turn whispers the message to the child sitting next to him, who in turn whispers the message to yet a fourth child, and so on until the message has been whispered to the last child in line. By the time the message reaches the last child, it has generally undergone significant change. We need to make sure that the message delivered by our security policies is consistent and unwavering. By design, our first policy, the *Information Security Policy Document Objective and Ownership policy,* unequivocally states the need for information security policies as well as who is responsible for creating, approving, enforcing, and reviewing policies.

The objective of the Information Security Document policy is to direct, approve, publish, and communicate the merits of an information security policy document. In other words, this is a policy about the need for written and managed policies. In addition to stating that an organization needs policies, it also outlines management's approach and commitment to information security.

Is There a Relationship Between the Organization's Security Policy Document and Federal Law?

Absolutely. In 2002, the Office of the President of the United States published the "National Strategy to Secure Cyberspace." The very first paragraph of the Executive Summary provides important clues about how federal regulations have and will impact the direction of information security policy:

> Our Nation's critical infrastructures are composed of public and private institutions in the sectors of agriculture, food, water, public health, emergency services, government, defense industrial base, information and telecommunications, energy, transportation, banking and finance, chemicals and hazardous materials, and postal and shipping. Cyberspace is their nervous system—the control system of our country. Cyberspace is composed of hundreds of thousands of interconnected computers, servers, routers, switches, and fiber optic cables that allow our critical infrastructures to work. Thus, the healthy functioning of cyberspace is essential to our economy and our national security.

Current regulations impact a variety of private sector organizations. One can surmise that the other critical infrastructures listed in the Executive Summary will soon be impacted by federal regulations. At this time, financial institutions are subject to the Financial Modernization Act, also known as Gramm-Leach-Bliley (GLBA). Healthcare service providers and covered entities are subject to the Health Insurance Portability and Accountability Act of 1996 (HIPAA). Publicly traded corporations are subject to Sarbanes-Oxley of 2002 (SOX). Educational institutions are subject to the Family Educational Rights and Privacy Act (FERPA). These four major pieces of legislation all require covered organizations to have in place written policies and procedures that protect their information assets. They also require the policies to be reviewed on a regular basis.

Many organizations are already finding that they are subject to more than one set of regulations. For example, publicly traded banks are subject to both GLBA and SOX requirements, while medical billing companies find themselves subject to both HIPAA and GLBA. Organizations that try to write their policies to match federal regulations find the task daunting. Fortunately, all of the regulations published to date have enough in common that a well-written set of information security policies based upon a framework such as the ISO 17799 can easily be mapped to multiple regulations. The Information Security Policy Document policy should reference the federal (and state) regulations the organization is subject to. Each individual policy should have a cross reference notation to the specific regulatory section.

FYI: The National Strategy to Secure Cyberspace

From the Whitehouse.gov Web site:

The *National Strategy to Secure Cyberspace* is part of our overall effort to protect the Nation. It is an implementing component of the *National Strategy for Homeland Security* and is complemented by a National Strategy for the Physical Protection of Critical Infrastructures and Key Assets. The purpose of this document is to engage and empower Americans to secure the portions of cyberspace that they own, operate, control, or with which they interact. Securing cyberspace is a difficult strategic challenge that requires coordinated and focused effort from our entire society, the federal government, state and local governments, the private sector, and the American people.

The complete document can be found at **www.whitehouse.gov/pcipb/**.

The Need for an Employee Version of the Security Policies

As an organization begins to develop a comprehensive security policy, the comment often made is that the policy document as a whole is too big, too complex, and too intimidating for the average employee to use effectively. A truer statement was never made. Handing an employee a binder chock-full of policies, most of which do not pertain to her, doesn't make sense. The entire policy document needs to be centrally managed by an assigned owner. The expectations should be that individual policies will be shared with appropriate departments and individuals (e.g., personnel polices are shared with the Human Relations department).

A separate document should be developed for the user community at large. This document is a succinct version of the comprehensive policy document that only includes instructions that pertain to the entire user base. The name of this document is important, as it reflects organizational culture. In many organizations, this document historically has been known as an *Acceptable Use Agreement*. A current trend is to name this document an *Employee Affirmation Agreement*. The document name should stress that protecting information assets is an integral part of everyone's job and that employees are affirming their individual commitment. We will discuss the contents and delivery of this agreement in upcoming chapters. For now, we just need to acknowledge the need for a separate end-user policy document.

Policies Are Dynamic

Because organizations change over time, policies sometimes need to be revisited. We introduced the concept of change drivers in earlier chapters. *Change drivers* are events within an organization that affect culture, procedures, activities, employee responsibilities, and relationships. Examples of change drivers include both positive and negative events such as acquiring a company, changing physical locations, introducing new technology, and employee layoffs. When any type of change occurs, there is the potential for a new set of risks and vulnerabilities. Change drivers should trigger risk and vulnerability assessments and ultimately a review of policies. Stale or outdated policies are of no use to an organization.

Who Is Responsible for the Information Security Policy Document? This is a key question. Policies are the foundation of a successful information security program. Generally, organizations assign policy "ownership" to either the Information Security Officer or a member of Senior Management. Ownership translates into developing, maintaining, and reviewing the policies and companion documents. The policy owner is not the final authority. Approval of policies belongs at a higher level. Depending upon the size, legal structure, and/or regulatory requirements of the organization, this might be owners, executive officers, or board members. The Information Security Policy Document policy defines both ownership and authority.

FYI: Policy Companions: Standards, Procedures, and Guidelines Refresher

Standards dictate specific minimum requirements in our policies. While standards are very definite, and required, guidelines are best thought of as suggestions for the best way to accomplish a certain task. A procedure provides a method by which a policy is accomplished; the instructions necessary to carry out a policy statement.

IN PRACTICE: Information Security Policy Document Objective and Ownership Policy

The goal of this goal is to deliver the message that the organization is committed to developing and implementing information security policies.

The *objectives* of this policy are to:

- Define the need for written information security policies.
- Assign ownership for the purpose of the management and maintenance of the written policies.
- List the relevant federal and state information security regulations with which the organization must comply.
- Ensure that the written policies are revisited when necessary as well as reviewed on a scheduled basis.

The audience is the entire organization.

TABLE 4.1 Sample Information Security Policy Document Policy.

Section X:	[COMPANY] Information Security Policy	Effective Date:
Subsection	Information Security Policy Document	Change Control #:
Policy	Information Security Policy Document Objective and Ownership	Approved By:
Objective	[Company] information is a valuable asset and must be protected from unauthorized disclosure, modification, or destruction. Prudent information security	

▸▸ CONTINUED ON NEXT PAGE

» CONTINUED	
	policies, standards, and practices must be implemented to ensure that the integrity, confidentiality, and availability of information are not compromised.
Purpose	The purpose of this policy is to communicate the direction of the organization's information security by providing relevant, accessible, and understandable definitions, statements, and explanations.
Audience	All Users are expected to understand and abide by established enterprise information technology security policies.
Policy	The Information Security Policy document, taken as a whole, shall explain the organization's security policies and compliance requirements.
	The Information Security Policy document shall outline specific responsibilities for information security management.
	The Information Security Policy Document shall serve as a reference document that will lead to additional, more detailed information when necessary (for instance, employee manuals, procedural documents, regulatory compliance documents, etc.).
	For the purpose of educating and gaining acceptance from the general user community, a summary version of the Information Security Policy document will be published.
	The Information Security Office shall be responsible for the maintenance and review of the policies defined in the Information Security Policy document. The ISO shall review the Information Security Policy document at least annually, or when significant changes take place to warrant review. Such changes include: Operational, Infrastructure, and Personnel changes.
	All changes to the Information Security Policy document will be brought to the Board of Directors for review and approval.
Exceptions	None
Disciplinary Actions	Violation of this policy may result in disciplinary action, which may include termination for employees and temporaries; a termination of employment relations in the case of contractors or consultants; or dismissal for interns and volunteers. Additionally, individuals are subject to civil and criminal prosecution.

4

Managing Organizational Security

Organizational security is best thought of as the management of security-related activities. Decisions need to be made about who is responsible for security management, the scope of their enforcement authority, and when it is appropriate to engage outside expertise. Since organizations do not operate in a vacuum, we also need to consider how we manage third parties such as business partners, vendors, and contractors in regard to our security objectives. The ISO 17799 standard suggests three categories of policies for this domain:

- Information Security Infrastructure

- Identification of Risks from Third Parties

- Security Requirements for Outsourcing

Taken together, these policies define the organizational structure and governance of our information security program.

Creating an Organizational Structure that Supports the Goals of Information Security

Designing and maintaining a secure environment is a huge undertaking that requires input from professionals throughout an organization. This includes members of management, developers, network engineers and administrators, human resources, and legal and financial communities. You will often hear the expression that "security is everyone's responsibility." What that really means is that everyone is expected to act in a manner consistent with good security practices. We don't expect the user community to make the rules—just follow them. Following the rules is possible only if the infrastructure is designed in such a way that following the rules is easy and doesn't hinder performance or productivity.

To accomplish this mission, we need a policy that addresses and encourages a multidisciplinary approach to information security, e.g., one that involves the cooperation and collaboration of managers, users, administrators, application designers, auditors and security staff, and specialist skills in areas such as insurance and risk management. A natural extension of this approach should be developing relationships with external security specialists. External specialists can be an invaluable resource regarding security knowledge as well as a source of advice, encouragement, and analysis.

FYI: Recommended External Resources

Many organizations have come to rely on external security professionals. The two main benefits of bringing in outside expertise are specialized knowledge and independence. Commonly used specialists include:

- Compliance specialists

- External auditors such as Certified Information Systems Auditors (CISA)

- Industry certified advisors such as Certified Information Systems Security Professionals (CISSP) or Certified Information System Managers (CISM)

- Disaster response and recovery planners

- Physical security designers

- Forensic and data recovery analysts

4

IN PRACTICE: Information Security Infrastructure Policy

The goal of this policy is to define the organizational structure responsible for and tasked with information security.

The *objectives* of this policy are to:

- Assign and communicate information security responsibilities.

- Outline a framework for interdepartmental security cooperation and coordination.

- Acknowledge the benefit of seeking independent expert advice outside of the organization.

The *audience* is management, directors, and information security officials.

▶▶ CONTINUED ON NEXT PAGE

▶▶ CONTINUED

TABLE 4.2 Sample Information Security Infrastructure Policy.

Section X:	[COMPANY] Information Security Policy	Effective Date:
Subsection	Organizational Security	Change Control #:
Policy	Information Security Infrastructure	Approved By:
Objective	To establish a framework for the management of information security within the organization.	
Purpose	The purpose of this policy is to protect all of the information assets within the organization by allocating responsibility and establishing an environment of cooperation and collaboration.	
Audience	This policy applies to all directors, managers, and security officials.	
Policy	Suitable management forum with management leadership will be established to approve the information security policy, assign security roles, and coordinate the implementation of security across the organization. A multidisciplinary approach to information security will be encouraged, e.g., one involving the cooperation and collaboration of managers, users, administrators, application designers, auditors and security staff, and specialist skills in areas such as insurance and risk management. The organization assigns responsibility for the overall application and management of the information security policy to the Chief Information Security Officer. A source of specialist information security advice should be established and made available within the organization. Contacts with external security specialists should be developed to keep up with industrial trends, monitor standards and assessment methods, and provide suitable liaison points when dealing with security incidents.	
Exceptions	None	

▶▶ CONTINUED ON NEXT PAGE

> **»CONTINUED**

Disciplinary Actions	Violation of this policy may result in disciplinary action, which may include termination for employees and temporaries; a termination of employment relations in the case of contractors or consultants; or dismissal for interns and volunteers. Additionally, individuals are subject to civil and criminal prosecution.

4

Who Else Has Access?

Security professionals by nature are usually control freaks. Nothing makes them more crazed than the idea of having folks outside of the organization accessing corporate data. Every day we become an increasingly interconnected society. Technology can be a double-edged sword. Take, for example, technologies such as WebEx™ (**www.webex.com**). WebEx™ started out as a collaborative tool for Web conferencing, video conferencing, and online meetings. Over time, it has expanded its scope to include desktop support. With permission, a third party can remotely run a desktop, download patches and updates, and even make configuration changes.

The benefits of this technology are obvious. Unfortunately, the risks may not be as obvious to the end user. Once a user "invites or gives permission for desktop support," we have effectively allowed an outside party into our network. While we hope their intentions are good, security is not built on hope but rather assurance. It is important for an organization to have a policy that controls the type of access that third parties can have to information and information systems. For the record, when we say "third parties," we are usually referencing a person or organization that is not on the direct company payroll. Third parties include business partners, vendors, and contractors (including temporary workers).

Don't Overlook Facility Access The main objective of a hacker or intruder is to get access to information and information systems. What easier way is there to gain access than to be allowed into an organization's information processing facilities? Significant damage can be done in a matter of moments. A Network Manager tells the story of being paged by his office while en route to the airport to take his family on vacation. It seems that users were getting "server not found errors" when trying to log in. Since he and his family had arrived early at the airport, he dropped his family off at the ticket check-in counter and drove back to his office. Upon arriving at his office, he immediately went to the server room, only to find no servers! The thieves posing as a computer repair crew were given access to the server room and took off with the equipment. His users were experiencing a literal "server not found" error.

Another trick employed by a would-be intruder is to pose as a potential job applicant. During the interview, the applicant requests a "tour" of the facility. All too often, interviewers are delighted to show off facilities and in the process play right into the hands of the intruder by providing valuable information that can be used to attack or steal corporate assets.

Where there is a legitimate business need for third-party access, a risk assessment should be carried out to determine security implications and control requirements. Controls should be agreed upon and defined in a contract with the third party. More common than you may suspect, third-party access may also involve other participants. Third parties often assign or subcontract their work out without notifying the client. This is why pre-engagement *due diligence* investigations and clearly stated contractual obligations are so important.

IN PRACTICE: Identification of Risks from Third Parties Policy

The goal of this policy is to reinforce the concept that all third-party access must be evaluated.

The *objectives* of this policy are to:

- Define the type of access to information systems allowed by third parties.
- Control access to information processing facilities by third parties.

The *audience* is management, directors, information security officials, legal advisors, compliance officers, human resource staff, and third parties.

TABLE 4.3 Sample Identification of Risks from Third Parties Policy.

Section X:	[COMPANY] Information Security Policy	Effective Date:
Subsection	**Organizational Security**	Change Control #:
Policy	**Identification of Risks from Third Parties**	Approved By:
Objective	To maintain the security of organizational information processing facilities and information assets accessed by third parties.	

▸▸ **CONTINUED ON NEXT PAGE**

▶ CONTINUED	
Purpose	To provide guidance on the information security issues that should be considered when using third-party resources to accomplish [Company] business.
Audience	This policy applies to all directors, managers, security officials, vendors, contractors, consultants, and auditors.
Policy	• A risk assessment will be carried out before any third-party access is granted and will consider the reasons for access as well as the necessary controls to be put in place. • Access to information classified as sensitive and/or confidential by third parties will be specifically agreed upon and documented in contracts. • Access of third parties to information processing facilities will be clearly spelled out in contracts; this access includes the scope of access to physical, logical, and network assets. • No third-party access will be granted without first having entered into a binding contract that clearly delineates the security responsibility of the third party. • The third party may not assign any portion of work to a subcontractor without the express permission of the Information Security Officer.
Exceptions	None
Disciplinary Actions	Violation of this policy may result in disciplinary action, which may include termination for employees and temporaries; a termination of employment relations in the case of contractors or consultants; or dismissal for interns and volunteers. Additionally, individuals are subject to civil and criminal prosecution.

Outsourcing Is a Growing Trend

Outsourcing is loosely defined as assigning internal work to external organizations, generally with the goal of cutting costs or gaining efficiency. In the last few years, many outsourced jobs have been awarded to **_offshore organizations_** in India or Southeast Asia. These jobs run the gamut from accounting to sales. In May of 2004, Forrester Research reported that over the next ten years, 3.4 million U.S. jobs—roughly

6.4%—will move offshore. The security implications of this trend are enormous. Whether U.S.- or foreign-based, corporations are allowing access to their information assets by users whom they do not directly manage, control, or in many cases ever even set eyes upon. To compound the problem, countries around the world view privacy and security violations in vastly different ways. As organizations make the strategic decision to outsource jobs, they must also put in place policies that ensure that their information will be protected from violations of confidentiality, integrity, and availability.

FYI: Security Around the Globe— European Union Security Standards

Similar to the United States Strategy to Secure Cyberspace is the European Union Initiative eEurope 2005. More information can be found at **http://europa.eu.int**.

IN PRACTICE: Security Requirements in Outsourcing Contracts Policy

The goal of this policy is to ensure that security requirements extend to all outsourced work.

The *objectives* of this policy are to:

- Provide guidance on security issues that must be considered when using outsourced resources to accomplish organizational business.
- Ensure that language specific to maintaining information security is a requirement of all outsourced contractual obligations.

The *audience* is management, directors, information security officials, legal advisors, compliance officers, human resource staff, and third parties.

▶▶ CONTINUED ON NEXT PAGE

>> CONTINUED

TABLE 4.4 Security Requirements in Outsourcing Contracts Policy.

Section X:	[COMPANY] Information Security Policy	Effective Date:
Subsection	Organizational Security	Change Control #:
Policy	Security Requirements for Outsourcing	Approved By:
Objective	To establish a policy to manage the security context and responsibilities of third parties that provide by contact outsourced services.	
Purpose	To provide guidance and direction in regard to the information security requirements of service providers.	
Audience	This policy applies to all management, directors, information security officials, legal advisors, compliance officers, human resource staff, and third parties.	
Policy	• All third parties that provide outsourcing services are expected to comply with the same policies, standards, and guidelines that are exercised internal to the organization. • All third parties that provide outsourcing services are expected to comply with any and all federal regulations to which the organization is subject. • All outsourcing agreements will contain information security provisions specifically tailored to the particular outsourcing initiative. • All third parties will be expected to participate in and complete information security training as assigned by the Office of the CISO.	
Exceptions	None	
Disciplinary Actions	Violation of this policy may result in disciplinary action, which may include termination for employees and temporaries; a termination of employment relations in the case of contractors or consultants; or dismissal for interns and volunteers. Additionally, individuals are subject to civil and criminal prosecution.	

4

Summary

The starting point for an information security program is defining and communicating the rules. In both public and private sector organizations, the rules are commonly known as *policies.* These policies are contained in a policy document. We have chosen to use the ISO 17799 standard as a framework for developing our policy document. Section 3 of ISO 17799 focuses on the requirement to have written policies that are authorized at the highest level possible. The policies should be assigned an owner to manage and maintain them; the owner must also be committed to communicating these policies. We have expressed these requirements in the statement of authority and the Information Security Policy Document policy.

Written policies alone are not enough. Organizations must build an infrastructure that supports the design and implementation of the policy goals and objectives. As we continue to use the ISO 17799 standard as our framework, we focused on the requirements outlined in Section 4–Organizational Security. The organizational security domain considers the prerequisites necessary for successfully implementing security both internal and external to the organization. We are asked to recognize that security decisions cannot be made in a vacuum. A multidisciplinary approach to security involving various departments and factions will ultimately result in a unified set of security requirements that can be successfully adopted throughout the organization.

Security is a fast-moving target. Organizations can clearly benefit from the advice and counsel of independent professionals with recognized security expertise. As corporations have begun to outsource many positions, it is the responsibility of the organization to clearly define expectations and requirements to all parties that have access to information assets. We presented three samples of organizational security policies: Information Security Infrastructure policy, Identification of Risks from Third Parties policy, and Security Requirements in Outsourcing Contracts policy.

Test Your Skills

MULTIPLE CHOICE QUESTIONS

1. The purpose of a statement of authority is to:

   A. intimidate users

   B. deliver a clear message of commitment

   C. relay punishment options

   D. use it as a marketing tool

2. A statement of authority should be signed by:

    A. the highest organizational authority (Owner, Chairman, CEO)

    B. the City Council where the company is headquartered

    C. the FBI

    D. the Information Technology Department

3. The statement of authority should be published and distributed to:

    A. the Board of Directors

    B. the user community

    C. vendors

    D. all of the above

4. In order for policies to be effective, they must be:

    A. written in strict legal code

    B. clearly written and widely distributed

    C. stored in one big binder

    D. available only upon demand

5. The most compelling reason to have an employee version of a comprehensive security policy is that:

    A. sections of the comprehensive policy may not be applicable to all employees

    B. it is unproductive to read the whole policy document

    C. the comprehensive document should be classified information

    D. the more understandable and relevant a policy is, the more likely users will positively accept it

6. Which of the following is a common element of all federal information security regulations?

    A. Organizations must implement appropriate policies and procedures to protect information assets.

    B. Organizations must use federally mandated technology.

    C. Organizations must store all records electronically.

    D. Organizations must use federally mandated policies.

7. An example of a *change driver* is:

    A. a business relocation

    B. a new Web-based product offering

    C. significant employee layoffs and downsizing

    D. all of the above

8. Policy *ownership* means that the owner:
   A. can charge a fee for using the policy
   B. retains rights to the policy and can sell it
   C. is responsible for maintaining the policy document
   D. can change the policy at will

9. Standards are best defined as:
   A. minimum requirements
   B. suggestions
   C. tasks
   D. instructions

10. Which of these is *not* an objective of the Information Security Policy Document policy?
    A. designing the document in such as way that it never has to be revised
    B. defining the need for written information security policies
    C. assigning ownership for the purpose of the management and maintenance of the written policies
    D. listing the relevant federal and state information security regulations with which the organization must comply

11. Organizational security can be described as:
    A. having security guards posted at the front entrance
    B. the management of security-related activities
    C. requiring employees to wear badges
    D. bullet-proof windows

12. The recommended method to design security policies is to:
    A. solicit input from throughout the organization
    B. purchase a set of policies on the Internet
    C. assign one person to the task
    D. make it a project for the summer college interns

13. External security specialists may include a:
    A. Certified Information Systems Security Professional (CISSP)
    B. law enforcement official
    C. former hacker who is now a bona fide security consultant
    D. all of the above

14. When an organization refers to a "third party," they mean:

    A. an independent candidate running for a government office

    B. any person not directly employed by the organization

    C. any employee who is not a member of management

    D. none of the above

15. Which of these is *not* an objective of the Information Security Infrastructure policy?

    A. assign and communicate information security responsibilities

    B. outline a framework for interdepartmental security cooperation and coordination

    C. assign ownership for the purpose of the management and maintenance of the written policies

    D. acknowledge the benefit of seeking independent expert advice outside of the organization

16. Access to information systems includes:

    A. network access

    B. physical access

    C. both A and B

    D. neither A nor B

17. Which of these *is* an objective of the Identification of Risks from Third Parties policy?

    A. influence third-party contract awards

    B. define the type of access to information systems allowed by third parties

    C. discourage the company from employing outside contractors

    D. make it harder for legitimate third parties to access information systems

18. The current trend toward outsourcing is a security concern because:

    A. it drives down costs

    B. it may require virtual private networks (VPNs) be implemented

    C. there is the potential for less control over who accesses data and where it may be stored

    D. the European Union has more stringent laws regarding privacy than the United States

19. Which of these is *not* an objective of the Security Requirements in Outsourcing Contracts policy?

    A. provide guidance on security issues that must be considered when using outsourced resources to accomplish organizational business

    B. ensure that language specific to maintaining information security is a requirement of all outsourced contractual obligations

    C. have outsourced employees embrace the organization's security policy

    D. save money

20. Organizations that choose to adopt the ISO 17799 framework must:

    A. use every policy, standard, and guideline recommended

    B. create policies for every security domain

    C. evaluate the recommendations and customize as appropriate

    D. register with the International Standards Organization

EXERCISES

Exercise 4.1: Information Security Policy at Your School

1. Locate a copy of your school's information security policy.

2. What steps did you take to locate the policy? Was the policy easily accessible?

3. Can you tell who wrote the policy?

4. Can you tell who "owns" the policy?

Exercise 4.2: Acceptable Use Agreements

1. Locate a copy of your school's acceptable use agreement.

2. Who is required to sign the agreement?

3. What is the punishment for violating the agreement?

Exercise 4.3: Who's In Charge?

1. Either by reading your school's policy or by asking the Administration, find out who is in charge of information security at your school.

2. If you were to assemble an information security team at your school to develop and/or recommend security policies, who would you choose and why? You must choose at least three people.

Exercise 4.4: You Be the Judge

Three students got together and created a Web design and Web hosting company called HTMLTips.net. They will be creating Web sites for their customers, from simple "Hello World" pages to full-fledged e-commerce solutions. One student is the technical guru, the second is the marketing genius, and the third is in charge of running the company. The students also have five Web developers working for them as contractors on a per-project basis. They need to create an information security policy document.

1. Who do you think should be the policy owner? Write a paragraph explaining your decision.

2. Who do you think should be the policy authority? Write a paragraph explaining your decision.

Exercise 4.5: Third Party?

The three entrepreneurs from Exercise 4 decide that they need to look closely at their organizational security, especially as it pertains to the security requirements for outsourcing. They do have five contractors working as Web developers, after all. While not all five developers usually work for them at the same time, they still have a high level of access to the company's Web servers, among other resources. All five developers are friends and classmates of the triumvirate who owns the company.

1. Based on this scenario, and on what was covered in this chapter, do you think that these five developers should be considered third parties or as employees of the company? Write a paragraph to justify your answer.

2. Based on what you answered in Question 1, would you recommend that the company create a specific third-party security policy?

3. What security measures would you recommend regarding network access for the five developers? Write two paragraphs on this matter.

PROJECTS

Project 4.1: Writing an Affirmation Agreement

1. Affirmation agreements can be used as a teaching tool with the goal being to convince the reader that security is important. Write an introductory paragraph explaining why information security is important at your school.

2. In the second paragraph, explain to readers what information assets need to be protected and why.

3. In the third paragraph, explain to readers their individual responsibilities.

Project 4.2: Information Security Management Job Descriptions

1. The ABC Hospital has decided to move responsibility for information security from the Information Technology department to the newly created Office of Information Security. In charge of the new Office of Information Security department will be a Chief Security Officer. By researching current job postings, write a job description for the new CSO.

2. The new CSO's first assignment is to review all information security policies. He needs to assemble a multidisciplinary committee to assist him. Who would you suggest he invite to be on the committee?

3. The hospital president has suggested that the CSO engage external resources to provide advice on HIPAA compliance in regard to policy development. Locate a local firm that has the expertise to provide this service.

Project 4.3: Evaluating Third-Party Risks

Jill's Computer Shop has been providing IT services to a local Real Estate Company (REC) for the past seven years. REC does not have any in-house technology expertise. Jill used to service her clients directly, but as demand for services has increased, Jill has expanded her staff. In addition, technology advances now allow Jill's staff to provide support services remotely. This past year, Jill added two new services that REC has signed up for—remote data backup and Web site hosting.

1. You have been asked to assess the risks associated with this relationship. Detail at least three areas of risk.

2. You have arranged to meet with Jill personally to discuss the risk assessment. What questions are you going to ask her?

3. You have decided to incorporate your security expectations into Jill's annual contact. Write a paragraph outlining Jill's responsibilities.

Project 4.4: Relationships Are Complicated

1. In Exercise 5, we looked at the relationship between a Web company and five contractors who worked on a per-project basis. Write a list of the top five issues you think the current relationship has from a security standpoint with no security policy clearly defined between these five contractors and the company. What would you call this document if it contained all the security issues, and not just the top five?

2. Based on your findings in Question 1, write a document outlining the policies that would alleviate those issues.

3. What types of documents do you think this company should make contractors sign before they are allowed to perform any work for the company?

Project 4.5: Interviewing and Training Third Parties

1. The Web company from Project 4 is growing well; it has secured new deals with several big clients. The three students who run the company have decided that their time would be better spent creating Web sites than cleaning up the office at night after hours. They have therefore decided to hire a cleaning firm. Write five security-related questions they should ask this third-party firm before hiring them.

2. The company has decided to train the janitors who will come on-site themselves when it comes to their security policy. List three items you think that these third parties should be made aware of.

3. The three student-owners have also been thinking about outsourcing their security needs to a third-party company. List five questions they should ask this company before hiring them. How many of your questions were in common with the questions you created in Question 1? Do you think that the list should be entirely the same? Justify your answer.

Case Study

A security consulting firm was hired to assess the Federal Agency of Debt compliance with ISO 17799. They began the process by evaluating the Security Policy document and the Organizational Structure. Listed below are their findings:

The Office of the Secretary of Federal Debt is committed to building and supporting a secure environment for information assets. Management throughout the Agency recognizes the need for security process and procedures. The general consensus is that security controls are currently lacking or are inadequate. There is significant concern in regard to confidentiality issues as they relate to regulations and public trust.

There is no agency-wide security policy; however, there are departmental policies.

There is no agency-wide security training.

There is no agency requirement for employees to acknowledge the acceptable standards of behavior in regard to information security. However, individual departments have implemented confidentiality agreements.

Implementation of internal technical security controls is the domain of the Office of Information Technology.

The Federal Department of Information Services (a separate Federal Agency) provides and manages Internet access and connectivity, including external e-mail. The Federal Department of Information Services outsources the e-mail services to a private company.

Security reviews are conducted as required by law.

One of the recommendations of the last review was creating the position of Information Security Officer.

You have been asked to create an Information Security Policy Document policy and an Informational Security Infrastructure policy that incorporate current practices and attitudes as well as the consultants' findings and recommendations. Use the samples provided in this chapter for guidance. Be prepared to present, explain, and defend your policies.

Chapter | 5

Asset Classification

Chapter Objectives

After reading this chapter and completing the exercises, you will be able to do the following:

- Assign information ownership responsibilities.
- Develop and use information classification guidelines.
- Understand information handling and labeling procedures.
- Manage an information classification program.
- Identify and inventory information systems.
- Recognize the goal and methodology of criticality assessments.
- Create and implement asset classification policies.

Introduction

Section 5 of ISO 17799 is dedicated to Asset Classification and Control, with the objective of maintaining appropriate protection of organizational information assets. In previous chapters, we discussed the key concepts of protecting the confidentiality, integrity, and availability of information. We saw that information can exist in many forms. Per the ISO, it can be written on paper, stored electronically, shown on film, or spoken in conversation. Whatever form it takes, there is a business imperative that information and the systems that store, transmit, and process it need to be appropriately protected.

Is it possible to protect something if we don't know how much it is worth and how sensitive it is? Until we classify the information, how do we know the level of protection required? Unless we determine the value to the organization, how can we decide the amount of time, effort, or money that we should spend securing the asset? Who is responsible for making these decisions? How do we communicate the value of our information assets to our employees and vendors?

In this chapter, we will be looking at the various methods and rating systems that organizations use to define, inventory, and classify their information and information systems. We will examine public and private sector classification systems that are used to communicate value and handling instructions. We will determine who is responsible for these activities. Lastly, we will put these best practices into policy.

What Are We Trying to Protect?

What exactly is an information asset and why protect it? An *information asset* is a definable piece of information, stored in any manner, which is recognized as having value to the organization. The information can range from a prospect database to the schematics for top secret military equipment. The type of information can vary as widely as there are types of organizations. The common characteristic is that the information is used by a company (regardless of size) to fulfill its mission or goal. A secondary characteristic is that the information may be used to support internal operations such as payroll. If the information is damaged, compromised, or stolen, the consequences could include embarrassment, legal liability, financial ruin, and even loss of life.

Examples of Information Assets:

- Databases: Information about customers, personnel, production, sales, marketing, finances.

- Data files: Transactional data giving up-to-date information about each event.

- Intellectual property: Drawings, schematics, patents, music scores, or other publications that have commercial value.

- Operational and support procedures: Detailed instructions on how to perform various activities.

- Research documentation: Proprietary information based upon experimentation or exploration.

- Archived information: Old information that organizations may be legally required to maintain.

- Business plans: Strategic, operational, and business continuity policies and procedures that uniquely define the organization.

Information Systems

Information systems are the supporting players. *Information systems* provide a way and a place to process, store, transmit, and communicate the information. These systems are generally a combination of hardware and software assets and associated services. Information systems can be garden variety off-the-shelf products or highly customized equipment and code. Support services may be technical services (voice communication and data communication) or environmental (heating, lighting, air conditioning, and power) as well as business partners. Fairly new to this list are Application Service Providers (ASP) usually accessed via the Internet. A current trend is to outsource applications rather than having to host and manage the information system internally.

Who Is Responsible for Information Assets?

This brings us to the question of ownership and our first policy in this domain. Every information asset must be assigned an owner. In Chapter 3, we defined information ownership as being liable and responsible for protecting the information and the business results derived from using that information. For example, you have a medical file at your doctor's office, which may contain your medical history, digital scans, lab results, and physician notes. The clinicians in the office use that information to provide you with medical care. Since the information is all about you, are you the owner? No. The medical staff uses the information to provide care, are they the owner? No. The information owner is the one responsible for protecting the confidentiality of your medical record, insuring the integrity of the information in your records, and making sure that it is available to the clinicians whenever you need care. In a small medical practice, the owner is generally a physician. In a clinic or hospital, the owner is a member of senior management. While it may seem obvious that every information asset needs an owner, it is not always apparent who should be or who is willing to assume the responsibility of ownership.

Accountability for Assets The ISO 17799 standard recommends that we have a policy that specifically addresses the need to account for our information assets and to assign an owner to the asset. The goal of an Information Ownership policy is to ensure that appropriate protection is maintained. Owners should be identified for all major assets and given the responsibility for the safeguarding of the information system. The owner is responsible for the security of the asset. However, the owner is not the one who will be tasked with implementing security controls. That responsibility can be delegated to the information custodians such as System Administrators.

The Role of the Information Security Officer The information owner is accountable for the protection of the information asset. The information custodian is responsible for managing the day-to-day controls. The role of the Information Security Officer (ISO) is to provide direction and guidance as to the appropriate controls and to ensure that controls are applied consistently throughout the organization. While information owners and custodians focus on specific information assets, the ISO is responsible for the security of the entire organizations. As such, the office of the ISO is the central repository of security information. The ISO publishes the classification criteria, maintains the information systems inventories, and implements broad strategic and tactical security initiatives.

FYI: Information Owners

The success of an information security program is directly related to the defined relationship between the data owner and the information. In the best case scenario, the data owner also functions as a security champion enthusiastically embracing the goals of CIA.

Security Role: *Data Owner*

Organizational Role: Owner, Director, Executive Management, Sr. Management

Responsibilities: Assign value to the asset.

Determine who should have access to the asset.

Define the level of protection necessary.

Delegate day-to-day tasks for implementation and maintenance of security controls.

Provide oversight and enforcement.

IN PRACTICE: Information Ownership Policy

This is an example of a policy that clearly states the importance of assigning information ownership and responsibilities.
The *objectives* of this policy are to:

- Require ownership for all major information assets.
- Hold information owners accountable for the protection of the information asset.

▸▸ CONTINUED ON NEXT PAGE

>> CONTINUED

The *audience* is directors, managers, and security officials.

TABLE 5.1 Sample Information Ownership policy.

Section X:	[COMPANY] Information Security Policy	Effective Date:
Subsection	Asset Classification & Control	Change Control #:
Policy	Information Ownership Policy	Approved By:
Objective	Accountability for information assets helps to ensure that appropriate protection is identified, implemented, maintained, and reviewed.	
Purpose	The purpose of this policy is to protect all of the information assets within the organization by requiring that all major information assets have an identified owner.	
Audience	This policy applies to all directors, managers, and security officials.	
Policy	Owners should be identified for all major assets. An inventory of information ownership will be maintained by the Office of the Information Security Officer. Owners are responsible for the protection of the asset as identified by the [COMPANY] information classification policy and information system criticality assessment. Implementation and maintenance of controls is the responsibility of the Office of the Information Security Officer; however, accountability will remain with the owner of the asset.	
Exceptions	None	
Disciplinary Actions	Violation of this policy may result in disciplinary action, which may include termination for employees and temporaries; a termination of employment relations in the case of contractors or consultants; or dismissal for interns and volunteers. Additionally, individuals are subject to civil and criminal prosecution.	

5

Information Classification

Information classification is the organization of information assets according to their sensitivity to disclosure. Classification is a reflection of who should have access to the information. Classification systems are labels that we assign to identify the sensitivity level. The natural outcome of the classification process is instructions on who can access the asset, how the asset is to be used, what security measures need to be in place, and ultimately the method in which the asset should destroyed or disposed of.

Let's make this personal. Over the years, you have kept a diary of your most personal and intimate thoughts. You want to retain control over who reads the diary and you most certainly wouldn't want someone editing your thoughts. Imagine how embarrassed you would be if someone got hold of your diary and published it on the Internet—especially if that person added entries that weren't even true!

The private sector, the government, and the military are all committed to protecting their information assets. A bank will allow a teller to view general account information and cash checks of reasonable amounts. That same teller is not allowed to view information about internal bank assets and most definitely can't access systems that would allow her to transfer millions of dollars. A hospital will allow a lab technician to access patient demographics and physician instructions but will not allow him to read the complete patient record. The military, based upon national security concerns, makes decisions to whom and how to make information accessible. They certainly do not want battle plans shared with the enemy. As a matter of fact, the military is the best example of an organization that relies extensively on a well-defined classification system. They classify not only information systems but people as well. Military and supporting civilian personnel are assigned clearance levels. The clearance level of the individual must match the classification of the data in order to be granted access. This structure is known as *Mandatory Access Controls (MAC).*

Government and Military Classification Systems

The government and the military have a vested interest in protecting the confidentiality, integrity, and availability of information systems. Over time, they have developed a plethora of complex classifications schemes. Experts have warned that the confusing number of schemes can have the opposite effect and create chaos where order is warranted. For the majority of information, the government and military use a multi-tiered three-level classification scheme as defined in Executive Order 12958: Top Secret,

Secret, and Confidential. Information that is not assigned one of these three classifications is referred to as *unclassified.*

Top Secret　Top Secret (TS) is applied to "any information or material the unauthorized disclosure of which reasonably could be expected to cause exceptionally grave damage to the national security. Examples of exceptionally grave damage include armed hostilities against the United States or its allies; disruption of foreign relations vitally affecting the national security; the compromise of vital national defense plans or complex cryptology and communications intelligence systems; the revelation of sensitive intelligence operations, and the disclosure of scientific or technological developments vital to national security."

Secret　Secret (S) is applied to "any information or material the unauthorized disclosure of which reasonably could be expected to cause serious damage to the national security. Examples of serious damage include disruption of foreign relations significantly affecting the national security; significant impairment of a program or policy directly related to the national security; revelation of significant military plans or intelligence operations: compromise of significant military plans or intelligence operations; and compromise of significant scientific or technological developments relating to national security."

Confidential　Confidential (C) is applied to "any information or material the unauthorized disclosure of which reasonably could be expected to cause damage to the national security. Examples of damage include the compromise of information that indicates strength of ground, air, and naval forces in the United States and overseas areas; disclosure of technical information used for training, maintenance, and inspection of classified munitions of war; revelation of performance characteristics, test data, design and production data on munitions of war."

Unclassified　Unclassified (U) is applied to "any information that can generally be distributed to the public without any threat to national interest." Sensitive But Unclassified (SBU) is a Department of Defense subcategory and is applied to "any information of which the loss, misuse or unauthorized access to, or modification of might adversely affect U.S. National Interests, the conduct of the Department of Defense (DoD) programs or the privacy of DoD personnel." Labeling in this category includes "For Official Use Only," "Not For Public Release," or "For Internal Use Only."

FYI: Freedom of Information Act

The Freedom of Information Act (FOIA) provides a powerful tool to advocates for access to information. Under the FOIA, anyone may request and receive any records from federal agencies unless the documents can be officially declared exempt based upon specific categories, such as top secret, secret, and classified. There are several avenues available to obtain government information, including the following government Web sites:

- **FirstGov**—U.S. Federal Government's primary Web portal (**www.firstgov.gov**)
- **Regulations.gov**—U.S. Federal Government's online portal for rulemaking (**www.regulations.gov**)
- **2002 Guide to the Freedom of Information Act** from the Department of Justice (**www.usdoj.gov/oip/foi-act.htm**)
- **A Citizen's Guide On Using The Freedom Of Information Act and The Privacy Act of 1974 To Request Government Records** from the Committee on Government Reform and Oversight (**www.tncrimlaw.com/foia_indx.html**)
- **How to Make a FOIA Request** from the National Security Archive (**www.gwu.edu/~nsarchiv/nsa/foia/howtofoia.html**)
- **The Freedom of Information Act: A Practical User's Guide** from the National Security Archive (**www.gwu.edu/~nsarchiv/nsa/foia_user_guide.html**)

Commercial Classification Systems

Private sector organizations tend to implement less complex and easier to understand classification systems. There is no one standard, so organizations are free to choose a system that works best for them and best reflects their corporate culture. Even the most familiar classifications are open to interpretation. The trend is to use four tiers. How many tiers is often directly related to whether or not the organization is subject to federal information security regulations such as HIPAA or GLBA. The more regulated the information, the more detailed the classification levels. Fairly universal classification includes: Confidential, Sensitive, Restricted, and Public. Not all information needs to be classified, hence the category "public." The criteria for choosing to classify information are generally based upon one or more of the following characteristics:

- The information is not public knowledge or public domain.

- The information has a demonstrated value to the organization.

- The information needs to be protected from those outside of the organization.

- The information is subject to government regulations.

Sometimes information that doesn't obviously meet the above criteria also needs to be protected due to its intelligence value to others. Information such as telephone and e-mail lists, discarded paperwork, purchase orders, evacuation routes, and the like can often reveal valuable information. This information may be used by hackers, thieves, competitors, or others with malicious intent. A question to consider when assessing information is "what's the worst thing that could happen if this information got into the wrong hands?" Very few documents require no access controls at all, unless specifically designed for public use.

5

IN PRACTICE: Footprinting and the Four-Step Hacking Process

Hackers use a four-step process to infiltrate a network: footprinting, scanning, enumerating, and attacking. The first step, footprinting, is the process of accumulating data regarding a specific logical or physical environment. Footprinting can reveal system vulnerabilities and pinpoint ways they can be exploited. Hackers use noninvasive techniques to gather information. Corporate Web pages may provide a wealth of information including a personnel directory, e-mail addresses, and leadership bios. Corporate trash bins may reveal financial data, network maps, contracts, and even payroll data. Accessible policy and procedure manuals may reveal hours of operation, off-site storage facilities, and even lock combinations.

An intruder uses this information to build a virtual map of the infrastructure. The intruder then begins the process of scanning the environment to test and validate his assumptions as well as gather more in-depth information. Once the intruder has located weaknesses and potential access points to the network, he begins the process of enumeration. Enumeration is gathering specific network data such as user names, shares, registry settings, and hardware configuration. The final step is to attack the network. Often, this is the easiest step of all as by now the intruder has a clear picture of the environment and its weaknesses. Remember, it all began with the process of culling clues from information that was readily available.

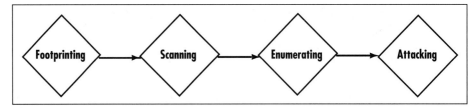

FIGURE 5.1 The four-step hacking process.

Confidential *Confidential information* is meant to be kept secret and restricted to only a small circle of authorized individuals. Confidential is the private sector equivalent to the government's Top Secret classification. The information is often essential to the technical and financial success of an organization. Loss, corruption, or unauthorized disclosure would cause significant financial or legal damage to the organization, and its reputation. Confidential information may include business strategies, financial positions, upcoming sales or advertising campaigns, laboratory research, or product schematics. The more confidential and/or valuable such information, the tighter its access controls must be.

Sensitive *Sensitive information* (sometimes referred to as personal or privileged) is information whose loss, corruption, or unauthorized disclosure would not necessarily result in significant business, financial, or legal loss but involves issues of personal credibility, reputation, or other issues of personal privacy. Most organizations restrict access to sensitive data on a demonstrated "need to know" basis. Sensitive data may include patient medical records, employee payroll records, financial statements, or sales forecasts. Access to sensitive information is often granted upon a role based model. Role-Based Access Control (RBAC) is security managed at a level that corresponds closely to the organization's structure. Each user is assigned one or more roles, and each role is assigned one or more privileges that are permitted to users in that role. A good example is your student record. Your student record includes your transcript, housing information, disciplinary actions, family financial data, and medical records. Who do you want to have access to those records? You expect that the financial aid officers will have access to your family financial record and that the Health Center care providers will have access to your medical records. But you wouldn't expect the opposite to be true. RBAC assignments would support your expectations. While you might not know who specifically has access, you can make assumptions based upon their role at the university.

Restricted *Restricted information* is business-related information that is to be used internal to the organization for the purpose of conducting company business. The information may relate to the organization itself or a third party. Loss, corruption, or unauthorized disclosure may impair the business or result in business, financial, or legal loss. Examples may include policy documents, procedure manuals, nonsensitive client or vendor information, employee lists, or organizational announcements. Also included in this classification is information protected by legal agreements such as nondisclosure agreements (NDA).

Public *Public information* is information that does not require protection or information that is specifically intended for the public at-large. Examples include annual reports, product documentation, list of upcoming trade shows, or published white papers. Also included in this category is information required by law to be either distributed or made available to the public, such as candidate campaign spending records.

IN PRACTICE: Information Classification Policy

This is an example of a policy that would be used in the private sector to classify data. It is applicable to organizations of any size. The *objectives* of this policy are to:

- Require a classification system.
- Define the classification levels.
- Require that all major information assets be classified.
- Assign responsibility for classification systems, identification, management and oversight.
- Acknowledge and allow for reclassification.

The *audience* is all individuals or organizations that have access to organizational assets.

TABLE 5.2 Sample Information Asset Classification policy.

Section X:	[COMPANY] Information Security Policy	Effective Date:
Subsection	Asset Classification & Control	Change Control #:
Policy	Information Asset Classification Policy	Approved By:
Objective	In support of information security, the [COMPANY] will use an asset classification system to determine the	

▸▸ CONTINUED ON NEXT PAGE

▶▶ CONTINUED	
	protective controls associated with each information asset.
Purpose	The purpose of this policy is to protect major information assets by providing a mechanism with which custodians and users can readily identify the security and handling requirements of such assets.
Audience	This policy applies to any individual or organization that has access to or comes in contact with [COMPANY] information assets.
Policy	The [COMPANY] must adopt and adhere to an information classification system.
	All major information assets will be classified and labeled according to [COMPANY] guidelines so that the information asset can be readily identified to determine handling and protection level for that information asset.
	The classification system shall remain as simple as is appropriate with a maximum of four classifications, so as to be easily understood and administrated. The classifications will be: Confidential, Sensitive, Restricted, and Public. The criteria for each level will be maintained by and available from the Office of the Information Security Officer.
	The asset information owner or their designate shall define the classification of the information.
	Each classification shall have handling and protection rules. The Office of the Information Security Officer is responsible for the development and enforcement of the handling and protection rules.
	The classification system will allow that classifications of information assets may change over time.
Exceptions	None
Disciplinary Actions	Violation of this policy may result in disciplinary action, which may include termination for employees and temporaries; a termination of employment relations in the case of contractors or consultants; or dismissal for interns and volunteers. Additionally, individuals are subject to civil and criminal prosecution.

Information Classification Labeling and Handling

Information owners classify information for the sole purpose of identifying the level of protection necessary and communicating that information to information custodians and information users. The level of protection extends to the key areas of access, modification, duplication, transport, storage, records management, and disposal.

Information Labeling

Labeling is the vehicle for communicating the sensitively level. Labels can take many forms: electronic, print, audio, or visual. Information may need to be labeled in many ways depending upon the audience. The labels you are most probably familiar with are safety labels. You recognize poison from the skull-and-crossbones symbol. You instinctively know to stop when you see a red stop sign. You know to pull over when you hear a police siren.

Familiar Labels

In order to protect information, classification level labels need to be as clear and universally understood as a skull-and-crossbones symbol or a stop sign. In electronic form, the classification should be a part of the document name, e.g., "F11 Airplane Plan Engine Drawing–CONFIDENTIAL." On written or printed documents, the classification label should be clearly marked on the outside of the document as well as in either the document header or footer. Media, such as backup tapes, should be clearly labeled with words and (where appropriate) symbols.

Information Handling

Information needs to be handled in accordance with its classification. Simply put, this means that information labeled *confidential* must have strict administrative, physical, and technical access controls, whereas information classified as *public* does not require significant levels of protection. We will be discussing access controls and access control policies in upcoming chapters. Asset classification policies assign the responsibility of defining protection to the information owner, the responsibility of implementing protection to the information custodian, and the responsibility of using the information in accordance with its label to the information user.

Information Classification Program Lifecycle

An information classification program lifecycle starts with assigning classification levels and ends with the process of declassification. The prerequisites to implementing this program are defining the classification levels that the organization is going to use and the criteria for each level.

Information Classification Procedures

For each information asset, the following procedures should be followed:

1. Define the information asset and the supporting information system.
2. Characterize the criticality of the information system.
3. Identify the information owner and information custodian.
4. Assign a classification level to the information (responsibility of the information owner). Define declassification criteria.
5. Determine and implement the corresponding level of security controls (responsibility of the information custodian).
6. Label the information and information systems appropriately.
7. Document handling procedures, including disposal.
8. Integrate the handling procedures into a information user security awareness program.
9. Declassify information when (and if) appropriate.

Reclassification/Declassification

Over a period of time, the need to protect information may change. An example of this can be found in the auto industry. Prior to a new car introduction, the design information is considered confidential. Disclosure would have serious ramifications to the automaker. After introduction, the same information is considered public and is published in the automotive manual. The process of downgrading sensitivity levels is known as ***declassification.***

Conversely, organizations may choose to strengthen the classification level if they believe that doing so is for the benefit of the organization or required by evolving regulations. The healthcare sector is currently in the process of reviewing electronic protected health information in light of HIPAA security regulations. The process of upgrading a classification is known as ***reclassification.*** If the information owner knows ahead of time when the information should be reclassified, then that date should be noted on the original classification label, e.g., *Confidential until date.*

At the time an organization is establishing the criteria for classification levels, it should also include a mechanism for reclassifying and declassifying information. This responsibility may be assigned to the information owner or subject to an internal review process.

TOP SECRET   NOFORN

OFFICE OF THE SECRETARY OF DEFENSE   **SPECIAL HANDLING**
WASHINGTON 25, D.C.

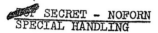
SECRET - NOFORN
SPECIAL HANDLING

19 February 1962

MEMORANDUM FOR THE CHIEF OF OPERATIONS, CUBA PROJECT

Subject: Tasks 33c and 33 d

The Joint Chiefs of Staff and Mr. Gilpatric

have approved the attached plans responsive to

Tasks 33 c and 33 d. This completes our action on

these Tasks.

WILLIAM H. CRAIG
Brig General, USA
DOD/JCS Representative
Caribbean Survey Group

Enclosure:
a/s

.1002

> EXCLUDED FROM AUTOMATIC
> REGRADING; DOD DIR 5200.10
> DOES NOT APPLY

SECRET - NOFORN
SPECIAL HANDLING

CSG wg 000054

TOP SECRET   NOFORN   SPECIAL HANDLING

FIGURE 5.2 Reclassified document from the Cuban Missile Crisis of 1962. (From the National Security Archive, www.gwu.edu/~nsarchiv/)

IN PRACTICE: Information Classification Handling and Labeling Policy

This policy is an example of how to identify and use classified information.

The *objectives* of this policy are to:

- Assign responsibility for developing and documenting handling and labeling standards.
- Assign responsibility for implementing handling and labeling procedures.
- Require that classified output, media, and devices be labeled appropriately.

The *audience* is all directors, managers, and security officials.

TABLE 5.3 Sample Information Classification Labeling and Handling policy.

Section X:	[COMPANY] Information Security Policy	Effective Date:
Subsection	Asset Classification & Control	Change Control #:
Policy	Information Classification Labeling and Handling Policy	Approved By:
Objective	In support of information security goals, [COMPANY] will adopt and use information labeling and handling procedures in accordance with its information classification policy.	
Purpose	The purpose of this policy is to address the issue of how information assets that have been classified should be labeled and handled.	
Audience	This policy applies to all directors, managers, and security officials.	
Policy	The Office of the Information Security Officer will develop and publish labeling and handling standards for all information systems in accordance with [COMPANY] information classification policy. Standards will be reviewed annually by the Board of Directors.	

▶▶ CONTINUED ON NEXT PAGE

>> CONTINUED

	Information system custodians will be responsible for developing and documenting handling for the following types of system activity:
	Processing
	Storage regardless of media type
	Transmission in any form
	Reuse
	Destruction / Disposal
	Output from systems containing information that is classified will carry an appropriate classification label.
	Media that contains classified information will carry an appropriate classification label.
	Devices that process, store, and/or transmit information will carry an appropriate classification label.
Exceptions	None
Disciplinary Actions	Violation of this policy may result in disciplinary action, which may include termination for employees and temporaries; a termination of employment relations in the case of contractors or consultants; or dismissal for interns and volunteers. Additionally, individuals are subject to civil and criminal prosecution.

5

Value and Criticality of Information Systems

Organizations classify information to identify the appropriate level of protection. Classifications are one of the elements in determining the overall value and criticality of information systems to the organization.

The value of the information and information system is relative to the organization and how the information is used. The asset's value needs to be determined before a reasonable decision can be made regarding how much money to spend protecting it. It stands to reason that it wouldn't make sense to spend $50,000 to protect information that could easily be replaced for $5,000. There are situations, however, in which it may not be possible to assign a hard dollar figure since the benefit may be "priceless." An example would be detailed customer information gleaned over the course of many years or information that is required to be protected by law or social mores.

In calculating the value of an asset, any or all of the following may be considered:

- Cost to acquire or develop the asset
- Cost to maintain and protect the asset
- Cost to replace the asset
- Importance of the asset to the owner
- Competitive advantage of the information
- Marketability of information (intellectual property)
- Impact on delivery of services
- Reputation
- Liability issues
- Regulatory compliance requirements

How Do We Know What We Have?

As amazing as it may seem, many organizations do not have an up-to-date inventory of information systems. This happens for any number of reasons. The most prevalent is a lack of centralized management and control. Departments within organizations are given the autonomy to make individual decisions, bring in systems, and create information independent of the rest of the organization. Corporate cultures that encourage entrepreneurial behavior are particularly vulnerable to this lack of structure. Another reason is the growth of corporations through acquisitions and mergers. During the Dotcom boom of the 1990s, companies were changing so rapidly that it became impossible to manage information effectively. Generally, the plan is to consolidate or merge information and systems, but in reality they often end up cohabitating.

Asset Inventory Methodology

Putting together a comprehensive physical inventory of information systems is a major task. The critical decision is choosing what attributes and characteristics of the information asset you want to record. The more specific and detailed the inventory, the more useful the inventory will be. Bear in mind that over time your inventory may have multiple purposes, including being used for criticality and risk analysis, business impact and disaster recovery planning insurance coverage, and business valuation.

Hardware Assets Hardware assets are visible and tangible pieces of equipment and media, such as:

- *Computer equipment:* Mainframe computers, servers, desktops, notebook computers, PDAs

- *Communication equipment:* Access points, firewalls, modems, routers, cabling, and transmission lines

- *Storage media:* Magnetic tapes, disks, CDs, DVDs, and DATs

- *Infrastructure equipment:* Power supplies, air conditioners, access control devices

Software Assets Software assets are programs or code that provides the interface between the hardware, the users, and the data. Software assets generally fall into three categories:

- *Operation system software:* Operating systems are responsible for providing the interface between the hardware, the user, and the application. Examples include Microsoft™ Windows, Novell™ Netware, Linux, Unix, and FreeBSD.

- *Productivity software:* The objective of productivity software is to provide basic business functionality and tools. Examples include the Microsoft Office™ Suite of Word, Excel, Publisher, and PowerPoint; Adobe™ Reader; Intuit™ Quick Book; and TurboTax.

- *Application software:* Application software is designed to implement the business rules of the organization and is often custom developed. Examples include programs that run complex machinery, process bank transactions, or manage lab equipment.

Asset Inventory Characteristics and Attributes

Unique Identifier Each asset should have a unique identifier. The most significant identifier is the device or program name. While you may assume that the name is obvious, we often find that the same information, system, or device is referred to differently by different users, departments, and audiences. Best practices dictate that the organization chooses a naming convention for its assets and apply the standard consistently. The naming convention may include the location, vendor, instance, and date of service. For example a Microsoft Exchange 5.5 server located in New York City and connected to the Internet may be named: MS_EX_5.5_NYC_I. A SQL database containing inventory records of women's shoes might be named SQL_SHOES_W. The name should also be clearly labeled on the device. The key is to be consistent, so that the names themselves become pieces of information. This is, however, a double-edged sword. We risk exposing asset information to the public if our devices are accessible or advertise themselves in any way. We need to protect this information consistent with all other valuable information assets.

Asset Description An asset description should indicate what the asset is used for. For example, devices may be identified as computers, connectivity, phone, or switching equipment. Categories can (and should) be subdivided. Computers can be broken down into servers, workstations, laptops, PDAs, Blackberries™, or even iPods™. Connectivity equipment might include firewalls, routers, proxy servers, or even Intrusion-Detection Systems (IDS).

Manufacturer Imprint For hardware devices, the manufacturer name should be recorded, as should the model number and part number. For example, a Hewlett-Packard Color LaserJet Printer would be recorded as HP Color LaserJet 3700n Printer (Q1322A). The manufacturer-assigned serial number should be included in the record. Software should be recorded by publisher or developer, version number, revision number, and, if applicable, patch level. Software vendors often assign a serial number or "software key," which should be included in the record.

Physical and Logical Address The physical address refers to the geographic location of the device itself or the device that houses the information. This should be as specific as possible. For example: APPS1_NYC is located at the East 21st Street office–2nd floor data center. The logical address is where the asset can be found on the organization's network. The logical address should reference the host name, the IP address, and, if applicable, the MAC address. Host names are "friendly names" given to systems that are accessed through the network. The host name may be the actual name of the system or an alias used for easy reference. The host names you might be most familiar are the ones found on the Internet. Let's say you wanted to find out when and where J. Lo's next concert was scheduled. You would most probably go on line and type **www.JenniferLopez.com** and, sure enough, you would be at her Web site. You accessed this information by using a "friendly name." The Internet Protocol or IP address is the unique network address location assigned to this system. The notation for an IP address is four octets separated by a period (x.x.x.x). Lastly, the Media Access Control or MAC address is a unique identifier assigned to network connectivity devices by the manufacturer of the device.

Controlling Entity In this case, control is related to money. The controlling entity is the department or business that purchased or paid for the asset and/or is responsible for the ongoing maintenance and upkeep expense. The controlling entity's capital expenditures and expenses are reflected in its budgets, balance sheets, and profit and loss statements.

System Characterization

The physical inventory provides basic documentation. To complete the picture, we need to define the relationships between the information, the information system, and the organization. This process is known as system characterization. ***System characterization*** articulates the understanding of the system, including the boundaries of the system being assessed, the system's hardware and software, and the information that is stored, processed, and transmitted. A key part of system characterization is the ranking of information and information system components according to their protection level and importance to the institution's operations. Information classification is one of the elements considered in the system characterization process. System characterization defines the importance of the information asset to the organization. An example would be a corporate Web site. The information itself would be classified as "public" or "nonclassified," meaning that is it available to whoever wants to read it. However, the site itself and the information presented may be extremely important to the company for marketing, sales, and reputation reasons.

The two criteria commonly used to rank the criticality of information assets are system impact and protection levels. *System impact* refers to how vital the information system/resource is to business processes and/or customer service. *Protection level* refers to the level of safeguards or control required. Protection can refer to any or all of the three attributes of security: confidentiality, integrity, or availability. For example, when a bank publishes Certificate of Deposit interest rates on its Web site, the information is meant to be widely disseminated; however, the rate information needs to be protected from an unauthorized change. Imagine the problems that would occur if an interest rate of 3% suddenly showed up as 30%! In this case, we are focused on protecting the integrity of the information.

Tables 5.4 and 5.5 define the levels commonly used to characterize an information asset. This type of ranking is known as a *qualitative approach,* meaning rankings are assigned based upon expert opinions rather than hard numbers. Who provides these expert opinions? We have found that the most successful approach brings together a cross-section of organizational management. This group is tasked with evaluating the criticality and sensitivity

TABLE 5.4 *System impact* refers to how vital the information system/resource is to business processes and/or customer service.

High	Breach or disruption of information system would have major business processing or customer impact	4 or 5
Medium	Breach or disruption of information system would have minor business processing or customer impact	3
Low	Breach or disruption of information system would have no business processing or customer impact	1 or 2

TABLE 5.5 *Information protection* refers to safeguarding the confidentiality, integrity, and availability of the information.

High	Compromise, disclosure, or loss of information stored or processed would have a significant negative impact	4 or 5
Medium	Compromise, disclosure, or loss of information stored or processed breach may have some negative impact	3
Low	Compromise, disclosure, or loss of information stored or processed would have minimal negative impact	1 or 2

of the information asset. The final score assigned to the information asset is a combination of the two. Organizations compile this information and organize it into tiers or levels (Table 5.6). The ranking tells the organization

TABLE 5.6 Information systems inventory and criticality ratings.

Information System	Description	System Impact	Information Protection	Criticality Rating
Tier I Critical Information Systems				
ABA	Core Banking Systems	5	5	10
Backup Unisys	Disaster Recovery Mainframe	5	5	10
Command	Virus Protection	5	5	10
WAN	Frame Relay / T1	4	5	9
Tier II High Priority Systems				
PBX	Telephone System	5	3.5	8.5
I-Banking	Outsourced I-Banking Presence	3	5	8
VIP Plus	Security Camera / Digital Photos	4	4	8
Tier III Medium Priority Systems				
Microsoft Exchange™	E-mail	3.5	2	5.5
ACT™	Sales Tracking Database	3	2	5
ADP™ Payroll	HR Payroll Processing	2	1	3

which information assets are most important and how allocated resources should be prioritized.

Criticality Ratings Criticality ratings are an incredibly useful metric. Most organizations do not have unlimited resources. Management is tasked with making thoughtful decisions on how to allocate time and money. They must balance controls with productivity. They must ensure they remain in compliance with local, state, federal, and international law. Criticality ratings provide the basis on which to prioritize and allocate resources. Criticality rating can also be used in risk analysis and management as well as in disaster recovery and business continuity planning. Criticality ratings should be revisited annually, as well as whenever a change driver is introduced.

IN PRACTICE: Inventory of Information System Assets policy

This goal of this policy is to require that information system assets are documented and analyzed. The outcome of this policy is the metrics necessary to make appropriate and prudent protection decisions.

The *objectives* of this policy are to:

- Require a documented inventory of information assets.
- Designate responsibility for the inventory.
- Require an annual criticality analysis.
- Involve executive management in the criticality analysis.

The *audience* is all directors, managers, and security officials.

TABLE 5.7 Sample Information System Asset Inventory policy.

Section X:	[COMPANY] Information Security Policy	Effective Date:
Subsection	Asset Classification & Control	Change Control #:
Policy	Information System Asset Inventory	Approved By:
Objective	In support of information security goals, [COMPANY] will compile a list of all its information assets, and establish the relative value and importance of each asset.	

▶▶ CONTINUED ON NEXT PAGE

▸▸ CONTINUED	
Purpose	The purpose of this policy is to ensure that protection is provided that is commensurate with the value and importance of each information asset.
Audience	This policy applies to all directors, managers, and security officials.
Policy	All information system assets shall be identified and documented with their classification, owner, location, and other details according to standards published by the Office of the Information Security Officer.
	All information system assets will be ranked to determine their system criticality. The ranking process will be conducted annually by the Office of the Information Security Officer and results presented to the executive management team.
	The office of the Information Security Officer will maintain the documentation.
Exceptions	None
Disciplinary Actions	Violation of this policy may result in disciplinary action, which may include termination for employees and temporaries; a termination of employment relations in the case of contractors or consultants; or dismissal for interns and volunteers. Additionally, individuals are subject to civil and criminal prosecution.

Summary

As security professionals, our task is to develop both a defensive and offensive strategy to protect and defend organizational information and information system assets. To adequately do so we must have a clear understanding of what they are, where they are located, how critical they are to the organization, how sensitive they are to compromise or disclosure, and who owns them. This chapter focused on Section 5 of the ISO 17799 framework: Asset Classification.

We began with defining information assets and information systems. We discussed the need for information classification and examined both public and private sector classification systems. We examined why classification is the responsibility of the information owner. We then looked at the elements to be included in a physical inventory of information assets. Finally, we brought it all together in a process known as criticality analysis.

The outcome of a criticality analysis is to assign a rating based upon business impact and protection level. The composite score provides the organization with the evidence necessary to allocate resources to protect and defend the information assets.

Test Your Skills

MULTIPLE CHOICE QUESTIONS

1. Asset Classification is Section 5 of:

    A. ISO 2001

    B. NIST 7799

    C. ISO 17799

    D. NIST SP 80-300

2. Which of the following is the best example of an information asset?

    A. customer database

    B. word processing program

    C. laptop

    D. server

3. Which of the following is the best example of an information system?

    A. router

    B. desktop computer

    C. fax machine

    D. SQL database server

4. An ASP provides which of the following services?

    A. programming

    B. application service provider hosting

    C. transcription

    D. all of the above

5. Information owners are responsible for:

    A. protecting information

    B. maintaining information

    C. using information

    D. registering information

6. Which of the following is responsible for implementing appropriate security controls?

   A. information owner

   B. information vendor

   C. information user

   D. information custodian

7. Information classification systems are used in which of the following organizations?

   A. government

   B. military

   C. financial institutions

   D. all of the above

8. Which of these classifications requires the most protection?

   A. Secret

   B. Top Secret

   C. Confidential

   D. Unclassified

9. Which of these classifications require the least protection?

   A. Secret

   B. Top Secret

   C. Confidential

   D. Unclassified

10. The Freedom of Information Act allows anyone to:

    A. access all government information just by asking

    B. access all classified documents

    C. access classified documents on a "need to know" basis

    D. access any records from federal agencies unless the documents can be officially declared exempt

11. Is it mandatory for all private businesses to classify information?

    A. yes

    B. only if they want to pay less taxes

    C. only if they do business with the government

    D. only if they are subject to federal regulations that require classification of data such as HIPAA or GLBA

12. Which of the following is not a criterion for classifying information?

    A. The information is not public knowledge or public domain. ✓

    B. The information has no value to the organization. ✓

    C. The information needs to be protected from those outside of the organization.

    D. The information is subject to government regulations. ✓

13. Confidential information is meant to be:

    A. kept secret

    B. restricted to a small circle of authorized users

    C. both a and b

    D. neither a nor b

14. Most organizations restrict access to sensitive data to:

    A. executives

    B. information owners

    C. users who have a demonstrated "need-to-know"

    D. vendors

15. "For Official Use Only" and "Not for Public Release" are labels used by the DoD for which classification?

    A. Sensitive

    B. Unclassified

    C. Sensitive but unclassified

    D. Classified

16. The two criteria commonly used to rank the criticality of information assets are:

    A. system impact and protection levels

    B. system impact and information classification

    C. protection level and replacement cost

    D. replacement cost and insurance premiums

17. A *qualitative approach* to an analysis uses:

    A. hard numbers

    B. statistics

    C. expert opinions

    D. general population surveys

5

18. The process of downgrading sensitivity levels is known as:
    A. declassification
    B. classification
    C. reclassification
    D. negative classification

19. The process of upgrading or changing sensitivity levels is known as:
    A. declassification
    B. classification
    C. reclassification
    D. negative classification

20. Criticality ratings are used to:
    A. determine the importance of an information asset
    B. test the strength of the safeguard
    C. determine the replacement cost
    D. none of the above

EXERCISES

Exercise 5.1: Assigning Ownership

Owners are responsible for the protection of assets. For each of the following assets, assign an owner and list their responsibilities in regard to protecting the asset.

1. The house you live in

2. The car you drive

3. The computer you use

4. The city you live in

Exercise 5.2: Ownership vs. Controlling Entity

You most probably have a cell phone or know someone who does. A cell phone contains information (e.g., address book, text messages) and is in itself an information system.

1. Who would you consider the information owner?

2. Who would you consider the information custodian?

3. Who would you consider the information system owner?

4. Who would you consider the information system custodian?

5. Does your answer depend upon who initially purchased the phone? For example, suppose you were given the phone as a gift. Write a paragraph explaining your answer.

6. Does your answer depend upon who pays the monthly cell phone bill? Write a paragraph explaining your answer.

Exercise 5.3: Creating an Inventory

You have been tasked with creating an inventory system for the Computer Lab at your school. You can create the inventory either on paper or using a database or spreadsheet.

1. For the hardware in the lab, list at least five characteristics that you will use to identify each asset.

2. For the software in the lab, list at least five characteristics that you will use to identify each asset.

3. Visit a classroom or lab and enter two hardware and two software assets into your inventory.

Exercise 5.4: Previously Top Secret

Recently classified documents from the Cuban Missile crisis were declassified and made available to the public via the National Archives. The documents can be found at **http://www.gwu.edu/~nsaarchiv/nsa/cuba_mis_cri/docs.htm** (Note: you may be redirected to GW Home Page. If this happens, search on "National Archives Cuban Missile Crisis documents.")

1. Access the National Archives Cuban Missile Crisis, 1962 site.

2. Locate and print one of each of the following:
   a. A declassified TOP SECRET document
   b. A declassified SECRET document
   c. A document that was always UNCLASSIFIED

Exercise 5.5: Color-Coded National Security

The Department of Homeland Security uses a color-coded advisory system to communicate threat levels to the public. This is an example of labeling.

1. What colors are used in the Threat Advisory System?

2. What does each of the colors mean?

3. Do you think these labels are an effective way to communicate threat information to the general public? Why or why not?

PROJECTS

Project 5.1: Owner vs. Owner

When you compose an e-mail, you have created an information asset. Develop a three-level classification system for your e-mail. Consider the type of e-mails that you send and who should be able to view, save, print, or forward your e-mail. For each classification, decide how you will label your e-mails to communicate the assigned classification.

Multiple information systems are used to process, transmit, store, and backup e-mail. Identify as many systems as possible involved in each step. For each system identified, document the person or position you would expect to be the information system owner.

Sometimes information system owners have different priorities than information asset owners. For example, your Internet Service Provider by law has the right to view/open all documents that are stored on or passed through its systems. The ISP may choose to exercise this right by scanning for viruses or checking for illegal content. Suppose you have sent e-mails that would harm your organization if they were disclosed or compromised. As the information asset owner, what do you see as your options?

Project 5.2: Classifying Your School Records

Over time, your school has accumulated a great deal of information about you and your family, including your medical records, finances (including tax returns), transcript, and student demographic data (name/address/date of birth/etc.).

1. Create a table listing each of the above information categories. Classify each one as either Confidential, Sensitive, Restricted, or Unclassified.

2. Include in your table a column defining the "Need to Know" criteria. (Hint: This is the reason someone should be granted access to the information.)

3. Even though the information pertains to you, you are not the owner. Include in your table a column listing who you would expect to be the information owner.

4. Choose one of the categories you have listed and find out where the information is actually stored, who is responsible for it, who has access to it, and what policies are in place to protect it. Compare this information with your answers to Parts 1, 2, and 3 of this project.

Project 5.3: Assigning Criticality Ratings

Imagine that you are the General Manager of a National Football League stadium. You have to decide how best to allocate resources. You will need to refer back to Tables 5.4, 5.5, and 5.6 to complete this project.

1. Assign business impact and information sensitivity ratings. Add the two together to get the criticality rating.

Information System	Description	System Impact	Information Protection	Criticality Rating
Ticket Plus	Front office system for issuing tickets to events			
FastFood$	Automated cash register system for the concession stands			
NoBurn	Computer system that controls the sprinkler and fire suppression systems throughout the facility			
Scorecard	System that tracks the scores and statistics and displays the information on the stadium scoreboards			
TeamWeb	The team's Web site			

2. Compare your results with another student's. You must come to agreement on ratings.

3. Prepare a presentation to the Board of Directors of the stadium explaining your decisions.

▶▶ Case Study

The Federal Deposit Insurance Corporation (FDIC) is responsible for auditing savings banks. Their goal is to make sure that the banks comply with all federal regulations, including those governing the privacy and security of customer information.

▶▶ CONTINUED ON NEXT PAGE

5

▶▶ CONTINUED

In January 2005, the FDIC began an audit of SouthEast Community Bank. SouthEast was founded in 1888. It is head-quartered in Atlanta, Georgia and has 15 branches located throughout the state. SouthEast provides a full range of services to both the consumer and commercial markets. The bank is a leader in e-commerce and virtually all services can be accessed via the Web. Southeast seems to be a model of security. Over the years, they have spent a fortune on firewalls; Intrusion-Detection Systems; programs that audit, monitor, and report access; biometric devices; and so forth. Although their information technology and security staff is small, they are a dedicated team of professionals.

At first, the audit team was very impressed. Then they began to wonder how protection decisions were made. It appeared to them that all information assets were being treated with equal protection, which meant that some were perhaps protected too much, while others were underprotected. They approached the bank president and asked her to explain how the bank made protection decisions. She replied that she left it up to the information technology and security team. The auditors then went to the members of the team and asked them they same question. They enthusiastically replied that the importance of the various information assets was "institutional knowledge." They were puzzled when the auditors asked if the information owners classified the information and authorized the protection levels. No, they replied, it had always been left to them. The auditors were not happy with this answer and expressed their displeasure in their report. They tasked the bank with completing both a classification and criticality analysis within the next six months or risk being shut down.

1. Who should take responsibility for this project?

2. Is this one project or two separate projects?

3. Who should be involved in this project(s)?

4. Would you engage external resources? Why or why not?

5. How would you gain consensus?

6. What involvement should the Board of Directors have?

Chapter | 6

Personnel Security

Chapter Objectives

After reading this chapter and completing the exercises, you will be able to do the following:

■ Describe the role of security in personnel practices.

■ Develop secure recruiting and interviewing procedures.

■ Evaluate confidentiality and employee security agreements.

■ Understand appropriate security education, training, and awareness programs.

■ Design an incident reporting program.

■ Create personnel-related security policies and procedures.

Introduction

This chapter is mapped to the ISO 17799 Section 6 and addresses personnel issues as they relate to information systems security. This domain is an example of how security management responsibilities transcend the information technology department. The policies and procedures in this domain are primarily the responsibility of the Human Relations department. Aspects of personnel security may involve the Training Department, Legal Counsel, and Employee Unions or Associations.

Employees are simultaneously an organization's most valuable asset and their most dangerous risk. For an organization to function, employees need access to information and information systems. Since we are exposing valuable assets, we must know our employees: their background, education, and potential vulnerabilities. Potential employees must also know what is expected of them; from the very first contact, the organization needs to deliver the message that security is taken seriously. We will begin this chapter with a discussion of job descriptions and hiring practices.

Once hired, employees need to understand their role and responsibilities as a steward of information as well as the consequences of violating policy. Information security and confidentiality are so important that at the time of hire a binding contract needs to be signed by the employee agreeing to the policies. To accomplish this task, organizations have confidentiality and security agreements. We will examine the substance of these agreements.

Even long-standing employees continually need to be re-educated about security issues. We will look at who is responsible for training and security awareness programs. We will examine the Security Education, Awareness, and Training model developed by the National Institute of Standard and Technology (NIST) and see how it relates to policy.

One of the key messages to be delivered in training and awareness programs is the importance of incident reporting. We need to train users on what constitutes suspicious behavior and how to report it. Users can be an organization's first line of defense against an attack. Educating users to recognize and report suspicious behavior is a powerful deterrent to would-be intruders. We will end this chapter with a discussion of incident reporting procedures and policies.

First Contact

The first direct contact many potential candidates have of their future employer is a help wanted advertisement. Historically, this advertisement was published in a newspaper or trade journal. The current trend is posting jobs on the Internet (e-posting) using an employment search engine such as Monster or Yahoo Jobs. The upside to this trend is reaching a wider audience of talent. The downside is that this exposure also reaches a wider audience of potential intruders and may have the unintended consequence of exposing information about an organization. In Chapter 5, we discussed the process of *footprinting*. Job postings are one of the sources that intruders often look to use. Why? Because job postings can be a wealth of information about an organization: personnel changes, product development, new services, opening of offices, as well as basic information like the name and phone number of the hiring manager. All of these can be used in social engineering attacks and provide a path to more in-depth knowledge. An idea to consider is having two versions of a job description. Version A is posted and/or published and has enough information to attract the attention and interest of a potential employee. Version B is more detailed and is posted internally and/or shared with candidates that have made the "first cut."

FYI: Internet-Based Job Hunting

According to a July 2002 report released by the Pew Internet Project, 52 million Americans have hit the Internet in search of a job. That's a 60 percent jump over the number of people who used the Internet in their online job searches in March 2000. On an average day, more than 4 million people search out new employment opportunities on the Net, which is 33 percent higher than the daily job-search traffic two years ago. Online job searching is also a young person's game. More than 60 percent of Net users between the ages of 18 and 29 have searched online for jobs, compared to 42 percent of people ages 30 to 49, and 27 percent of those ages 50 to 64.

Popular sites include:

- Monster.com (**www.monster.com**)
- The Riley Guide (**www.rileyguide.com**)
- Yahoo! HotJobs (**http://hotjobs.yahoo.com**)
- Excite Careers & Education
  (**www.excite.com/careers_and_education/**)

6

Job Descriptions

Version B of a job description needs to be detailed enough to convey the facets of the position and has the following characteristics:

- Conveys the mission of the organization.

- Describes the position in general terms.

- Outlines the responsibilities of the position.

- States the organization's expectations regarding confidentiality, safety, and security. The goal of this characteristic is to deliver the message that the organization has a commitment to security and that all employees are required to honor that commitment.

What should not be in either version of the job description is information regarding specific systems, software, security features, or access controls.

The Interview

Interviewers often reveal much more than they should to job candidates. They do so for a variety of reasons. Sometimes they are trying to impress a sought-after candidate. They may be proud of (or dismayed with) the organization. Sometimes they simply do not realize the confidentiality of the information they are sharing. For example, an interviewer might reveal that the organization is about to launch a new Internet-based shopping portal and that they know little about how to secure it! One of the worst mistakes that an interviewer can make is taking an early-stage job candidate on a tour of the facility. A candidate should never be allowed access to secure areas without prior authorization by the information system owner. Even then, the candidate should be required to obtain the requisite level of clearance.

FYI: Social Engineering

Social engineering is defined by the Gartner Research Group as "the manipulation of people, rather than machines, to successfully breach the security systems of an enterprise or a consumer." Social engineering is used to compromise all sorts of information, such as passwords, user IDs, Social Security numbers, etc. Phishing is one popular mechanism used, as criminals continue to reinvent old scams using better technology (e.g., mimicking bank websites/logos and redirecting users to nonbank sites where they're requested to enter old passwords). In October 2004, Gartner released a report concluding that the "greatest security risk facing large companies and individual Internet users over the next 10 years will be the increasingly sophisticated use of social engineering to bypass IT security defenses." For more information, visit **www.gartner.com/security**.

IN PRACTICE: Job Recruitment and Descriptions Policy

The goal of this policy is to integrate security controls into the recruiting and hiring process.

The *objectives* of this policy are to:

- Protect sensitive and/or confidential information.
- Acknowledge the security requirements of the organization and the position.

The *audience* is all users.

▶▶ CONTINUED ON NEXT PAGE

▸▸ CONTINUED

TABLE 6.1 Sample Job Recruitment and Descriptions Policy.

Section X:	[COMPANY] Information Security Policy	Effective Date:
Subsection	Personnel Security	Change Control #:
Policy	Job Recruitment and Descriptions	Approved By:
Objective	In support of information security, the [COMPANY] will ensure that job descriptions do not reveal sensitive information and that the security requirements of the position are included.	
Purpose	The purpose of this policy is to ensure [COMPANY] resources are protected during the recruitment process and that personnel security responsibilities are clearly defined at the recruitment stage and during an employee's tenure.	
Audience	All users are expected to understand and abide by established enterprise information technology security policies.	
Policy	• Any information that is classified as sensitive or confidential will not be included in job postings or job descriptions. • Candidates will not be allowed access to any secure area unless authorized in writing by the information owner. • General security responsibilities will be included in all job descriptions according to established standards. • Specific security requirements appropriate to the position will be included in job descriptions according to established standards. • The Office of the Information Security Office and the Office of Human Resources will be jointly responsible for the implementation and enforcement of this policy.	
Exceptions	None	

6

▸▸ CONTINUED ON NEXT PAGE

▸▸ **CONTINUED**

| Disciplinary Actions | Violation of this policy may result in disciplinary action which may include termination for employees and temporaries; a termination of employment relations in the case of contractors or consultants; or dismissal for interns and volunteers. Additionally, individuals are subject to civil and criminal prosecution. |

Who Is This Person?

You are a business owner. You've spent the last ten years toiling night and day to build your business. You've invested your personal financial resources. Your reputation in the community is intertwined with the actions of the business. How much do you need to know about your newest salesperson?

You are the Chief Executive Officer (CEO) of a Fortune 1000 financial services company. You are responsible to the stockholders and accountable to the government for the actions of your business. How much do you need to know about your new Chief Financial Officer?

You are the Head of Medicine at your local hospital. You are responsible for maintaining the health of your patients and for guaranteeing their right to privacy. How much do you need to know about the new emergency room intake nurse?

In all three cases, the information owner wants assurance that the user will treat the information appropriately in accordance with its classification and criticality. Earlier, we defined *information classification* as the organization of information assets according to their sensitivity to disclosure and *criticality* as the ranking of information assets in terms of their importance to the organization. One of the standards in determining who should have access is defining the user criteria. These criteria extend to their background: education, experience, certification/license, criminal record, and financial status. In addition, we must consider the amount of power or influence the employee will have in the organization.

For example, we expect that a Chief Financial Officer will have access to confidential financial records and sensitive corporate strategy documents. In addition, the CFO has the power to potentially manipulate the data. In this case, we need to be concerned about both the confidentiality and the integrity of the information. It seems obvious that the CFO needs to be held to a high standard. He should have a spotless criminal record and not be under any financial pressure that may lead to inappropriate activities such as embezzlement. Unfortunately, as corporate scandals such as Enron and Adelphia have shown us, those in power do not always act in the best interest of the organization. The organization needs to proactively protect itself by conducting background checks on potential employees and directors. The same holds true for positions of less prominence, such as a salesperson or intake nurse. While these positions may have less power, the potential for misuse still exists.

The government takes this concept to the next level. Similar to information having classifications, in government, people have clearances. Based upon a preset criteria and an extensive background check, personnel are assigned a clearance level. While each government agency has its own standards, in general a security clearance investigation is an inquiry into an individual's loyalty, character, trustworthiness, and reliability to ensure that he or she is eligible for access to national security information. In order to obtain access to data, clearance and classification must match. For example, in order to view Top Secret information, the person must hold Top Secret clearance. However, merely having a certain level of security clearance does not mean one is authorized to access the information. To have access to the information, one must possess two elements: a level of security clearance, at least equal to the classification of the information, and an appropriate "need to know" the information in order to perform their duties.

6

FYI: Sarbanes-Oxley: A Response to Misuse of Power

Posted on the Securities and Exchange Web site (**www.sec.gov/about/laws.shtml**):

"On July 30, 2002, President Bush signed into law the Sarbanes-Oxley Act of 2002, which he characterized as 'the most far reaching reforms of American business practices since the time of Franklin Delano Roosevelt.' The Act mandated a number of reforms to enhance corporate responsibility, enhance financial disclosures and combat corporate and accounting fraud, and created the 'Public Company Accounting Oversight Board,' also known as the PCAOB, to oversee the activities of the auditing profession."

The full text of the Act is available at **www.sec.gov/about/laws/soa2002.pdf**. You can find links to all Commission rule-making and reports issued under the Sarbanes-Oxley Act at **www.sec.gov/spotlight/sarbanes-oxley.htm**.

Types of Background Checks

Not all potential employees need to undergo the same level of scrutiny. It is the responsibility of the information owner to set standards based upon level of information access and position. It is important to have a policy that sets the minimum standards for the organization yet affords information owners the latitude to require additional or more in-depth background checks or investigations. This is an example of a policy that in the development stage may need to involve outsiders such as legal counsel or employee representatives. Many organizations have union labor. The union contract may forbid the background checks. This policy would need to be incorporated into the next round of negotiations.

Workers' Right to Privacy There are legal limits on the information you can gather and use when making employment decisions. Workers have a right to privacy in certain personal matters, a right they can enforce by suing you if you pry too deeply. Make sure your inquiries are related to the job. Stick to information that is relevant to the job for which you are considering the worker.

Getting Consent While not always required by law, conventional wisdom recommends asking candidates to agree to a background check. Most organizations include this request on their application forms and require the applicant to agree in writing. By law, if a candidate refuses to agree to a reasonable request for information, you may decide not to hire the worker on that basis.

Rules To Be Aware Of

- **Educational Records.** Under the Family Educational Rights and Privacy Act (FERPA) schools must have written permission in order to release any information from a student's education record. For more information on obtaining records under FERPA go to **http://www.ed.gov**.

- **Motor Vehicle Records.** Under the federal Drivers Privacy Protection Act (DPPA), the release or use by any state DMV (or any officer, employee, or contractor thereof) of personal information about an individual obtained by the department in connection with a motor vehicle record is prohibited. The latest amendment to the DPPA requires states to get permission from individuals before their personal motor vehicle record may be sold or released to third-party marketers.

- **Financial History.** According to the Federal Trade Commission (FTC), you may use credit reports when you hire new employees and when you evaluate employees for promotion, reassignment, and retention — as long as you comply with the Fair Credit Reporting Act (FCRA). Sections 604, 606, and 615 of the FCRA spell out employer responsibilities when using credit reports for employment purposes. These responsibilities include the requirement of notification if the information obtained may result in a negative employment decision. For more information on using credit reports and the FCRA go to: **http://www.ftc.gov**.

- **Bankruptcies.** Under Title 11 of the U.S. Bankruptcy Code, employers are prohibited from discriminating against someone who has filed for bankruptcy. While employers can use a negative credit history as a reason not to hire, employers cannot use bankruptcy as a sole reason.

- **Criminal History.** The law on how this information can be used varies extensively from state to state.

- **Workers' Compensation Records.** In most states, when an employee's claim goes through Workers Compensation, the case becomes public record. An employer may only use this information if an injury might interfere with one's ability to perform required duties. Under the federal Americans with Disabilities Act, employers cannot use medical information or the fact an applicant filed a Workers' Compensation claim to discriminate against applicants.

TABLE 6.2 Types of Background Checks.

Educational Verification	Confirming that all educational credentials listed on the application, resume or cover letter are valid and have been awarded.
Employment Verification	Verifying all relevant previous employment as listed on the application, resume, or cover letter.
License/Certification Verification	Authentication of all relevant licenses, certifications or credentials.
Credit History Check	Checking the credit history of the selected applicant or employee. Federal laws prohibit discrimination against an applicant or employee as a result of bankruptcy. Federal law also requires that applicants be notified if their credit history influences the employment decision.
Criminal History Check	Verifying that the selected applicant or employee does not have any undisclosed criminal history.

IN PRACTICE: Personnel Screening Policy

The goal of this policy to make sure that the company really knows who it is hiring.

The *objectives* of this policy are to:

- Protect sensitive and/or confidential information.
- Define screening and verification required of applicants.
- Define screening and verification required of employees who change positions.
- Assign screening and verification responsibilities.
- Assure that all screening and verification will be done in accordance with all applicable local, state, and federal laws and regulations.

The *audience* is all users.

TABLE 6.3 Sample Personnel Screening Policy.

Section X:	[COMPANY] Information Security Policy	Effective Date:
Subsection	Personnel Security	Change Control #:
Policy	Personnel Screening	Approved By:
Objective	In support of information security, the [COMPANY] will carry out initial and periodic screening of employees, temporaries and contractors with the degree of which being determined by the sensitivity of systems that the person accesses.	
Purpose	The purpose of this policy is to ensure that information assets are protected from personnel who may not be able to be trusted with the responsibilities associated with security protection and handling.	
Audience	All users are expected to understand and abide by established enterprise information technology security policies.	

Policy	• The policy requires that all employees, temporaries and contractors be screened, prior to starting, for
	  • One personal character reference,
	  • One business character reference,	

▸▸ CONTINUED ON NEXT PAGE

CONTINUED

- Confirmation of professional qualifications,

- Confirmation of academic qualifications,

- Independent identity checks (passport or similar document),

- State criminal check.

- The screening of new personnel shall be carried out by Human Resources Department.

- If the person will have access to sensitive or highly confidential information, additional screening may be required at the discretion of the information owner. This screening will be carried out by Human Resources Dept. This includes new staff or those who might be moved into such a position from a less-sensitive position.

- If temporary or contractor staff is provided by an agency, the contract will clearly specify the agency's responsibilities for screening.

- If contractor staff is provided through an outsourcing contract, the contract will clearly specify the contractor's responsibilities for screening.

- Managers will evaluate employees for changes in personal circumstances that might present additional security threats. Such changes will be immediately reported to the Information Security Officer.

- All screening and supervision shall be in accordance with appropriate legislation in the relevant jurisdiction.

- Human Resources will publish guidelines of relevant legislation.

Exceptions	None
Disciplinary Actions	Violation of this policy may result in disciplinary action which may include termination for employees and temporaries; a termination of employment relations in the case of contractors or consultants; or dismissal for interns and volunteers. Additionally, individuals are subject to civil and criminal prosecution.

6

The Importance of Employee Agreements

It is common practice to require employees, contractors, and outsourcers to sign two basic agreements: a confidentiality agreement (also known as a nondisclosure agreement) and an acceptable use agreement. Confidentiality agreements are in place to protect from unauthorized disclosure of information and are generally a condition of work regardless of access to information systems. Acceptable use agreements traditionally focus on the proper use of information systems and cover such topics as password management, Internet access, and e-mail etiquette. A growing trend is to replace traditional acceptable use agreements with employee information security affirmation agreements. The goal of an employee information security affirmation agreement is to teach the employee the importance of security, obtain commitment, and install organizational values.

Confidentiality Agreements

Confidentiality agreements are contracts entered into by the employee and the organization in which the parties agree that certain types of information remain confidential. The type of information that can be included is virtually unlimited. Any information can be considered confidential—data, know-how, prototypes, engineering drawings, computer software, test results, tools, systems, and specifications.

Confidentiality agreements perform several functions. First and most obviously, they protect sensitive technical or commercial information from disclosure to others. Second, they can prevent the forfeiture of valuable patent rights. Under U.S. law, and in other countries as well, the public disclosure of an invention can be deemed as a forfeiture of patent rights in that invention. Third, confidentiality agreements define exactly what information can and cannot be disclosed. This is usually accomplished by specifically classifying the information as such and then labeling appropriately (and clearly). Fourth, confidentiality agreements define how the information is to be handled and for what length of time. Last, they state what is to happen to the information when employment is terminated or, in the case of a third party, when a contract or project ends.

Information Security Affirmation Agreements

While a traditional acceptable use agreement is a document that simply details what those rules are, an information security affirmation agreement focuses on explaining why the policies have been established and how important compliance is. The agreement is, in essence, a teaching tool that provides guidance for the user when faced with a situation not explicitly covered in the agreement. The following are excerpts from agreements that illustrate ways of using this document as a teaching tool.

". . . These rules are in place to protect the public, our employees, and the [COMPANY]. Inappropriate use of our information resources exposes the [COMPANY] to risks including virus attacks, compromise of network systems and services, and legal issues. . . ."

". . . E-mail use has become the standard method of communication, used in 75 percent of all business communications. E-mail is inherently insecure, and messages can easily be intercepted and read or changed. Additionally, e-mail is the number one doorway to viruses and worms, which infect and destroy valuable information. These policies are intended to offer rules of usage that will protect our information. . . ."

". . . All of the work we are doing at [COMPANY] to secure the public's information will be ineffective if the most important aspect of information security, the daily users of our information resources, have weak passwords. Though we recognize that it is initially inconvenient, using a strong password is the most important way you can protect our information resources. We would like to think of passwords as a "shared secret" between you and [COMPANY]'s information resources. . . ."

Another way to think about the information security affirmation agreement is that it is a condensed version of the entire information security policy document specifically crafted for employees. It contains only the policies that pertain to them and is written in language that they can easily and unequivocally understand.

Components of an Affirmation Agreement

- The affirmation agreement should be prefaced with a statement of authority. The statement of authority sets the tone for the agreement and emphasizes the commitment of the leadership of the organization. In Chapter 4, you will find a sample statement of authority.

- The body of the affirmation agreement should address at a minimum the following areas:
  - Acceptable use of information resources
  - Internet use
  - E-mail use
  - Incidental use of information resources
  - Password management
  - Portable computers

- The document should conclude with a commitment paragraph acknowledging that the user has read the agreement, understands the agreement and the consequences of violation, and agrees to abide by the policies presented.

- The agreement should be dated, signed, and witnessed.

- An appendix of any definitions that the reader may be unfamiliar with should be included.

- Sample confidentiality agreements and employee information security affirmation agreements can be found in the Appendix to this text.

IN PRACTICE: Personnel Agreements Policy

The goal of this policy is to create a security contract between users and the organization as well as to demonstrate management's commitment.

The *objectives* of this policy are to:

- Require confidentiality and information security affirmation agreements as a condition of employment.

- Assign responsibility for the development and maintenance of agreements.

- Assign responsibility for the execution of the agreements.

The *audience* is all users.

TABLE 6.4 Sample Personnel Agreements Policy.

Section X:	[COMPANY] Information Security Policy	Effective Date:
Subsection	Personnel Security	Change Control #:
Policy	Personnel Agreements	Approved By:
Objective	In support of information security the [COMPANY] will require both confidentiality and information security affirmation agreements from all employees and third party staff not otherwise covered by third party contracts.	
Purpose	The purpose of this policy is to protect the assets of the organization by clearly informing personnel of their	

▸▸ CONTINUED ON NEXT PAGE

»CONTINUED	
	roles and responsibilities for keeping the organization's information confidental and information resources secure.
Audience	All users are expected to understand and abide by established enterprise information technology security policies.
Policy	• This policy requires that staff sign a confidentiality agreement and an information security affirmation agreement as a condition of employment and prior to being granted access to any sensitive information or systems.
	• The documents provided to the employee will clarify the employees' responsibilities both during employment and post-employment.
	• The employee's legal rights and responsibilities will be included in the document.
	• The Office of Human Resources is responsible for developing, maintaining and updating the confidentiality agreement.
	• The Office of the Information Security Officer is responsible for developing, maintaining and updating the information security affirmation agreement.
	• Agreements will be reviewed with the staff member when there is any change to the employment or contract, or prior to leaving the organization.
	• The agreements will be provided to the employee by the Office of Human Resources.
Exceptions	None
Disciplinary Actions	Violation of this policy may result in disciplinary action which may include termination for employees and temporaries; a termination of employment relations in the case of contractors or consultants; or dismissal for interns and volunteers. Additionally, individuals are subject to civil and criminal prosecution.

6

Training Important?

In October 2003, the National Institute of Standards and Technology (NIST) released Special Publication 800-50, "Building an Information Technology Security Awareness and Training Program" (**http://csrc.nist. gov/publications/nistpubs/800-50/NIST-SP800-50.pdf**). In the introduction, the NIST succinctly defines why security education and training is so important:

"Federal agencies and organizations cannot protect the confidentiality, integrity, and availability of information in today's highly networked systems environment without ensuring that all people involved in using and managing IT:

- Understand their roles and responsibilities related to the organizational mission;

- Understand the organization's IT security policy, procedures, and practices;

- Have at least adequate knowledge of the various management, operational, and technical controls required and available to protect the IT resources for which they are responsible.

"The 'people factor'—not technology—is key to providing an adequate and appropriate level of security. If people are the key, but are also a weak link, more and better attention must be paid to this 'asset.'

"A strong IT security program cannot be put in place without significant attention given to training agency IT users on security policy, procedures, and techniques, as well as the various management, operational, and technical controls necessary and available to secure IT resources. In addition, those in the agency who manage the IT infrastructure need to have the necessary skills to carry out their assigned duties effectively. Failure to give attention to the area of security training puts an enterprise at great risk because security of agency resources is as much a *human issue* as it is a technology issue.

"Everyone has a role to play in the success of a security awareness and training program but agency heads, Chief Information Officers (CIOs), program officials, and IT security program managers have key responsibilities to ensure that an effective program is established agency wide. The scope and content of the program must be tied to existing security program directives and established agency security policy. Within agency IT security program policy, there must exist clear requirements for the awareness and training program."

FYI: Who Is NIST?

NIST stands for National Institute of Standards and Technology. Founded in 1901, NIST is a nonregulatory federal agency within the U.S. Commerce Department's Technology Administration. NIST's mission is to develop and promote measurement, standards, and technology to enhance productivity, facilitate trade, and improve the quality of life.

The Computer Security Division (CSD)–(893) is one of eight divisions within NIST's Information Technology Laboratory.

The mission of NIST's Computer Security Division is to improve information systems security by:

■ Raising awareness of IT risks, vulnerabilities, and protection requirements, particularly for new and emerging technologies.

■ Researching, studying, and advising agencies of IT vulnerabilities and devising techniques for the cost-effective security and privacy of sensitive Federal systems.

■ Developing standards, metrics, tests, and validation programs:

- to promote, measure, and validate security in systems and services;

- to educate consumers; and

- to establish minimum security requirements for Federal systems.

■ Developing guidance to increase secure IT planning, implementation, management, and operation.

The CSD's Computer Security Resource Center (CRSC) is a comprehensive portal to information security resources and is located at **http://csrc.nist.gov**.

6

SETA for All

The phrase *security education* is really a catch-all for three different programs: security education, training, and awareness. NIST SP 800-16 refers to this as the SETA model and assigns specific attributes to each program.

TABLE 6.5 NIST SP 800-16 SETA model.

Security	Education	Training	Awareness
Attribute	Why	How	What
Level	Insight	Knowledge	Information
Objective	Understanding	Skill	Awareness
Teaching Method	Discussion, Seminar, Reading	Lecture, Case Study, Hands-on	Interactive, Video, Posters, Games
Test Measure	Essay	Problem Solving	T/F, Multiple Choice
Impact Timeframe	Long-term	Intermediate	Short-term

Influencing Behavior with Security Awareness

Awareness is defined in NIST Special Publication 800-16 as follows: "Awareness is not training. The purpose of awareness presentations is simply to focus attention on security. Awareness presentations are intended to allow individuals to recognize IT security concerns and respond accordingly."

Security awareness programs are designed to remind the user of appropriate behaviors. In our busy world, sometimes it is easy to forget why certain controls are in place. For example, an organization may have access control locks to secure areas. Access is granted by entering a PIN on the lock pad or perhaps using a swipe card. If the door doesn't click shut or someone enters at the same time, the control is effectively defeated. A poster reminding us to check and make sure the door is shut completely is an example of an awareness program.

Teaching a Skill with Security Training

Training is defined in NIST Special Publication 800-16 as follows: "training seeks to teach skills, which allow a person to perform a specific function." Examples of training include teaching a system administrator how to create user accounts, training a firewall administrator how to close ports, or training an auditor how to read logs. Training is generally attended by those tasked with implementing and monitoring security controls. You may recall from previous chapters that the person charged with implementing and maintaining security controls is referred to as the *information custodian*.

Security Education is Knowledge Driven

Education is defined in NIST Special Publication 800-16 as follows: "The 'Education' level integrates all of the security skills and competencies of the various functional specialties into a common body of knowledge, adds a multidisciplinary study of concepts, issues, and principles (technological and social), and strives to produce IT security specialists and professionals capable of vision and pro-active response." Education is management oriented. In the field of Information Security, education is generally targeted to those who are involved in the decision-making process: classifying information, choosing controls, evaluating and reevaluating security strategies. The person changed with these responsibilities is often the information owner.

Investing in Training

In times of corporate prosperity, SETA is often well funded. Unfortunately, the opposite is true as well. In times of economic downturn, these programs are scaled back or eliminated. That is a mistake. In hard times, there is even more temptation for industrial espionage, embezzlement, and thievery. This is the time information assets need the most protection. One way to ensure the continuation of SETA programs is to codify their importance in policy. The policy makers in Washington, DC, understood this reality and included training and security awareness requirements in both Gramm-Leach-Bliley and HIPAA.

IN PRACTICE Information Security Education, Training, and Awareness Policy

The goal of this policy is to focus on SETA and why it is important to the organization.

The *objectives* of this policy are to:

- Require general and departmental information security programs at orientation.
- Require annual mandatory security awareness programs.
- Support security training for technical personnel.
- Support security education for management personnel.

The *audience* is all users.

▸▸ CONTINUED ON NEXT PAGE

» CONTINUED

TABLE 6.6 Sample Information Security Education, Training, and Awareness Policy.

Section X:	[COMPANY] Information Security Policy	Effective Date:
Subsection	Personnel Security	Change Control #:
Policy	Information Security Education, Training, and Awareness	Approved By:
Objective	In support of information security, the [COMPANY] will regularly provide employees and appropriate third parties with information security education and training.	
Purpose	The purpose of this policy is to ensure that all employees are appropriately trained in regard to information security issues and policies appropriate to their position.	
Audience	All users are expected to understand and abide by established enterprise information technology security policies.	
Policy	All employees will be trained and educated on the [COMPANY] security policies and procedures prior to receiving access to information or services.	
	Under the direction of the Information Security Officer, the Human Resources Department is responsible for initial training and education on the organization's security policies.	
	The initial security training will include both the policies and responsibilities and uses of equipment, software, and facilities.	
	Subsequent training will be conducted at the departmental level. Users will be trained on the use of departmental systems appropriate to their specific duties to ensure the confidentiality, integrity, and availability of information is safeguarded.	
	Annual information security training will be conducted by the Office of the Information Security Officer. All staff is required to participate and attendance will be	

» CONTINUED ON NEXT PAGE

▸▸ CONTINUED

	documented. At a minimum, training will include the following: Security awareness of current threats and risks Updates to security policies and procedures Reporting of security incidents Technical staff entrusted to protect [COMPANY] information resources will be trained to a level of competence that matches their duties and responsibilities. The [COMPANY] will support the ongoing education of information security management by funding attendance at conferences, tuition at local colleges and universities, subscriptions to professional journals, and membership in professional organizations.
Exceptions	None
Disciplinary Actions	Violation of this policy may result in disciplinary action, which may include termination for employees and temporaries; a termination of employment relations in the case of contractors or consultants; or dismissal for interns and volunteers. Additionally, individuals are subject to civil and criminal prosecution.

6

Security Incident Reporting Is Everyone's Responsibility

A security incident can happen anywhere, anyplace, anytime. A *security incident* is defined as any adverse event whereby some aspect of an information system or information itself is threatened: loss of data confidentiality, disruption of data integrity, disruption or denial of service. Users need to be vigilant as it is most likely that those who are in the front line on a daily basis will be the ones to notice that something is amiss. Suspicious activity can take many forms. It may be an e-mail requesting the user link to a site and change his password. It may be a caller asking unusual questions. It may be a person posing as a contractor attempting to gain entry.

Security incident reporting is the foundation of a successful response and recovery process. The key is to create a culture of users who are sensitive to potential incidents and who are so invested in the security of the organization that they are willing to take time out of their busy day to report suspicious activities. Sadly, it seems that it is human nature not to want to get involved. Organizations need to overcome that inertia. A security incident reporting program has three components:

- Training users to recognize suspicious incidents.

- Implementing an easy and nonintimidating reporting system.

- Having staff follow through with investigations and report back their findings to the user.

Incident Reporting Training

What to watch for and how to report an incident should be integrated with the training and awareness programs presented at orientation and annually. One of the key elements is to stress to users how important they are in the process. Without them, the majority of incidents might go unnoticed and undiscovered. It is critical to deliver the message that all reports will be taken seriously; that employees will never be made to feel foolish and will never experience any repercussions. The organization has a responsibility to act accordingly.

Security Reporting Mechanisms

If we are to expect the general population to report suspicious activity, then we must make it easy for them to do so. This may be a designated person to contact, a number to call, or a form to complete. Posting a form on the organization's intranet and then creating a favorites link directly to it is an efficient way for users to report potential incidents.

Reporting with Ease It is not enough just to publish an easy-to-use form. We must get users to actually remember to use it. We suggest providing all users laminated instruction cards and requiring the cards to be posted in a visible location. The instructions should remind users what they are looking for and how and whom to report to.

Testing the Procedures

The best way to know if a process is working is to test it. This includes security incident procedures. While the testing should always be done with the consent of senior management, it should also be carried out in relative secrecy. To do otherwise would impact on the validity of the test. Tests should include a variety of breaches or suspicious activities. The tests should target a functional and geographical cross-section of the population. There are two outcomes that should be evaluated. First (and most important), how did the users react to the suspicious activity? Second, did they report the activity? The results should be documented and used to evaluate the effectiveness of the program. The goal of testing is continuous improvement. No one should ever lose her job based upon a test.

IN PRACTICE: Security Incident Awareness and Reporting Policy

The goal of this policy is to make sure that the first line of defense (users) know how to react to and report suspicious activities.
The *objectives* of this policy are to:

- Assign responsibility for developing and maintaining the security incident reporting process
- Require formal incident response procedures
- Require incident response training and testing
- Require a closeout and feedback process

The *audience* is all users.

TABLE 6.7 Sample Security Incident Awareness and Reporting Policy.

Section X:	[COMPANY] Information Security Policy	Effective Date:
Subsection	Personnel Security	Change Control #:
Policy	Information Security Education, Training, and Awareness	Approved By:
Objective	In support of information security, the [COMPANY] will regularly provide employees and appropriate third parties with information security education and training.	
Purpose	The purpose of this policy is to ensure that all employees are appropriately trained in regard to information security issues and policies appropriate to their position.	
Audience	All users are expected to understand and abide by established enterprise information technology security policies.	
Policy	All employees will be trained and educated on the [COMPANY] security policies and procedures prior to receiving access to information or services.	
	Under the direction of the Information Security Officer, the Human Resources Department is responsible for initial training and education on the organization's security policies.	

▶▶ CONTINUED ON NEXT PAGE

6

▶▶ CONTINUED

	The initial security training will include both the policies and responsibilities and uses of equipment, software, and facilities.
	Subsequent training will be conducted at the departmental level. Users will be trained on the use of departmental systems appropriate to their specific duties to ensure the confidentiality, integrity, and availability of information is safeguarded.
	Annual information security training will be conducted by the Office of the Information Security Officer. All staff is required to participate and attendance will be documented. At a minimum, training will include the following:
	Security awareness of current threats and risks
	Updates to security policies and procedures
	Reporting of security incidents
	Technical staff entrusted to protect [COMPANY] information resources will be trained to a level of competence that matches their duties and responsibilities.
	The [COMPANY] will support the ongoing education of information security management by funding attendance at conferences, tuition at local colleges and universities, subscriptions to professional journals, and membership in professional organizations.
Exceptions	None
Disciplinary Actions	Violation of this policy may result in disciplinary action, which may include termination for employees and temporaries; a termination of employment relations in the case of contractors or consultants; or dismissal for interns and volunteers. Additionally, individuals are subject to civil and criminal prosecution.

Summary

Employees can be an organization's strongest line of defense or its weakest link. It is the responsibility of the organization to deliver the message that security is a priority even before an employee joins the organization. Job postings, job descriptions, and even the interview process need to reflect an organizational culture committed to information security.

Confidentiality and information security affirmation agreements should be a condition of employment. Security awareness programs, security training, and education all serve to reinforce the message. Organizations will reap significant benefits from training users to be sensitive to and report suspicious actives and potential incidents.

Test Your Skills

MULTIPLE CHOICE QUESTIONS

1. At which phase of the hiring process should personnel security practices begin?
    A. interview
    B. offer
    C. recruitment
    D. orientation

2. An organization's commitment to security should be included in which of the following job descriptions?
    A. management
    B. all users
    C. developers
    D. systems administrators

3. A published job description for a Web designer should not include:
    A. job title
    B. compensation
    C. version of the Web development application the company is using
    D. company location

4. During the course of an interview, a job candidate should be given a tour of:
    A. the entire facility
    B. public areas only unless otherwise authorized
    C. the server room
    D. the wiring closet

5. Which of these facts is it permissible for an interviewer to reveal to a job candidate?

   A. detailed client list

   B. home phone numbers of senior management

   C. security weaknesses

   D. duties and responsibilities of the position

6. The reason for conducting background checks is to:

   A. verify the truthfulness, reliability, and trustworthiness of the applicant

   B. find out if the applicant ever got in trouble in high school

   C. find out if the applicant has a significant other

   D. verify the applicant's hobbies, number of children, and type of house she lives in

7. Under the Fair Credit Reporting Act (FCRA), which of these statements is true?

   A. Employers cannot request a copy of an employee's credit report under any circumstances.

   B. Employers must get the employee's consent to request a credit report.

   C. Employers cannot use credit information to deny a job.

   D. Employers are required to conduct credit checks on all applicants.

8. Which of these records is an employer allowed to request?

   A. private medical records

   B. sealed criminal records

   C. basic military service records

   D. confidential mental health records

9. Which of the following statements is NOT true about confidentiality agreements?

   A. Confidentiality agreements protect from unauthorized disclosure.

   B. Confidentiality agreements are generally considered a condition of work.

   C. Confidentiality agreements are considered to be contracts.

   D. Confidentiality agreements should only be required of top-level executives.

10. Which if the following would you NOT expect to find in an acceptable use agreement?

    A. password management

    B. lunch and break schedule

    C. Internet access use rules

    D. e-mail etiquette

11. NIST is a(n):

    A. United States government agency

    B. research university

    C. privately held organization

    D. book publisher

12. SETA is an acronym for:

    A. Security Education Teaches Awareness

    B. Security Education Training Awareness

    C. Security Education Tells All

    D. Security Education Training Acceptance

13. Posters are placed throughout the facility reminding users to log off when leaving their workstations unattended. This is an example of a:

    A. security education program

    B. security training program

    C. security awareness program

    D. none of the above

14. A network engineer attends a one-week hands-on course on firewall configuration and maintenance. This is an example of a:

    A. security education program

    B. security training program

    C. security awareness program

    D. none of the above

15. The Board of Directors has a presentation on the latest trends in security management. This is an example of a:

    A. security education program

    B. security training program

    C. security awareness program

    D. none of the above

6

16. Which one of these would NOT be considered a "security incident"?
    A. loss of confidentiality
    B. disruption of integrity
    C. denial of service
    D. user password expired

17. It is important that all users know how to:
    A. investigate security incidents
    B. recover from security incidents
    C. report security incidents
    D. all of the above

18. Incident response testing should:
    A. be done only with the consent of management
    B. evaluate both initial reaction and reporting process
    C. be used to improve the process
    D. all of the above

19. Social engineering techniques:
    A. never involve people
    B. always involve people
    C. focus on firewalls
    D. aren't very useful

20. Best practices dictate that incident reporting training be offered at least at:
    A. orientation and monthly
    B. orientation and every five years
    C. orientation and annually
    D. orientation only

EXERCISES

Exercise 6.1: Job Descriptions

1. Access an online job-posting service.

2. Find and print out two technology-related job postings.

3. Review the job descriptions. Are security responsibilities mentioned as a part of the jobs? If not, what do you think should be added?

Exercise 6.2: Footprinting

1. Access on online job-posting service.

2. Search for jobs related to "information security." Hint: Use *information security* as a key word in your search.

3. Print out two job postings.

4. Highlight any information that you think could be used for "footprinting." Explain your answer.

Exercise 6.3: Phishing

1. Access **www.antiphising.org**.

2. In your own words, explain the terms *phishing* and *pharming*.

3. On the site, locate the activity chart. What is the general trend?

Exercise 6.4: Background Checks

1. Go online and locate one company that provides credit checks.

2. Can you tell if the company you found sells to businesses or to consumers only? How much does the company charge? What is the promised delivery time?

3. Locate one company that will provide criminal background information.

4. How much does the company charge? What is the promised delivery time?

5. Summarize your findings. Include how trustworthy you believe the companies are.

Exercise 6.5: Acceptable Use Agreement

1. Ask the Information Technology department at your school for a copy of its acceptable use agreement.

2. Within the agreement, locate and highlight sections that pertain to the following:

   - Internet use
   - E-mail use

6

- Portable computer use
- Password management

3. Write a short critique of the agreement. Do you think that it includes enough detail? Does it explain why certain activities are prohibited or encouraged? Does it encourage users to be security conscious?

Exercise 6.6: Security Awareness Training

1. Either at your school or place of work, locate at least one instance of a security awareness campaign.

2. Note in writing its purpose and effectiveness.

3. If you can't locate an example of a security awareness campaign, compose a memo to senior management suggesting one.

PROJECTS

Project 6.1: The Hiring Process

1. Call a local business and ask to speak with the personnel manager. Explain you are a college student working on a project. Request a 15-minute meeting.

2. At the meeting, ask the personnel manager to explain the company's hiring process. Be sure to ask what (if any) background checks the company does and why. Also ask for a copy of a job application form. Be sure to thank the person for his time.

3. After the meeting, review the application form. Does it include a statement authorizing the company to conduct background checks?

4. Write a report that covers the following:

- Summary of meeting logistics (who you meet with, where, when)
- Summary of hiring practices
- Summary of any information shared with you that you would classify as sensitive or confidential

Project 6.2: Employee Agreements

1. As Information Security Officer, you have been tasked with reviewing employee agreements. You have recently been reading about the new trend in affirmation agreements. Write a memo to senior management proposing that the organization discontinue use of the traditional agreement and instead develop an affirmation agreement.

2. Senior management has agreed to your proposal. Write the opening paragraph of the new agreement. Focus on why information security is important.

3. Since this is a new agreement, all users should be expected to review and sign it. In your opinion, what is the best way to distribute the new agreement? Who should be responsible for distribution? Who should be responsible for tracking the return of the signed agreements? Where should the agreements be stored?

Project 6.3: E-mail Is Just a Postcard

E-mail is transmitted across the Internet in clear text. The most powerful analogy is to think of an e-mail as a postcard available to be read by anyone who has access to it. The message is that users should never write anything in an external e-mail that they wouldn't write on a postcard.

1. Create a security awareness campaign focused on this topic. Include in this plan specifics on how you intend to deliver the message.

2. Create at least one piece of supporting collateral.

3. Design a way to test the effectiveness of your message.

Project 6.4: Incident Reporting

1. The Chief Security Officer has classified the following incidents as high priority, requiring immediate reporting and response. You have been tasked with training all users to recognize these types of incidents. Your first step is to write a one- to two-sentence explanation of each incident plus one example per incident.

2. Your second task is to create a PowerPoint presentation that will be used to train all users to recognize these incidents and how to report them.

High Priority Incidents:

- Confidential data at risk
- Business continuity at risk
- Unauthorized use of a system for any purpose
- Changes to system hardware, firmware, or software without the system owner's authorization
- Denial of service attack
- Property destruction related to a computer incident greater than $10,000

- Download of P2P files or programs
- Download of unauthorized software
- Downloading or accessing pornography
- Computer virus/worm (server-based or multiple systems)
- Suspicious person in secure areas
- Unfriendly employee termination

▶▶ Case Study

AutoAll is a Fortune 1000 company that writes consumer auto loans. AutoAll's systems process, store, and transmit confidential data on hundreds of thousands of consumers and small businesses. The company is acutely aware of its responsibility to ensure the confidentiality and integrity of the information. AutoAll recently developed a full security incident program including reporting, response, recovery, and investigative policies and processes. Earlier this year, the company conducted mandatory training sessions for all users on how to spot suspicious activity and how to report the activity. To make it easy, a link to an online reporting form was created on the company intranet. To remind employees to use the form, a laminated instruction card was posted at every cubicle and private office. The company hired an outside organization to test the effectiveness of the program. What follows is a report on the testing. After reading the report, you need to compose a report to AutoAll's Board of Directors. Your report needs to address the following:

- Would you characterize the incident reporting program as successful? Why or why not?

- Why do you think the reporting form was not used?

- What modifications would you suggest to the program?

Incident Reporting Test Results

PHASE I: Phone-based Social Engineering

The premise: The ISO provided the social engineer with various locations and their corresponding phone numbers. The aim was to call and pretend that that the social engineer was a member of a "mainframe support team" calling to try and isolate an

▶▶ CONTINUED ON NEXT PAGE

▸▸ CONTINUED

issue between one machine and the mainframe to at least the location in which that machine was located. To do so, he would ask the end user to run various commands and to provide the information returned on their screen.

There were two goals to this exercise:

1. To ensure that no employee would actually agree to "blindly" run commands and divulge the results of those commands to a complete stranger over the phone.

2. To see if the phone call would prompt the users to fill out the incident response form.

Results as provided by the Social Engineer "Bob":

1st call: Branch Office 1:

Called the branch office and talked to Customer Service Rep Sue. Told her that I was Bob, a member of the mainframe support team, and that we had an issue that we were trying to identify. I did not give her a last name, nor did I mention the actual name of the company. I told her that we were looking at all locations to try and isolate the location of the faulty machine. I asked her if she could help me with this issue.

I did not have the time to finish my little intro speech. Sue cut me off and said that she "would love to help me out." I asked her to run a command for me, but she informed me that she was not in front of a computer. She put me on hold and by the time she was indeed in front of a computer, she had become suspicious. Whether she spoke to someone in the meantime, or whether her training kicked in, I do not know. She asked me who I was again, and who I worked for. I repeated the info I had already given her—Bob, working for the mainframe support team. She said that she needed to clear the call with John Boyd, that she was not authorized to answer my questions. Gave me Mr. Boyd's name and phone number, and asked me to clear it with him.

I asked her if, in the event that I would not be able to reach Mr. Boyd, I could call her back and if she would help me with the issue at hand. She answered that she would help me reach Mr. Boyd. I ended the call by thanking her for her time, and told her that I would be contacting Mr. Boyd.

Note: No Incident Report Filed.

▸▸ CONTINUED ON NEXT PAGE

▶▶ CONTINUED

2nd call: Branch Office 2:

Called branch office 2 and spoke with Hilda, who transferred me to a Customer Service Representative. Liz picked up my call next. Told her that I was Bob, a member of the mainframe support team, and that we had an issue that we were trying to identify. I did not give her a last name, nor did I mention the actual name of the company. I told her that we were looking at all branches to try and isolate the location of the faulty machine. I asked her if she could help me with this issue.

Liz asked me if it was related to the issue that they had been having that day. This was a great opening for me. This was volunteered information that I could build on. I told her that my feeling was that her issues—"inability to export" is what she described it as—was probably a by-product of the original reason for my call. I told her that if she could help me fix my issue, then hers would resolve itself as well.

Liz finally asked me what company I worked for. I volunteered the same information: the mainframe support team. She then asked me who referred me to call. I told her that I did not know, that my boss had taken the original call from AutoAll, and that I was just calling back to try and solve the issue that I had been assigned. I told her that we were a third-party company. She put me on hold. When she came back, I asked her how long the issue with exporting had been happening to try and divert her attention back to her problem and away from the legitimacy of the call. She answered—since that morning—but promptly offered to take my phone number so that she could call me back.

Since my previous call had produced Mr. Boyd's name as a person in charge, I used his name and said that I had a call in for him, had left a voicemail, and was waiting for a call back. I also stressed the fact that it was already mid-afternoon on Friday, that I wanted to have this fixed before the weekend if possible, and that it was difficult for me to wait for Mr. Boyd to get the message and call back.

Liz said she was sorry, but that without a call from Mr. Boyd, there was nothing she could do. I thanked her and hung up the phone.

Note: No Incident Report Filed, Supervisor was alerted.

▶▶ CONTINUED ON NEXT PAGE

▶▶ CONTINUED

3rd Call: Main Office:

Called and asked for Tim Libby, Asst. VP of Operations. Tim answered and then quickly excused himself, saying he had to go. I inquired about his reasons, and he let me know that he was late for his child's baseball game. I asked about the gender of the child, and was told, as a complete stranger, that it was a daughter. I decided against pressing for more personal details at that stage, having formed a sort of a "bond" with this person upon sharing that I had kids as well, and talking quickly and generically about the fun of having children. Kept all banter very positive and upbeat, then urged him to put me on hold for someone else so that he could get to the game.

His assistant, Camille, got back on the phone. Camille flatly declined to help until Mr. Boyd authorized her to do so. Cited policy and training, saying that for her to do so would be against the policies of the company. I congratulated her on that strong stance, and told her that I wished more companies would enforce such efficient policies. I then mentioned that I had already attempted to contact Mr. Boyd and that I so far had had no luck other than leaving an as-of-yet unanswered voicemail. I explained that the issue was time sensitive, and that her immediate help would be really appreciated. Still refused to do anything until prior authorization from Mr. Boyd.

I went on to explain that the commands I wanted her to run were actually extremely nonintrusive, and that during the whole process she would retain complete control of the session: she would be the one deciding to run the commands or not, the one to decide whether to tell me the results or not. That way, I would be able to rule out her network segment as being where the problem was, and would be out of her hair. She still refused, quoting one more time that the policy precluded her from agreeing to this.

Note: No Incident Report Filed, Security Officer contacted directly.

Chapter 7

Physical and Environmental Security Policies and Procedures

Chapter Objectives

After reading this chapter and completing the exercises, you will be able to do the following:

- Define the concept of physical security and how it relates to information security.

- Evaluate the security requirements of facilities, offices, and equipment.

- Understand why it is critical to identify, authenticate, and authorize access to secure areas.

- Understand the environmental risks posed to physical structures, areas within those structures, and equipment.

- Enumerate the vulnerabilities related to reusing and disposing of equipment.

- Develop policies designed to ensure the physical security of information, information systems, and information processing and storage facilities.

Introduction

As illustrated by the Chapter 4 anecdote about the infamous "server not found" error message, which turned out to be a physical reality, information security must include physical security. Section 7 of the ISO 17799 is dedicated to physical and environmental security. Of course, when we speak about *environmental security,* we do not mean keeping the habitat of the spotted owl safe. Instead, we are referring to the workplace environment, which includes the design and construction of the facilities, how and where people move, where equipment is stored, how the equipment is secured, and so forth.

Section 7 of the ISO 17799 has three main sections, including secure areas, equipment security, and general controls. In this chapter we will discuss the importance of physical and environmental security and related policies and procedures.

Designing Secure Areas

In previous chapters we have discussed risk analysis and risk management. We have introduced the idea that to properly protect organizational information we must first know where it is, and how critical it is to the life of the organization. Just as we shouldn't spend as much money or resources to protect noncritical information as we would to protect critical information, so it goes that we shouldn't spend the same amount to protect a broom closet as we should to protect information processing facilities such as data centers or server rooms, or even offices containing client computers.

All of the controls we can implement to physically protect our information are dictated first by a thorough analysis of our risks or vulnerabilities, the likelihood of a threat exploiting those vulnerabilities, and the value of the information we are trying to protect. Though many may think physical security is not related to information security, in fact it is one of the most important domains of a comprehensive information security program.

A cursory examination of our physical security needs will not reveal the many things we need to think about to best address this domain. For example, suppose I want to place all of my domain servers in one room where I can protect them all at once. I have a room large enough, currently being used as a simple storeroom. I invest in a double-steel door, card-reading locks, and a camera outside the door. Sounds pretty thorough, doesn't it? Let's take another look. What are the walls made of? Are there any windows? Is this room in the normal walking path of the public or even of employees who have no reason to be near our server room? What is the environment like as it pertains to fire suppression, air conditioning, and power availability? Is there a raised floor to protect cabling? All of these questions need to be considered in designing a secure area. A *secure area* is one where the assets are protected from man-made and natural harm.

Why would I care what the walls are made of? Well, spending $1,000 on a door, and twice that much on the lock and camera, will count for little if I have a room constructed of Sheetrock and wood framing. Why be concerned about walking traffic? Because we don't want anyone to un-knowingly stumble upon our most protected system resources in case they may wish to knowingly do so in the future.

By the same logic, we want our most critical information processing facilities to be inconspicuous. They should not have signage relating to their purpose, nor should their outward appearance hint at what may be inside. We should also be careful that any processing facilities managed by third parties are separated from those managed by staff in-house.

There's still more to consider in the secure areas section of this do-main. The human element must be considered, so we will need a policy defining the work environment in secure areas. How will people be allowed access, how will they be supervised and monitored, and what will be done to secure these areas when there are no personnel present?

This brings us to the first section in the physical and environmental security domain, secure areas: the physical security perimeter.

Securing the Perimeter

Depending on the size of the organization, information processing facilities can range from a closet with one server to an entire complex of buildings with several hundred or more server computers. No matter the organiza-tion's size, however, these systems are always highly critical. In addressing physical security, we need to think of the most obvious risks such as theft and other malicious activity, but we also must think of accidental damage and damage from natural disasters.

We can think of the security perimeter as a barrier of protection. To protect against unauthorized access, we can create a manned reception desk, man traps, card-reading locks, heavy doors, and exterior walls that are made of heavy solid materials and provide fire resistance.

FYI: What's a Man Trap??

A man trap is a series of two or more sets of doors designed so that one set of doors cannot be opened until the other is closed, and both can be locked to trap an intruder.

To protect against environmental damage, we make sure all barriers extend from real-floor to real-ceiling, as opposed to those extending only to drop ceilings. These barriers will aid in case of flood or fire, whereas barri-ers extending only as far as the bottom of a drop ceiling leave a significant avenue for damage.

IN PRACTICE: Physical Security Perimeter Policy

Securing the exterior is the first line of defense against external physical attacks. The goal of this policy is to require perimeter controls as appropriate.

The *objectives* of this policy are to:

■ Prevent unauthorized access and/or damage to business facilities.

■ Assign responsibility for perimeter security risks.

The *audience* is the entire organization.

TABLE 7.1 Sample Physical Security Perimeter Policy.

Section X:	[COMPANY] Information Security Policy	Effective Date:
Subsection	Physical & Environmental Security	Change Control #:
Policy	Physical Security Perimeter	Approved By:
Objective	In support of information security, [Company] will establish physical security perimeters around business premises.	
Purpose	The purpose of this policy is to build a barrier to prevent unauthorized access, damage, or interference to the business facilities.	
Audience	This policy applies to all facilities.	
Policy	• A risk assessment of all business premises and information processing facilities will be performed to determine the type and strength of the security perimeter that is appropriate and prudent. The facility manager in conjunction with the Office of Information Security will conduct the risk assessment. • The facilities manager will be responsible for the implementation and maintenance of all physical security perimeter controls.	
Exceptions	None	

▶▶ CONTINUED ON NEXT PAGE

» CONTINUED

Disciplinary Actions	Violation of this policy may result in disciplinary action, which may include termination for employees and temporaries; a termination of employment relations in the case of contractors or consultants; or dismissal for interns and volunteers. Additionally, individuals are subject to civil and criminal prosecution.

Implementing Physical Entry Controls

Our next area to consider is physical entry controls. What does it take to get in, and how will we know who did? These are the big questions to be answered. This policy should include rules for employees, visitors, and vendors. It should also call for the regular review of access rights to secure areas.

Visitors should be required to wear some kind of identification that can be evaluated from a distance. For instance, we might choose to have three different colored badges for visitors, which tell our employees what level of supervision should be expected even if they view the person from across a one-hundred foot room. If a blue badge denotes close supervision, and I see someone wearing a blue badge without any supervision, I know immediately to be suspicious without having to confront or even come within close proximity to the individual.

7

IN PRACTICE: Physical Entry Controls Policy

The process of identification should begin as soon as a person attempts to gain entry. The goal of this policy is to require authorized users to be authenticated and visitors to be identified, labeled, and authorized.

The *objectives* of this policy are to:

- Prevent unauthorized access to nonpublic areas.
- Require all authorized users to be properly identified.
- Ensure that audit trails are created either manually or automatically to track access to critical facilities.

The *audience* is the entire organization.

» CONTINUED ON NEXT PAGE

>> CONTINUED

TABLE 7.2 Sample Physical Entry Controls Policy.

Section X:	[COMPANY] Information Security Policy	Effective Date:
Subsection	Physical & Environmental Security	Change Control #:
Policy	Physical Entry Controls	Approved By:
Objective	In support of information security, [Company] will institute physical entry controls to protect all secure areas.	
Purpose	The purpose of this policy is to prevent unauthorized access and to secure facilities.	
Audience	This policy applies to all facilities.	
Policy	• Access to sensitive information and information processing facilities will be restricted to authorized persons only. • Authentication controls will be used to authorize and validate entry. • All visitors to secured areas will be supervised and only allowed in for authorized purposes. • A visitors' log will be in place at all secure areas to record date and time of entry and exit. • All persons will wear identification that is visible when in secure areas or facilities. • Access rights to secure areas will be reviewed periodically and updated as necessary.	
Exceptions	None	
Disciplinary Actions	Violation of this policy may result in disciplinary action, which may include termination for employees and temporaries; a termination of employment relations in the case of contractors or consultants; or dismissal for interns and volunteers. Additionally, individuals are subject to civil and criminal prosecution.	

Securing Offices, Rooms, and Facilities

In addition to securing the building in general, the organization needs to secure the workspaces within the facilities. The policy must address not only intentional crime, but also environmental hazards posed by natural disasters and any proximal neighbors who might pose a threat.

Here is where we address the way buildings are marked, ingress and egress for vehicular traffic, what kind of alarm systems will be required, and even the rules for locking doors, cabinets, and other storage areas within the secure areas.

IN PRACTICE: Securing Offices, Rooms, and Facilities Policy

It is not unusual to have offices and facilities that require an additional level of security. This policy recognizes that there may be offices, areas, or equipment that need a higher degree of protection.

The *objectives* of this policy are to:

■ Protect all secure areas from unauthorized access.

■ Protect organizational information assets.

■ Prevent damage to, and interference with, business information and information processing through malicious acts or natural disasters.

■ To ensure that support equipment such as copiers and fax machines are sited to avoid demands for access that could compromise information assets.

The *audience* is the entire organization.

TABLE 7.3 Sample Securing Offices, Rooms, and Facilities Policy.

Section X:	[COMPANY] Information Security Policy	Effective Date:
Subsection	Physical & Environmental Security	Change Control #:
Policy	Securing Offices, Rooms, and Facilities	Approved By:
Objective	In support of information security, [Company] will secure offices, rooms, and facilities to protect all secure areas and organization's information assets.	
Purpose	The purpose of this policy is to protect information assets to prevent unauthorized access or damage to secure offices, rooms, and facilities.	

▸▸ CONTINUED ON NEXT PAGE

» **CONTINUED**

Audience	This policy applies to all facilities.
Policy	• A risk assessment will be made of secure areas to determine the type of control that is appropriate and prudent. • Rooms in facilities containing sensitive assets will be locked when not in use. • Windows and doors will be kept locked and have protection from intrusion or environmental factors. • Intrusion alarms will be in place and maintained to the vendors' standards. • Sensitive documents will be locked in file cabinets or other protective furniture that takes into account the results of the risk analysis. • Support functions and equipment will be situated away from the public and unauthorized personnel.
Exceptions	None
Disciplinary Actions	Violation of this policy may result in disciplinary action, which may include termination for employees and temporaries; a termination of employment relations in the case of contractors or consultants; or dismissal for interns and volunteers. Additionally, individuals are subject to civil and criminal prosecution.

Working in Secure Areas

What special rules should apply to work performed in secure areas? The goal is to define behavioral and physical controls for the most sensitive workspaces within information processing facilities. We will need to address the levels of supervision necessary for internal personnel as well as visitors and vendors. The controls called for by this policy are considered additional to any other physical controls—not in place of them—unless the use of a more restrictive control happens to supersede a similar control used in areas not considered secure areas.

The organization may also wish to include language restricting the materials or equipment that can be brought in to the facility, such as cameras or recording devices.

IN PRACTICE: Working in Secure Areas Policy

It is not enough to just physically secure an area. Close attention must be paid to who is allowed to access the area and what they are allowed to do. This goal of this policy is to restrict the knowledge of, the access to, and actions within secure areas.

The *objectives* of this policy are to:

- Dictate the level of supervision for secure areas.
- Restrict third-party and vendor access to critical areas within processing facilities.
- Ensure the protection of information from unauthorized duplication through photographic or other recording methods.

The *audience* is the entire organization.

TABLE 7.4 Sample Working in Secure Areas Policy.

Section X:	[COMPANY] Information Security Policy	Effective Date:
Subsection	Physical & Environmental Security	Change Control #:
Policy	Working in Secure Areas	Approved By:
Objective	In support of information security, [Company] will monitor and control the work of personnel and third parties that are working in secure areas.	
Purpose	The purpose of this policy is to protect information assets to prevent unauthorized access or damage to secure areas.	
Audience	This policy applies to all facilities.	
Policy	• All work in secured areas will be supervised. • Third parties will not be given access to secured areas or information processing facilities unless specifically authorized by the system owner or Information Security Officer. • Third-party access to secured areas will be monitored.	

▶▶ CONTINUED ON NEXT PAGE

▶▶ **CONTINUED**	
	• Mobile data storage devices or recording equipment of any kind are prohibited and may not be allowed in secure areas without the authorization of the system owner or Information Security Officer.
Exceptions	None
Disciplinary Actions	Violation of this policy may result in disciplinary action, which may include termination for employees and temporaries; a termination of employment relations in the case of contractors or consultants; or dismissal for interns and volunteers. Additionally, individuals are subject to civil and criminal prosecution.

Securing Equipment

Now that we have defined how facilities and work areas will be secured, we must address the security of the equipment within these facilities. This means defining the protection of company-owned equipment by dictating how equipment should be used, sited, maintained, and even disposed of.

In this area we need to consider how the organization will avoid problems related to power outages and power spikes. We will require any number of controls such as uninterruptible power supplies, redundant power feeds, and fail-over generators, which provide instant automatic power in case of power failure, to ensure we do not lose processing abilities in case of natural disaster or accidental damage to power lines.

This policy will also be the best place to define how the organization will protect cabling. Cabling is subject to many risks, from "tapping" by malicious persons seeking to listen to activities right down to squirrels chewing through data cables. We may choose to run data cable through a steel conduit, or at least use shielded cabling. We must also protect our data cables from the interference common to proximal location to power cables. We will also have to adhere to any state and federal codes relating to cabling, such as the requirement of Plenum cabling in ceilings to retard fire hazards.

Like other mechanical devices, all the equipment related to information processing requires regular maintenance. If you own a computer that has never been cleaned of dust, there is a significant risk of damage from static electricity. Optical media devices such as CD-ROM drives also require regular maintenance. Proper maintenance for information processing equipment will ensure the longest possible life and greatly reduce the risk of downtime due to equipment failure. All maintenance should be according to manufacturer recommendations and should be completely documented.

An organization that frequently has equipment removed from its premises would address the use and care of such equipment in this section. For example, an insurance company that sends adjusters out in the field with laptop computers would create a policy to control how those computers are allocated, stored, and returned.

Equipment Siting and Protection

Where am I going to put it, and how will I protect it in its place? Perhaps you have many people in the organization who are fond of drinking soft drinks around the mainframe? This is a bad idea. Smoking? Another bad idea. Did you know that one particle of smoke can destroy a hard drive? This is not to say that your hard drive is in imminent danger from your cigarette smoking, as all drives are sealed to prevent exposure. We only include this bit of trivia to exemplify the very sensitive nature of computer equipment.

Organizations that use computers in areas that are inherently hazardous to electronic equipment may wish to include language related to special shielding, such as keyboard membranes or protection for CRT monitors, especially if the equipment is being used in an industrial environment.

In some cases, it is less costly to isolate critical equipment to reduce the cost of additional protection measures required for systems exposed to greater hazards or risks from unauthorized access.

7

IN PRACTICE: Equipment Siting and Protection Policy

Equipment is vulnerable to environmental damage. The goal of this policy is to make sure the organization pays attention to potential environmental hazards and threats.

The *objectives* of this policy are to:

- Protect sensitive equipment from environmental risks.
- Prevent damage to sensitive equipment from careless behavior.
- Require that equipment be sited to shield it from unauthorized access and from conditions that may adversely affect electronic equipment.
- To ensure that extra measures are taken as needed to protect equipment from inherently dangerous conditions that exist by the nature of the organization's normal activities.

The *audience* is the entire organization.

▸▸ CONTINUED ON NEXT PAGE

▶▶ **CONTINUED**

TABLE 7.5 Sample Equipment Siting and Protection Policy.

Section X:	[COMPANY] Information Security Policy	Effective Date:
Subsection	Physical & Environmental Security	Change Control #:
Policy	Equipment Siting and Protection	Approved By:
Objective	In support of information security, [Company] will site and protect equipment from environmental threats and hazards.	
Purpose	The purpose of this policy is to protect the organization's assets from harm or unauthorized access by placing controls on the environment where the equipment is situated.	
Audience	This policy applies to all facilities.	
Policy	• Environmental conditions will be monitored for changes that can adversely affect equipment or premises. • Equipment will be placed in areas that minimize unnecessary traffic or access. • Smoking, eating, and drinking will not be permitted in areas where equipment is situated. • Protective controls will be used in areas where there is risk to equipment.	
Exceptions	None	
Disciplinary Actions	Violation of this policy may result in disciplinary action, which may include termination for employees and temporaries; a termination of employment relations in the case of contractors or consultants; or dismissal for interns and volunteers. Additionally, individuals are subject to civil and criminal prosecution.	

No Power, No Processing

No power, no processing—it's that simple. Long before computers took over the business world, organizations have been taking steps to ensure that power is available. Of course, it is now more important than ever. We all absolutely rely on clean, consistent, and abundant supplies of electrical power.

Potential Power Problems To function properly, our systems need consistent power delivered at the correct voltage level. Unfortunately, power problems such as surges, brownouts, and blackouts are a fact of life. ***Power surges*** are an increase in the voltage. ***Brownouts*** are periods of low voltage. ***Blackouts*** are interruptions or failure of power.

We use power protection devices for several good reasons, including:

- To "condition" power feeds for consistency.
- To allow a properly controlled shut-down of computer systems in the event of power failure.
- To provide power for critical systems in times of failure.

There are four basic types of power protection devices: surge suppressors, line conditioners, uninterruptible power supplies (UPS—also known as battery backups), and generators.

IN PRACTICE: Power Supply Policy

Without power, information systems come to a halt. The goal of this policy is to ensure that organizations recognize the importance of as well as the inherent danger from electrical power. The *objectives* of this policy are to:

- Protect equipment from damage caused by power fluctuations or interruptions.
- Ensure that equipment controlling the power supply is regularly tested for effectiveness.

The *audience* is the entire organization.

TABLE 7.6 Sample Power Supply Policy.

Section X:	[COMPANY] Information Security Policy	Effective Date:
Subsection	Physical & Environmental Security	Change Control #:
Policy	Power Supply	Approved By:
Objective	In support of information security, [Company] will protect information systems equipment from damage caused by electrical problems.	

▸▸ CONTINUED ON NEXT PAGE

7

▶ CONTINUED	
Purpose	The purpose of this policy is to prevent loss, damage, or interruption to information processing assets.
Audience	This policy applies to all facilities.
Policy	• A risk assessment should be done to determine the best method(s) to provide clean, reliable power to information systems. • UPS systems will be tested regularly for functionality and capacity. • Back-up generators will be tested regularly according to manufacturer's instructions. • All equipment will be serviced according to manufacturer's instructions. Logs will be kept of all service and routine maintenance.
Exceptions	None
Disciplinary Actions	Violation of this policy may result in disciplinary action, which may include termination for employees and temporaries; a termination of employment relations in the case of contractors or consultants; or dismissal for interns and volunteers. Additionally, individuals are subject to civil and criminal prosecution.

Secure Disposal and Reuse of Equipment

So we come to one of the most overlooked and underserved areas of information security. Not only do many people labor under the misapprehension that formatting a hard drive actually renders all data unrecoverable, but many people don't stop to think about what might become of that old computer they throw in the dumpster, or gave to their cousin's best friend. In fact, many organizations have taken the time and care to create donation policies for decommissioned computers, which do nothing to address how the information resident on those machines will be destroyed.

To give you an idea of how easy it is to recover information from a formatted hard drive, simply "Google" on the phrase *data recovery* and see what comes back to you. Utilities are available for less than $50 that are quite capable of recovering data from formatted drives. If the drive has been formatted twice, it is still relatively easy to get the data back. Even if a drive has been formatted and a new operating system installed, the data is recoverable.

FYI: *Private Data on Discarded Hard Drives*

Two MIT graduate student researchers, Simson Garfinkel and Abhi Shelat, purchased 158 disk drives from a variety of sources: on-line auction services, swap meets, and stores selling used computer equipment. A review of the drives revealed over 5,000 credit card numbers, medical records, financial records, detailed personal and corporate information, and a massive amount of e-mail. The results of the study have been published by the IEEE Computer Society in the January/February 2003 issue of IEEE Security and Privacy, titled "Remembrance of Data Passed: A Study of Disk Sanitation."

Key findings of the report include:

■ 17% of the drives showed no evidence of attempts to delete data.

■ 92% of the drives were not properly sanitized.

■ There is a general lack of awareness and understanding regarding effective techniques to permanently delete data.

7

IN PRACTICE: Secure Disposal and Reuse of Equipment Policy

All too frequently organizations dispose of information without considering the consequences. The goal of this policy is to require that all information and information systems be disposed or recycled in a secure manner.

The *objective* of this policy is to:

■ Prevent unauthorized access to information through improper disposal or re-use of equipment.

The *audience* is the entire organization.

▸▸ CONTINUED ON NEXT PAGE

▶▶ CONTINUED

TABLE 7.7 Sample Secure Disposal and Reuse of Equipment Policy.

Section X:	[COMPANY] Information Security Policy	Effective Date:
Subsection	Physical & Environmental Security	Change Control #:
Policy	Secure Disposal and Reuse of Equipment	Approved By:
Objective	In support of information security, [Company] will securely dispose of or reuse equipment.	
Purpose	The purpose of this policy is to prevent loss, damage, or compromise of data or equipment when the equipment is no longer needed, being recycled or redeployed.	
Audience	This policy applies to all equipment.	
Policy	• Disposal of equipment shall be done in accordance with all applicable state and federal surplus property and environmental disposal laws, regulations, or policies to prevent unauthorized exposure of data. • Storage devices shall be securely overwritten so the information is unrecoverable (not simply deleted) or physically destroyed. • All devices containing storage media shall be overwritten, and/or data or software removed prior to disposal or redeployment. • A risk assessment of all damaged storage devices that contain sensitive material should be performed to determine whether items should be repaired, destroyed, or discarded.	
Exceptions	None	
Disciplinary Actions	Violation of this policy may result in disciplinary action, which may include termination for employees and temporaries; a termination of employment relations in the case of contractors or consultants; or dismissal for interns and volunteers. Additionally, individuals are subject to civil and criminal prosecution.	

General Controls

The broad objective of general controls is to prevent theft of information. The conditions that lead to information theft arise from unattended equipment and paper records, and even the position of computer monitors.

To those of us who don't spend our time trying to steal other people's information, it may seem absurd that there are individuals whose entire reason for being is to look for opportunities to do just that. We seem ready to accept that there are those who steal property, yet we resist the idea that these same people steal information. During any security awareness training, the instructor will invariably be met with disbelief when this topic is covered. Yes, there are people walking around airports watching you at ATM machines and telephones, hoping to look over your shoulder on the chance that you will be typing something they can use for self-gain. Not only in airports do these shadowy types seek to commit their crimes, but in every organization of every size at one time or another, they are there to see how careless we will be.

Clear Desk and Clear Screen

What happens to all those papers, CD-ROMs, floppy disks, and all the other hard copy information at the end of the working day? What happens to this material when workers go to lunch, take breaks, or go to meetings? This depends on whether or not the organization has adopted the Clear Desk and Clear Screen policy.

If not, anything can happen. Anyone who has seen the movie *Wall Street* remembers Charlie Sheen's character buying into a partnership in an office-cleaning company with the specific purpose of getting a look at a law firm's files. Though the example may be somewhat extreme, the lesson is right on the mark.

Shoulder surfing, the act of looking over someone's shoulder to see what is displayed on her computer monitor, is a physical attack. Other physical attacks include looking at papers on desks, taking the last document out of a copy machine, reprinting the last document from the fax machine, stealing digital media such as CD-ROMs, and other such avoidable acts.

The way to avoid these kinds of attacks is to have and enforce a policy that requires certain behavior. When leaving a desk for any length of time, papers should be locked in file cabinets or in desk drawers. Password-protected screen savers should be automated to engage automatically, or users should be required to log off completely from the network. Copy and fax machines should be locked out and new habits need to be formed to always make sure the last copied and last faxed documents are removed from the machines. If network printers are centrally located, all users should be required to clear their documents immediately after printing.

7

IN PRACTICE: Clear Desk and Clear Screen Policy

All too often, organizations make it "easy" for unauthorized users to view information. The goal of this policy is to remove information from plain sight.

The *objectives* of this policy are to:

■ Prevent theft of information from documents and media in plain view.

■ Prevent common physical attacks perpetrated on unattended equipment, hard copy documents, and digital media.

■ Instill protective habits in workers that protect organizational information.

The *audience* is the entire organization.

TABLE 7.8 Sample Clear Desk and Clear Screen Policy.

Section X:	[COMPANY] Information Security Policy	Effective Date:
Subsection	Physical & Environmental Security	Change Control #:
Policy	Clear Desk and Clear Screen	Approved By:
Objective	In support of information security, [Company] will instill behavior and procedures to protect information from undue exposure and theft.	
Purpose	The purpose of this policy is to minimize the exposure of the organization's information resources to unauthorized access as well as protect them from damage or destruction.	
Audience	This policy applies to all facilities and uses.	
Policy	• When left unattended or particularly during nonworking hours, desks shall be clear of all critical business information. • Sensitive or critical business information (media, documents, etc.) shall be locked away in secure and appropriately protective office furniture. • When left unattended, workstations shall be logged off and protected by access controls.	

▶▶ CONTINUED ON NEXT PAGE

▶▶ CONTINUED

	• Incoming mail and outgoing drops shall be in protected areas. • Photocopies of sensitive materials shall be removed immediately. • Sensitive print jobs shall be retrieved immediately.
Exceptions	None
Disciplinary Actions	Violation of this policy may result in disciplinary action, which may include termination for employees and temporaries; a termination of employment relations in the case of contractors or consultants; or dismissal for interns and volunteers. Additionally, individuals are subject to civil and criminal prosecution.

Removing Company Property

Even in smaller organizations, it is difficult to keep track of equipment and other property. This section is very simple and brief. If workers need to remove any company property from the premises, it must be signed out and logged. The logs should be maintained so that at any time an audit will account for the location and possession of every piece of equipment or information.

7

IN PRACTICE: Removal of Property Policy

Company assets should be accounted for at all times. The goal of this policy is to maintain an up-to-date record of the whereabouts of all information assets.

The *objectives* of this policy are to:

■ Prevent unauthorized removal of company property.

■ Provide for the accounting of all equipment and information taken off of company premises for any reason.

The *audience* is the entire organization.

▶▶ CONTINUED ON NEXT PAGE

▶▶ **CONTINUED**

TABLE 7.9 Sample Removal of Property Policy.

Section X:	[COMPANY] Information Security Policy	Effective Date:
Subsection	Physical & Environmental Security	Change Control #:
Policy	Removal of Property	Approved By:
Objective	In support of information security, [Company] shall control the removal of equipment and information assets.	
Purpose	To ensure that the location of equipment, information, and/or software can be immediately determined and protected from unauthorized removal.	
Audience	This policy applies to all facilities.	
Policy	• Removal of equipment, information, and/or software from [Company] must be authorized by appropriate management. • Authorized removal of items shall be logged out and logged back in when returned. • Management will carry out periodic random spot checks to detect unauthorized removal of property.	
Exceptions	None	
Disciplinary Actions	Violation of this policy may result in disciplinary action, which may include termination for employees and temporaries; a termination of employment relations in the case of contractors or consultants; or dismissal for interns and volunteers. Additionally, individuals are subject to civil and criminal prosecution.	

Summary

In this chapter we discussed the many aspects of physical and environmental security. We began at the security perimeter and worked our way gradually inward to discuss the threats posed by simply leaving private documents in plain view at the end of the work day. The subject of physical security at first seems a one-dimensional topic, yet upon some reflection we see all the less obvious aspects of making sure we are securing our information from myriad physical and environmental risks. From power problems; to flood, fire, and other threats to our sensitive computing environment; to the materials used to construct information processing facilities; the protections we must consider are many and varied.

We discussed the importance of logging access to these facilities, and logging the use of equipment that in many cases must be removed from the protections afforded on premises to satisfy the normal demands of businesses activities. We also learned that there are those whose purpose in life is to sneak glances at computer screens or papers left on desks to promote their own gain.

Test Your Skills

MULTIPLE CHOICE QUESTIONS

1. A security perimeter is:
    A. the widest imaginary circle around a facility
    B. a barrier of protection
    C. the field around which security alarms can monitor activity
    D. none of the above

2. Physical security controls should be driven by:
    A. educated guesses
    B. industry survey
    C. risk analysis
    D. risk management

3. CPTED stands for:
    A. crime prevention through environmental design
    B. crime prevention through environmental designation
    C. criminal prevention through energy distribution
    D. criminal prosecution through environmental design

4. Which of the following is a CPTED strategy?
    A. natural surveillance
    B. territorial reinforcement
    C. natural access control
    D. all of the above are CPTED strategies

7

5. The purpose of colored badges is to:

   A. make it easy for visitors to find their destination by matching colors

   B. enable observers to know which day of the week matches each color

   C. enable observers to know the proper level of supervision required for visitors

   D. none of the above

6. UPS stands for:

   A. United Postal Service

   B. uninterruptible power surplus

   C. uninterruptible power supply

   D. unintended power surplus

7. Shielded data cabling provides protection from:

   A. interference from electrical cabling

   B. eavesdropping from data wire taps

   C. both A and B

   D. neither A nor B

8. Plenum data cables provide protection from:

   A. eavesdropping

   B. electrical storms

   C. interference from electrical cabling

   D. fire

9. It is often advisable to _____ systems rather than spend a great deal securing them.

   A. insulate

   B. isolate

   C. enclose

   D. hide

10. Equipment siting refers to:

    A. how equipment is positioned in a room

    B. where equipment is located

    C. how easy it is to see equipment

    D. watching over sensitive equipment

11. Fail-over generators provide:

    A. monitoring for generators that fail

    B. power to failing generators

    C. alerting for failing power supplies

    D. instant automatic power in case of power failure

12. Formatting a hard drive will do all of the following EXCEPT:

    A. make data formerly on the drive irretrievable

    B. not make data formerly on the drive irretrievable

    C. allow for a clean installation of an operating system

    D. leave data formerly on the drive retrievable by unauthorized parties

13. The only way to ensure that data on a hard drive is irretrievable is to:

    A. format the drive

    B. format the drive twice

    C. destroy the drive physically

    D. format the drive and perform a clean installation of an operating system

14. What is shoulder surfing?

    A. the act of standing on another's shoulders while surfing

    B. the act of looking over someone's shoulders to see what is on a computer screen

    C. the act of positioning one's shoulders to prevent fatigue

    D. none of the above

15. What is the purpose of a Removal of Property Policy?

    A. to allow for the easy and efficient removal of decommissioned computers

    B. to ensure that all equipment will be removed according to government regulations

    C. to ensure that hazardous computer equipment is removed according to federal guidelines

    D. to ensure that the location of equipment, information, and/or software can be immediately determined and protected from unauthorized removal

7

EXERCISES

Exercise 7.1: Analyzing Risks

1. Conduct a physical risk analysis of your own computer. Determine the dangers your computer faces from possible power problems, maintenance problems, and location. For instance, laptop computers are easily stolen.

2. Make a list of these risks.

Exercise 7.2: Identifying Current Controls

1. Using the list of risks you created in Exercise 1, compare them to any current controls you have against those risks.

2. Create a table with one column for the risks, another for the current controls, and a third blank column. For instance, if you have identified that power outage is a possible risk, but you have a surge suppressor or UPS device, either one would be considered a current control against the risk of power failure.

Exercise 7.3: Action Items or Future Controls

Now that you have identified the physical risks and your current controls, it is time to make plans to control risks further.

1. Identify which risks lack current controls.

2. Use the third column in your table to note controls you could implement to reduce the risks lacking controls. Title this column "Action Items." (Note: Sometimes action items in column three will include research or simple controls such as moving the computer.)

Exercise 7.4: Locating the Data Center

1. Locate the data center or information processing facilities of your school.

2. Is the facility marked with signage? How easy was it to find? What controls are in place to prevent unauthorized access? Write a paragraph about your findings.

Exercise 7.5: Making Clear Desk/Clear Screen a reality

1. Review the Clear Desk and Clear Screen Policy (Table 7.8). The concept seems simple and straightforward until you try to implement it. Why do you think users react defensively to this policy?

2. What resources can an organization provide to users to support the implementation of this policy?

3. What technical, physical, or administrative controls can an organization implement to support compliance with the policy?

PROJECTS

Project 7.1: Your Physical Security Policy

1. Using the risk analysis from the exercises above, write a physical security policy for your computer.

2. Your policy will take into account all current controls and future controls.

3. Your policy must contain an objective, purpose, audience, exception, enforcement, and of course policy statements.

4. Your policy must also contain a statement of authority that clearly explains the need for your policy to the intended audience.

5. Your policy should be no longer than two pages.

Project 7.2: Physical Controls for a Data Center

1. You have been tasked with designing the environmental and physical controls for a *new* Data Center to be built at your school. You are expected to present a report outlining your recommendations to the Chief Information Officer. The first part of your report should be a synopsis of the importance of Data Center physical security.

2. Your report should address three areas: location, access control, and power. You are expected to include diagrams, equipment descriptions, and cost estimates:

   a. Location recommendations should include: where the data center should be built and construction details (floor, wall, ceilings). Be sure to consider the security and accessibility of the location.

   b. Access control recommendations should address entry controls, monitoring controls, and emergency access.

   c. Power safeguards should consider both normal and emergency operating conditions.

Project 7.3: Securing the Perimeter

1. The security perimeter is a barrier of protection from theft, malicious activity, accidental damage, and natural disaster. Almost all buildings have multiple perimeter controls. We have become so accustomed to perimeter controls that they often go unnoticed, e.g., security guards.

    Begin this project with developing a comprehensive list of perimeter controls.

2. Conduct a site survey by walking around your city or town. You are looking for perimeter controls. Include in your survey results the address of the building, a summary of building occupants, type(s) of perimeter controls, and your opinion as to the effectiveness of the controls. In order to make your survey valid, you must include at least ten properties.

3. Choose one property to focus on. Taking into consideration the location, the depth security required by the occupants, and the geography, comment in detail on the perimeter controls. Based upon your analysis, recommend additional physical controls to enhance perimeter security.

Case Study

A fast-growing bank must expand its data/information process-ing facilities. There are many barriers to the simple task of lo-cating a facility large enough to accommodate the bank's needs. The bank is located in a flood plane and there are fre-quent power outages from violent storms such as tornados and hurricanes.

These problems weren't as much of a concern for the bank's prior facilities as data/information processing tasks were out-sourced to a company providing all the protections required. Now the bank has outgrown the outsourced company's abilities and must build its own facility.

How will you address the bank's unique needs? Will you build a new facility that can withstand all the possible natural risks of the area? Will you locate the facility in a remote area not as sus-ceptible to natural disaster? If you choose a remote location, what method of connectivity will you choose? If you choose to build locally, how will you construct the building(s) to withstand the adverse conditions? Will you work with local power providers and other resources? What redundancies will you include to maintain service to your growing bank? How will you balance the need for protection from the adverse environment and the need for access protections?

Write at least two pages describing your new facility and the methods and means you would use to achieve your goal. Include policy considerations as the primary way to express these meth-ods and means.

7

Communications and Operations Management

Chapter Objectives

After reading this chapter and completing the exercises, you will be able to do the following:

- Author useful standard operating procedures.

- Implement change control processes.

- Develop an incident response program.

- Protect against malware.

- Advocate for formal backup and restore procedures.

- Manage portable storage devices.

- Secure the transport, reuse, and disposal of media.

- Protect the integrity of information published on publicly available systems.

- Recognize the unique security requirements of e-mail and e-mail systems.

- Write policies and procedures to support operational security.

Introduction

Section 8 of the ISO 17799 standard is Communications and Operations management. This domain focuses on the daily use and protection of information assets and information systems. The array of topics that are covered in this area are staggering. In this chapter, we are going to focus on activities that are common to corporate environments. We are also going to assume that information assets have been properly classified, access controls have been assigned, and physical controls are in place.

We will begin with a discussion of standard operating procedure documentation and why this is a foundation of operations security. We will acknowledge that environments are dynamic and that change is inevitable. We will discuss ways to manage change. We know that unplanned and unexpected events occur even in the most prepared environments. We will discuss the importance of a comprehensive incident response program.

We will examine the various ways that information can be compromised during the course of relatively normal use, including malware, portable storage devices, and improper media reuse and disposal. We will recognize the need for an organized backup and restore process for the purpose of recovery. Lastly, we will discuss the unique confidentiality, integrity, and availability considerations in regard to e-mail communication.

Throughout the chapter, we will introduce policies and procedures required to create and maintain a secure operational environment.

Standard Operating Procedures

Standard operating procedures (SOPs) provide direction, improve communication, reduce training time, and improve work consistency. These documents are the official way for the company to do business. They are the "rules of the game."

Why Document Operating Procedures?

Well-written standard operating procedures reduce organizational dependence upon individual and institutional knowledge. The very process of creating standard operating procedures requires us to look in detail at what we do, why we do it that way, and hopefully, how we could do it better. This is critical in terms of business continuity. A business process should not depend upon what a single individual knows. What if that person suddenly becomes unavailable due to illness, death, or a change of plans? How can a business expect to continue operating efficiently (if at all) without written, approved direction on how to perform various tasks and functions?

Imagine a situation where a law firm decides to outsource its information systems administration and management and awards ABC Network Engineers a one-year contract. ABC dedicates a network engineer 40 hours a week to this project. The engineer does a fabulous job redesigning, administering, and supporting the network. Everyone agrees that the network is now in better shape than ever. At the end of the year, the law firm evaluates the cost and decides that it would be more cost-effective to bring the position back in-house. Unfortunately, the engineer has not documented any of the work for the past year. The law firm now finds itself with no guidance or procedures on how to support and maintain its network.

Similarly, it is not uncommon for an employee become so important to a small business that losing that individual would be a huge blow to the company. Imagine that this person is the only one performing a critical task and that there is no documentation as to how he performs this task. Now suppose that this employee chooses to leave the organization. The company is now faced with the situation of having lost a valuable employee, no documentation as to how he performed critical tasks, and no one on staff to either step in directly or train a new employee.

Consider the situation where an employee is promoted, or perhaps the task exceeds the capacity of a single person. In both cases, organizations need a way to train the new employee as well as maintain consistency of operations. From these simple examples, we can see that proper documentation of all operating procedures is not a luxury: it is a business requirement.

Developing Standard Operating Procedure Documentation

Standard operating procedures (SOPs) are instructions that should be understandable to everyone who uses them. SOPs should be written as simply as possible. It is best to use short, direct sentences so that the reader can quickly understand and memorize the steps in the procedure. Procedures should include all steps that are essential and that should be performed the same way by all personnel. Omitting any of these essential steps may lead to confusion or performance variation among different workers. On the other hand, procedures should not be so detailed that they become cumbersome and impractical for everyday use.

There are four common ways to organize and format SOPs. The goal is to create a document that is easy for the reader to understand and helpful for the work at hand. Two factors determine what type of SOP to use. First, how many decisions will the user need to make during the procedure? Second, how many steps and substeps are in the procedure? Routine procedures that are short and require few decisions can be written using the simple steps format. Long procedures consisting of more than ten steps, with few decisions, should be written in hierarchical steps format or in a graphic format. Procedures that require many decisions should be written in the form of a flowchart.

Simple Step Format   The simple step format uses sequential steps. These are generally rote procedures that do not require any decision making and do not have any substeps. The simple step format should be limited to ten steps.

Hierarchical Format   The hierarchical format is used for tasks that require more detail or exactness. The hierarchical format allows the use of easy-to read steps for experienced users while including more detailed substeps as well. Experienced users may only refer to the substeps when they

Many Decisions?	More Than 10 Steps?	Recommended SOP Format:
No	No	Simple Step
No	Yes	Hierarchical or Graphic
Yes	No	Flowchart
Yes	Yes	Flowchart

FIGURE 8.1 SOP methods.

Backup Tape Transport Procedures	
Procedure	**Completed**
Note: These procedures are to be completed by the night operator by 6:00 am Monday-Friday. Please initial each completed step.	
1. Remove backup tape from tape drive.	
2. Label with the date.	
3. Place tape in tape case and lock.	
4. Call ABC delivery at 888-555-1212.	
5. Tell ABC that the delivery is ready to be picked up.	
6. When ABC arrives, require driver to present identification.	
7. Note in pickup log, driver name.	
8. Have driver sign and date log.	

FIGURE 8.2 Simple step format.

need to, while beginners will use the detailed substeps to help them learn the procedure.

Graphic Format When writing procedures for very long activities, managers should consider using a graphic format. The graphic format breaks long processes into shorter subprocesses that consist of only a few steps. Workers can learn several short subprocesses more easily that one long

New User Account Procedures	
You must have the HR New User Authorization Form before starting this process.	
Procedures	**Detail**
Launch Active Directory Users and Computers ⟶	a. Click on TS icon b. Provide your login credentials c. Click on ADUC icon
Create a New User ⟶	a. Right click on the Users OU folder b. Choose New User
Enter Required User Information ⟶	a. Enter User first, last and full name b. Enter User login name, click Next c. Enter User's temporary password d. Choose User Must Change Password at Next Login, click Next
Create an Exchange Mailbox ⟶	a. Make sure Create and Exchange Mailbox is checked b. Accept defaults, click Next
Verify Account Information ⟶	a. Confirm that all information on summary screen is correct b. Choose Finish
Complete Demographic Profile ⟶	a. Double click on the User Name b. Complete the information on the General, Address, Telephone and Organization tabs. (Note: Info. should be on the HR request sheet)
Add Users to Groups ⟶	a. Choose the Member of tab b. Add groups as listed on the HR request sheet c. Click OK when completed
Set Remote Control Permissions ⟶	a. Click on Remote Control tab b. Make sure Enable Remote Control and Require User's Permission boxes are checked. c. Level of control should be set to Interact with the Session
Advise HR re: Account Creation ⟶	a. Sign and date HR request form b. Send to HR via interoffice mail

8

FIGURE 8.3 Hierarchical format.

procedure. Another possibility for the graphic format is to use photographs, diagrams, or screenshots to illustrate the procedure. Pictures truly are worth a thousand words, and they are helpful regardless of the literacy level or native language of a worker.

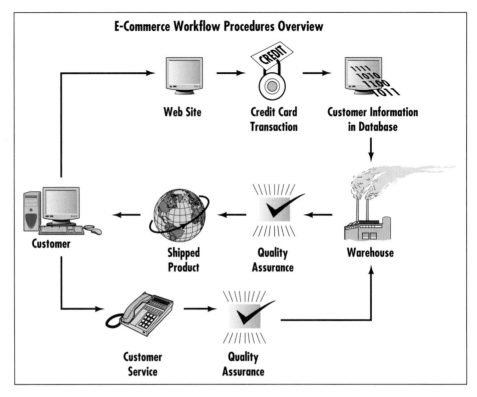

FIGURE 8.4 Graphic format.

Flowchart A flowchart is simply a graphic way to present the logical steps in a decision-making process. A flowchart provides an easy-to-follow mechanism for walking a worker through a series of logical decisions and the steps that should be taken as a result. When developing flowcharts, you should use the generally accepted flowchart symbols.

Flowcharting is a language all its own. Special shapes are used to represent actions, steps, and decisions. SmartDraw® has a free online tutorial on basic flowcharting: **www.smartdraw.com/tutorials/flowcharts/basic.htm**. An excellent reference on developing flowcharts is *Flowcharts: Plain & Simple: Learning & Application Guide by Joiner Associates Staff* (Oriel, Inc.: 1995 ISBN 1-88473-103-1).

FYI: Writing Resource

A recommended resource for learning how to write procedures is *Procedure Writing: Principles and Practices* by Douglas Wieringa, Christopher Moore, and Valerie Barnes (Battelle Press: 1998–2nd ed. ISBN 1-57477-052-7).

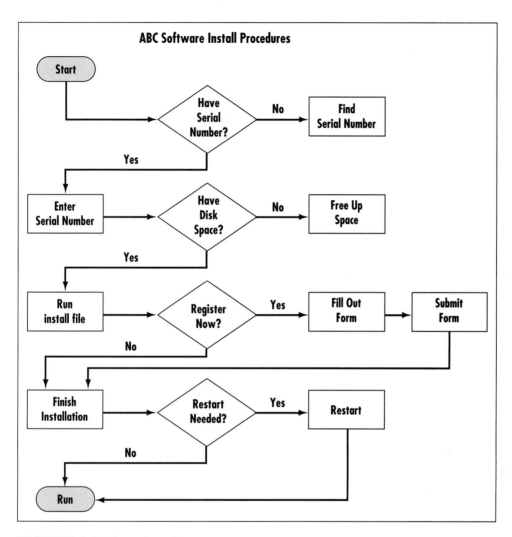

FIGURE 8.5 Flowchart format.

Authorizing SOP Documentation

Once a procedure has been thoroughly researched and documented, it should be reviewed, tested, and authorized before being presented as an official procedure to ascertain the veracity of the information it contains. The reviewer should be independent of the documentation project. The reviewer is reading for clarity and understanding. Final authorization should come from the information system owner or designee.

Protecting SOP Documentation

Mechanisms should be put in place so that the integrity of the document cannot be tampered with. Imagine a case where a business-critical procedure is documented. A disgruntled employee gets hold of that document and changes key information. If the tampering is not discovered, it could lead to a disastrous situation for the company.

SOP Change Management

The documentation process does not end with approval and authorization. Many procedures are dynamic and will evolve over time. That means that the document will need to be revised. Revisions, not unlike the original documents, must be approved, tested, and authorized by the information system owner before they can be considered official. This control protects the integrity of the document from unauthorized changes.

IN PRACTICE: Standard Operating Procedures Documentation Policy

The goals of this policy require that the organization develop and authorize standard operating procedures for all information systems.

The *objectives* of this policy are to:

- Ensure the secure operation of information systems through the documentation of standard operating procedures.

- Assign responsibility for authorization, management, and maintenance of SOPs.

The *audience* is all individuals with access to information resources.

TABLE 8.1 Sample Standard Operating Procedures Documentation Policy.

Section X:	[COMPANY] Information Security Policy	Effective Date:
Subsection	Communications and Operations Management	Change Control #:
Policy	Standard Operating Procedures Documentation	Approved By:
Objective	To ensure the secure operation of information systems through the documentation and maintenance of standard operating procedures.	

▸▸ CONTINUED ON NEXT PAGE

▸▸ CONTINUED	
Purpose	The purpose of this policy is to ensure the correct and secure management of all information systems.
Audience	The standard operating procedures documentation policy applies equally to all individuals granted access privileges to any information resources.
Policy	• Standard operating procedures and responsibilities for all information processing systems will be tested, documented, and maintained. • The information system owner must authorize the official version of all standard operating procedures. • Formal authorization from the information system owner is required prior to any changes made to the documentation.
Exceptions	None
Disciplinary Actions	Violation of this policy may result in disciplinary action, which may include termination for employees and temporaries; a termination of employment relations in the case of contractors or consultants; or dismissal for interns and volunteers. Additionally, individuals are subject to civil and criminal prosecution.

8

Operational Change Control

Operational change is inevitable. Change occurs because circumstances around businesses change. Change can be internal: new employees, new business endeavors/opportunities, new application systems being deployed, new features added to existing application systems, and so forth. Change can also be external, as seen in past years with the introduction of federal regulations such as HIPAA, GLBA, and Sarbanes-Oxley.

Change control is an internal procedure by which only authorized changes are made to software, hardware, network access privileges, or business processes. The starting point is an analysis of the need, followed by a formal request for change. This request should be reviewed by the data owner or designee prior to being authorized. Implementation should be monitored to ensure security requirements are not breached or diluted and that unsuccessful changes can be rolled back or recovered. All changes (successful and unsuccessful) should be documented.

Step 1: Assessment

The first phase of the change control process is a formal assessment of the existing situation, the goal of the change, and the impact of the change. Based on those three criteria, a plan can be created to map the proper course of action that will need to be followed.

Consider this scenario: Windows XP Professional is installed on a mission-critical workstation. The System Administrator installs a service pack. A service pack often will make changes to system files. Now imagine that for a reason beyond the installer's control, the process fails halfway through. What is the result? An operating system that is neither the original version, nor the updated version. In other words, there could be a mix of new and old system files, which would result in an unstable platform. The negative impact on the process that depends upon the workstation would be significant. Take this example to the next level and imagine the impact if this machine were a network server used by all employees all day long. Consider the impact on the productivity of the entire company if this machine were to become unusable because of a failed update. It now becomes obvious that the risks associated with changes must be considered, and there should be a tested and approved recovery plan.

Step 2: Logging Changes

An essential element of change control is logging. The following information should be made documented for all changes:

- Who requested the change?
- Who approved the change?
- What was the system state prior to the change?
- What were the reasons that prompted the change?
- Specifically, what changes were made?
- What was the system state after the change?
- Was the change successful?
- If not, how was the system recovered?
- Date and time of the change.
- Name and contract information of the implementer.

Step 3: Communication

The need to communicate to all relevant parties that a change has taken place cannot be overemphasized. Take the example of a department such as Billing or HR that has been dutifully saving all their documents to a specific server that is backed up every night. Maybe it has been decided that this server will be dropped from the backup rotation, and that the members of the aforementioned department now need to save their information to another server that is still being backed up. Maybe the list of employees impacted by this change was not as exhaustive as it should have been, and three users are still backing up data to the old server as they always have in the past. Three weeks later, that older server is taken offline and the drives are erased for security purposes. Safe to say, all the data that the three employees worked on for the past three weeks is now lost because they were not apprised of a simple change. A strategy must be in place to make sure that such an event does not occur.

IN PRACTICE: Operational Change Control Policy

The goal of this policy is to integrate the process of change control into the culture of the organization.
   The *objectives* of this policy are to:

- Support information security by instituting a formal change management process.

- Define the framework for the change control process.

The *audience* is all individuals with access to information resources.

TABLE 8.2 Sample Operational Change Control Policy.

Section X:	[COMPANY] Information Security Policy	Effective Date:
Subsection	Communications and Operations Management	Change Control #:
Policy	Operational Change Control	Approved By:
Objective	In support of information security, the [COMPANY] will institute a formal change management process.	
Purpose	The purpose of this policy is to prevent system or security failures by establishing a formal process for change, integrating operational and application change control procedures, and logging all changes.	

▶▶ CONTINUED ON NEXT PAGE

>> CONTINUED	
Audience	The operational change control policy applies equally to all individuals granted access privileges to any information resources.

Policy	• There shall be a formal assessment and approval process for proposed changes which will be developed by the office of the Information Security Officer.
	
	• Prior to any operational change, there shall be a risk assessment that:
	
	  • Identifies significant changes
	
	  • Records significant changes
	
	  • Assesses the potential impact of such changes
	
	  • Documents procedures and responsibilities for aborting and recovering from unsuccessful changes
	
	• Changes shall be communicated to all relevant persons. The system owner shall approve and manage this process with the assistance of the Information Security officer.
	
	• All changes shall be logged.

Exceptions	None
Disciplinary Actions	Violation of this policy may result in disciplinary action, which may include termination for employees and temporaries; a termination of employment relations in the case of contractors or consultants; or dismissal for interns and volunteers. Additionally, individuals are subject to civil and criminal prosecution.

Incident Response Program

Military personnel do not start to design a plan of battle when the bullets start flying around them. At least those who would like to survive do not. The same applies to companies. The simple truth is that incidents happen. The reasons are many and varied. Incidents may be caused by a malicious intruder or by an untrained, well-meaning employee. Incidents may occur because an organization did not take proper precautions or implement appropriate controls. Conversely, incidents are bound to happen even in the most prepared environments. Risk-free environments simply do not exist.

However, the impact can be minimized by a risk management process. ***Risk management*** is the formal process in which a risk is identified, assessed, and mitigated by implementing a control. Ignoring a risk is a refusal to face the facts. Ignoring a risk is dangerous and irresponsible.

The key is to be ready to respond and recover. An ***incident response plan*** is a roadmap of reporting, responding, and recovery actions. Incident response procedures are detailed steps to take to implement the plan. Taken together, these are referred to as an incident response program.

Incidents and Severity Levels

Not all incidents are created equal. Some are more severe than others. After all, incidents run the gamut from a seldom-used file being corrupted on the network to a fire raging through the facilities, endangering employees and data alike.

A well-designed incident response program begins with an assessment in which all foreseeable incidents are identified, reviewed, and assigned a severity level. The severity level is based upon the operational, reputational, and legal impact to the organization. Executive management should be tasked with assigning the severity. Severity levels should be organized into tiers. Procedures should be developed for each tier that address the response time and response responsibilities. The assignee of response responsibilities is also referred to as the *designated incident handler.*

What Is a Designated Incident Handler?

A ***designated incident handler*** is the person (or group) responsible for responding to, investigating, and overseeing a recovery and documenting the resolution of a particular incident. Severity levels should have designated handlers. For example, a violation of regulatory compliance would be assigned to a member of senior management, while a virus outbreak would be assigned to the Help Desk.

The designated incident handler is tasked with:

- Responding within the designated time frame.

- Involving the personnel necessary to contain and/or eradicate the problem.

- Managing problem resolution.

- Identifying and assessing the evidence in detail and maintain a chain of custody.

- Controlling access to the evidence.

- Completing and submitting the appropriate documentation for review and analysis.

TABLE 8.3 Incident severity level matrix.

An information security incident is any adverse event whereby some aspect of an information system or information itself is threatened: loss of data confidentiality, disruption of data integrity, disruption or denial of service. The types of incidents have been classified into tiers depending on the severity. The level of consequence of an incident refers to the relative impact it has on an organization. Each tier has a specific response time and responsible party.

Severity Level	Explanation	Examples
Tier I *Immediate response*	**Tier I Incidents** are the most serious and are considered *Major.* Because of the gravity of the situation and the high potential for harm, these incidents should be handled as soon as possible. Tier I incidents are defined as those that could have long-term effects on business, critical systems, and regulatory compliance.	Confidential data at risk Business continuity at risk Unauthorized use of a system for any purpose Changes to system hardware, firmware, or software without the system owner's authorization Denial of Service attack Property destruction related to a computer incident > $10,000 Personal theft Download of P2P files or programs Download of unauthorized software Download of or accessing pornography Computer virus/worm (server-based or multiple systems) Suspicious person in secure areas Suspicious activity in any area Any violation of law Unfriendly employee termination

▶▶ CONTINUED ON NEXT PAGE

» **CONTINUED**

Tier II *2-4 hours response*	**Tier II Incidents** are more serious and should be handled the same day the event occurs (normally in two to four hours of the event). For purposes of reporting, they are classified as *Major.* Tier II incidents are defined as an incursion on noncritical systems or information; detection of precursor to a focused attack; believed threat of an imminent attack, or antivirus software unable to eradicate infection.	Violation of special access by vendors or employees Computer virus/worm (workstation) Property destruction related to a computer incident < \$10,000 Explicit/covert violation of a control that is not an immediate threat Threats of personal harm via e-mail Compromise of personal password Loss of personal equipment (laptop/PDA) Unsuccessful scans/probes
Tier III *Within 24 business hour response*	**Tier III Incidents** are considered less severe and should be handled within one working day after the event occurs. A Tier III incident is defined as an incident that can be resolved by the system user or operator with no damage to the system or company data.	Excessive bandwidth use Suspected sharing of user accounts Unintentional violation of a control, such as logging in after specified hours Copyright infringement Unsolicited adult content Warning of potential exploit via internal monitoring
Tier IV *Within 3 business day response*	**Tier IV Incidents** are proactive high priority. Tier IV incidents are defined as a threat of future attack; detection of reconnaissance.	Vendor alert: Potential Exploit Industry alert: Potential Exploit
Tier V *Unspecified*	**Tier V Incidents** are proactive low priority. Tier V incidents are defined as an unsubstantiated rumor or security incident.	

8

Incident Reporting, Response, and Handling Procedures

A well-defined incident response program includes reporting, response, handling, and recovery procedures. These procedures should be clear, with no ambiguous terms or syntax. An employee should not need to reread it several times to discover the intent, nor should any room be left for interpretation.

Incident Reporting Procedures Incident reporting is best accomplished by implementing simple mechanisms that can be used by all employees to report the discovery of an incident. Again, the point here is to make the process easy and straightforward. Nobody wants to remember what form number she is supposed to be looking for to report a raging fire! Incident reporting should never depend on the severity level of the incident. Regardless of the assigned severity level, any discovered incident should be reported *immediately.* This is an important practice since the person who discovers an incident may not have the skill, knowledge, or training to properly assess the level of severity inherent to that incident.

People frequently fail to report issues because they are afraid of being wrong and looking foolish, they do not want to be seen as a complainer, or they simply don't care enough and don't want to get involved. These reasons may be understandable, but they must be met with an effective response from management. Management needs to deliver the message that this procedure is in effect to save the company from some potentially disastrous situations, and that their help is not only sought, it is required.

Employees must be assured that even if they were to report a perceived incident that ended up not being an actual incident, they would not be ridiculed or met with annoyance. On the contrary! Their willingness to get involved for the greater good of the company is exactly the type of behavior that the company needs. If anything, they should be supported for their efforts, and made to feel valued and appreciated for doing the right thing. This is a cultural element that needs to be established as early in the process as possible for the incident response program to yield the best results.

Incident Response Procedures Incident response procedures address who and within what time frame an incident report should be responded to. Here is where the designated incident handler is specified as well as response time. Commonly used response times are immediate, within 2-4 hours, within 4-8 hours, within one business day, and within three business days. There may be times when external resources need to be involved in the response. External resources include law enforcement, forensic experts, legal counsel, security consultants, and regulators. The response procedures should clearly state under what circumstances it is appropriate to engage these resources, who has the authority to authorize contact, and how contact should be made.

Incident Handling Procedures Incident handling focuses on *containment, eradication,* and *recovery.* The goal of containment is to limit the scope and magnitude of an incident to keep the incident from getting worse. The goal of eradication is to ensure that the problem is eliminated and vulnerabilities are addressed. The goal of recovery is to return to a fully operational status.

Containment, eradication, and recovery methods are highly dependent on the type and scope of the security incident. It is impossible to document handling procedures for every type of incident. Procedures should address sample scenarios and provide general guidance.

Analyzing Incidents and Malfunctions

Once an incident has been successfully handled, it is essential for the company to determine what new controls can be deployed to prevent such an incident or malfunction from ever happening again. Additionally, while the incident is fresh in everyone's mind, this is an appropriate time to review and assess the response and recovery process.

This is the old concept of feeding a man as opposed to teaching him how to fish. The company cannot be content with simply handling incidents as they arise, every time they arise. Preventing them from arising is a lot more cost-efficient, both in terms of cost related to resolving issues and loss of productivity. Which would you prefer: that every time a tire explodes on your car, your mechanic replaces it with a new one, or that your mechanic finds out *why* your tires keep exploding and prevents further incidents?

Reporting Suspected or Observed Security Weaknesses

The rule here is simple. If an employee comes in contact with a network or application system security weakness, be it actual or suspected, she is to report it immediately. Such weaknesses, however minimal as they may appear, can potentially be exploited and escalate into direct threats to the confidentiality, integrity, and/or availability of the company's sensitive data. Because most employees cannot differentiate between a more "benign" issue and a full-fledged exploitable vulnerability, any weakness must be reported immediately upon observation. It should be described in the information security policy as the responsibility of all employees. It should also be noted that failure to report an observed or perceived vulnerability can be met with disciplinary actions ranging up to termination of employment or criminal prosecution.

Because employees use systems directly in their everyday jobs, as opposed to developers who create them and then move on to another project, they often know a great deal about those systems. With this experience comes an increased chance that they will stumble upon a weakness that had not been identified yet, hence the responsibility assigned to all employees to report such weaknesses as soon as they are observed.

8

Testing Suspected or Observed Security Weaknesses

Only authorized employees or authorized third-party contractors should be allowed to test suspected security weaknesses. Authorization needs to come from the highest levels of management. Other employees should be forbidden to test suspected security weaknesses, and doing so will be seen as blatant and intentional misuse of the system. It is very difficult to distinguish between a user "testing a weakness" and a user "abusing a weakness" to see if he can get away with it and perhaps later even profit from it. The acceptable use or affirmation agreement should clearly and unequivocally state the importance of complying with this policy.

IN PRACTICE: Incident Response Program Policy

The goal of this policy to require a comprehensive Incident Response program.

The *objectives* of this policy are to:

- Assign roles and responsibilities.
- Mandate the development of an incident response plan.
- Mandate the development of incident response procedures.
- Forbid unauthorized testing of security weaknesses.

The *audience* is everyone who uses company information resources.

TABLE 8.4 Sample Incident Response Program Policy.

Section X:	[COMPANY] Information Security Policy	Effective Date:
Subsection	Communications and Operations Management	Change Control #:
Policy	Incident Response Program	Approved By:
Objective	To ensure that the organization develops, implements, supports, and maintains an incident response program.	
Purpose	The purpose of this information security policy is to provide guidance to [COMPANY] employees, officers, contractors, and vendors to enable quick and efficient response to and recovery from security incidents.	

▶▶ CONTINUED ON NEXT PAGE

▶▶ CONTINUED	
Audience	This policy applies to all [COMPANY] locations and to all employees, officers, contractors, consultants, affiliates, and government representatives that use, process, and/or manage [COMPANY] information.

Policy	• [COMPANY] employees and officers have predefined roles and responsibilities, which can take priority over normal duties.
	
	• The Information Security Officer will document all foreseeable incidents. An Executive Management committee will assign incident severity levels. Severity levels will be used to determine appropriate response.
	
	• The Information Security Officer will document an incident reporting and handling procedure, which will include:
	  • A process for all users to communicate breaches of security and other incidents
	  • Documented escalation procedures to inform the appropriate personnel quickly
	  • Response and recovery procedures
	  • A close-out and feedback process to communicate back to the appropriate user when the incident is resolved
	  • A process to report incident types, severity levels, access details, and involvement
	
	• Users of information services are required to note and report any observed or suspected security weaknesses in, or threats to, systems or services immediately upon observation.
	
	• Users shall not under any circumstances test suspected security weaknesses. Any unauthorized testing by users shall be considered misuse of the system and be subject to disciplinary measures.
	
	• Analysis of incidents and malfunctions will be done to determine new controls that can be established to prevent future incidents.

Disciplinary Actions	Violation of this policy may result in disciplinary action, which may include termination for employees and temporaries; a termination of employment relations in the case of contractors or consultants; or dismissal for interns and volunteers. Additionally, individuals are subject to civil and criminal prosecution.

8

Malicious Software

Malicious software, or *malware,* comes in many flavors these days, from computer viruses to worms, from spyware to browser hijacking, from Remote Access Trojans to key loggers.

What Is Malware?

Malware stands for malicious software and encompasses a range of programs and code including the following.

- A *virus* is a self-replicating program that spreads by infecting other programs. In other words, it needs a host on the target machine. An infamous example of a virus is Melissa, which spread across the world attached to Microsoft Word documents sent as e-mail attachments.

- A *worm* is a piece of malicious code that can spread from one computer to another without requiring a host file to infect. Worms represent a greater threat than viruses and are characterized by their being designed to exploit known vulnerabilities. Infamous examples of worms are Nimda (admin in reverse), Slammer, and Code Red.

- *Spyware* is a relatively newer type of malware. Spyware is code that is installed on users' machines without their consent, usually via a legitimate download, or what is perceived by the user as a legitimate download. Once installed, spyware can track all Web surfing activity (and report on it to its masters), create a profile of shopping habits and preferences for a given user, hijack the browser so that the start page is redirected to another page than the one originally set up by the user, disallow access to some Internet content against the user's wishes, and so forth. Spyware is at best an invasion of users' privacy, and at worst no less than a Denial of Service attack.

- *Trojan horses* are potentially destructive programs that masquerade as legitimate and benign applications. For example, a user downloads what she thinks is a simple computer game. She is unaware that, although the game is fully functional, it really served as a conduit for the download of nefarious code. One of the typical activities attributed to Trojans is to open connections for an outside attacker through the use of listening ports. If a RAT (Remote Access Trojan) was downloaded, the attacker will be notified once it is installed, and will be able to take over control of the infected machine. In fact, many hackers will tell you that once they've successfully installed a RAT on a target machine, they have more actual control over that machine than the very person interactively seated at that same machine! Examples of Trojan tools include Back Orifice and SubSeven, among many others.

- *Key loggers* are applications that run discreetly on a target machine and record each and every key entry that takes place in a session. That way, an attacker simply has to bring up that text file with all the recorded keystrokes and harvest such information as user names and passwords.

- *Logic bombs* are code that is loaded but lies dormant unless a specific, predetermined event either happens or fails to happen, depending on the instance. The typical example of a logic bomb is for a person to install malicious code that will check the payroll list every month. Were it to fail to find the name of the person who loaded the malicious code–meaning that this person is no longer on the payroll–the attack would be launched.

Malware Controls

The Information Security Office or the Information Technology department is generally tasked with the responsibility of employing a strong anti-malware defense in depth strategy. In this case, *defense in depth* means implementing prevention and detection controls coupled with a security awareness campaign.

Prevention and Detection Controls The goal of a prevention control is to stop the attack before it even has a chance to start. One of the most effective prevention controls is limiting the number of users who are allowed and/or able to install software on their company-provided computers. Additionally, not allowing users to have administrative rights to their workstations will prevent malware from running in a powerful security context.

Detection should occur at multiple levels: at the entry point of the network; between the Wide Area Network and the Local Area Network; at the e-mail server; at the file, print, and application servers; and at the desktop.

Specifically, each computer on the corporate network—including all workstations and servers—should be equipped with an anti-malware solution. It is important that the antivirus solutions be configured upon installation to automatically update at least once a day, as many new pieces of malicious code are released and detected every day around the world. These updates must be automatic, because the vast majority of users would probably forget to run those updates manually everyday, thereby endangering the whole network.

Antivirus Software Architecture A common mistake made by computer users is to believe that if an antivirus solution is installed on their machine, then they must be all set and protected against the worst code floating around the Internet looking for a next victim. While that may be true–if the installation was performed correctly, including automatic daily updates–it may also be a classic case of overconfidence. This misconception exists because the architecture of an antivirus solution is not necessarily well understood by those users.

The first part of antivirus solution is known as the "engine." It is the basic program. On top of this engine are layered definition files, also known as *DAT files*. Those files require daily updates. The engine may also be updated, but it usually lasts at least a year. The DAT files are where the latest discovered malicious code entries are stored, along with all the already-known malicious code entries.

Suppose an antivirus company shipped DAT files made of almost 70,100 different virus definitions. One month later, that same file would include at least 70,210 virus definitions, but the engine will likely be the same. So if a user purchased a new computer, brought it home, installed an antivirus, and never updated it after that, not only would he not be protected against all known viruses (to the tune of 110 multiplied by the amount of months since the latest update), but he would also be operating *under the impression that he is in fact protected,* which is even more dangerous than not being protected at all but knowing it.

FYI: The Impact of Worms

You may remember reading in the paper about three Category 4 worms that were released within 12 days. Their names were Blaster, Welchia, and Sobig. What you may not remember is that they quickly infected millions of computers all over the world—not to mention that the cost of those three worms alone was estimated to be $2 billion.

Many worms and RATs will open known and identified ports once they are successfully unleashed. In situations where the malicious code may have been able to defeat the preventive controls, it may still be possible to catch them by looking for suspicious open ports. All unauthorized ports reported by a port scan should be immediately logged and investigated. Be aware that false positives may be reported, especially if custom application systems are deployed. It is not rare for such applications to use the same port as a port also used by a known piece of malicious code. In other words, not all ports reported by a port scan will mean that malicious code was successfully installed on a host. But it does mean that if an unauthorized port is picked up during a port scan, it must be determined as soon as possible whether that port is linked to a legitimate application—or if it is the manifestation of malware.

FYI: Ports Explained

Ports and IP addresses are to computers, respectively, what extensions and phone numbers are to phone systems. If a server runs both as a mail and a Web server, and a packet stream comes in, how would that computer know whether to direct the packet stream to the Web interface or to the mail interface? The target IP address in the packet stream got that stream all the way to the server itself. The port number associated with this packet stream—80 for Web traffic, and 110 for incoming mail, for example—will tell the computer which service should handle this traffic.

Compare this with the following situation: A client calls your company on the phone. For this, she uses your company's phone number (the server's IP address in the previous example). Once connected to the PBX, the caller has a choice of basically talking to all employees of the company. The way to connect to the one person she actually wants to talk to is through the use of an extension number for that particular person (i.e., the port number for that particular service).

Security Awareness *Security awareness* must be a focus of all companies when it comes to fighting malware. Users must be trained on the matter as thoroughly as possible. The training must be augmented with regular security awareness campaigns, including reminders in the form of e-mail, posters in common shared areas, and newsletters.

8

IN PRACTICE: Malicious Software Policy

The goal of this policy is to ensure a company-wide effort to prevent, detect, and contain malicious software.

The *objectives* of this policy are to:

- Prevent the introduction of malicious software into the organization's computing environment.
- Detect the introduction of malicious software.
- Contain the impact of malicious software.
- Assign roles and responsibilities.

The *audience* is all employees.

▶▶ CONTINUED ON NEXT PAGE

>> CONTINUED

TABLE 8.5 Sample Malicious Software Policy.

Section X:	[COMPANY] Information Security Policy	Effective Date:
Subsection	Communications and Operations Management	Change Control #:
Policy	Malicious Software	Approved By:
Objective	Implement prevention, detection, and containment controls to lessen the impact of malicious software.	
Purpose	The purpose of this policy is to protect the integrity of software and information by mitigating the risks of malicious software.	
Audience	The malicious software policy applies equally to all individuals, information assets, and information systems.	
Policy	• The Information Security Officer is responsible for ensuring that security awareness, prevention, and detection controls are utilized to protect all information and information systems against malicious software. • The Department of Information Technology is responsible for recommending and implementing prevention, detection, and containment controls. • The Department of Human Resources is responsible for developing and implementing security awareness training, which will include virus control procedures, including recognizing hoax e-mails.	
Exceptions	None	
Disciplinary Actions	Violation of this policy may result in disciplinary action, which may include termination for employees and temporaries; a termination of employment relations in the case of contractors or consultants; or dismissal for interns and volunteers. Additionally, individuals are subject to civil and criminal prosecution.	

Information System Backup

A company that exists without a tested backup and restore solution is like a flying acrobat who works for a circus–without a net. If he were to miss that trapeze, we would be best advised to close our eyes for the next ten seconds.

Not backing up data simply is not an acceptable solution. Backing up data is a way to protect data availability and data integrity. It protects data availability, because if I lose the data that I had prior to the last backup, I can retrieve and restore it.

Note that if data is entered after the latest backup, and consequently lost, the backup solution will not be able to be of service. Therefore, backup solutions do not offer 100 percent insurance against data loss.

Backing up data also protects against data integrity issues. Let's say an employee just found out that she is about to be fired. Upset, she maliciously edits several documents. The data integrity of those documents has been compromised. Restoring these documents from backup would restore the data integrity.

Defining a Backup Strategy

Several factors should be considered when designing a data backup strategy. Reliability is paramount; speed and efficiency are also very important, as are simplicity and ease of use. These factors will all define the criteria for the type of backup device, tapes, and rotation.

Deciding what data to back up is based upon a simple premise: Can the company afford to lose this specific instance of data and not suffer in any way? If not, what is the cost associated with losing this data? For archival and retrieval purposes, it is recommended to keep the last three generations of backed-up information. This backed-up data should be relocated to an off-site facility, in an environment where it is secure from theft, the elements, and natural disasters such as floods and fires.

Grandfather-Father-Son Generations of Backup A universally accepted rotation is known as "Grandfather-Father-Son." The goal of this three week rotation is to have separate tapes for daily, weekly, monthly, and quarterly backups. To use this procedure, you will need four daily tapes (labeled Monday-Thursday), five weekly tapes (labeled Week 1-Week 5), and three monthly tapes (labeled Month A-C).

The Importance of Test Restores

The whole point of backing up data is that it can be restored if that data is lost or tampered with. In other words, more than the value of the backup to the company is in the knowledge that running a restore operation will yield success and that the data will once again be available for production and business-critical application systems.

Just as proper attention must be paid to designing and testing the backup solution, the restore strategy must also be carefully designed and tested before being approved as the official strategy.

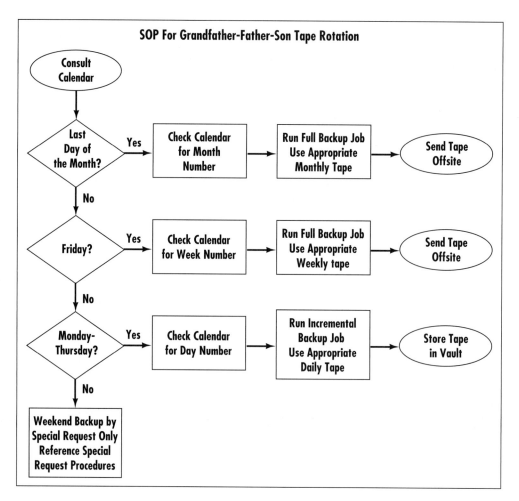

FIGURE 8.6 SOP for Grandfather-Father-Son rotation.

The following basic rules should be a part of a restoration policy:

- The restoration procedures must be tested, documented, and officially approved.

- Once approved, an updated copy must be kept with the actual backup tapes at the remote location.

The only way to know whether a backup operation was successful and can be relied upon is to test it. It is recommended that test restores of random files be run at least monthly.

IN PRACTICE: Information System Backup Policy

The *objectives* of this policy are to:

- Regularly back up adequate copies and generations of all software, documentation, and business information and store it off-site.
- Regularly test backups to ensure the quality and usability of backed-up media.

The *audience* is all users of information systems.

TABLE 8.6 Sample Information Backup Policy.

Section X:	[COMPANY] Information Security Policy	Effective Date:
Subsection	Communications and Operations Management	Change Control #:
Policy	Information System Backup	Approved By:
Objective	To regularly back up [COMPANY] information assets as well as to ensure the reliability and integrity of the backup media.	
Purpose	The purpose of this policy is to maintain the availability and integrity of information resources in the case of error, compromise, failure, or disaster.	
Audience	The information system backup policy applies to all users of information systems.	
Policy	• Backups of all essential [COMPANY] electronically-stored business data must be routinely created and properly stored to ensure prompt restoration in the event of disaster. At least three generations of backup information shall be retained at a remote location for all business applications. • Restoration procedures will be documented and tested to ensure that they are effective and comply with restoration time requirements. They shall be kept with the backup copies at the remote location. • Backup media shall be tested to ensure the backup can be relied upon.	

▶▶ CONTINUED ON NEXT PAGE

8

►► CONTINUED	
	• System owner's delegate shall be responsible for ensuring that backups are tested.
Exceptions	None
Disciplinary Actions	Violation of this policy may result in disciplinary action, which may include termination for employees and temporaries; a termination of employment relations in the case of contractors or consultants; or dismissal for interns and volunteers. Additionally, individuals are subject to civil and criminal prosecution.

Managing Portable Storage

Portable storage devices (PSD) are transportable drives or disks that can be moved easily from one computer to another. Portable storage devices are often referred to as *removable media*. Open any computer magazine, or surf to any online computer equipment retailer, and look at the options available to a buyer: recordable CDs and DVDs, USB hard drives, FireWire hard drives, USB pen drives–with storage capacities of up to 4GB at the time of writing–all kinds of backup tapes, ZIP drives, Jazz drives, compact flash cards, memory sticks, microdrives, secure digital cards, SmartMedia cards, and don't forget the old reliable floppy disk. There is a plethora of options for removable computer media on the market, and while demand for such hardware has dramatically increased, costs have been falling equally as dramatically in the past year. A USB thumbdrive with 1GB of built-in storage now retails for below $80, making this item not only a bargain, but also a very real risk for all computers equipped with a USB port–which, basically, is all computers currently on the market.

The risks are real: Technology analyst Gartner warns that portable devices containing a USB or FireWire connection are a serious new threat to businesses. In a July 2004 report, Gartner named removable media devices as a significant security risk in the workplace and advised that these can be used both to download confidential data and also to introduce a virus into the company network.

Consider the threat introduced by thumbdrives. Thumbdrives are very small, measuring a couple of inches or less. They are easy to conceal. They do not require a cable as they come with a built-in USB connector. They can be used in many different ways: to copy confidential data to the built-in memory space, to carry infected files to download onto a target machine, or even to carry a complete, bootable, and ready-to-use operating system. There is a release of Linux based on DSL that will fit, complete with an emulator, on a 128MB thumbdrive. All that is needed is to plug in the USB drive into the target computer's USB port, open the contents of it from such a utility as Windows Explorer, double-click on the emulator, and the Linux operating system loads in memory. There is no access to the local hard drive, and there is no need to reboot the machine for this OS to load. Once loaded, all local partitions can be mounted and all data saved to those partitions are accessible, even if Windows file system permissions have been assigned. All local access control lists (ACLs) will be bypassed and are rendered useless in such a scenario. The cost of such a solution? The operating system is free for the download. As for the 128MB thumbdrive, they cost around $10.

FYI: But . . . It's Only an MP3 Player!

Or is it? MP3 players are all the rage lately. Suddenly, everyone has to carry their entire CD collection on a player the size of an audio tape. Many people bring them to work, set them up on their desk, hook them up to a little computer speaker system, and enjoy music all day long while at work. There is nothing wrong with that activity on the surface . . . until we start to pay better attention to the device in question.

MP3 players mostly come in two versions. One comes with limited storage space–up to 1GB–and are usually equipped with some kind of internal flash memory chip. Then there are players that come with built-in mini hard drives, allowing up to 40GB of space for songs . . . or just about any other type of files. Remember, a song is nothing but a computer file with a specific format. But at the core, it is a computer file. And so is an internal confidential memo or a sensitive spreadsheet. Just computer files. Most if not all MP3 players come equipped with a USB port and are basically seen by a computer to which they are plugged as a removable hard drive.

In other words, it is conceivable that someone could come to work with an MP3 player under the guise of listening to some music, and could end up copying 40GB worth of confidential, company-owned data to the internal drive and never be suspected of doing anything illegal. It's only an MP3 player, right?

8

This being said, removable media has a place and a role to play in most companies. The point is not to condemn all use of removable computer media, just to present it as what it is: a valuable tool that can be turned into a potential threat to network security if not monitored and regulated properly.

Controlling Non-Company-Owned Removable Media

Network security used to be almost solely equated with perimeter security. In other words, if you could protect yourself from the outside threats, you won the battle. That is why many companies felt safe from threats by deploying firewalls and hardening all Internet-facing devices such as Web servers, routers, FTP servers, e-mail servers, and so forth.

Now that we know that most attacks actually originate from inside of the network, the importance of perimeter security is not as all-encompassing as it once was. To further illustrate this point, let's look at all the everyday items that have also contributed to making perimeter security become only *one* element of the overall network security strategy.

Cell phones now come with digital built-in cameras and full PDA capabilities. Yet, from the outside, and to the casual, unsuspecting user, they just look like a regular cell phone. But these devices are allowed daily into most companies and can be used to upload data, either as files or as screenshots taken with the built-in camera. Because they obviously have remote connectivity capabilities, they can also be used to transmit that information to an offsite contact.

PDAs are becoming more and more sophisticated. Personal Digital Assistants also come with plenty of storage space, wireless and blue tooth remote connectivity capabilities, and built-in cameras. The same issues we have with cell phones are duplicated here, including that they are small and therefore easy to conceal, and that they are perceived more as "gadgets" than spying tools.

Thumbdrives, as we saw, can contain complete operating systems and can be used to access data located on a local machine by bypassing all security measures such as ACL and encryption. They are small, easy to conceal, and inexpensive.

MP3 players are nothing but hard drives waiting to be filled with computer files, be they of the musical or sensitive variety. While on the topic of hard drives, many manufacturers now sell cheap solutions that feature a small, laptop-sized hard drive hooked up to a USB cable. These are roughly half the size of a CD case, and just as flat. They require no drivers for most modern operating systems, and are therefore extremely easy to install. Pretty much all it takes is to plug in the USB cable and wait a couple of seconds. From there, it is far too easy to simply fill them up with data. And with storage capacities of up to 250GB, that's a lot of sensitive data that can be pilfered.

This list is not exhaustive, nor is it meant to be. It is simply an effort to outline how important it is for the information security policy to include a section dealing with whether users—including vendors, contractors, and even visitors—are allowed to bring in removable media such as those we described in this section. While it may be unrealistic to tell employees, contractors, vendors, or visitors that they cannot have a PDA or a cell phone, many companies have now taken this stand and are enforcing it. Additionally, technical control can be implemented. These controls include disabling workstation and server USB and SCSI ports. Recently, software has been introduced that enforces removable media read and write access policies by user and by computer.

Let us now focus on how to secure the legitimate use of this technology.

Controlling Company-Owned Removable Media that Leaves Company Premises

The rule here is simple: No company-owned removable media should be allowed to leave the company premises unless it was previously authorized. Furthermore, all such authorized instances should be logged to create an audit trail.

There are two kinds of circumstances that fall under this rule: Those situations where the removable media will be regularly taken off the premises, and single-instance cases. For the former, in order to not flood the ISO with requests, a policy should be created that clearly states that the removable media are authorized to be taken offsite as long as they follow the specific procedures. While each instance does not require an individual authorization request, it should still result in individual log entries. A simple example of this would be the daily transfer of backup tapes to an offsite facility.

As for the individual situations that require transporting removable media outside of company facilities, they should, without exception, receive individual authorization prior to taking place. They should also result in individual entries in the appropriate log.

It is, as always, extremely important that all employees be trained on this topic. While the term "removable computer media" is a bit generic, it can conceivably be extended to include such equipment as company-provided laptop computers and PDAs, both of which can contain sensitive information and are easy to steal or lose. In other words, the management team must create a company culture in which users are aware that they are entrusted with potentially sensitive information. While many of us may take for granted that a laptop is "just a laptop," it should also be considered as the container for sensitive information, and as such, must be treated as a resource that should be protected.

Storing Removable Media

If it can potentially contain sensitive information, then it should be stored securely. The examples here range from backup tapes to archived data on tape, CD-R, DVD-R, and other removable media solutions. For the sake of simplicity, we will focus on backup tapes for the rest of this section.

Backup tapes should be stored at a remote location for safekeeping. That way, if a building where all the servers are located were to be completely destroyed, the tapes would be located somewhere else and be available to start the restore procedure.

A serious concern with backup tapes is theft or misappropriation. With that in mind, and remembering that removable media are easy to carry and conceal, it is imperative that wherever the tapes are actually stored, they be stored securely. Inside a locked room is the most basic requirement. That room should not have windows and should be equipped with a secure door and lock configuration. Access to that room should be limited to those authorized to gain access. Access to that room should also be logged, either manually or automatically. Some lock systems use a key that comes with an internal chip. When that key is used to open the door, the date and time, along with the identity of the key holder, are automatically logged.

Because of the importance of their guaranteed availability, backup tapes should always be protected from fire and other natural disasters. Most server rooms are equipped with sprinklers and/or additional fire-suppressing systems, which can harm tapes directly exposed to them. Traditionally, the recommendation is that tapes be stored inside a fireproof safe, itself located inside a locked room as described in the previous paragraph. Access to the safe should also be monitored, authorized, and logged.

If a tape is to be disposed of, its contents must be thoroughly destroyed so that it cannot be retrieved later by someone else.

IN PRACTICE: Management of Portable Storage Devices and Removable Media Policy

The goal of this policy is to regulate the use of portable storage devices.

The *objectives* of this policy are to:

- Control company-owned PSD or removable media.

- Disallow the use of non-company-owned PSD or removable media.

The *audience* is all users of information assets.

▶▶ CONTINUED ON NEXT PAGE

>> CONTINUED

TABLE 8.7 Sample Management of Portable Storage Devices and Removable Media Policy.

Section X:	[COMPANY] Information Security Policy	Effective Date:
Subsection	Communications and Operations Management	Change Control #:
Policy	Management of Portable Storage Devices and Removable Media	Approved By:
Objective	To regulate the use of portage storage devices and removable media.	
Purpose	To protect the confidentiality, integrity, and availability of data either stored on removable computer media, or potentially at risk of being copied to unauthorized removable computer media.	
Audience	The management of portable storage devices and removable media policy applies equally to individuals with authorized and nonauthorized access to information assets.	
Policy	• All company-owned removable media leaving the company premises must be authorized by the ISO and logged prior to actual removal. • All removable media shall be stored in a secured environment and protected from fire, water, and other environmental threats. • Employees, vendors, contractors, and visitors are not allowed to bring removable storage solutions inside company premises without prior written consent from the ISO.	
Exceptions	None	
Disciplinary Actions	Violation of this policy may result in disciplinary action, which may include termination for employees and temporaries; a termination of employment relations in the case of contractors or consultants; or dismissal for interns and volunteers. Additionally, individuals are subject to civil and criminal prosecution.	

8

Secure Reuse and Disposal of Media

The information security policy must include a section detailing the officially approved methods of removing information and discarding media that is no longer needed by the company. Some media are broken, some are obsolete, and some are simply replaced on a schedule. It is important to realize that the reason why some media is discarded does not matter: It still cannot just be thrown in the trash and be considered "securely discarded."

FYI: How Resilient Is that Media, Anyway?

A couple of years ago, a company shipped servers from its facilities in New York City to Western Europe. The servers were shipped by boat. Halfway across the Atlantic Ocean, the boat sank. It took several months to locate the boat, organize a 'rescue mission,' and finally get the servers out of the freezing, salty water in which they had been resting. Most people would probably assume that these servers were not able to function anymore. However, the company that owned the servers hired a third-party company located in California to see if it could retrieve some of the data that was stored on the servers' hard drives. That company took the contract and retrieved more than 60 percent of the data originally stored on those drives, even though they were immersed in cold, salty water for several months.

In other words, it is not safe to throw a hard drive in the trash just because it seems not to be functioning anymore. The data that is stored on defective drive can still be retrieved—and the confidentiality of that data is very much still at risk.

The key to secure disposal is to destroy the information. Destruction methods include physical destruction, high powered magnets, cremation, zeroization (overwriting each sector on each track of each platter of a hard drive with zeros), or randomization (overwriting all sectors with random data a specific number of times).

Remember, however, that media is not limited to digital media or computer-related media. It also includes paper—which should be shredded before it is thrown away—recordings, carbon paper, one-time-use printer ribbons, and so forth.

The information security policy should include a list of all media used in the company as compiled during the risk assessment, and should include one or more approved methods of destruction for each media type listed.

Outsourcing Media Removal

Some companies specialize in providing media removal services for organizations that do not wish to deal with the issue themselves. Contracting one of these third-party companies may seem like the "easy way out," but it still implies a range of security-related measures that need to be taken.

First of all, a due diligence report must be compiled on the company hired to provide the data removal service so it can be included in the chain of trust as a business partner. Such information as the company's reputation, how long it has been in business, its financial situation, its direct experience in the type of media destruction the company needs, and ownership details are all valid items that should be researched prior to contracting a third-company to handle the task of media removal and destruction.

Furthermore, all media must be secured inside the company until the contractor comes to remove it. For example, paper awaiting the shredding service should be placed in locked containers so that it cannot be retrieved before it is shredded.

When in Doubt, Check the Log

It is always recommended to log all important aspects of doing business. Media removal, whether handled internally or via a third-party contractor, should also be logged to create a valid audit trail.

No company wants to be in a situation in which it is uncertain whether sensitive financial data was indeed securely deleted. When in doubt, it should be as simple as looking up a log and finding the date, time, and identity of the employee/contractor who handled the task.

IN PRACTICE: Secure Reuse and Disposal of Media Policy

The goal of this policy is to protect make sure that media is properly reused and/or disposed.

The *objectives* of this policy are to:

- Commit to the secure reuse of media.
- Commit to the secure disposal of media.
- Create a system of accountability.

The *audience* is all users of information resources.

▶▶ CONTINUED ON NEXT PAGE

>> CONTINUED

TABLE 8.8 Sample Secure Reuse and Disposal of Media Policy.

Section X:	[COMPANY] Information Security Policy	Effective Date:
Subsection	Communications and Operations Management	Change Control #:
Policy	Secure Reuse and Disposal of Media	Approved By:
Objective	To ensure that confidentiality and integrity of data is not put at risk via the media disposal process.	
Purpose	The purpose of this policy is to ensure that all company-owned media is disposed of in a secure fashion.	
Audience	The secure reuse and disposal of media policy applies equally to all users of information resources.	
Policy	• All media no longer needed by the company must be disposed of securely. • All media slated for reuse must be securely sanitized. • If the removal of media is going to be outsourced, due diligence must be extended when selecting the business partner who will handle the task. • All disposed of media must be logged to create a valid audit trail.	
Exceptions	None	
Disciplinary Actions	Violation of this policy may result in disciplinary action, which may include termination for employees and temporaries; a termination of employment relations in the case of contractors or consultants; or dismissal for interns and volunteers. Additionally, individuals are subject to civil and criminal prosecution.	

Security of Media While in Transit

Making sure that media is secure while in transit directly impacts all three tenets of network security: confidentiality, integrity, and availability. If a tape is stolen, and access to the data is gained by an unauthorized user, confidentiality of that data is clearly compromised. Similarly, if a tape is stolen, and data on that tape is tampered with maliciously, integrity of that data is lost. Finally, if a tape is stolen, and a restore job is needed that requires that particular tape to be complete, data availability is threatened.

From that standpoint, it becomes obvious that particular attention must be paid to the security aspect of transporting media from one facility to another.

Only Authorized Couriers Need Apply

Generally, the Information Security Officer will be responsible for selecting and authorizing couriers to transport media from one location to another. Whether the process is handled by an in-house courier or a third-party company, they must be authorized to act as couriers. Furthermore, depending on the solution chosen, the ISO may also choose to design an identification method for the courier to prove that they are indeed authorized, especially if third-party contractors are used.

Instead of relying on the third-party company to provide its own identification method—with which most of your employees will not be familiar—consider designing an ID internally and distributing it only to those

---

FYI: Corporate Badges and Business Cards

Employees should be trained not to believe in business cards or shirts with official badges or embroidered company names. After all, those are very cheap and easy to duplicate and do not guarantee that the person who displays them actually is employed by that company. Employees should be trained to alert management when they doubt anyone's authenticity.

Unfortunately, that is not human nature, hence the need for training on this matter. For example, imagine a situation where a car alarm can be heard. A tow truck is driving past a group of ten people with a Mercedes hooked to the back. The alarm is coming from the Mercedes. Of those ten people, how many will simply think to themselves that some guy just got his Mercedes towed away? How many of those same ten people will wonder if some guy with a tow truck helped himself to the Mercedes?

We are conditioned to accept the obvious, because we are fundamentally trusting. This predisposition is potentially dangerous when it comes to network security. It only takes about ten minutes to make a stack of fake business cards with a cheap color laser printer.

8

third-party consultants authorized to transport media. This method features several advantages:

- Only couriers authorized by this company will have those credentials, as opposed to all couriers working for a third-party company having some form of ID from their own company, regardless of whether or not they were authorized by the company.

- When/if a new company is selected to replace the original contractor, the same IDs are used. Employees do not have to get used to new IDs and start the process anew.

- The exact IDs can be used in training, and since they are issued by the company, they are easier for employees to recognize.

Physically Protecting the Media During Transport

Media that is moved from one facility to another becomes exposed to more and/or different physical threats than if it had stayed in its original location. Case in point: How many times have you broken a glass that was safely stored in a cupboard? How many have you broken while washing dishes or emptying a dishwasher?

Therefore, all media must be packed in a way that protects it from whatever it is especially vulnerable to. Dropping a stack of paper on the floor never broke paper. Dropping a stack of hard drive on a cement floor, on the other hand, can be pretty harmful to the hard drives. And sprinkling water on either a stack or paper or a stack of hard drives will damage both. In other words, depending on what media is being transported, a risk assessment should be conducted to determine the measures that should be taken to physically protect the media for the duration of the transport.

Security Controls Related to Transporting Media

Compromise of media in transport potentially threatens all three tenets of network security. Therefore, it may not be surprising that the security controls deployed in such circumstances go from the obvious to controls that could appear in a spy movie.

Locked containers are a simple way to protect media. Clearly, if the media is locked inside a box, and that box is stolen, it is only a matter of time before the box is broken and the media is accessed. While this does not stop a dedicated hacker or thief, it is a first layer of protection that will stop a "casual" thief. Most people may not go through the hassle of planning a heist, but if a cash drawer is wide open in front of them and nobody is there to look at their actions, they might be tempted by the opportunity to line their pockets with someone else's cash. This is such a simple and cheap control that not using it makes little sense. We all know that real robbers can probably unlock most any commercial lock, but this does not stop us from locking our doors everyday when we leave the house. One key aspect—pun intended—of this control is that the courier should not have a key (or combination, or smart card, depending on the lock type) to the container, so that only the people sending and receiving the box should be able to open it. Similarly, the lock should be complex enough that it can't be opened with a toothpick and a paper clip.

Use tamper-evident locks/containers so that it is easy to identify if someone did attempt to gain access to the media while in transport.

Do not allow packages just to be "dropped off." Instead, require the courier to deliver the package to an actual person, and to have that person sign for the package. That way, there is an auditable log of the passing of the package from being the responsibility of the courier to being the responsibility of the company. This settles many issues, such as:

- The courier says that he delivered the container but did not.

- The courier did leave the container in the approved drop location, but someone else swiped it before the legitimate and authorized person could pick it up.

- The courier did leave the container, but not in the approved drop location, and it remains available for anyone to steal until it is finally located. It also means that, until it is located, it is not available and usable by the company, which can have productivity-related repercussions.

8

IN PRACTICE: Security of Media in Transit Policy

The goal of this policy is to make sure that media is protected through the transportation cycle.

The *objectives* of this policy are to:

- Require security controls

- Assign responsibilities

The *audience* is all users of information resources.

▶▶ CONTINUED ON NEXT PAGE

>> CONTINUED

TABLE 8.9 Sample Security of Media in Transit Policy.

Section X:	[COMPANY] Information Security Policy	Effective Date:
Subsection	Communications and Operations Management	Change Control #:
Policy	Security of Media in Transit	Approved By:
Objective	To secure media during pickup, transport, and delivery.	
Purpose	To ensure that confidentiality, integrity, and availability of data is not put at risk during transportation of media from one facility to another.	
Audience	The security of media in transit policy applies equally to all users of information resources.	
Policy	• Only authorized couriers should be used. The ISO will be responsible for the process of authorizing couriers. • Proper packaging methods and material must be used to protect the media during transport. • Appropriate security controls must be deployed for safe transport of all media.	
Exceptions	None	
Disciplinary Actions	Violation of this policy may result in disciplinary action, which may include termination for employees and temporaries; a termination of employment relations in the case of contractors or consultants; or dismissal for interns and volunteers. Additionally, individuals are subject to civil and criminal prosecution.	

Securing Data on Publicly Available Systems

Only unclassified information should ever be posted on a publicly available system. Even then, the information owner should authorize publication. In this situation, controls need to be implemented that protect the integrity of the information and the availability of the information system.

In other words, the focus is not on whether data should be placed on publicly-available systems or not, as much as it is accepting the fact that information will be placed on publicly-available systems, and that there is therefore a need to create an environment as safe as possible for this data.

Publishing Data and Respecting the Law

When information is made available on a publicly available system, the entity that publishes this information is also responsible for its content. Companies must create a policy that makes clear to employees that all material posted to such systems must fully comply with local, state, and federal law. Because this data is posted in the name of the company, the company is directly responsible for this material.

FYI: Copyrighted Material

Not all material is safe to post on a publicly available system. There is plenty of material out there that is of great quality, but is protected by copyright laws, and cannot therefore be reproduced unless prior licensing agreements have been accepted. Failure to do so would place the company in a situation where it could be sued.

Some years ago, a large computer company had so many Web servers that it forgot to monitor them all. One server was soon identified and targeted by unscrupulous people looking for free Web space. These people allegedly uploaded hundreds of different software titles, all copyrighted, to this server and made them available for free downloads. It took several weeks for this company to realize that one of its Web servers was being used to distribute pirated software. While this situation did not escalate beyond the embarrassment stage–the company finally discovered the site and acted on it before anyone else could–it remains a perfect example of how a company can expose itself to both criminal and civil prosecution by not keeping a tight reign over its publicly available systems.

The Need for Penetration Testing

Because each and every publicly available system is by default a potential target for a hacker, companies must make sure that those systems are as protected against malicious attacks. Penetration testing is highly recommended for publicly available systems. Penetration testing is a live test of the security defenses. Penetration testing subjects a system or device to real-world attacks. The goal of a pen test is to identify the extent to which a system can be compromised before the attack is identified and responded to.

IN PRACTICE: Publicly Available Systems Policy

The goal of this policy is to require that the integrity of all external facing systems is protected.

The *objectives* of this policy are to:

- Require appropriate authorizations prior to publication.

- Require controls to protect the information published on publicly available systems.

The *audience* is all users of external facing information resources.

TABLE 8.10 Sample Publicly Available Systems Policy.

Section X:	[COMPANY] Information Security Policy	Effective Date:
Subsection	Communications and Operations Management	Change Control #:
Policy	Publicly Available Systems	Approved By:
Objective	The purpose of this policy is to ensure that all company data published on public systems is first authorized for publication, and that it is not modified by unauthorized users.	
Purpose	To ensure that confidentiality and integrity of data is not threatened when data is published on public systems.	
Audience	The publicly available systems policy applies equally to all users of external facing information resources.	
Policy	• Only data that has been approved for publication by both the ISO and the data owner will be published on public systems. • Only data that is in full compliance with local law will be published on public systems. • Penetration testing must be performed by third-party consultants for all systems used by the company to publicly publish information.	
Exceptions	None	

▶▶ CONTINUED ON NEXT PAGE

▶▶ **CONTINUED**	
Disciplinary Actions	Violation of this policy may result in disciplinary action, which may include termination for employees and temporaries; a termination of employment relations in the case of contractors or consultants; or dismissal for interns and volunteers. Additionally, individuals are subject to civil and criminal prosecution.

Securing E-mail

The good news is that e-mail is an efficient business tool. The bad news is that basic e-mail is a very insecure way to communicate. Regardless, e-mail has become the most widely used application in the world. Organizations need to make policies that address the responsible use of e-mail, decide what classifications of information are appropriate to e-mail, and determine how best to implement protection controls.

When used in the context of a corporate environment, the rule is that e-mail should always be treated as a formal means of communication, whether it is used internally between employees of the same company, or with recipients from outside the company. Nothing should be committed to e-mail that wouldn't be appropriate in a letter featuring corporate letterhead.

Employees should be trained in this regard, and reminded that e-mails sent using the corporate e-mail solution involve the responsibility, and potentially the liability of the company.

Is E-mail Different than Other Forms of Communication?

Most people find that e-mail is more convenient than voice mail or faxes, and quicker than postal mail. And this can make it seem less formal than these other forms of communication. But e-mail follows many of the same "rules."

- Like faxes, letters, or phone calls, e-mail messages can be intercepted and read so they are not inherently secure.

- Letters and faxes may be considered legally binding documents under many circumstances. Under some circumstances, e-mail messages may be as well. When you send an e-mail message to a business associate or even to someone within your own business, be aware that commitments may be protected by law, and that the electronic trail your message leaves behind is practically impossible to erase.

- The federal E-Sign law, passed in 2000, states that "a signature, contract or record relating to [a] transaction may not be denied legal effect, validity, or enforceability solely because it is in electronic form."

■ When you write an e-mail, you should think about the content in the same way as when you write a letter or fax, or when you make a phone call.

Although many of the issues affecting e-mail are similar to those affecting other forms of communication, important differences do exist.

■ When you send an e-mail, the route that it takes in transit is unpredictable and relatively unregulated.

■ When you're talking to someone, you can clarify something that you say relatively easily. But it's difficult to reword an e-mail message after it has been sent.

■ Storing and retrieving e-mail is easy (and commonplace), so e-mails may well be more permanent than a phone call or fax.

■ It's almost impossible to know if anyone has read your e-mail in transit—at least with a letter, you can see if it has been opened!

E-mail is Transmitted in Clear Text E-mail is usually transmitted as clear text across the Internet, which is an unregulated, public network. Because e-mail messages going from one destination to another pass between multiple computers on their way, any information sent that hasn't been properly encrypted may be read by third parties, resulting in a breach of confidentiality.

Outgoing Attachments May Contain Hidden Information Documents sent as e-mail attachments might contain more information than the sender intended to share. The files created by many office programs contain hidden information about the creator of the document, and may even include some content that has been reformatted, deleted, or hidden.

Keep this in mind if:

■ You recycle documents by making changes and sending them to new recipients (e.g., a boilerplate contract or a sales proposal).

■ You use a document created by another person. In programs such as Microsoft Office, the document might list the original person as the author.

■ You use a feature for tracking changes. Be sure to accept or reject changes, not just hide the revisions.

Incoming Attachments May Contain a Dangerous Payload File attachments to e-mail messages can be a huge e-mail security risk because they can include computer viruses and other malicious scripts.

Every year, a vast amount of money is lost, in the form of support costs and equipment workload, due to hoaxes sent by e-mail. A hoax may be a fake virus warning or false information of a political or legal nature, and often borders on criminal mischief.

Some hoaxes ask recipients to take action that turns out to be damaging—deleting supposedly malicious files from their local computer, sending uninvited mail, randomly boycotting organizations for falsified reasons, or defaming an individual or group by forwarding the message on.

We Can Be Our Own Worst Enemy

The three most common mistakes that impact the confidentiality of e-mail are sending the right e-mail to the wrong person, choosing "reply all" instead of "reply," and using "forward" inappropriately.

It is easy to mistakenly send e-mail to the wrong address. This is especially true with e-mail clients that finish addresses for the user based on the first three or four characters entered. All users must be made aware of this, and must pay strict attention to the e-mail address entered in the To: field, along with the CC and BCC fields when used.

The consequence of choosing "reply all" instead of "reply" can be significant. The best case scenario is embarrassment. In the worst cases, confidentiality is violated by distributing information to those who do not have a "need to know." In regulated sectors such as healthcare and banking, violating the privacy of patients and/or clients is against the law.

Forwarding has similar implications. Assume that two people have been e-mailing back and forth using the "reply" function. Their entire conversation can be found online. Now suppose that one of them decides that something in the last e-mail is of interest to a third person and forwards that e-mail to her. In reality, what that person just did was forward the entire thread of e-mails that had been exchanged between the two original people. This may well have not have been the person's intent and may also violate the privacy of the original correspondent.

Compromising the E-mail Server

In addition to protecting the information, the information system needs special protection from the obvious breaches of confidentiality and integrity. As dependence upon e-mail increases, availability of the e-mail server becomes more critical. E-mail servers need to be protected against Denial of Service attacks.

Relay Abuse and Blacklisting The role of an e-mail server is to process and relay e-mail. The default posture for many e-mail servers is to process and relay *any* mail sent to the server. This is known as "open mail relay." The ability to relay mail through a server can (and often is) taken advantage of by those who benefit from the illegal use of the resource. Spammers conduct Internet searches for e-mail servers configured to allow relay. Once they locate an open relay server, they use it for distributing spam. The spam e-mail appears to come from the company whose e-mail server was misappropriated. Spammers often use this technique to hide their identity. This is not only an embarrassment but can also result in legal and productivity ramifications.

In a response to the deluge of spam, blacklisting is becoming a standard practice. Blacklisting is a process of actively monitoring the Internet for reports of e-mail sources sending unsolicited commercial e-mail (spam). Many Internet Service Providers and independent organizations then use these blacklist reports as a filter applied to their inbound mail servers to deny receipt of e-mail. Simply, the receiving e-mail server checks the incoming e-mails against a list of blacklisted servers, and when a match is found, the e-mail is denied. Obviously, no legitimate organization wants this to happen to it and must take steps to ensure that its servers do not behave in this manner.

IN PRACTICE: E-mail and E-mail Systems Policy

The *objectives* of this policy are to:

- Assign e-mail risk assessment responsibilities.
- Assign e-mail standards development responsibility.
- Assign control implementation, maintenance, and monitoring responsibility.
- Require all users to be trained of the secure and proper use of e-mail communications.

The *audience* is all users of e-mail and e-mail systems.

TABLE 8.11 E-Mail and E-Mail Systems Policy.

Section X:	[COMPANY] Information Security Policy	Effective Date:
Subsection	Communications and Operations Management	Change Control #:
Policy	E-mail and E-mail Systems Security	Approved By:
Objective	To assess the security risks associated with the use of electronic mail as a business tool.	

▶▶ CONTINUED ON NEXT PAGE

▶▶ CONTINUED	
Purpose	The purpose of this policy is to require that all the organization assess the risks associated with e-mail.
Audience	The e-mail and e-mail systems security policy applies equally to all e-mail and e-mail systems.
Policy	• The office of information security in conjunction with the department of technology is responsible for analyzing the risks associated with e-mail and e-mail systems. The office of information security is responsible for creating e-mail security standards. The department of information technology is responsible for implementing, maintaining, and monitoring appropriate controls. • E-mail containing information classified as sensitive or confidential information must conform to [Company] encryption standards as defined by the office of information security. • All users will be trained in the proper use of e-mail.
Exceptions	None
Disciplinary Actions	Violation of this policy may result in disciplinary action, which may include termination for employees and temporaries; a termination of employment relations in the case of contractors or consultants; or dismissal for interns and volunteers. Additionally, individuals are subject to civil and criminal prosecution.

8

Summary

This security domain is all about day-to-day operational activities and their impact on the security of information assets and information systems. We started with documentation of standard operating procedures. We discussed that well-written standard operating procedures (SOPs) provide direction, improve communication, reduce training time, and improve work consistency.

We saw that, while change is inevitable, it must be controlled. We were reminded that the worst time to start planning a response to an incident is when it has already occurred. A well-documented incident response program is critical to the continued success of an organization.

We looked at various ways that information can be compromised, including malware, portable storage devices, and attacks on publicly available systems. We examined the need for an organized backup and restore process for the purpose of recovery. We reviewed the importance of unique confidentiality, integrity, and availability considerations in regard to e-mail communication.

Throughout the chapter, we focused on policies and procedures required to create and maintain a secure operational environment.

Test Your Skills

MULTIPLE CHOICE QUESTIONS

1. Which of the following is true about documenting standard operating procedures?

    A. it promotes business continuity

    B. the documentation should be officially authorized before it is approved

    C. both A and B

    D. neither A nor B

2. If a standard operating procedure includes multiple decision-making steps, which documentation method is most effective?

    A. simple

    B. hierarchical

    C. graphic

    D. flowchart

3. What is the first step in the change management process?

    A. a formal risk assessment

    B. the ISO must authorize the change

    C. the system owner and the data owner must authorize the change

    D. the CEO must authorize the change

4. Which of the following would you generally NOT include in a change control log?

    A. who made the change

    B. why the change was made

    C. cost of the change

    D. date and time of the change

5. Prior to implementing a change that has the potential to impact business processing, what should happen?

   A. the system should be backed up

   B. the change should be thoroughly tested

   C. a rollback or recovery plan should be developed

   D. all of the above

6. Who should assign severity levels to incidents?

   A. executive management

   B. help desk

   C. users

   D. consultants

7. When an incident occurs:

   A. the business should close

   B. all computers should be shut off

   C. all doors should be locked

   D. it should be reported immediately using a defined mechanism

8. When it comes to incidents and severity levels, which of the following is true? Choose all that apply:

   A. All incidents have the same severity level: important.

   B. Each incident has a different severity level and cannot be classi-fied by degree of severity.

   C. Executive management should be involved with all incidents.

   D. Incidents' severity levels have no bearing on when the incident should be reported.

9. Who should draft the incident reporting program?

   A. the CEO

   B. the CTO

   C. the head of IT

   D. the ISO

10. Employees should report what kind of incidents?

   A. those that are confirmed

   B. those that are suspected

   C. both A and B

   D. neither A nor B

8

11. Which of these is NOT a goal of incident response and recovery?

    A. containment

    B. eradication

    C. recovery

    D. procurement

12. Who should test the network for security weaknesses?

    A. all users

    B. employees and consultants who are explicitly authorized by management

    C. business partners

    D. hackers

13. Which of the following is NOT a part of a malware defense in-depth strategy?

    A. security awareness

    B. prevention controls

    C. detection controls

    D. portable storage devices

14. Which of the following are parts of an antivirus solution?

    A. the engine and definition files

    B. the handler

    C. the Trojan

    D. the virus

15. What is true about hoax e-mail?

    A. It is less dangerous than virus-infected e-mail.

    B. It is as dangerous as virus-infected e-mail.

    C. It contains malicious code.

    D. It contains malicious attachments.

16. Generally speaking, how often should the restore process be tested?

    A. hourly

    B. daily

    C. weekly or monthly depending upon the criticality

    D. annually

17. Which of these devices would be considered a Portable Storage Device?

    A. IPod

    B. PDA

    C. Laptop

    D. all of the above

18. Employees should not be allowed to leave company premises with company-owned removable media unless they have received proper authorization from:

    A. the CEO

    B. the ISO

    C. their direct manager

    D. their department manager

19. A workstation is being donated to a non-profit organization. What should be done to the hard drive?

    A. the drive should be either thoroughly sanitized or removed and destroyed

    B. nothing

    C. confidential files should be deleted

    D. the drive should be renamed

20. When transporting media, care should be taken to:

    A. protect the media from human hazards

    B. protect the media from physical hazards

    C. protect the media from environmental hazards

    D. all of the above

EXERCISES

Exercise 8.1: Operating Procedures Documentation

1. Standard operating procedures are not restricted to use in information technology and information security. Cite five examples where SOP documentation is important.

2. Choose a procedure that you are familiar enough with that you can write SOP documentation.

3. Decide which format you are going to use. Write one paragraph explaining your reasons.

4. Create the documentation.

Exercise 8.2: Incident Response and Malware

1. Your roommate just called you and said all kinds of weird new applications are appearing on your computer. He also can't find the song he just downloaded a few minutes earlier. Write one or two paragraphs telling what you think happened.

2. Your roommate wants to know what to do. Complete the grid below by detailing your recommended action.

Process	Action
Containment	
Eradication	
Recovery	
Analysis	

Exercise 8.3: Information System Backup and Removable Media

1. You store all of your schoolwork on your laptop. Write one or two paragraphs about what would happen if your laptop crashed, was misplaced, or stolen.

2. The information is really critical to your success at school. Without it, you probably would not be able to complete your graduation requirements. You decide that perhaps you should begin backing up your data. Research your options and answer the following questions.

   • How are you going to back up your data?
   • How much will it cost?
   • Where are you going to store the copy?
   • How often are you going to update the backup?
   • What do you need to do to test the restore/recovery process?
   • How often will you test the restore/recovery process?

Exercise 8.4: Securing Publicly Available Systems

1. Launch your favorite Web site.

2. Carefully review the site. Make a list of any information you find that might be considered confidential or sensitive or could be used in footprinting.

3. View the source data. If you are using Internet Explorer, from the Menu Bar choose View, Source. Review the source code for sensitive or confidential information.

4. Download a copy of Sam Spade (**www.samspade.org**). *Note:* Always have an up-to-date virus program active before downloading any files. Install Sam Spade for Windows. Use the Web crawler tool to see if you can find any additional information about the organization.

Exercise 8.5: E-mail Hoaxes

1. The U.S. Department of Energy-Office of CyberSecurity maintains a Web site dedicated to e-mail hoaxes. Access this site at **http:// hoaxbusters.ciac.org**.

2. On the site, find answers to the following questions:
   - How do you calculate the cost of a hoax e-mail?
   - How do you recognize a hoax e-mail?
   - What is a Malicious Code hoax?
   - What is an Urban Myth?

PROJECTS

Project 8.1: Secure Disposal of Media

1. You are the ISO for a statewide company called ABC Toys. Your company is spending a lot of money in research and development to create new gizmos that can be sold to other companies to market. Because innovations are the lifeblood of the company, data confidentiality is a high priority for ABC Toys. Write a policy detailing what must happen to printed documents produced by the company. Help yourself in this process by including some of these items:

   Will printed media disposal be handled by a third party or by the company?

   Will all printed media be disposed of the same way?

   How often will the media disposal process take place?

   What will happen to the printed documents in between disposal sessions?

   Who will be ultimately responsible for overseeing this process?

2. The company burns a lot of CDs as an archiving solution. However, because of version control problems that can arise from such a practice, it is decided that CDs older than six months will be discarded. Write a policy that addresses this situation.

3. The company has decided to replace all computers currently serving as workstations in the coming twelve months. ABC plans to donate the hard drive from each replaced workstation to a local charity. Do you need to write a policy dictating what must be done to these hard drives, or is the policy you created in Step 2 applicable? If not, revise the policy.

4. One of the branch offices of ABC Toys was acquired from another company. Consequently, this office has always had a different culture than the rest of ABC Toys. You decide to visit this office and discover that employees throw away everything they don't need into trashcans that are located outside in the back of the building. Create a PowerPoint presentation to deliver to the branch employees explaining why the trashcans are not secure, and what could happen if someone found company printouts in those unsecured trashcans. (*Hint:* Research "dumpster diving.")

Project 8.2: Malicious Software

1. You have been tasked with recommending anti-malware controls for ABC Toys. Since your organization has five locations, you want centrally managed solutions. You network is a Windows 2003 domain. You have a mix of Windows XP, Linux, and Macintosh workstations. Your messaging platform is Microsoft Exchange 2003. Your firewall is a Cisco Pix. Begin with making a list of the type of detective and preventative controls you believe are appropriate.

2. Research available options. Be sure to consider cost, interoperability, support, and management.

3. Based upon your research, develop a proposal to be submitted to the CEO, clearly articulating your recommendations.

Project 8.3: Security of Media in Transit

1. As the ISO for ABC Toys, you are responsible for ensuring the security of backup tapes as they are transported to your designated backup recovery site. You need make sure that this transfer of backup tapes—and therefore sensitive corporate information—is handled securely. The first decision you need to make is whether this transfer will be handled via an in-house courier, or a third-party contractor. For increased convenience, you decide to go with the latter. Outline the risks that can potentially be attached to this decision and what must be done to mitigate those risks.

2. You hire Best Way Transport to be your courier. One of your employees reports an incident that took place where the courier did not log in the tapes, but instead dropped it at the reception desk and took off. What should you do?

3. You want to make sure that the tapes are safe both from prying fingers/eyes and from damage during transport. You plan to contact Best Way Transport and ask for a container to be used for your tapes. Research and recommend the type of container you would like Best Way to provide.

4. To further increase security for the transport of your backup tapes, you decide that the courier should be wearing an official badge that uniquely identifies him. How would you issue this badge? What would prevent it from being counterfeited?

Project 8.4: Securing Data on Publicly Available Systems

1. You own DMJ Marketing. DMJ creates Web sites for its clients. IT Online has selected DMJ to create a new Web site for a company. The site will provide information about IT-related topics. The information that will be displayed comes from multiple sources: Some is proprietary to the company, some was found on other commercial Web sites, some was found on Web sites that belong to the open source movement. DMJ is not sure if this is legal and has asked you to find out if copyright laws are applicable. DMJ is also looking for guidance on how it can best protect its own proprietary information. What would you tell DMJ?

2. IT Online also hired DMJ Marketing to create an online shopping portal for a company. The portal consists of a front-end Web server and a back-end application server. Prior to go-live, you recommend that IT Online should hire a third-party consultant to run a penetration test against both the Web server and the application system. IT Online is not happy about the expense and argues that DMJ should be conducting the pen test. Write a memo explaining why DMJ should not conduct the test. Be sure to stress the importance of running the penetration test in the first place.

Project 8.5: Securing the Electronic Mail Solution

1. E-mailWiz, Inc., is a company that specializes in setting up e-mail solutions for its customers. You work as a security consultant for E-mailWiz. One of your clients recently commissioned a new mail server to be deployed in the coming week. You recommend that this

8

client hire you as a trainer for both the staff and the members of the IT department. You are meeting with the client this afternoon. Create an outline of the talking points you are going to use regarding the risks of e-mail and benefit of training.

2. The client is sold on the training, but not on your idea that it should monitor e-mails sent by its employees. How would you respond? Be prepared to present your answer to the class.

3. In preparing the training, you decide to research instances where individuals lost their jobs due to e-mail violations. You open a Web browser and point it to your favorite search engine. You run a search for these terms together: *+e-mail +mistake +fired*. Read the first ten articles you find that are related to someone being fired over an e-mail gaffe. Create a list of what the "offenses" were that got those people fired.

4. Create a list of five rules that employees should be aware of when writing an e-mail from a corporate network. Use of examples is recommended.

Case Study

How does a company react when it realizes that some sensitive data was stolen? What are their priorities once the incident is discovered? How do they communicate the news to the public? Let's look at a real-life case and examine those—and other—questions.

On April 13, 2005, LexisNexis revealed that criminals may have breached computer files containing the personal information of 310,000 people since January 2003. The company said the fraud did not involve hacking but rather improper use of IDs and passwords. The next day Kurt Sanford, President of Lexis-Nexis, testified at a Senate Judiciary hearing. Senator Dianne Feinstein asked Sanford about whether LexisNexis had security breaches before 2003 that they haven't disclosed. Sanford replied that, "I believe there may have been a security breach in LexisNexis prior to 2003 that involved personal data." No details were provided.

In a press release from LexisNexis dated April 12, 2005, the company announced that based upon an in-depth analysis they have concluded that "unauthorized persons, primarily using IDs and passwords of legitimate customers may have acquired personal-identifying information such as Social Security numbers or Driver's License numbers of individuals in the United States in some 59 incidents. LexisNexis is notifying all individuals whose information may have been compromised."

Industry analysts have speculated that these incidents would have gone unreported if not for the California Security Breach Information Act (SB 1386). SB 1386 mandates the public disclosure of computer security breaches in which confidential information of any California resident may have been compromised. SB 1386 went into effect July 1, 2003. Many in Congress are advocating for a national version of the California law.

1. What happened?

2. How did the attackers gain access to the data?

3. Do you agree that the company should notify all potential victims?

4. What would you do if you received this type of notification?

5. Do you support national legislation modeled after SB 1386?

Chapter | 9

Access Control

Chapter Objectives

After reading this chapter and completing the exercises, you will be able to do the following:

- Apply the concepts of default deny, need-to-know, and least privilege.
- Secure user accounts throughout the employee lifecycle.
- Understand secure authentication.
- Protect systems from risks associated with remote access and telecommuting environments.
- Monitor and log all access-related activities and events.
- Develop policies to support access control to information assets.

Introduction

The ninth section of the ISO 17799 is dedicated to Access Control. What could be more fundamental than controlling who has access to information? This domain contains some of the broadest ranging concepts in information security: deny all, least privilege, and need-to-know. These concepts provide the basis of an organization's security posture. Supporting these concepts are user account, authentication, and password management.

The Access Control domain extends beyond the boundaries of the internal network; it also includes access to portable devices, mobile commuting, and telecommuting. Organizations have the dual task of providing multiple methods of secure access while simultaneously denying access to unauthorized users. At each entry point, specific controls must be implemented. Organizations must audit and monitor access to information assets and information systems to be altered to potential security violations.

In this chapter, we will focus on user access to information. We will cover a spectrum of users, ranging from system administrators to telecommuters. We will develop policies that guide user behavior, define physical environments, and control access to resources.

What Is a Security Posture?

What do we mean by *security posture*? A security posture is the organizational attitude toward security that is reflected in its default position. The two fundamental postures are secure (default deny) and reactive (default permit). Every access control decision is based upon the organization's security posture.

To Deny All or Not To Deny All ... That Is the Question

Did you know that prior to the release of the Microsoft™ Windows 2003 operating systems™, the security posture of all Microsoft operating systems was permit all? This means that, right out of the box, organizations were implementing unsecured systems. Very often, they weren't even aware of how vulnerable the systems actually were. While this had been a major complaint in the technology community, it is important to remember that Microsoft was responding to the market demands of interoperability and ease of use. This model supported the business requirements of "ease of use" and "productivity above all." Security was barely a consideration.

The shift from mainframe computing to the client/server model and the explosive growth in the uses of technology coupled with increasing awareness of vulnerabilities created a shift in the market. Organizations became more security conscious and began to demand more secure products from their vendors. Microsoft responded by turning 180° from a state of "default permit" to the more appropriate security posture of "default deny." *Default deny* (also referred to as *deny all*) means that access is unavailable until a rule, control list, or setting is modified to allow access. In Windows 2003, this not only affected the default state of operating system access control lists, but also which application services were included in a default operating system installation as well as how these default services were configured.

Just as it is better to start a running race with a posture that supports a quick take-off, it is far better to start a security program with a posture that supports securing information. So common sense would dictate that we should always begin in the most secure state possible, which is no access, or default deny. From this posture, we can then begin to define reasons for and methods of access.

Least Privilege to Perform Business Activities

Again, there is an old model that must be torn down before we can put ourselves into the right posture. The old model went something like this: If a user needs access to one folder, give her access to the entire drive. This way we won't have to come back over and over to escalate privilege. It is important to view this old model through the lens of what was most important at the time, productivity and efficiency. Fortunately, users finally realized that if we leave security out of the picture, the cost to both efficiency and productivity will be far greater, due to the disruption caused by breaches in security.

There is a balance to be achieved. Security cannot be so restrictive as to stop the wheels of business from turning. Organizations are not in business to be secure after all; they are in business to accomplish the mission of the organization. But organizations needed to realize that security plays a major role in accomplishing that mission, even though it is not the mission itself.

Least privilege means that a user is given the least amount of access required to perform the functions of his job or role, and no more. This is not always convenient. However, when balanced correctly with the need for productivity, it is the most effective posture considering the nature of the Internet and the whole of our computer-centered business environment.

If you are a teller in a bank, you have no need for access to customer mortgage information. Likewise, if you are the member of the Information Technology department whose job it is to manage printers, you do not need access to logon account management functions. By maintaining the least privilege principle, we continue to support the best possible posture for a sound information security principle.

Do You Need to Know, or Just Want to Know?

This brings us to the third control principle, namely the "need-to-know." *Need-to-know* means having a demonstrated and authorized reason for being granted access to information. There are two sides or two protections gained by exercising this principle: (1) the organization is protected by having the fewest number of people with knowledge critical to its operations and (2) individual users are protected from knowing more than they should, thereby reducing their liability to the absolute minimum as a natural extension of their job function. Though it is in direct opposition to our natural curious nature, in business it is best to build the need-to-know principle into the culture of any organization.

How Do We Know Who Needs What?

This is where we tie up some of the different concepts discussed thus far in this book. Earlier we discussed the three main models of access control:

- Mandatory Access Control (MAC): Data is classified and people are given clearance according to the sensitivity of information.

- Discretionary Access Control (DAC): Data owners decide who should have access to what information.

- Role-Based Access Control (RBAC): Access is based on positions (roles) within an organization.

We also discussed classification models, including:

- Top Secret, Secret, and Confidential: Generally used in the public sector.

- Sensitive, Confidential, and Public: Generally used in the private sector.

Once we have decided our access and classification models, we can properly apply the foundational principles through our access controls policies. For example: If I have a Top Secret clearance, I may be granted access to Top Secret information. However, access assignments are tempered by both a demonstrated need-to-know and least privilege to accomplish the tasks. When using DAC and RBAC, access principles provide information owners with the guidance necessary to make secure access assignments.

Who Decides Who Needs What?

This seems an easy question to answer, and it is. The challenge is in making sure the policy is adhered to. System or information owners must create the access rules. Other people, such as an Information Security Officer, are normally involved in the process, but ultimately the rules are created by the liable parties. Simply put, those with the most to lose make the rules.

It is irresponsible for any information owner to leave the creation of access rules to any person or persons with no liability stake. It is also an unfair burden to place on those without the authority to enforce policies.

Consider for a moment the law firm of Smith and Jones. This firm specializes in medical malpractice litigation. As you can imagine, the information the firm works with is very sensitive and confidential. Professional ethics dictate that all client-attorney exchanges of information are protected. An information leak could not only damage a case but could leave them personally liable to breaches of confidentiality. In this case, we would consider Mr. Jones and Ms. Smith to be information owners. They would be the ones to decide who should have access to information and what those individuals should be able to do with it. Whenever they take on a new case, Smith and Jones confer with the network administrator. The network administrator creates a new set of folders with the appropriate access rights. At the completion of the case, the network administrator is instructed to archive the information to CD and securely remove the network files. The CDs are stored in a bank vault for safekeeping.

IN PRACTICE: Access Control Policy

The goal of this policy is to ingrain the key access control principles in the culture of the organization. This policy is applicable to organizations of all sizes and types.

The *objectives* of this policy are to:

- Serve the access control principles of least privilege, need-to-know, and default deny.
- Assure access control is aligned with information classification policies.
- Maintain access control through organizational changes such as promotions and terminations.
- Ensure access control rules are created by liable parties with authority.
- Require periodic review of access control.

The *audience* is the entire organization.

TABLE 9.1 Sample Access Control Policy.

Section X:	[COMPANY] Information Security Policy	Effective Date:
Subsection	Access Control Policy	Change Control #:
Policy	Access Control Criteria	Approved By:
Objective	In support of information security, [Company] will create access controls to serve the concepts of default deny, need-to-know, and least privilege.	
Purpose	The purpose of this policy is to define access controls to information systems and resources for [Company].	
Audience	This policy applies to all individuals granted access privileges to any [Company] information resources.	
Policy	• Default access privileges will be set to "deny all" prior to any specific permissions being granted. • Access will be given that is consistent with security levels and classifications. • Access privileges shall be granted on the basis of specific business need (need-to-know basis). • Access privileges shall be restricted to the minimal amount required for business need (least privilege basis).	

▶▶ CONTINUED ON NEXT PAGE

▶▶ CONTINUED	
	• The authority to grant access to [Company] information resources will be provided by the information owner. Access rules for each system will be developed by the ISO and system owner. • Access control privileges should be reviewed at least once a year by the information owner.
Exceptions	None
Disciplinary Actions	Violation of this policy may result in disciplinary action, which may include termination for employees and temporaries; a termination of employment relations in the case of contractors or consultants; or dismissal for interns and volunteers. Additionally, individuals are subject to civil and criminal prosecution.

Managing User Access

Now that we have defined the issues surrounding access controls, we must address how users are given access to organizational information. There are many questions to answer in addressing this function. How will user accounts be created? Who will create them? How will this function be logged? What happens when users change positions or leave the organization? How will we treat those whose accounts have special privilege? How will we ensure that each person's user account is unique within the organization?

Our user access management policy must answer all of these questions.

One to Authorize, Another to Implement, and Another to Keep Watch

User access management transcends departmental boundaries. Critical to successful user access management is the involvement of and communication between the Human Resources (HR) department, the Information Technology (IT) department, and the Information Security Officer, as shown in Figure 9.1.

User Access Management

User accounts are the first target of a hacker who has gained access to an organization's network. Diligent care must be used when designing procedures for creating accounts and granting access to information. Word of mouth is not the way to go. This function should be one of the more strictly controlled functions of user management.

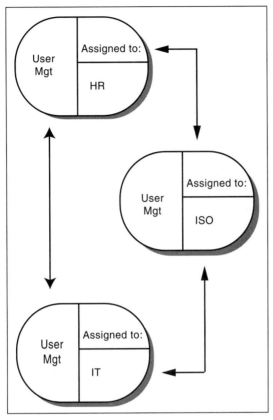

FIGURE 9.1 A successful user access management model.

The first point of contact for a new employee is generally the Personnel or Human Resources department. Human Resources should be tasked with the responsibility of generating the initial paperwork (request form) that will culminate with a user account being created and access rights assigned. The request form should include demographic information, role, access, and equipment requirements. The request form should then be routed to the appropriate management or supervisory personnel for authorization.

Depending upon the level of access being granted, the Information Security Officer may also need to approve the account. After authorization, the form is routed to the IT department or the department responsible for creating new user accounts. No privileges should ever be granted until authorization is complete.

Within the department responsible for user account management, there must be a position accountable for all aspects of user accounts such as creating, modifying, and deleting those accounts. This can either be one dedicated person, or several people. The goal is to be able to trace events back to the accountable person. This accountability can be assured by the process of logging activity. It is preferable that this logging process be automated and operates in the background. A separate person or department should be required to regularly review all of the activity related to user account management.

Promotions, Terminations, and Other Changes

Changes in position are another area where HR and IT need to work closely together. Strictly from a productivity standpoint, it is important to have procedures in place to address promotions, lateral moves, or demotions within the company. If my job/role changes and my access doesn't, I may not be able to perform my new job as I still have access rights associated with my old job. Conversely, for the sake of security, access rights associated with the old position may no longer be appropriate and need to be revoked.

Layoffs and terminations present yet another challenge. Formal procedures must exist between the HR and IT departments to communicate all personnel changes expediently. There must be a mechanism for disabling accounts should relations end between the organization and any of its employees. The best case scenario is that HR alerts IT prior to termination. If that is not possible, then IT should be notified as soon as possible. Unfortunately, HR departments are often understaffed and this communication falls through the cracks. In response to this known problem, IT can be proactive. An effective mechanism for verification of accounts is a regular report from the IT department to the HR department containing a list of user names that have not been used in a predetermined period of time. This will allow the HR department to verify employment status and direct the deletion of accounts for people who may have left the organization. The last thing any organization wants is to have fired an unruly employee only to leave his account active and ripe for compromise. This is not uncommon, and therefore even more important that our policy accounts for it.

With Privilege Comes Responsibility

Every organization has employees who require user accounts with special privileges. For example, by the nature of their position Systems Administrators must have elevated privileges. The creation of accounts with special privilege must be subject to a higher level of control and authorization.

Generally, a senior person in the IT or IS departments is allowed to authorize the creation of special privilege (administrative) accounts. This authority may also reside with the Information Security Officer. Accounts with special privileges should be monitored and audited for use and misuse.

Special privilege accounts should be used only when the activity being performed requires the special privilege. There is no need to use this type of account to perform routine activities such as checking e-mail, writing reports, performing research on the Internet, and other activities for which a basic user account will suffice. Why is this important? Consider this: Viruses, worms, and other malicious code will run in the security context of the logged-in user. So, if I am logged in as a system administrator and my computer is infected with a virus, then the virus has administrative privilege as well. To address this very real risk, every person with a special privilege account should also have a basic user account with which to perform duties that do not require escalated privileges.

IN PRACTICE: User Access Management Policy

The goal of this policy is to establish a framework for both user and administrative account management throughout the lifecycle of the account.

The *objectives* of this policy are to:

- Control the creation, modification, and deletion of user access accounts.
- Ensure account management functions are closely monitored and periodically audited.
- Ensure a formal process, including documentation, is in place for account management functions.
- Ensure accounts with special privilege are also subject to special controls.

The *audience* is the entire organization.

TABLE 9.2 Sample User Access Management Policy.

Section X:	[COMPANY] Information Security Policy	Effective Date:
Subsection	Access Control	Change Control #:
Policy	User Access Management	Approved By:
Objective	In support of information security, a formal documented process for granting access to information systems is required.	
Purpose	The purpose of this policy is to protect and maintain the security of access to the organization's information resources through the complete lifecycle of the user.	

▶▶ CONTINUED ON NEXT PAGE

9

Audience	This policy applies to all individuals granted access privileges to any [COMPANY] Information Resources.
Policy	• All privileges shall be granted only with formal written authorization provided to the Information Technology Department from Human Resources by the Information Owner. No privileges shall be granted until authorization is complete.
	• An authorized member of the Information Technology department staff will create the user account.
	• All users will be given unique user IDs.
	• Formal records of all access rights granted for each system shall be maintained by the Information Technology department.
	• Human Resources must notify the IT department in writing whenever a user changes positions. Access rights will then be modified by an authorized member of the Information Technology department. Modifications must be approved by the information owner.
	• Human Resources must notify the IT department in writing immediately when a user leaves the organization. The account will be disabled for a period of three months and then deleted.
	• All user-ID creation, deletion, and privilege change activity performed by systems administrators and others with administrative access should be securely logged and periodically reviewed by management.
	• The Information Technology department will provide Human Resources a weekly report of users who have not logged in for the last fourteen days. Human Resources will review the report and notify the Information Technology department of any changes that need to be made in regard to user accounts.
	• All users who require administrative privileges will be assigned two accounts; one with administrative privileges and one with basic user rights. Administrative accounts are only to be used for administrative activities. All other activities shall be done using the basic user account.

» CONTINUED ON NEXT PAGE

▶▶ CONTINUED	
	• Administrative privileges will be restricted to those directly responsible for system management and/or information security. All administrative accounts must be approved by the Office of the Information Security Officer. • Privileged access rights shall be reviewed monthly to make sure that all are authorized and remain appropriate and that no unauthorized privileges have been gained.
Exceptions	None
Disciplinary Actions	Violation of this policy may result in disciplinary action, which may include termination for employees and temporaries; a termination of employment relations in the case of contractors or consultants; or dismissal for interns and volunteers. Additionally, individuals are subject to civil and criminal prosecution.

Keeping Passwords Secure

Our perspective thus far in this chapter has been focused on the organizational challenges and responsibilities regarding access to information resources. All the controls in the world are useless if the end users don't hold up their end of the bargain.

The most crucial bit of information every user is entrusted with is his unique and hopefully secret authentication credential, the humble password. Our password use policy will require adherence to certain standards as well as mandate specific behaviors.

Don't Ask, Don't Tell

All users are required to keep their passwords confidential. This means they are not allowed, under any circumstances, to share their password with any other person. This also means they are not allowed to write their password on a yellow sticky note and affix it to their computer monitor. Nor are they allowed to name desktop application icons with the user name and password used to access the application.

There are many reasons people should maintain unique passwords, and they are all related to protection. Not just protection of information, but also of the password owners. Since all user activities are theoretically subject to accountability, which means that they can be traced to their original source, users must make sure that they actually performed the activities carried out under their unique user ID and password. Whether it is the result of a malicious act or the more common accident, any compromise of organizational information must be traceable to its source. So, two or more people who share credentials potentially open themselves to liability on either side of the equation. They may be blamed for things they didn't do.

Protecting the Key

Most organizations use single factor authentication. ***Single factor authentication*** means using only one way to verify a user's identify. The most common method of single factor authentication is the password. In this case, the password provides the key to access. Protection of that key is paramount. We always advise people to think of their password as a shared secret. The secret is shared between the user and the system. This subtle shift is important because every person knows the dynamics of a secret. If you tell anyone a secret, it is no longer a secret. Also, the longer a secret is kept, the greater the chances it will eventually be told or discovered.

Passwords (shared secrets) must be changed periodically as a control against password guessing and password cracking attacks. This seems obvious given what we just mentioned about the nature of secrets. However, there are other situations where changing or reissuing passwords is required.

Generally, when a user is initially granted access to information system she is given a temporary password. This password is issued by an organization to enable a user to perform her first log on into a system. Most systems have an administrative mechanism that will force the user to change her password at her first or next log on attempt. It is the responsibility of the organization to protect the temporary password and relay it to the user in a secure manner. All too often, organizations use extremely vulnerable passwords, such as the company name, for this process. An even worse practice is using the same temporary password for all users. By protecting the temporary password, the organization delivers the message that securing passwords is important.

No one should know a user's password: not the boss, and not the system administrator.

As any Help Desk person will tell you, users forget their passwords with amazing regularity. This has become more of an issue since the advent of the "strong" password. If a user forgets his password, there needs to be a process for reissuing passwords including verification that the requester is indeed the original owner.

Another reason to change a password is in response to a compromise of that password. At the slightest suspicion of compromise, a password must be changed. This means that if a user suspects that another person has for any reason learned her password, it has been compromised and must be changed.

You will notice that, in the password use policy example shown in Table 9.3, there is no mention of complexity requirements, password history remembered, or other criteria specific to password use. These elements would be covered in the organization's password standard, which is referenced in the policy but developed separately.

Other Password Policy Issues

It may seem very convenient and helpful when a Web site or software package offers to remember a user's log on credentials or provide an automatic log on to a system, but this practice should be strictly prohibited. There are two reasons for this policy. First, if a user allows Web sites or software applications to automate his log on, then unattended equipment can be used by unauthorized people to gain access to information resources. Second, it is human nature to use the same or similar passwords for multiple systems, which means that if one password is captured, it is very likely that that this same (or similar) password can be used to gain entry to other unrelated systems.

FYI: NSA Security Configuration Guidance

The National Security Agency (NSA) division of Information Assurance has published numerous security configuration guides for both proprietary and open sources software, hardware, and operating systems. These unclassified documents are available to the public free of charge. For more information, visit **www.nsa.gov**.

Password recommendations, excerpted from the NSA Guide to Securing Windows 2000 Group Policy: Security Configuration Tool Set, v1.2.1 12/1/2003, are available on this book's companion Web site.

9

IN PRACTICE: Password Use Policy

The goal of this policy is to demonstrate the organizations commitment to secure password management and to outline requirements.
The *objectives* of this policy are to:

- Protect the organization from password-related security risks.
- Instill "best practice" password use habits in all users of information resources.
- Support the organization's best defense against any compromise of critical information.

The *audience* is the entire organization.

▸▸ CONTINUED ON NEXT PAGE

» CONTINUED

TABLE 9.3 Sample Password Use Policy.

Section X:	[COMPANY] Information Security Policy	Effective Date:
Subsection	**Access Control**	**Change Control #:**
Policy	**Password Use Policy**	**Approved By:**
Objective	The cooperation of authorized users is essential for effective security. Users should be made aware of their responsibilities for maintaining effective access controls, particularly regarding the use of passwords and the security of user equipment.	
Purpose	The purpose of this policy is to protect the organization's information resources from unauthorized access by requiring secure authentication and proper password management.	
Audience	This policy applies equally to all individuals granted access privileges to any [Company] information resources.	
Policy	• All users will keep their passwords confidential and store them securely (i.e., not on the computer and not on paper unless they can be protected). • Passwords shall not be shared. • Passwords shall be changed whenever there is a chance of compromise. • Users will report compromise to the system owner and administrator immediately. • Passwords will conform to [Company] password standards. • Regular passwords shall be changed according to [Company] standards. • Privileged passwords shall be changed according to [Company] standards. • Passwords cannot be reused during a minimum time period to be stated in [Company] password history standards. • Temporary passwords will be changed at first log on. • Passwords will not be stored in computer or used in a macro for sign on.	

» CONTINUED ON NEXT PAGE

▶▶ CONTINUED	
	• [Company] information system users should refuse all offers by software and/or Internet sites to automatically login the next time that they access those resources.
Exceptions	None
Disciplinary Actions	Violation of this policy may result in disciplinary action, which may include termination for employees and temporaries; a termination of employment relations in the case of contractors or consultants; or dismissal for interns and volunteers. Additionally, individuals are subject to civil and criminal prosecution.

User Authentication for Remote Connections

It is one thing to address user authentication for a local network, and quite another when we decide to open our internal networks to access from outside the perimeter. Remote access into internal networks requires an additional analysis of risks that must be addressed with additional controls specific to remote access. Once a risk assessment has been performed, management will need to choose controls based on the need for protection of each system to which remote access will be allowed.

There are many technology choices available for remote access, and as many security measures to consider, from proprietary controls like Cisco Systems' TACACS+ to the more platform-independent RADIUS services, VPN technologies, and a host of other possibilities. A comprehensive risk assessment will yield the most significant issues, which will in turn drive management toward one or more available technologies.

One of the most important things to remember about allowing remote access is that our perimeter protections are often circumvented. When dialing into a remote access server using a modem, I am connecting directly to that server and bypassing firewall devices. This is an important aspect of the risk assessment and analysis that will guide an organization to select the proper controls.

IPSec and the Virtual Private Network

A *Virtual Private Network (VPN)* provides a secure tunnel for transmitting data through an unsecured network such as the Internet. This is achieved using tunneling and encryption in combination to provide high security remote access without the high cost of dedicated private lines.

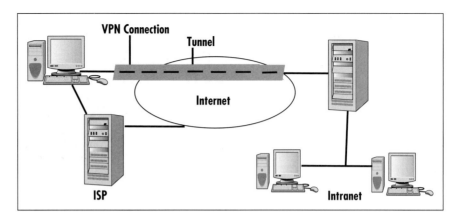

FIGURE 9.2 Virtual Private Network.

IPSec (short for IP Security) is a set of protocols developed by the Internet Engineering Task Force (IETF) to support secure exchange of packets at the IP layer. IPSec is most commonly associated with Virtual Private Networks (VPN) as the protocol providing encapsulation and encryption for VPN connections between physical sites or between a site and a remote user.

Tunneling or encapsulation is achieved by enclosing standard TCP-IP datagrams within other variations of protocols such as Point-to-Point Protocol, which is a standard used in dial-up connections. The tunnel can be thought of as a virtual pathway between systems within the larger pathway of the Internet. To form this pathway, both sides must be aware of each other in at least three ways: Each must have (1) the IP address of the other's public side, (2) the IP addressing scheme of the other's private side, and (3) a key used for encryption and authentication.

In a site-to-site VPN, two firewalls are configured with a Security Association (SA) containing the information described previously about the remote network. The tunnel is created using Internet Key Exchange (IKE), which is the means of authentication between sites. The two firewalls contact each other using knowledge of the other's IP address, and they exchange keys. If the keys match, the tunnel is established. Once the tunnel is established, the private networks on either side of the connection act as if they are one network.

RADIUS and TACACS+

Remote Authentication Dial-In User Service (RADIUS) and *Terminal Access Controller Access Control System (TACACS+)* are both remote authentication protocols. Both use a distributed architecture to authenticate remote users on private information resources. Though they are different, they use the similar architecture of a remote access server and an authentication server. Both use these two layers to authenticate a user and authorize use of information resources.

RADIUS allows a company to maintain user profiles in a central database that all remote servers can share. Having a central service also means that it's easier to track usage. Created by Livingston (now owned by Lucent), RADIUS is a de facto industry standard and is a proposed IETF standard. TACACS+ provides similar services to RADIUS but many believe it is more reliable and secure as authentication and authorization information are kept separate.

Hardware Tokens

Many organizations choose to use hardware tokens as a security measure for remote access. A hardware token is carried by any users requiring remote access to information resources. The hardware token displays a set of characters that change according to a predefined interval. This set of characters corresponds to a set of characters on the remote system and is synchronized. To gain access to the remote system, the user will need the set of characters on the token before she will be able to enter a user name and password. This technique is referred to as *Multi-Factor Authentication* and requires the use of more than one of the three types of authentication, which include:

- Something you know: such as user name and password.

- Something you have: such as a token or key-card.

- Something you are: a biometric characteristic such as a fingerprint or retinal scan.

Challenge/Response Protocol

Challenge and Response Protocol (CHAP) or *Microsoft Challenge and Response Protocol (MS CHAP)* are used to challenge any remote host attempting access to a private system. The primary value of both of these protocols is to prevent man-in-the-middle, hijacking, and IP spoofing attacks. Both protocols challenge the identity of the remote system while allowing a user simply to input user name and password. The authenticating server sends a challenge sting to the remote client computer, which is then encrypted with the user password and returned to the authenticating server.

The authenticating server also has the password, which it will use to decrypt the challenge string and authenticate the user.

This is also known as the three-way CHAP handshake. The user requests authentication, the server challenges the user's client computer, and the user sends the challenge back for authentication.

Both protocols use encryption technologies to secure the communication between hosts, but MS CHAP is more secure as it doesn't allow for storage of the password in a reversible form.

Private Lines

Although quite costly, private lines are very secure. If an organization wishes to connect sites, it may choose to purchase private data lines, usually T1, between sites. The term *WAN* (Wide Area Network) refers to sites connected by private lines.

Unlike VPN technologies, WAN connections use lines that are not accessible by the public; consequently, the risks associated with use of public lines are eliminated.

The reason for the rapid growth of VPN deployments, however, is directly related to the expense of private line technologies such as T1. When an organization deploys private lines, it must purchase these lines from a phone company or Internet Service Provider. Not only is the organization charged for the connection itself, referred to as a "circuit," but it is also charged for the amount of bandwidth and the equipment to manage the connection on either side.

Address Checking and Dial-Back Controls

The last two of the many options available are similar means of authenticating the remote host by a predetermined criterion. Phone numbers and IP addresses are similar forms of identification.

In address checking, a computer serving remote connections will authenticate the remote host by checking its IP address against a database of allowed IP addresses. In dial-back, the server will answer a call from a remote host through the use of telephone modems on either side. As soon as the call is answered, the server will then disconnect and immediately call back on the expected phone number. Both of these controls require that the remote host's phone number or IP address appear in a database of allowed phone numbers (for dial-back) or IP addresses (for address checking).

Testing, 1, 2, 3

Of course with any risk-based controls, we cannot simply rely on the marketing material to trust a control. Any proposed security control must be thoroughly tested before it is used in any production environment.

The goal of this policy is to acknowledge that remote access poses additional risks and requires supplementary controls.

The *objectives* of this policy are to:

- Require careful risk assessment for remote connections.
- Ensure the proper controls are selected based on this risk analysis.
- Protect the organization from risks associated with allowing remote connections to information resources.

The *audience* is all remote connections.

TABLE 9.4 Sample User Authentication for Remote Access Policy.

Section X:	[COMPANY] Information Security Policy	Effective Date:
Subsection	Access Control	Change Control #:
Policy	User Authentication for Remote Connections	Approved By:
Objective	In support of information security, the [Company] will secure all user connections that are authorized to access information resources.	
Purpose	The purpose of this policy is to prevent unauthorized access to the [Company] information and system resources.	
Audience	This policy applies to all remote connections.	
Policy	• A risk assessment shall be performed to determine the appropriate level of protection for various systems. • The system owners and system custodians, in coordination with the ISO, shall select from the following options, based upon the results of the risk assessment: • Cryptography • Hardware tokens • Challenge/response protocol • Dedicated private lines	

▸▸ CONTINUED ON NEXT PAGE

▶▶ CONTINUED	
	• Network user address checking • Dial-back procedures and controls (without call forwarding) • All procedures and controls shall be thoroughly tested prior to use.
Exceptions	None
Disciplinary Actions	Violation of this policy may result in disciplinary action, which may include termination for employees and temporaries; a termination of employment relations in the case of contractors or consultants; or dismissal for interns and volunteers. Additionally, individuals are subject to civil and criminal prosecution.

Mobile Computing

Mobile computing refers to use of information resources outside the controlled environment of organizational facilities. It is said that, due to the numerous options available today in mobile computing devices, the security perimeter has vanished. Even our cell phones have some capacity, such as built-in cameras and memory, to store many image files. We have multiuse portable music players with as much as 40GB or more available storage, and of course PDAs and laptop computers are becoming more and more popular.

Yet Another Risk Assessment!

No surprise here. How will we protect these devices and their communication? What are the issues? For starters, physical security is a major concern. Next might be access control, followed by securing the communications. Perhaps we should also consider how the data stored on these portable devices will be backed up.

A thorough assessment of risks will again direct the organization to the best controls to maintain security. Information owners and executives will decide which controls will be implemented, and end users will be well trained not only on the policies but on the procedures and guidelines dictated by those policies.

Approved or Prohibited?

Given the risks associated with portable devices, one of the most important requirements must be standardization. We must standardize not only the types of devices allowed, but also the data stored on these devices and the means used to access the organization's information resources.

Approved Devices Management must decide which manufacturers and models of portable devices will be used by their employees. This is important for many reasons. The devices themselves are chosen for their functionality, which is dictated by the organizational need to accomplish normal business functions. Once the devices are chosen, the next most important factor in allowing only approved devices is standardization.

Standardization not only allows for the most efficient administration of these devices, but also the software used for these devices can be secured in a standard fashion. PDAs use synchronization software to maintain change control between data residing on internal servers and the devices themselves. Whenever data is manipulated on a portable device, it will be synchronized the next time the device is connected to the network to ensure the latest version is present on both the network server and the device.

If an organization doesn't standardize, it will be open not only to security problems but also to an unacceptable administrative burden in trying to support users on different devices. To ensure that only approved devices are being used, an organization can employ any of several software auditing tools available commercially.

How Data Will Be Stored on Portable Devices As a rule, it is wise to prohibit the storage of data on portable devices. For laptop users, we can require that any use of organizational information be secured through the use of VPN and other remote access technologies. This way no data is actually stored on the laptop; if the computer is compromised, only generic data will be resident. This is also possible for PDA users as most PDA devices come standard with full networking ability in the form of wired and wireless network interface controllers.

However, one of the most useful functions of portable devices is that users can bring useable data off-site where connectivity may not be possible. In this case, data stored on any portable device must be encrypted using company-approved encryption standards.

Mandating the Means of Connectivity Just as we require certain controls for remote access from other sites, we must do so for remote access or internal access for portable devices. The most common method of connectivity for portable devices is through wireless technologies. Default wireless communications is inherently insecure. So again we will require company-approved methods only.

Don't Forget the Protection Additional precautions are necessary to protect mobile equipment. All devices, even cell phones, are vulnerable to virus and worms and require malware protection. Portable devices should be held to even more stringent standards than stationary equipment as they have more opportunity to be exposed to unprotected environments.

FYI: Sophos Reports First Ever Pocket PC Virus

In July of 2004, virus researchers at Sophos reported the discovery of the first ever virus to infect the Microsoft Pocket PC operating system. The W32/Dust-A virus infects PDAs running the Pocket PC operating system. The Duts virus requires users to deliberately send it to other Pocket PC PDA owners. If the infected file is run it displays a message:

"WinCE4.Dust by Ratter/29A"
"Dear User, am I allowed to spread?"

Only if the user agrees will it attempt to infect other executable programs on the user's PDA.

Due to their size and frequent use devices such as PDAs and cell phones are easily lost or misplaced. All devices must be password protected or otherwise secured so that the information isn't easily accessible.

Last but not least is the physical protection of portable devices. Users must be required to take great care in the use and storage of any portable device in their possession. Portable devices are easy targets for theft. Even leaving a laptop unattended for a few minutes in a conference room can lead to unintended consequences.

FYI: PC Theft and Recovery Statistics

Total laptop theft losses for 2004 increased to over $6.7 million. *CSI/FBI Computer Crime and Security Survey, 2004*

Over 600,000 PCs were stolen in 2003. *Safeware The Insurance Agency 2004*

Theft ranks as the number two cause for overall PC loss. *Safeware The Insurance Agency 2003*

Laptop theft has been attributed to 59% of computer attacks in government agencies, corporations, and universities during 2003. *Baseline 2004*

Computer crime statistics reveal that approximately 80% of computer crime consists of "inside jobs" by disgruntled employees. *Gartner Group*

80% of those surveyed acknowledged financial losses due to computer breaches. *CSI/FBI 2002*

97% of stolen computers are never recovered. *FBI*

The average loss due to laptop theft is $61,881. *CSI/FBI Computer Crime and Security Survey, 2001*

IN PRACTICE: Mobile Computing Policy

The goal of this policy is to address the unique protection requirements of mobile computing.

The *objectives* of this policy are to:

- Ensure efficient administration and security for all portable devices.
- Require approved devices and behavior to be employed by end users.
- Standardize methods of communications and storage pertaining to portable computing devices.
- Involve executive management in the criticality analysis.

The *audience* is all employees granted remote access privileges to information resources.

TABLE 9.5 Mobile Computing Policy.

Section X:	[COMPANY] Information Security Policy	Effective Date:
Subsection	Access Control	Change Control #:
Policy	Mobile Computing	Approved By:
Objective	In support of information security, the [Company] will implement formal controls, policies, and procedures for the secure use of mobile computing equipment.	
Purpose	The purpose of this policy is to ensure that business information is not compromised by use of such devices as notebooks, laptops, palmtops, and mobile telephones in an unprotected environment and to provide users with controls for and awareness of the potential risks.	
Audience	This policy applies to all individuals granted remote access privileges to any [Company] information resources.	

Policy	• A risk assessment will be performed on the potential threats associated with the various forms of mobile computing. The risk assessment will consider the following issues:
	  • Physical protection of the device
	  • Access control	

▸▸ CONTINUED ON NEXT PAGE

▸▸ CONTINUED

- The use of cryptographic techniques
- Back-up schedules, procedures, and media protection
- Protection from viruses and malicious software
- Based upon the risk assessment, the Office of the Information Security Officer will determine appropriate controls and procedures.
- Users shall be trained in the policies, procedures, and controls.
- Only [Company]-approved portable computing devices may be used to access [Company] information resources.
- [Company] data should not be stored on portable computing devices. However, in the event that there is no alternative to local storage, all sensitive [Company] data must be encrypted using approved encryption techniques.
- [Company] data must not be transmitted via wireless to or from a portable computing device unless explicitly approved by the Office of the Information Security Officer.
- All remote access (dial-in services) to [Company] must be either through an approved modem pool or via an Internet Service Provider (ISP).
- Unattended portable computing devices must be physically secure. This means they must be locked in an office, locked in a desk drawer or filing cabinet, or attached to a desk or cabinet via a cable lock system.

Exceptions	None
Disciplinary Actions	Violation of this policy may result in disciplinary action, which may include termination for employees and temporaries; a termination of employment relations in the case of contractors or consultants; or dismissal for interns and volunteers. Additionally, individuals are subject to civil and criminal prosecution.

Telecommuting

This section is closely related to the mobile computing section, but it addresses not the devices but their means of communication and the infrastructure concerns associated with networks that are not under organizational controls.

As explained by the American Telecommuting Association, "telecommuting can be broadly defined to include any method for working productively 'at a distance' from the traditional office. The title of 'telecommuter' can be applied to everyone from computer programmers in Denver reporting to an employer in Australia, to an executive who stays at home one morning to study a complex contract, to a data-entry clerk who works on a desktop in her spare bedroom, to a sales person who rarely leaves the territory in which he lives and works."

Telecommuting policy is meant to address more permanent remote users, just as the remote access policy addresses those who connect from different remote locations on a periodic or situational basis. It addresses the risks associated with permanent remote locations in which regular workers connect to internal organizational infrastructure as a normal part of their jobs (i.e., working from home).

The Telecommuting Environment

From what location will our teleworkers be allowed to connect and how will we ensure that their facilities are reasonably as secure as those on company premises? We must ensure the following:

- Controls to ensure the confidentiality, integrity, and availability of the information assets and information systems must achieve the same goals as "on-premises" systems.

- Telecommuting facilities should be protected from neighbors, roommates, and family members. If workers are accessing company information resources from home, measures must be in place to secure equipment from accidental and intentional misuse.

- Telecommuting equipment is not to be used for nonbusiness purposes.

- Information classification guidelines must carry through to the remote facility.

- Equipment used from telecommuting facilities must be secured physically in the same manner as "on-premises" equipment.

The goal is to establish a remote environment that most closely resembles the organization's internal environment. Specific authorization must be given for use and storage of company data at the remote site. The hours of access must be authorized and controlled and the work itself, performed by the teleworker, must be authorized. Adequate security, storage, and communications ability must be in place.

Also a concern of great importance is the nature of the controls in place at the remote telecommuting site. Activities should be audited and monitored by the same methods as the main facilities, as well as data back-ups that must conform to the organization's standards for backing up data. Lastly, the organizational business continuity plans must account for the telecommuting environment.

IN PRACTICE: Telecommuting Policy

The goal of this policy is address the unique protection require-ments of Telecommuting.
The *objectives* of this policy are to:

- Ensure that permanent remote workers are subject to the same security controls as local organizational staff.
- Ensure that telecommuting environments are as secure as on-premises facilities.
- Ensure the same controls to protect data are in place in telecommuting environments.

The *audience* is all permanent remote workers.

TABLE 9.6 Sample Telecommuting Policy.

Section X:	COMPANY] Information Security Policy	Effective Date:
Subsection	Access Control	Change Control #:
Policy	Telecommuting	Approved By:
Objective	In support of information security, the [COMPANY] will strictly control and protect the [COMPANY] information resources against the possible threats associated with telecommuting.	
Purpose	The purpose of this policy is that the [COMPANY] information resources are not compromised by those that access them from premises that are not under the control of the [COMPANY] by requiring authorization, controls and monitoring the telecommuting.	
Audience	This policy applies to all telecommuting privileges to any [COMPANY] information resources.	

▸▸ **CONTINUED ON NEXT PAGE**

▶▶ CONTINUED

Policy

- All telecommuting shall be authorized by management.
- A risk assessment of each location where the proposed telecommuting will occur will be done to review the risks associated with:
  - Theft of equipment or information;
  - Disclosure of information;
  - Unauthorized remote access to organization's facilities.
- All teleworking equipment shall have appropriate safeguards to ensure the confidentiality, integrity and availability of the information assets and information systems. These controls must achieve the same goals as "on-premises" system controls.

In addition to the above the following conditions must be satisfied prior to telecommuting being authorized:

- Access:
  - The telecommuting facility will be physically secure from free from nonemployee threat.
  - The threat of nonemployees gaining access to resources (family, friends) must be controlled.
  - Communication requirements will be secured and in line with those required by the information to be accessed classification.
  - The telecommuting equipment will be properly stored in furniture that locks or in accordance to the standards to which it would be subjected if it were within the organization.
- Authorization:
  - All telecommuting will be specifically authorized.
  - The hours of telecommuting will be specifically authorized.
  - The access to sensitive information shall be specifically authorized.
  - The storage of sensitive information shall be specifically authorized.
  - The work performed by the teleworker shall be specifically authorized.

9

▶▶ CONTINUED ON NEXT PAGE

>> CONTINUED

- Adequate resources:
  - The teleworker shall have adequate and secure communications equipment.
  - The teleworker shall have adequate storage and work furniture.
  - The teleworker shall be given access to hardware and support and maintenance services.
- Controls:
  - The teleworker shall be monitored and audited by [insert name and title] and by [insert method(s)].
  - The teleworker shall back up information in a manner consistent with the organization's policies.
  - Business continuity plans shall reflect the telecommuting environments.
  - Revocation of access rights shall be immediate as soon as telecommuting ceases.

Exceptions	None
Disciplinary Actions	Violation of this policy may result in disciplinary action which may include termination for employees and temporaries; a termination of employment relations in the case of contractors or consultants; or dismissal for interns and volunteers. Additionally, individuals are subject to civil and criminal prosecution.

Monitoring System Access and Use

On what could we rely if we simply implemented a bunch of controls and hoped they were all working out? How would we improve our environment without the ability to assess the efficacy of the controls? How would we know if we have been, or are in the process of being, compromised?

Monitoring access and use is a pillar of information security. What is most unfortunate is that many organizations deploy elaborate systems to gather data from many sources and then never look at the data. This is such a waste of time and money, and such an irresponsible way to protect information.

Enabling log files and installing monitoring software and tools is the easy part. The challenge is in the regular and periodic review and auditing of all of the information generated by all the systems on any given network. Network devices, network servers, and even workstation computers are very "talkative." They have the ability to log every event, and invariably they do so in a very cryptic manner with language that even the most dedicated geeks may find unintelligible.

So, our policy must define what we will monitor as well as who will review all the logs generated, how often they will review them, and how long we will retain these logs should we need to go back and look at them again.

What Will We Need to Monitor?

There are four main areas for monitoring: authorized access, privileged operations, unauthorized attempts, and system alerts or failures. Under each of these main categories are several more specialized areas, which we will explain here.

Authorized Access We need to know when users and systems that have proper authorization connect and use information resources. The information gathered must include the identification of the user or system performing the authorized actions. We also need to know the date and time of each important event, what kind of an event it was, and which program or utility was used.

There are many kinds of events associated with authorized access. Security events include all of the possible audited events in a server operating system. Microsoft operating systems include the following security audit options:

- Account logon events

- Account management events

- Directory service access

- Logon events

- Object access

- Policy change

- Privilege use

- Process tracking

- System events

For each of these there is an option for logging success or failure or both. All of these events are written to the Security Event Log.

Privileged Operations Some events have a higher place within the broad spectrum of security events. These are events related to operations and activities reserved for those with special privilege to perform critical operations.

The use of supervisory or administrative computer accounts must be closely monitored. System administrators have an almost absolute level of access to information. They create and change user accounts, issue passwords, implement and maintain software security policies, perform data back-up and systems maintenance activities, and a host of other critical activities. Since these accounts are so powerful, they are the prime target for anyone with intentional malice or the desire to obtain information. With great power comes great responsibility, though in the information technology age we can't afford to simply trust, so we monitor!

Other critical events related to privilege include system start-up and shut-down and the attachment of devices, installation of hardware and software, and other such activities.

Unauthorized Attempts Unauthorized attempts include failed attempts at access, and access policy violations such as attempts to access information without authorization. Also included here are firewall logs, which contain a record of every single incoming and outgoing connection attempt, successful or otherwise. We also include logs from any manner of intrusion detection systems.

Reviewing these kinds of logs requires an amazing amount of time and resources. This is why there are several packages available to bring all of these disparate types of information into convergence with tools to generate reports to make the data useable and understandable. These applications are not an option, and for monitoring and auditing to be successful, they must be treated with careful configuration and regular review themselves.

System Alerts or Failures System alerts generated by issues such as such as hardware failures, application failures, and power problems need to be logged and closely monitored. While alerts and alarms provide immediate feedback, logs provide us with the information necessary to spot trends. By proactively extrapolating the information, it may be possible to avert the next crisis. At a minimum, the information should be incorporated into the risk analysis process.

Review and Retention

The last issue related to monitoring is review and retention of the information gathered by system monitoring. Not only must we require how often the information should be reviewed, but we must identify the person or group who will perform these reviews.

Lastly, we must require by policy how long these logs will be stored for future reference. The practice of saving information for a specified period of time is known as *retention.*

Is Monitoring Legal?

In respect to monitoring system and user activity, courts have favored employer rights to protect their interests. Among the reasons given in the *Defense Counsel Journal:* (1) the work is done at the employer's place of business; (2) the employer owns the equipment; (3) the employer has an interest in monitoring employee activity to ensure the quality of work; and (4) the employer has the right to protect property from theft and fraud.

Court rulings suggest that reasonableness is a standard applying to surveillance and monitoring activities. Electronic monitoring is reasonable when there is a business purpose, policies exist to set the privacy expectations of employees, and employees are informed of organizational rules regarding network activities and understand the means used to monitor the workplace.

Affirmation (acceptable use) agreements should include a clause informing users that the company will and does monitor system activity. A commonly accepted practice is to present this statement to system users as a legal warning during the authentication process. Users must agree to company policies as a condition of logging on.

IN PRACTICE: Monitoring System Access and Use Policy

9

The goal of this policy is to establish the parameters for auditing and monitoring user and system activity.

The *objectives* of this policy are to:

- Ensure that critical events related to resource access are logged.
- Ensure that the use of privilege is closely monitored.
- Ensure that logs are reviewed regularly and periodically by authorized personnel.
- Ensure that the organization has a predetermined historical record of logged events.

The *audience* is all employees with access to company information.

▶▶ CONTINUED ON NEXT PAGE

>> CONTINUED

TABLE 9.7 Sample Monitoring System Access and Use Policy.

Section X:	[COMPANY] Information Security Policy	Effective Date:
Subsection	Access Controls	Change Control #:
Policy	Monitoring System Access and Use	Approved By:
Objective	In support of information security, [COMPANY] will log all security-relevant events or exceptions.	
Purpose	The purpose of this policy is to detect unauthorized activities and ensure that users are only performing the functions and gaining access to information to which they are authorized.	
Audience	This policy applies to all individuals granted access privileges to any [COMPANY] Information Resources.	

Policy	• Areas for monitoring include:
	   • Authorized access
	   • Privileged operations
	   • Unauthorized attempts
	   • System alerts or failures
	• The Information Security Department shall be responsible for implementing and maintaining the log programs and log files.
	• The Office of the Information Security Officer shall be responsible for timely monitoring of the logs.
	• All logs will be retained for a minimum of six months.	

Exceptions	None	
Disciplinary Actions	Violation of this policy may result in disciplinary action, which may include termination for employees and temporaries; a termination of employment relations in the case of contractors or consultants; or dismissal for interns and volunteers. Additionally, individuals are subject to civil and criminal prosecution.	

Summary

By now it is surely clear that access control is a highly complex domain. Access to information is possibly the most sensitive of all security concerns. We have learned the importance of managing user access and also unauthorized access. We covered the critical nature of managing passwords and the user's responsibility to protect them.

We also discussed the importance of additional risk assessment relating to remote access into systems, the use of mobile computing devices, and the many new risks associated with them. We learned also that telecommuting environments should be subject to all the same protections as organizational facilities. Lastly, we covered the importance of monitoring all of the above regarding access into systems and access to information including that which comes through the front door, direct remote connections, and also attempts at unauthorized access into our vital systems.

Test Your Skills

MULTIPLE CHOICE QUESTIONS

1. Access control security focuses on:
   A. access to information
   B. access to facilities
   C. access to equipment
   D. all of the above

2. Before Windows 2003, Microsoft operating systems had the default access control equivalent to the _____ posture.
   A. allow many
   B. allow none
   C. allow all
   D. disallow all

3. Giving a user the minimum access required to do their job is the:
   A. least access concept
   B. less protocol concept
   C. least privilege concept
   D. least process concept

9

4. Prohibiting access to information not required for one's work is the:
   A. access need concept
   B. need-to-monitor concept
   C. need-to-know concept
   D. required information process concept

5. Which is NOT a sound principle of access control security?
   A. need-to-know
   B. default allow all
   C. least privilege
   D. default deny all

6. If an organization is using MAC and a user has been granted Top Secret clearance, it means that:
   A. the user can automatically access all Top Secret information
   B. the user can access only Top Secret information
   C. the user can access Top Secret information that he has a demonstrated need to know
   D. the user can only access information up to the Top Secret level

7. What rights should a user be granted who only needs to view a document?
   A. read, write
   B. full access
   C. read only
   D. read, modify

8. A member of the Information Technology Department has been given the responsibility of creating new accounts. She cannot delete accounts. Therefore she has been granted read and create rights to the User Account Management program. This is an example of:
   A. need-to-know and least privilege
   B. default allow all and need-to-know
   C. least privilege
   D. default deny all

9. Access controls are created by:
   A. information custodians
   B. information auditors
   C. information owners
   D. data users

10. The creation of user accounts falls under which section of access control?
    A. user access management
    B. user accountability management
    C. user responsibilities
    D. end user management

11. These two departments must have clear communications procedures between them:
    A. Human Resources and Security
    B. Human Resources and Accounting
    C. Human Resources and Information Technology
    D. Information Technology and Accounting

12. Reasons to change a password include:
    A. to comply with a password age policy
    B. to strengthen security in case of any compromise of the password
    C. to create a unique password after logging on to a system for the first time
    D. all of the above

13. It is important to implement a password history policy because:
    A. users need to be able to reuse passwords more than six months old
    B. users must be required to create new and unique passwords, and not use passwords they have used before
    C. administrators must have a comparative record or user password use
    D. none of the above

14. Virtual Private Network uses the Internet to:
    A. create a secure channel for remote network access
    B. provide a cost effective remote access solution
    C. both A and B
    D. neither A nor B

15. The primary function of RADIUS is to:
    A. authenticate remote users
    B. assign file level access rights
    C. create new accounts
    D. encrypt data

16. Which is an example of multifactor authentication?
    A. using a password
    B. using a token
    C. using a finger scanner
    D. none of the above

17. Which of the following statements is NOT true of portable devices?
    A. They are vulnerable to viruses.
    B. They are easy targets of theft.
    C. They are more secure than stationary devices.
    D. They are easy to lose.

18. Which of the following statements BEST describes telecommuting?
    A. An employee who talks on the telephone.
    B. An employee who uses his cell phone to access the Internet.
    C. An employee who works from home.
    D. An employee who uses a mobile device.

19. Which is generally NOT a reason for monitoring administrative access?
    A. Administrators can absolutely not be trusted.
    B. Monitoring mitigates the risks associated with misuse of privileges.
    C. Monitoring can determine if an unauthorized administrative account has been created.
    D. Monitoring can provide oversight of administrative activities.

20. Retention refers to:
    A. storing log files for future review
    B. maintaining controls over user access
    C. creating security reports
    D. none of the above

EXERCISES

Exercise 9.1: Access Control Concepts

In your own words, define and provide an example for each of the following terms:

- deny all security posture

- need-to-know security posture
- least privilege security posture

Exercise 9.2: User Account & Password Management

In your own words, explain why each of the following is bad practice:

- shared user accounts
- unique user accounts, no password required
- unique user accounts, password never needs to be changed
- administrators have used their privileged accounts to perform basic user activities

Exercise 9.3: Multifactor Authentication Devices

Multifactor authentication requires two forms of authentication. Use the Internet to find a picture of the following:

- Example of an authentication device that is "something you have."
- Example of an authentication device that proves "something you are."

Exercise 9.4: Portable Devices

One of the most popular portable devices is USB Thumb Drives.

1. Write a paragraph explaining the dangers of these drives to organizational security. Consider the use of these drives by both authorized and unauthorized users.

2. Write a paragraph justifying the authorized use of USB devices and how you would suggest securing them.

Exercise 9.5: Mobile Equipment Security

Mobile office professionals need to take steps to ensure the safety and security of their mobile gadgets. Create a security awareness campaign that includes at least three ways to secure mobile equipment. Include at least one statistic on mobile device theft.

Exercise 9.6: Telecommuting

The high cost of real estate and long commute times are but two of the reasons telecommuting is becoming more popular. Write an article explaining the benefits of telecommuting. You may want to reference the Web site of the American Telecommuting Association at **http://www.knowledgetree. com/ata.html**. In your article, address the security concerns related to telecommuting.

PROJECTS

Project 9.1: The IT-HR Connection

1. As Personnel Manager, you have been asked to work with the Information Security Officer and the Information Technology manager to develop user account management processes. You are pleased to be involved in this project. Write a memo to your boss, the Director of Human Resources, explaining what you hope to accomplish.

2. At your first meeting, it was decided that you would design a "user access authorization form." Develop a form that will be used by the HR department to inform the IT department that a new user account needs to be created.

3. Modify the form you created in Step 2 so it can be used to notify IT of any changes in position (e.g., new job assignment) or change in status (e.g., medical leave).

4. Modify the form to include notification of termination.

5. Modify the form to include inventory of all information assets (e.g., laptop, PDA, pager) as well as a way to verify recovery upon termination.

Project 9.2: Responsible Administrative Access

1. Assume the role of a Network System Administrator. Make a list of all of the different types of activities that you perform that require administrative or escalated privileges.

2. Make a second list of daily activities that require basic user rights.

3. Best practices dictate that you should have two accounts—one for administrative access and one for basic user activities. Write a memo to the Information Security Officer explaining how having two accounts impacts your productivity as well as how you believe the dual accounts can best be implemented.

Project 9.3: Telecommuting Best Practices

1. Your organization has decided to allow users the option of working from home. Make a list of six security issues that must be considered. For example, is the company going to provide computers? If not, will the employees be expected to provide their own?

2. Note your recommendations for each issue and detail any associated security control.

3. Assume that your recommendations have been accepted. You have now been tasked with training the telecommuters. Create a PowerPoint presentation entitled "Telecommuting and Security." The goal of the presentation is to explain the expected security behavior of telecommuters.

9

Case Study

You are the Security Officer for a biomedical research organization (BRO). BRO has recently been audited by the National Institute for Health and the auditor has documented several access control security concerns. If these concerns are not addressed, BRO will lose its government funding.

Currently the organization has very few procedures in place to address access control. The following is a list of concerns developed by the auditor. You must create security policies to address each of the issues given below. The policies will be presented to the Board of Directors at their next meeting.

1. Each department manager contacts the IT department when a new employee begins work. The department manager calls IT on the phone to request the new user account.

2. The new account is assigned a password, which is used permanently.

3. Remote users are permitted access by dialing a modem. There is no database of acceptable phone numbers. Users dial direct.

4. Auditing is enabled. Audit logs are set to overwrite as needed. There is no procedure to archiving log files before the log is full, so many events are overwritten.

5. Laptop computers are available for researchers. If a laptop is available, a researcher can take it home without signing it out or back in.

6. Users are allowed to use PDAs, but they must supply their own. Researchers store confidential data on their PDAs.

7. There is a firewall, but it is not set to log activity.

8. Administrators use their one administrative account for everything they do.

9. There is no communication between the Human Resources and IT departments.

Chapter 10

Systems Development and Maintenance

Chapter Objectives

After reading this chapter and completing the exercises, you will be able to do the following:

- Appreciate the importance of creating new software solutions with security in mind from the genesis of the project.

- Build code that protects the security of the sensitive data on which it relies.

- Use cryptography in application systems.

- Understand the intricacies of patch management and system availability as they relate to both operating system files and application system files.

- Apply policies related to systems development and maintenance.

Introduction

Section 10 of ISO 17799 is dedicated to Systems Development and Maintenance with the objectives of making sure that line-of-business applications and mission-critical software do not become a security threat to the rest of the organization's assets. While an organization may come to depend on the software that it runs to generate revenue, those applications and software may bring as much negative impact to the organization as they bring positive value. This dichotomy exists because organizations sometimes unwisely cut corners to ensure profits. In some cases, the people in charge simply do not know any better. This chapter aims to provide these decision-makers with a framework that balances the belief in the mirage—i.e., instant profit—with an understanding of the importance of information security.

In this chapter, we will focus on different yet complementary aspects of security as it pertains to application development. From building the application systems to updating them, not forgetting securing the data that they provide, systems development and systems maintenance is an area of the security policy that is central to keeping the organization, and the data it relies upon, productive yet secure.

What Are the Risks to the Organization?

What exactly are the risks to the organization stemming from improper code, or from "upgraded" code? The answer is as simple as it may appear to be overly dramatic: potentially disastrous. Consider a company that relies on a Web-based application linked to a back-end database. If the code that was used to create the Web-based application was not thoroughly tested, it may contain loopholes that would allow a hacker to bring the application down with a Denial-of-Service attack, run code on the server hosting the application, or even trick the database into publishing classified information. It may sound like science fiction at first, but the simple truth is that these three examples are the basic goals that hackers attempt to achieve when they encounter an application that includes weak code.

The repercussions that could stem from one or several of the incidents we just described come in two flavors: direct and indirect. The direct repercussions are, of course, linked to the loss of productivity inflicted upon all the employees and/or business partners who rely on the application to conduct normal business. The indirect repercussions include, but are not limited to, the loss of trust in the company from existing and potential customers alike after the incidents become public. In an age where perceptions often wield more power than reality in the mind of the public, bad P.R. can be disastrous for any organization's bottom line.

Systems Development

In our context, **systems development** is related to code that is created from scratch to create a line-of-business application. Whether this code is written in-house or outsourced to a third party does not change the fact that security must be included in the design process from the very beginning of the project.

Systems Maintenance

Systems maintenance is related to the fact that no code should remain static over the years. Indeed, new vulnerabilities are regularly discovered, new features are required/added, which in turn can introduce new vulnerabilities, and so forth. Note that this is not limited to custom applications. Most commercial applications also need to be updated regularly.

Systems maintenance is also related to the platform on which the code runs. The operating system—Windows 2000, XP, 2003, Linux, and so forth—also need to be regularly updated with add-on pieces of code called *hotfixes,* service packs, and patches. Again, this process needs to be tested: Does updating the operating system introduce new vulnerabilities for the code that we run on that platform? Does the update jeopardize the stability of the relationship between the platform on which the line-of-business application is running and the application itself?

Security Requirements of Systems

You may have heard the expression "There is no better time to think about selling your house than right before you actually buy it." The same holds true for the relationship between building applications and security: There is no better time to think about the security of the code you are writing than before you start to write it. In other words, security should remain one of the high-priority items during the design phase of any new application creation project.

If a developer attempted to retroactively "inject" security into existing code, without actually rewriting the whole code, all that would probably do is introduce a couple of new vulnerabilities for each vulnerability that the new code would have "fixed." It is a losing battle. Since part of what this chapter is concerned with is creating brand new code, why not create this code with security in mind right from the start? Again, to take another real estate example, why bother building a roof if a foundation has not been poured yet?

Risk Assessments

Section 10 of the ISO 17799 standard strongly recommends that risk assessments be performed "to evaluate the security requirements for new systems and upgrades." A risk assessment is a formal process that takes place at the beginning of the project. The aim is to identify and document all potential risks associated with the project. In keeping with the three tenets of IT security, the risk assessment will focus on those risks to the confidentiality of the data, the availability of the systems, and the integrity of the data accessible via the systems. Risk management decisions are based upon the outcome of the risk assessment, the classification of the information, the sensitivity of the information, and the business value of the information.

Independent Third-party Consultants: A Requirement?

Companies are usually reluctant to bring in third-party consultants for a simple reason: they add cost to the overall project. Some IT professionals might also worry that they will be blamed for mistakes that the third-party

10

consultants may find. This feeling may be understandable, but it should not enter the equation. This process is not about personal ego. It is about making sure that the code that is being developed is secure and does not threaten the confidentiality, integrity, and/or availability of the sensitive business data it relies on.

The advantages of bringing in third-party consultants are multiple. For one thing, it's a fresh pair of eyes. How many times have you labored over a crossword puzzle, desperately looking for that elusive five-letter word, when a friend came up to you, glanced at the puzzle, and told you what that darned word was? It's not that your friend was smarter than you; it's just that she had a fresh perspective on the problem and was able to use what you had already written as a clue. The same phenomenon occurs when third-party consultants bring a fresh brain, a different background, and a fresh pair of eyes to the problem.

A best practice is the requirement for third-party oversight to ensure that those who verify the code for security purposes are not the same people who actually wrote the code. This is an example of the principle of separation of duties. Separation of duties as defined by NIST in special publication 800-12 refers to the division of roles and responsibilities so that a single individual cannot subvert a critical process. Imagine for example, a bank that creates an in-house application to process loans. A coder hired for the project could simply leave himself a backdoor into the application, and be able to monitor/steal/tamper with all the data handled by the application. Having an independent third-party review the code is a simple way to make sure that such a security breach is not going to materialize.

Adding Controls After Implementation

Adding controls *after* implementation is a really bad idea. At best, it shows a breakdown in the process we have previously outlined in this section. It means that some risk or vulnerability was not correctly assessed, or was not correctly mitigated. The coders now need to backtrack and inject code that should have already been a part of the finished application. As was previously stated, this sort of retroactive code injection often can fix one issue and create a couple of other problems. Fixing those collateral issues can in turn create more potential risks, and this is an exponential risk increase that can really plague an application.

On the flip side, the risk identified after implementation cannot simply be ignored. Once identified, this risk needs to be either accepted or dealt with. At this stage, a choice will have to be made based on the degree of sensitivity of the data potentially involved in the risk, the cost associated with fixing this risk (including the loss of availability of the application, if it comes to that), and the probability of the risk actually becoming an exploited threat.

FYI: The Risk of Moving Past This Part of the Project

Let's face it: For developers, the coding is the "fun part" of the project. All the planning—especially the peripheral planning, such as incorporating security into the actual application—sometimes feels burdensome. Because of this, many developers fall in the trap of not spending enough time planning and refining the security design of their applications.

While enthusiasm for the application is understandable and expected, enthusiasm for creating clean and secure code must also be a part of the equation. It may be the responsibility of the team leader, the head of the Development Team, or the head of IT to make sure to create a culture that stresses and values the importance of clean and secure code. Not all pride is shameful. There is pride to be had in knowing that no corners were cut, that code was developed in a responsible way. This is another example of a concept we have already outlined: Network security, and in this case code development security, has a human face and is culture-based. That should not be overlooked. It should, in fact, be turned into a strength—not a liability—by the team leaders and by management.

IN PRACTICE: Security Requirements of Systems Policy

The goal of this policy is to influence the culture of the organization with the end result that security is a priority in all application development.

The *objective* of this policy is to:

- Ensure that security is built into information systems, including infrastructure, business applications, and user-developed applications.

The *audience* is network administrators, system developers, and members of the technical support staff.

▶▶ CONTINUED ON NEXT PAGE

10

▶▶ **CONTINUED**

TABLE 10.1 Sample Security Requirements of Systems Policy.

Section X:	[COMPANY] Information Security Policy	Effective Date:
Subsection	System Development and Maintenance	Change Control #:
Policy	Security Requirements of Systems	Approved By:
Objective	In support of information security goals, [COMPANY] will secure all hardware devices and software including operating systems and applications.	
Purpose	The purpose of this policy is to ensure that the [COMPANY'S] security requirements are met with any new implementations and do not have to be retrofitted.	
Audience	This policy applies to all Network Administrators and System Developers, along with all members of the Technical Support Staff.	
Policy	• A risk assessment will be performed to evaluate the security requirements for new systems or upgrades. • The system owner in conjunction with the Information Security Officer and Department of Information Technology will specify the security requirements of all new implementations prior to their final approval. • The controls and requirements will reflect the classification and value of the information assets. • Independent consultants will be brought in to assist in evaluations if deemed necessary. • Whenever possible, all controls will be required in the system prior to selection or implementation and not added after the implementation.	
Exceptions	None	
Disciplinary Actions	Violation of this policy may result in disciplinary action which may include termination for employees and temporaries; a termination of employment relations in the case of contractors or consultants; or dismissal for interns and volunteers. Additionally, individuals are subject to civil and criminal prosecution.	

The Things that Should Never Happen to Sensitive Data!

By definition, sensitive data needs to be protected. In some cases, this data belongs to the company: proprietary data, research and development data, and so forth. In other cases, the data is entrusted to the company by another entity. A simple example of that would be your medical files. You have entrusted your physician with your medical information. Your physician keeps it on file to better provide you with health services.

If a company creates an application system that handles sensitive data, the application system must not put the information in question at risk. Speaking of risk, let's look at all the frightful things that can happen to that data because of an unsecured application system.

Data Loss

Data loss is a nightmare waiting to happen. It simply means that whatever data we had, we have no way to get back. Stating that such a situation can quickly become disastrous is like saying the Titanic did not just get involved in a run-of-the-mill fender bender. For example, imagine a small community bank with a loan department. Let's pretend that a hacker compromised the bank's network and deleted each and every tidbit of information related to loan activities. We basically have a bank that has lent millions of dollars and has no idea to whom, or how much is still owed on those loans. Ouch!

Data Modification

Data modification means that the data is still there. It's just that the data is not accurate and has been tampered with. In other words, while there is data in the system, it cannot be trusted. How dramatic this can be is directly related to whether the data owners are aware that the data cannot be trusted.

For example, imagine that someone is registered with his local hospital for a simple procedure. Maybe he is going to have an appendectomy. While this is not exactly anyone's idea of a fun time, it is a pretty routine procedure. Now imagine that a hacker has compromised an application system that handles medical files and changed the scheduled appendectomy into a leg amputation. I gather that you are starting to sense that unless the data modification has been spotted on time, our friend will wake up with an intact appendix but without a left leg, simply because the data was trusted and used to proceed with the wrong surgical procedure.

In other, not-so-graphic words, if a company is going to rely on sensitive data to make business decisions, it must inherently trust the veracity of the sensitive data involved in the decision-making process if it wants to avert disastrous situations.

10

Data Misuse

Data misuse is a slightly different take on the problem. The data is not lost; it is still very much there. It has not been the victim of tampering, either; therefore, the data integrity has not been threatened. The data is for all intents and purposes valid and legitimate. It is the way in which it is used that is not legitimate.

Again, let's use a "real world" example. Suppose an employee gains access to insider, sensitive information regarding an upcoming merger involving her company. The application system that handled this sensitive data was not correctly secured, and while the employee was not looking for this information, she still came across it. She quickly realizes that this is potentially profitable information. For example, she might buy shares of the company in anticipation of seeing prices soar once the information is made public, or she might sell the information to a corporate rival. Or she could do the right thing and inform management that she has accessed information that is "above her pay grade," and that she is afraid that another, less honest employee might do the same.

It is the employee's responsibility to alert the Information Security Officer or designee that the application is faulty and divulging information that should not be made public. Failing to do so in the hopes of duplicating the process and gaining access to more sensitive information is a crime.

Sloppy Code vs. Secure Code

In the world of developers, there are two types of code released by programmers: sloppy code and secure code. Sloppy code is sometimes the result of an amateurish effort, but more often than not it reflects a flawed process. Secure code, however, is always the result of careful planning that considered security as an element of the coding process from the beginning of the design phase onward.

System Owners

System owners must be aware of the fact that deploying secured application systems is their responsibility. It is therefore important to clearly identify who the system owners are, and to make certain that they understand their responsibilities and what those responsibilities imply. If employees need proper training to reach these goals, then it must be done at the earliest stage of development.

Input Validation: An Introduction

Input validation is a keyword used in correlation with secure coding. It is really quite a simple concept once we look at it for what it is. What's more, it is a concept that does not really require actual coding knowledge.

Imagine a Web page with a simple form that contains fields corresponding to your physical address information, such as street name, zip code, and so on. Upon hitting the "submit" button, the information you entered in the fields is sent to the Web server and entered into a back-end database. Input validation deals with the kind of information that is entered in those fields and, maybe even more importantly, the kind of information that will *not* be allowed to be entered.

To stick with our example, let's focus on the zip code field. We all know how zip codes are formatted: They consist of numbers only, and the basic ones only include five digits. This example will focus on this type of zip code.

A first valid level of input validation would look at how many characters are entered in that field. Let's assume that the developer limited the field to six characters. This limitation would prevent the user from entering more than six characters, but what would happen if fewer than six characters were entered? In this case, if five or fewer characters were entered, the format would be wrong and the form should not attempt to send that data to the back-end server.

Furthermore, there is no reason why a zip code field should be used to enter anything other than numbers. Neither letters, ASCII characters, nor anything else belongs in that field. The next level of input validation should therefore refuse to send any content that is not strictly numbers-only.

If a coder really wanted to take this process to its logical conclusion, he could add a third level of input validation that would correlate the information in the zip code field with the information in the town/city and state fields, making sure that the entered zip actually matched the zip that goes with that combination of city and state.

You may wonder: why bother to go through all this? Who cares if a user sends the wrong zip? Who cares if the information entered in the zip code field includes letters and/or ASCII characters? Hackers care. Hackers attempt to pass code in those fields to see how the database will react. They want to see if they can bring down the application (DoS attack against that application), bring down the server on which it resides (DoS against the server, and therefore against all the applications that reside on that server), or run code on the target server to manipulate or publish sensitive data. Proper input validation is therefore a way to limit the ability of a hacker to try and "abuse" an application system.

10

Advanced Input Validation

By now, you have a pretty good handle on what input validation is. Let's add to this knowledge by examining different layers to the concept.

The generic idea behind input validation, as we have seen, is to use logic checks in correlation with the data that needs to be passed via the application interface. In other words, we look at the characteristics of the expected data, and we make sure that the actual data entered matches those characteristics before we allow for that data to be transmitted to the back-end database.

But hackers are devious, and we therefore need to be more refined than that in the way we protect our data. Imagine an application system that requires our users to authenticate by logging on. Traditionally, this is achieved from a technical perspective by using a "token." If this token is compromised, how do we still protect our sensitive data? By making sure that the token itself is not limited just to predictable information such as username and password. A simple method is to encrypt the token using a key that also includes a time stamp, for example. When the token is replayed by a hacker, once the system decrypts it, it gets a time stamp that does not match the current time stamp. The attempt to run what is referred to as a "replay attack" will be foiled by proper examination of the information passed via the application system interface.

Testing the Plausibility of Data Inputs

Many application systems are designed to rely on outside parameter tables for dynamic data. For example, it is easy to imagine an e-commerce solution with a shopping cart that would enter the sales tax automatically based on the zip code entered. Input validation is also involved in the process of checking that the sales tax rate entered is indeed the one that matches the state entered by the customer. What is tricky in this type of situation is that the information pulled from the outside table is real and legitimate—it is just that it does not apply to the situation at hand. This is a lot harder to track than when the data input is clearly wrong, such as when a letter is entered in a zip code field.

Dynamic data is also something that we need to be careful with as it relates to our application systems. By dynamic data, we mean data that changes over time. A simple example of this is the value of a certain stock, or the exchange rate for a particular currency. These values can potentially change all day, every day. This dynamic character needs to be kept in mind. Saying that a Euro equals $1.30 might be right today, but it might be totally off tomorrow. If the transaction involves a large sum, the difference can translate into a fair amount of money!

Output Validation

In this section, we have repeatedly looked at input validation, not output validation. You need to be aware of output validation, however, especially as it relates to hacker discovery techniques. We have already discussed that the first step of the hacking process is footprinting. In other words, what is known by criminals the world over as "casing the joint." Finding out as much as possible about the target victim prior to proceeding with the actual misdeed provides some of the most enjoyable moments of Hollywood-produced cinema. In the real world, it can be a very boring endeavor, but one that is still necessary and cannot be overlooked. You can rest assured: efficient hackers do not overlook this step.

One of the first things that a hacker needs to find out about a targeted application system is how it reacts to systematic abuse of the interface. A hacker will learn a lot about how the application reacts to errors if the developers did not run output validation tests prior to deployment. They may, for example, learn that a certain application is vulnerable to SQL Injection attacks, or buffer overflow attacks, and so on. The answer an application gives about an error is potentially a pointer that can lead to a vulnerability, and a hacker will try and make that application "talk" to better customize the attack.

Developers therefore need to run their own tests by feeding erroneous data into the interface to see how it reacts and what it reveals about the underlying code. They need to edit those answers to not allow the application system to reveal anything that could put the sensitive data it handles at risk of being compromised. The more time spent on this activity, the less likely hackers will gain the advantage they are seeking.

Speaking of Hollywood, there was recently a movie where the main protagonist went to a hotel and asked for a guest. He didn't know what room number that guest—the target—had been given, so he simply walked to the front desk and asked for a phone call to be placed to the guest's room. The concierge complied with the request, and used a machine to dial the room directly. This machine was running an application system that connected the front desk phone to a room phone by simply inputting the room number. The only issue was that the screen on this machine displayed the room number in clear text as it was entered. Bingo! Our man had the information he wanted, simply by using the machine the way it was supposed to be used. The output validation had not been thought out to protect the confidential data represented by the room number of a guest and the privacy to which the guest was entitled.

IN PRACTICE: Security in Application Systems Policy

This policy clearly defines for developers what is expected of all code written by or for the organization. The benefit is that is supports the effort to write "clean code."

The *objectives* of this policy are to:

■ Prevent loss, modification, or misuse of user data in application systems.

■ Design appropriate controls and audit trails into application systems.

The *audience* is network administrators, system developers, and members of the technical support staff.

TABLE 10.2 Sample Security in Application Systems Policy.

Section X:	[COMPANY] Information Security Policy	Effective Date:
Subsection	System Development and Maintenance	Change Control #:
Policy	Security in Application Systems	Approved By:
Objective	In support of information security goals, [COMPANY] will require appropriate controls to prevent loss, modification or misuse of user data in application systems.	
Purpose	The purpose of this policy is to ensure all code written by the [COMPANY] is inherently secure.	
Audience	This policy applies to all Network Administrators and System Developers, along with all members of the Technical Support Staff.	
Policy	• All code developed or customized by the [COMPANY] is to be tested and validated during development, prior to release and whenever a change is implemented. • System owners are responsible for oversight of secure code development.	

▶▶ CONTINUED ON NEXT PAGE

» CONTINUED

Exceptions	None
Disciplinary Actions	Violation of this policy may result in disciplinary action which may include termination for employees and temporaries; a termination of employment relations in the case of contractors or consultants; or dismissal for interns and volunteers. Additionally, individuals are subject to civil and criminal prosecution.

Risk Assessments and Cryptography

Cryptography is defined as the process that takes plain text and transforms it into what is known as *cipher text*. Cipher text is text that cannot be read without applying an algorithm and a predetermined value to turn it back into plain text. The predetermined value is known as the **key.** Simply put, the key specifies what part of the algorithm to apply, in what order, and what variables to input. In other words, if you don't have the key, cipher text will remain unreadable until you can find a way to either obtain a copy of that key, or a way to break (or figure out) the key.

This highlights the two weaknesses of cryptography: keys that are not secured properly, and keys that are so weak that they can be broken easily.

IN PRACTICE: Breaking the Caesar Cipher

Let's take the time here to quickly go through a fun little cryptography example. Let's say that you came across the following text:

htslwfyzqfyntsx dtz gwtpj ymj hfjxfw hnumjw

Since that does not seem to be just a sentence written in a foreign language—at least not one used on this planet—it must be cipher text. If it is cipher text, we know that it was generated using some key. Therefore, cracking that key is what stands between us and clear text. The number one lesson we learn in cryptology is to work from what we do know to try and make sense of what we don't know. Look at the example of cipher text above. What do we know? We know that there are six groups of letters separated by blank spaces, just like six words in a sentence would be. So let's treat them as individual words until proven otherwise. You may also have noticed that there are no numbers or ASCII special characters. It's all letters in there. Furthermore, all those letters are in lowercase, and there are no punctuation signs either. Starting with the smaller words, we see that there are two words that are

» CONTINUED ON NEXT PAGE

10

▸▸ **CONTINUED**

only made of three letters, namely *dtz* and *ymj*. The most common three-letter word in the English language is the word "the." Let's see if we can use that tidbit of knowledge to our advantage.

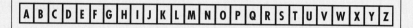

| A | B | C | D | E | F | G | H | I | J | K | L | M | N | O | P | Q | R | S | T | U | V | W | X | Y | Z |

FIGURE 10.1 The alphabet

You have no doubt recognized the series of letters above as being the alphabet. Now let's say that *ymj* in the cipher text stands for "the." We don't know that yet, we are just assuming, just to see what we get. Let's add to our alphabet:

| A | B | C | D | E | F | G | H | I | J | K | L | M | N | O | P | Q | R | S | T | U | V | W | X | Y | Z |
| | | | | | | | | | E | | | H | | | | | | | | | | | | | |

FIGURE 10.2 Letters pushed to the right

What do we notice? That between line 1 and line 2, the letter E was pushed 5 squares to the right. We also notice that the letter H was pushed 5 letters to the right. And what do you know? The same applies to the letter T. This pattern is not a coincidence. It is the key to our encryption method. Let's now complete the second line:

| A | B | C | D | E | F | G | H | I | J | K | L | M | N | O | P | Q | R | S | T | U | V | W | X | Y | Z |
| V | W | X | Y | Z | A | B | C | D | E | F | G | H | I | J | K | L | M | N | O | P | Q | R | S | T | U |

FIGURE 10.3 The completed second line

Now that we have completed this part of the exercise, we have the complete transposition cipher. To use it, simply replace the letters in the top line by the one directly below it in the second line.

htslwfyzqfyntsx dtz gwtpj ymj hfjxfw hnumjw

therefore becomes this:

Congratulations you broke the Caesar cipher

By the way, if you are interested in cryptography, and learning more about the Caesar cipher, use your favorite search engine and run searches on such topics as "cryptanalysis," "cryptography challenge," "Caesar cipher," and so on.

Risk Assessment

A thorough risk assessment should already have been conducted for any application system development project, and one of the goals of such an assessment is to determine what data should never be sent in clear text between an application and a back-end file or database server. A rule of thumb is that any data that was classified as sensitive should always be transferred in encrypted format. Sensitive data, as you may remember, is data that should never be divulged to the public. More often than not, sensitive data should not even be divulged to all employees of the company, but only to the select few authorized users cleared for such data.

It may be tempting just to resort to encrypting all traffic between the application system and the back-end server, but remember that encryption means "overhead," meaning that encrypted information takes longer to be transmitted and processed by all the computers involved in the transaction. The data needs to be encrypted prior to the transaction, and again decrypted by the target computer before it can be displayed or stored. It is therefore recommended to encrypt only data that needs this security feature.

Confidentiality, Integrity, Authentication, Nonrepudiation

The first use of encryption is obvious: cipher text is safe from prying eyes. A simple example is the use of e-mail, which, by default, sends messages in clear text. If a hacker intercepts the message using a packet sniffer such as Ethereal, for example—**www.ethereal.com**—any message that was sent is hers to read as it was sent in clear text. If all it includes is the coming week's menu at the company's cafeteria, no harm was done. If the message was listing the password for the administrative account for the entire network, it's a disaster. Encryption ensures that the confidentiality of the data being transmitted is protected, and that only those users authorized to read this data can access it in plain text. In the "real world," this is achieved by using digital certificates.

Data integrity, as you know by now, is the assurance that the data has not been tampered with. Let's keep the example of e-mail to illustrate this point. Let's say a user sends an e-mail to his boss, in which he praises him for his hard work and leadership. A hacker—a disgruntled coworker, maybe?—intercepts the message, replaces the text with something akin to "I've known goats who smelled better than you," and sends it back on its way to the boss. While this is more a prank than anything else, it could result in our friend losing his job. The answer? If confidentiality is not needed, just the assurance that the data integrity of the message is beyond question, using a digital signature will do the trick.

A *digital signature* is basically digital code that is appended to an e-mail. Because that digital code was signed using a user's private key, I know that she indeed sent the e-mail. And because the original plain text message was run through a hash function before it was signed, upon reception of the e-mail it is run through the same hash function. If the two results match, then I know beyond a shadow of a doubt that the message is legitimate and was not tampered with. In other words, digital signatures accomplish two things for us: They prove that the data integrity of the message is intact and that the person who sent the e-mail really is who I think she is. Since using her public key decrypts the signature that was encrypted using her private key, she must be who she says she is and the e-mail is therefore deemed legitimate. Again, I want to stress that a digital signature does NOT provide confidentiality—just authenticity.

FYI: Public Keys, Private Keys, Hash Functions, and Message Digests

It is clearly not the aim of this book to delve too much into the technical aspects of encryption, but since some of these notions have been used in the examples, let's quickly review what they are.

Public keys and private keys: Think of private and public keys as two keys to the same lock—one used to lock and the other to unlock. The private key never leaves the owner's possession. The public key is given out freely. In the case of digital signatures, the private key is used to "sign" or lock the message. The sender's corresponding public key is used by the recipient to unlock the message. Since only these two keys match, the recipient can be assured the message came from the sender. For example, Joe has a unique private key. He digitally signs a message with it. He sends me the message. I use Joe's public key to decrypt the message. Because Joe's public key can only decrypt messages encrypted using Joe's private key, I know that the e-mail indeed came from Joe. Nonrepudiation is proven.

Hash functions and message digests: Running text through a hash function creates a message digest. A hashing function turns a variable-length input into a fixed-length output. If two people have the same hashing function, and they run the same text into it, then they should get the same message digest in return. If I run the text of an e-mail through a hash function, I obtain a certain message digest. If I send you that same e-mail, and you run it through the same hash function, you should end up with the same message digest I did. If that is the case, then the integrity of the message sent is proven. If the message digests are not the same, then the message was edited/tampered with during transport, and the contents of the message cannot be trusted.

Keepers of the Keys

One of the weaknesses of encryption is how we protect the keys used in correlation with encryption. If a hacker gets a hold of the keys used by a company, all cipher text that company will send will basically be clear text for this hacker. In other words, there is no more confidentiality. And if the hacker compromised those keys unbeknownst to the company, the company will continue to send text that it believes is encrypted when it is not. The repercussions of this situation can be disastrous. What if the hacker decides to sell those keys to a corporate rival? This rival is now able to read all encrypted data belonging to the company as if it were clear text.

Whoever is responsible for protecting those encryption keys plays an extremely important strategic role in the company. More often than not, that role falls to some senior people in the IT department, in correlation with the Information Security Officer.

Key Management

Key management involves many different functions, from acquiring the digital certificates, to assigning them to different application systems or people, to maintaining the revocation lists, and finally retiring keys. There are two kinds of digital certificates: those issued by a third-party certificate authority, and those created in-house for internal use. The rule of thumb is that if the keys are only going to be used for internal application systems, then internal certificates can be used. If, however, the application systems will be used to interface with the public, as in the case of a Web site for example, then the digital certificates should be purchased from a trusted certificate authority. And remember that the trust that will be put in the digital certificate is actually the trust that is placed in the certificate authority that issued it. Therefore, it is recommended to purchase digital certificates only from the proven leaders in the industry.

It is recommended to use a key for only one given application system and not reuse that key for another application system. Although the savings can be considerable to use one digital certificate for all application systems, the downside is that if that one digital certificate is compromised, then all the application systems are wide open to an attacker. Furthermore, one user may be allowed to use one application system but not another. Assigning the same key to both systems would create a risk that our user might take it upon himself to go see what the second application system is all about—and what encrypted data he can pilfer. A certificate policy should be drafted. A certificate policy is a document that identifies the exact situation in which a given digital certificate will be used.

Digital certificates have an expiration date, usually one year after they were released. While it is possible to renew them, this is not a good idea. A digital certificate is like a secret. The longer it exists, the greater the chance

10

that it will be leaked and broken. Simply renewing a certificate for another year is the same as issuing a certificate for two years!

Certificates can be revoked. This is usually a very bad sign. At the very least, it means that there is a chance the keys have been compromised. The rule of thumb here is that if there is the slightest chance that a key may have been compromised, then the digital certificates need to be revoked and removed from service as soon as possible. This may prove in the long term to be an overreaction, but it remains the secure and responsible thing to do. Again, digital certificates work only on the basis of trust. If I can't trust that the keys have not been compromised, how can I place any real trust in the certificate?

The primary method used to communicate that a digital certificate has been revoked is through the use of certificate revocation lists. The security policy needs to clearly mention who is in charge of revoking a certificate.

Note that a certificate may also be suspended. This is a pretty rare occurrence, put into effect when a digital certificate is known to be out of service for the foreseeable future. Indeed, if a certificate is not used for a while, the certificate authority may revoke it. Instead, it is recommended to suspend the certificate until it will be used again.

Key destruction is another phase of key management. Let's pretend that a company uses a dedicated server to create its own digital certificates. Later on it decides to upgrade to another server and plans to donate the old server to a local school. Prior to doing so, the company must overwrite all the key data on the hard drive. This process is known as *zeroization,* because all the data will be overwritten three times with zeros until it is deemed to be unrecoverable.

Encryption and Business Partners

A company frequently needs to allow another company access to a specific array of data. This type of situation requires tightened security, because only those authorized, third-party contacts should be able to gain access to this data.

Imagine a situation where a company sells automotive parts. Let's call this fictitious company AutoParts. AutoParts purchases the parts from a wholesaler and stores them in a warehouse. Every day, the wholesaler connects to a Web site owned by AutoParts and checks which items were sold the day before and need to be replenished.

Note that this Web site—also referred to as an "extranet"—is not accessible to the public. It is accessible only to those authorized users identified by AutoParts. Because the data should not be traveling between the Web server and the Web client using plain HTTP—which sends data in clear text—some encryption method should be employed. HTTPS, which is a secure version of HTTP that relies on SSL and digital certificates for encryption purposes, would be an obvious technical answer to this problem by taking care of protecting the confidentiality of the data being exchanged.

FYI: Encryption: It's All About the Strength of the Keys

While it is beyond the scope of this book to look in-depth into encryption issues, you still need to understand a very basic concept: What matters when it comes to encryption is the strength of the keys used for encryption purposes. A rule of thumb is that the key should be at least of 128-bit strength or it will be not be strong enough to prevent being cracked by a hacker—which pretty much negates the whole purpose of encryption.

Weak keys are an inherent weakness of some applications, notably wireless technologies used to access network over the 802.11 standard. If you use a wireless network at home—most people do so from a laptop to be able to roam around the house and still be able to access the Internet, for example—you may be familiar with WEP, or Wired Equivalent Privacy. While WEP touts the use of a 128-bit encryption scheme, the truth is that one of its components actually uses a 24-bit key. This flaw means that no one takes WEP very seriously. Tests show that WEP-encrypted packets can be cracked in about two hours. So much for a true security measure!

10

IN PRACTICE: Cryptographic Controls Policy

The goal of this policy is to require an organization think about their internal and external communications and, when necessary, apply cryptographic controls.

The *objective* of this policy is to:

■ Protect the confidentiality, authenticity, and integrity of sensitive data

The *audience* is all network administrators, system developers, and members of the technical support staff.

▶▶ CONTINUED ON NEXT PAGE

▶▶ CONTINUED

TABLE 10.3 Sample Cryptography Controls Policy.

Section X:	[COMPANY] Information Security Policy	Effective Date:
Subsection	System Development and Maintenance	Change Control #:
Policy	Cryptographic Controls	Approved By:
Objective	In support of information security goals, [COMPANY] will implement cryptographic controls as appropriate.	
Purpose	The purpose of this policy to secure the confidentiality, authenticity and integrity of at-risk information assets.	
Audience	This policy applies to all Network Administrators and System Developers, along with all members of the Technical Support Staff.	
Policy	• A risk assessment will be done to determine the level of protection that sensitive information should be given. • Encryption will be implemented when needed per the results of the risk assessment to cover confidentiality and/or authentication and integrity. • The Office of Information Security will determine the appropriate level of control. • The Department of Information Technology will be in charge of implementation and key management.	
Exceptions	None	
Disciplinary Actions	Violation of this policy may result in disciplinary action which may include termination for employees and temporaries; a termination of employment relations in the case of contractors or consultants; or dismissal for interns and volunteers. Additionally, individuals are subject to civil and criminal prosecution.	

Operating System and Application Software Stability

Application software does not usually stand by itself as an all-inclusive solution. More often than not, it is built to run on top of an existing environment called an *operating system.* Windows 2000, 2003, and XP, Novell NetWare, and a plethora of versions of Linux are all examples of commonly used operating systems.

Because of the dependent relationship between the OS and the applications, the stability of the OS is paramount to the availability of the application. Indeed, if a server cannot boot because a system file is corrupt, no one can use the applications that execute on this server. Compare this to a car equipped with a special feature such as a Global Positioning System (GPS). The car is the OS, and the GPS is the application system. Well, if the car doesn't run, who cares how accurate the GPS really is? It's not like the car is about to move anyway, so all the built-in maps and directions that the GPS can deliver are basically useless, not because they are wrong, but because the platform on which they rely to have a role to play is out of order.

The policy items we will outline in this section can therefore apply to both the OS and the application system. To avoid redundancy, we have compiled a common list that we will present in the rest of this section.

Only Stable Versions Should Be Deployed on Production Servers

When software is created, it exists in two states: stable and in development. You may have heard of the expression "beta release." It means that this particular software is not ready to be truly released yet, and is still being worked on. It is close to being "ready for prime time," but there are still some bugs and other issues. Because those issues and bugs threaten the stability of the software, and usually manifest themselves in untimely crashes, such "unfinished" code is not acceptable for live production servers where stability is a must. Indeed, an application crash and a server crash can both result in loss of data (loss of availability) and corrupted data (loss of data integrity).

Conclusion: Only stable and tested software releases should be deployed on production servers to protect data availability and data integrity.

Updates: Required, Dangerous, or Both?

Software updates require their own policy, known as patch management policy. Note that there is a difference between a software update and a software upgrade: A software update is just fixing a known issue of an installed release; a software upgrade involves moving on from one software release to another.

Typical reasons to update software are:

- A security vulnerability has been discovered, and new code has been created to eradicate that vulnerability

10

- A new feature is needed, and a new module is added onto the core application

- A nonsecurity-related "bug," or issue with the software, has been discovered, and new code has been created to relieve the issue.

Regardless of why new code has been created, just because it exists does not mean that it must be installed. This point is also valid for both OS files and application system files.

So, if new and improved code has been released, why should it not be installed on production servers? Because it has not been tested on an environment similar to that in which this new code will be deployed. For example, a new system file might work perfectly fine with 99 percent of the software out there, but what if one of the line-of-business applications deployed on the same server falls in the remaining 1 percent? This can have a disastrous effect on the availability, and potentially on the integrity, of the data. This risk, however minimal it may appear, should not be taken.

Conclusion: No updates should be deployed either on the OS or on the application side until they have been thoroughly tested in a lab environment and declared to be safe to be released on production servers. The bottom line is simple: There is a reason why servers are either production or test servers and using a production server as a test server is a very bad idea.

FYI: Patch Updates and Rollback Policies

Let's say that we have a software update that has been tested, documented, and declared fit for deployment on live production servers. Before this deployment can actually take place, a rollback policy should be designed, tested, and documented. A rollback policy is an additional insurance policy: It is designed to bring a server or an application to the stable state in which it was prior to the patch being deployed. Even though the patch has already been thoroughly tested, we still need to prepare for the unforeseen and make sure that we have a tested and documented exit strategy to get back to that previous stable state in case the worst were to happen.

Some say that only the paranoid survive in this business. It's a bit of an exaggeration, but the observation is not all that farfetched! The simple reality is that data integrity and availability have a (potentially very high) cost, and therefore must not be taken lightly.

Updates: When Should They Be Applied?

Beyond the obvious point we just spent some time making—updates should be deployed only after they have been tested and approved, and only after an appropriate rollback strategy has also been tested and approved—there are a couple of aspects of patch management timing that need to be taken into account. First, even if an update has been tested, there is still a chance of failure. Adequate time should be allowed for recovery procedures such as a restore or rollback.

If an update requires a system reboot, it should be delayed until the reboot will have the least impact on business productivity. Typically, this means after hours and weekends, although if a company is international and has users who rely on data located in different time zones, this can get a bit tricky.

If an update does not require a system reboot, but will still severely impact the level of system performance, it should also be delayed until it will have the least impact on business productivity.

However, some other mitigating factors may force an administration team to ignore—or at least forgo—the previous recommendation:

- A new security vulnerability has been identified on either a server or an application system and must be patched as soon as possible because attacks against the vulnerability have already been reported.

- An application system or an operating system has been behaving more and more erratically, threatening data integrity and availability to the point where it is decided that a little down time now is better than the impending crash that is sure to result from ignoring the situation any longer.

Conclusion: There is a time for everything, and this platitude also applies to patch deployment. A careful examination of the impact of the patch installation—based on the information gained from the test deployments that should already have taken place—should dictate the best time to install a patch, unless a crisis such as a security vulnerability or an unstable application already exists.

Updates: Who Should Apply Them?

Only authorized users should be allowed to apply patches to either the OS or the application systems. These users should be properly trained and officially in charge of this important task. In most cases, they will either be in-house members of the IT Department or third-party technical consultants.

10

Whoever is in charge of patch deployment should work closely with the coders who developed the application and the patch. You will notice that we said work closely *with* coders, not abdicate responsibility *to* coders. Best security practices dictate a separation of duties between developers and operations. Developers should not be allowed to unilaterally apply their own patches or upgrades. All instances should be subject to a change management review and authorized by information system owners.

Conclusion: Not just any tech should be given the task of patch management. The patch management policy should clearly state who will be assigned this task. If it is a third-party consultant, she will need to be approved by the company not only on the merit of her technical abilities, but also on her willingness to sign a nondisclosure agreement in case she was to come into contact with some sensitive, proprietary information or technology.

Testing Environment Concerns

We have already outlined several times the importance of testing in regard to patch deployment. However, we have only alluded to testing from a conceptual perspective. We have not looked at it from a practical point of view yet.

The Testing Environment The worst case scenario for a testing environment is that a company simply does not have one, and basically treats production servers as test servers. As we have already seen, that's really not a commendable idea, although it is a widely used practice—primarily because testing costs money. Potentially a lot of money, especially if the testing environment is set up as a perfect mirror image of the production environment, software and hardware included. That would be the best case scenario, and frankly it is rarely a reality. It is, however, a goal for which to aim.

The equation is simple: The closer to the production environment the test environment is, the more we can trust the test results. The more we can trust those test results, the less likely it is that bad surprises will pop up (and the more money we will save by eliminating potential disastrous situations). This becomes a basic situation where we need to compare the cost of setting up the test environment to the cost of losing data availability and potentially data integrity. The relationship between these costs will dictate how much money should reasonably be spent to create that test environment.

Conclusion: Testing environments should be totally separate from production environments.

Don't Use Live Data in a Testing Environment Imagine a medical practice with an Electronic Medical Records (EMR) database replete with patient information. Imagine the security measures that have been put in place on the live server to make sure that the confidentiality, integrity, and availability of the database are protected. Since this database is pretty much the lifeblood of this practice and is protected under law, it is to be expected that those security measures are pretty extensive. It is also to be expected that those same extensive, and therefore potentially costly, security measures have not been deployed on the test environment. That means that if we are using the live database in the test environment, it is now put at serious risk from not being protected to the same degree as it is on the live network. The data is potentially exposed to those who do not meet the criteria of "need to know." This is a serious violation of confidentiality.

So, if live data isn't used, how do we validate the testing results? The answer is simple—with simulated data, often referred to as *dummy data*. Simulated data takes the same form as live data but is in essence fictional. For example, rather than using actual patient data to test an EMR database, fake patient data would be entered into the system. That way the data could be tested but there would be no violation of confidentiality.

Conclusion: Simulated or dummy data should be used on test systems.

IN PRACTICE: Security of System Files, Development, and Support Processes Policy

The goal of this policy is implement a secure framework inside of which all systems maintenance and support activities occur. Again, this is a case of influencing the organization's culture and creating an overall mindset of security.

The *objectives* of this policy are to:

- Ensure that IT projects and support activities take place in a secure fashion.

- Maintain the security of all application systems during maintenance functions.

The *audience* is all network administrators, system developers, and members of the technical support staff.

▶▶ CONTINUED ON NEXT PAGE

10

▶▶ **CONTINUED**

TABLE 10.4 Sample Security of System Files, Development, and Support Processes Policy.

Section X:	[COMPANY] Information Security Policy	Effective Date:
Subsection	**System Development and Maintenance**	**Change Control #:**
Policy	**Security of System Files, Development, and Support Processes**	**Approved By:**
Objective	In support of information security goals, the stability and integrity of information systems will be protected.	
Purpose	The purpose of this policy is to protect the [COMPANY'S] information resources by minimizing the risk for operational system corruption.	
Audience	This policy applies to all Network Administrators and System Developers, along with all members of the Technical Support Staff.	
Policy	• Only stable versions of both Operating Systems and Application Systems should be deployed on production servers. • The Department of Information Security is responsible for designing and implementing a patch management process that reflects the organizational commitment to security, integrity and availability. • Patch management activities must be documented in accordance with the [COMPANY] change control process. • No live data shall be deployed on non-production systems.	
Exceptions	None	
Disciplinary Actions	Violation of this policy may result in disciplinary action which may include termination for employees and temporaries; a termination of employment relations in the case of contractors or consultants; or dismissal for interns and volunteers. Additionally, individuals are subject to civil and criminal prosecution.	

Summary

Corporate America relies more and more on computer networks and on line-of-business applications. This reliance implies that the availability of those solutions must be protected to avoid severe losses in revenue. Custom applications should be built with security in mind from the start. When applications and operating systems are updated, the code should first be tested to make sure that it will not have a disastrous impact on the overall solution. When application systems conduct transactions that involve sensitive information, they should do so in an encrypted fashion to protect data confidentiality. Appropriate policies must be designed and deployed to make sure that these goals are achieved to help maximize the positive use of those important application systems.

Test Your Skills

MULTIPLE CHOICE QUESTIONS

1. When is the best time to think about security when building an application?

   A. Build the application first, then add a layer of security.

   B. As you start planning for the application, the focus should already be on creating secured application.

   C. Start the application development phase, and when you reach the halfway point, you have enough of a basis to look at to decide where and how to set up the security elements.

   D. No security needs to be developed inside of the code itself. It will be handled at the operating system level.

2. Which of the following should be handled first when developing new application systems?

   A. a risk assessment to determine how the sensitive data will be handled by the new application system

   B. a patch management strategy

   C. the level of access third-party consultants will have to the source code

   D. determine when the security controls will be added to the final product.

10

3. Adding security controls to an application system after implementation is:

A. normal: that's when they are added

B. not a good thing: they should have been developed from the start

C. not a good thing: they should have been developed at the halfway point of development

D. not a good thing: security controls should not be added to an application because they are handled at the operating system level

4. Which of the following should never happen to sensitive data handled by an application system?

A. data loss

B. data modification

C. data misuse

D. all of the above

5. Which of the following statements about digital signatures is true?

A. Digital signatures guarantee confidentiality only.

B. Digital signatures guarantee integrity only.

C. Digital signatures guarantee integrity and nonrepudiation.

D. Digital signatures guarantee nonrepudiation only.

6. When unauthorized data modification occurs, which of the following tenets of security is directly being threatened?

A. confidentiality

B. integrity

C. availability

D. authentication

7. The act of limiting the characters that can be entered in a Web form that is a part of an application system is known as:

A. output validation

B. input validation

C. output testing

D. input testing

8. The act of limiting the information that is displayed by application system when errors are entered on purpose is known as:

   A. output validation

   B. onput validation

   C. output testing

   D. input testing

9. Which of the following statements about encryption is true?

   A. All encryption methods are equal: just choose one and implement it.

   B. The encryption method chosen must rely on a strong enough key.

   C. Encryption is not needed for internal applications. It should only be used for applications that link the inside of the network to the outside of the network.

   D. Encryption guarantees integrity and availability, but not confidentiality.

10. Which of the following statements about patch deployments is true?

    A. Patch deployment should take place as soon as the patch is made available.

    B. Patch deployment should take place as soon as the patch has been tested.

    C. Patch deployment should take place as soon as the patch has been tested, and a rollback strategy has been tested.

    D. Patch deployment should take place as soon as the patch has been tested, and a rollback strategy has been deployed.

11. Live production data should be:

    A. deployed on production servers only

    B. deployed on production and test servers

    C. deployed on test servers only

    D. deployed on neither test nor production servers

12. Which of the following statements about patches is true?

    A. Patches should only be installed by developers.

    B. Patches should only be installed by in-house engineers.

    C. Patches should only be installed by third-party consultants.

    D. None of the above.

10

13. Which of the following statements about software is not true?

    A. Beta versions of software should be installed on live servers.

    B. Stable versions of software should be installed on live servers.

    C. Beta versions of software can be installed on test servers.

    D. Beta and stable versions of software can be installed on test servers.

14. A rollback strategy is:

    A. when an application system is reloaded with the previous version of the software

    B. when an application system is reloaded with the beta version of the software

    C. when an application system is brought back to the state it was in prior to a patch installation

    D. when an application system is being patched

15. Which of the following statements about a hash function is true?

    A. It takes a variable-length input and turns it into a fixed-length output.

    B. It takes a variable-length input and turns it into a variable-length output.

    C. It takes a fixed-length input and turns it into a fixed-length output.

    D. It takes a fixed-length input and turns it into a variable-length output.

16. When is it acceptable not to have a test environment?

    A. when only beta versions are used

    B. when only stable versions are used

    C. when the cost of having one would be higher than the cost of loss of data availability

    D. when the cost of having one would be lower than the cost of loss of data availability

17. A test environment should:

    A. always be the exact same as the live environment

    B. be as cheap as possible no matter what

    C. be as close to the live environment as possible and still be cost-efficient

    D. include live data for true emulation of the real-world setup

18. Which of the following statements about dummy data is true?

    A. It should appear only on production servers.

    B. It should appear only on test servers.

    C. It should appear on both test and production servers.

    D. It should not appear on either test or production servers.

19. Why should live data not appear on a test server?

    A. because data can be corrupted on a test server

    B. because security measures on the test server may not be as strong as on the live server

    C. both A and B

    D. neither A nor B

20. Which of the following would be a reason not to deploy a patch?

    A. It has been tested and approved.

    B. It negatively impacts the performance of the server while being installed, and should therefore be installed at a later, more opportune time.

    C. It requires a reboot and should therefore never be applied.

    D. All of the above.

EXERCISES

Exercise 10.1: Building Security into Applications from the Start

1. List three reasons why security should be a concern from the onset of the code creation effort. Write a paragraph for each.

2. List two important issues that can arise from not developing applications with security in mind from the start. Write a paragraph for each.

3. CarRental USA hired you as a consultant. They are building an in-house application system that will pull data from a database located on one server, and display it via a Web-based interface running on another server. Write a paragraph about the perceived security issues that could plague this solution if not attended to.

Exercise 10.2: Input Validation

1. In your own words, write a paragraph defining input validation and why it is important.

2. You have developed an election results application. The purpose of the application is to record the vote of registered voters electronically. The first use of this application will be at your university. Specifically, there are three people running for class president. Only registered students should be allowed to vote. The application system interface will have fields where authorized voters will enter their first and last name and the name of the person for whom they are voting. Write a paragraph for each field, explaining how you would set up input validation.

3. A fourth field needs to be added per the request of the university president. This field will feature a number from 1 to 4 dedicated to recording which university year the voter is attending: freshmen will enter "1," sophomores "2," juniors "3," and seniors "4." What input validation method would you use in this example? Write a paragraph to substantiate your answer.

Exercise 10.3: Input Validation II

In this exercise, we will build on what you already created in Exercise 2.

1. One of the problems generated by our election results application is that many students have the same first and last name. What differentiating measure could we add to the existing "first name" and "last name" fields already present?

2. One of the coders offers to add a field for the middle initial. What input validation measure would you recommend in this circumstance? Write a paragraph to justify your position.

3. Another coder, afraid that there might be students with the same first name, last name, and middle initial, objects to that solution, and says that students should enter the name of their hometown and state to further identify themselves. What input validation method would you now recommend to secure these two new fields? Draft a paragraph to outline your opinion.

Exercise 10.4: Cryptography

1. In your own words, write a couple of paragraphs to explain why encryption is needed, what encryption is, and the importance of key strength in encryption.

2. Open an Internet search engine and run a search for "Caesar cipher." Create your own cipher with a character transposition of 6 letters as opposed to the regular 3. Write out the new letter grid you come up with.

3. Using the grid you created in the previous step, create a cipher text from this plain text quote from the great Mark Twain:

"The human race has one really effective weapon, and that is laughter."

Exercise 10.5: Updates and Systems Maintenance

1. In your own words, write a paragraph or two explaining why only stable operating versions should be deployed on production servers.

2. Write a paragraph to describe what steps should be taken after a network administrator found out that a new patch was released for the stable operating system that is installed on all the servers across the enterprise.

3. In your own words, describe what a rollback policy is, and explain why it is an important feature that should be included in any patch management policy.

PROJECTS

Project 10.1: Creating a New Application System

1. You are creating a new Web site that will allow your friends to upload the title of all the DVDs in their collection so that they can track what they own. This Web site will include two main elements: the Web-based interface and a back-end database. For now, you only want a select group of people to upload their collection titles to the database, and you want to make it browsable only to those same people. What authentication method could you use to achieve this goal? Write a paragraph explaining why your choice is easy and obvious.

2. One of your friends who is interested in using your application tells you that it takes too much time to enter the full title of each DVD. He mentions that each DVD is shipped with its own UPC number listed on the back of the DVD case. He would like to use that instead of the full title. You realize that all UPC codes are made of numbers only. Based on this knowledge, write a paragraph to explain what input

10

validation steps you could take to secure your application if you were to implement entering DVDs into the system via their UPC codes.

3. While surfing the Internet for some research for this project, you realize that there is a table that can be purchased that features all UPC codes for all DVDs ever produced that links the code to the title and most features of the DVD, such as screen format, subtitles, etc. Your application already features fields for both screen format and subtitles. If you were to acquire this table, how could you use it to bolster your input validation solution?

4. You want to add a new feature to your application: The ability for your users to exchange messages via the application. The aim is to facilitate trade requests from one member to the other. However, you want to make sure that those messages remain confidential. What do you need to implement to make sure that those messages cannot be intercepted by a potential hacker? Write a paragraph to justify your answer.

5. Your users are really enjoying this new application. They have one request: They would like to be able to enter a review of each movie either in their own collection, or in another member's collection. Based on the characteristics of a review—basically text that may include punctuation, letters, and numbers—how does this impact the difficulty level of an input validation method?

Project 10.2: Maintaining an Application System Solution

1. You have been hired as a member of the Information Technology department of a local small business. This company relies on a database system to enter insurance claims. This application is directly responsible for 90 percent of the company's revenue and is therefore vital. Simply put: The company cannot afford for this application to be unavailable. You are tasked with creating a policy to follow when new patches are released by the original coders for this application.

2. Write a couple of paragraphs to explain why the application should be updated from a generic standpoint. This will be used to show the nontechnical members of upper management why the IT department needs to maintain the database system by adding new code even when it is perceived as running perfectly well as is. Possible reasons include new features and security.

3. Because of the importance of this database system, you decide that a proper test strategy is required prior to installing any new code onto the application system. Write a couple of paragraphs detailing why

you are asking the company to invest in new hardware and software to create the test environment that you perceive is required. These two paragraphs will be the basis of a presentation that you will make to all members of upper management to convince them to approve this investment.

4. As a result of your presentation, management has decided to approve the creation of a new test environment. One of the team members that you assigned to help with this project does not see the value of a rollback strategy, stating that if all testing comes back positive, there is no reason why there would be a need for a rollback strategy in the first place. Write a couple of paragraphs to refute that short-sighted team member before you thank him for his time and hire another team member to replace him.

5. As part of the writing process, you are torn between two situations: What if a patch installation requires the application to be unavailable for 30 minutes, yet must be installed as soon as possible because it fixes a security hole that was recently exploited on a similar database used at another company? Write two paragraphs detailing what should be done in this case: Install now and lose 30 minutes of uptime during production hours, or take a chance that nothing will happen until after production hours when it is not inconvenient and costly to run the update.

Project 10.3: Encryption

1. The security firm that employs you has been hired by a new customer. This customer developed an in-house, custom application system that archives paper forms in electronic format, complete with a Web-based document locator function that works as follows: Users type in keywords in a search engine, related to the document that they are looking for. The application returns several possibilities. Users can then click on the appropriate document title, and it is downloaded from the back-end database and displayed on the user's screen. It is noteworthy that the users are not employees of the company in question. This company offers this application as a third-party service. All its clients are medical practices that use the application as on offsite electronic medical records solution. They are linked to the application via their Internet connection and a regular Web browser.

2. After spending a day with the developers responsible for this application reviewing the code, your first recommendation is that since all the information that is transmitted is in fact defined as Protected

10

Health Information (PHI), all transactions should be encrypted. As it presently stands, the application system is sending all the documents between the database server and the users' desktop via HTTP (i.e., in clear text). Write a couple of paragraphs making a case that the first thing that should be done to the application system is to retrofit an encryption solution.

3. It is settled that the application will be sending all information via HTTPS, the secure version of HTTP that relies on SSL to guarantee confidentiality. You know that there are two choices to set up HTTPS: Either use certificates bought from a certificate authority such as VeriSign, or use digital certificates created in-house. Write a couple of paragraphs on the matter, specifically listing the pros and cons of each solution. Finally, make a recommendation of using one or the other method.

4. One of the medical practices that contracted to use this application system as its EMR solution is located outside of the United States, but still requires 128-bit encryption. Explain in a paragraph how that can be an issue. Research U.S. federal regulations that govern exporting encryption technology on the Internet for more information on this topic if necessary.

5. Another need that you identified through the audit that you ran against this application system is that e-mails are being sent between clients and managers. However, the integrity and nonrepudiation of the e-mails sent is not currently guaranteed. Write a paragraph to outline a solution that could be deployed to remedy this issue.

Project 10.4: An Online Forum Solution

1. Nick is a geek and has decided that he is going to share his passion and knowledge by running a Web site dedicated to IT. The site will be free and will feature regular articles and "labs" where he will write step-by-step instructions on how to set up various services for his visitors to get some hands-on experience. One of the features that he wants his site to have is an online forum, or message board. This dynamic, interactive tool will allow his users to share messages and information about almost anything related to IT.

2. Nick is afraid of replay attacks where a user may log on using her own username and password, and have a hacker get hold of the token that was created for this session. This hacker could then feed the same token to the server and be authenticated as that other user. He decides that the token should be a little more complex than it is right

now, and include other information that would make it unique. Write a paragraph to explain how adding a timestamp to the information gathered to create the token would help fight replay attacks.

3. One of the users on Nick's message board posted a message asking for help with a specific situation. Namely, this user's company is rolling out a new application system that will only be available from the inside of the network to authorized and authenticated users. The user further volunteers that she will be using digital certificates. She tried to explain to her boss that since the system will be for internal use only, there is no need to purchase a digital certificate from a commercial CA. Instead, the company should simply set up its own certificate authority. Write a couple of paragraphs supporting Nick's Web site member in her claim.

4. Another member, this one going by the nickname Enforcer, is tasked with preparing a paper on encryption and when to use it. Help him start by creating a quick, two-paragraph overview of what type of data should be encrypted and why, versus which type of data does not require encryption. Use examples if it is easier to make your points.

5. A third member, BradyFan from Boston, MA, brings forth his own issue in hopes of getting some help. His issue is related to the fact that he was provided a copy of the ISO 17799 by his boss, and that he is not too sure that he understands the part that deals with the use of live data on a test environment. Write a quick policy explaining the restrictions of use of live data on nonproduction servers.

Project 10.5: Online Banking

1. The security firm that employs you has been hired by a local community bank. To its credit, the bank is extremely security-conscious and has resisted offering an online banking solution up to now because of the security issues inherent to such solutions. Your first assignment is to run a mini risk assessment, listing all the issues that could be related to running such an online banking solution. Write a paragraph centered on confidentiality issues related to online banking. Start by defining confidentiality, then list threats as you perceive them.

2. Your boss is presumably very satisfied with your assessment, and assigns you another one, looking for the same level of quality—not to put the pressure on you, or anything. Write a paragraph focused on data integrity issues related to online banking. Start by defining integrity, then list threats as you perceive them.

3. Ever more impressed, your boss decides that you have done such a wonderful job so far that you should be allowed to write the third part of this assessment. Write a paragraph about availability issues related to online banking. Start by defining availability, then list threats as you perceive them.

4. Looking at the three paragraphs you created, decide which one of the three security tenets would be more important in this scenario. This decision is important as it will dictate what priorities the coders will face when creating the actual online banking application system. So, according to you, what is more important: confidentiality, integrity, or availability of the application system? Justify your answer in at least two paragraphs.

5. Optional: Organize a debate with two other students who chose the other two tenets. Remember to remain civil in your debate!

Case Study

You have recently been promoted to Manager of the Development Department. Although you are not a coder yourself, you will supervise a group of five developers.

The first order of business is to make sure that the developers are all on the same page when it comes to building security into the code that they create. For that reason, you are waiting for the next project to start. You will use this project to emphasize the new rules, which up to now were mentioned but never enforced.

In preparation for the first project that will be handled under your leadership, you need to create a generic policy that will focus on security in application systems. You will create it based on, but not limited to, the following points:

- Outline the need for security to be a part of the code creation process from the start.

- Theorize on the need for different levels of input validation in application systems.

- Detail what encryption is, what it can do for an application system, and when it is beneficial to use.

▸▸ CONTINUED ON NEXT PAGE

▶▶ CONTINUED

- Focus on the dichotomy between the need for maintenance and updates of both operating system and application system files, and the quest for stability and uptime. Especially show that, while updates are meant to ensure stability, they can also threaten it if not appropriately deployed.

Each policy item that you create should be accompanied with a narrative to further exemplify the points being made by the separate policy items. You can certainly use some of the provided sample policies, although do try and use your own words as much as possible.

10

Chapter | 11

Business Continuity Management

Chapter Objectives

After reading this chapter and completing the exercises, you will be able to do the following:

- Define *disaster.*
- Understand the process for developing a business continuity plan.
- Describe the four components of a business continuity plan.
- Delineate the roles and responsibilities of leadership, the business continuity team, users, and business partners.
- Be familiar with testing, maintenance, and auditing techniques.

Introduction

Section 11 of the ISO 17799 is Disaster Recovery and Business Continuity. The focus of this domain is availability. The primary objective of disaster response, recovery, and business continuity policies, plans, and procedures is to ensure continued operations by providing for the safety of employees and customers, protecting the organization's assets, and restoring operating services after a business interruption. In other words, sustaining business processes.

Emergencies, disruptions, disasters, accidents, and injuries can occur any time. Being prepared physically, technically, and psychologically to handle emergencies is an individual as well as organizational responsibility. Response and recovery plans and procedures need to be made to ensure that all operations can adequately recover from damage to critical data, hardware, software, people, and facilities. Processes need to be developed and tested so the impact of any emergency or business disruption on people, products, and services is minimized. Business continuity plans for each operational area need be created, tested, and ready to be put into place at a moment's notice.

In this chapter, we will begin by defining what a disaster is and how the impact to the organization can be predetermined. We will discuss the need for disaster preparedness. We will look at the structure of response and recovery plans, procedures, and responsibilities. We will determine what needs to be incorporated into business continuity plan as well as who should develop, test, and update the procedures. Lastly, we will codify the requirements in policy.

What Is a Disaster?

A *disaster* is a disruption of normal business functions where the expected time for returning to normalcy would seriously impact the organization's ability to maintain operations, including customer commitments and regulatory compliance. This disruption could result from a natural event, a human mistake, or willful damage. Disruptions can occur any time without warning. If is often said that a disaster is an incident of significant proportions. Just as we prepare for incidents, we need to prepare for disasters.

Each of the threats shown in Table 11.1 affects operations differently. Each organization must define its tolerance for disruption. Risk assessments and business impact analyses (BIAs) are used to classify disaster scenarios.

TABLE 11.1 Threats to operations.

Threat	Examples
Malicious Activities	Fraud, Blackmail, Sabotage, Terrorism
Environmental/Natural	Fire, Flood/Water Damage, Severe Weather, Air
Technical/Logistical	Contaminants, Chemical Spills, Communication (WAN, Phone) Failure, Power Failure, Hardware/Software Failure, Transportation Disruption, Personnel Error, Personnel Unavailability

Risk Assessment and Business Impact Analysis (BIA)

Until this chapter, we have discussed risk assessments in the context of normal business operations. In this domain, the purpose of a risk assessment is to determine the threats that can disrupt operations, the likelihood of occurrence, and the mitigating controls we can put in place.

The risk assessment step is critical and has significant bearing on whether response, recovery, and continuity planning efforts will succeed. As a part of the risk assessment, organizations should develop realistic threat scenarios that may potentially disrupt their business processes and ability to meet their clients' expectations (internal, business partners, or customers).

Once threats have been documented, the next step is to determine the impact the disruption has on the organization. This process is known as a ***business impact analysis (BIA).*** Executive management is responsible for the oversight of the business impact analysis. Properly done, a BIA analyzes a threat by focusing on its impact on the business, not the nature of the threat. For example, the effects of certain threat scenarios can be reduced to business disruptions that affect only specific work areas, systems, facilities (i.e., buildings), or geographic areas. Additionally, the magnitude of the business disruption should consider a wide variety of threat scenarios based upon practical experiences and potential circumstances and events. There is a major difference between an outage that affects an informational Web site and an outage that affects a core processing system. Additionally, systems have differences in downtime tolerance. A marketing database may have a downtime tolerance of seven days while an e-mail system may have a tolerance that can be measured in minutes. Other considerations, such as date and time of day, matter. Consider the outcry if a payroll system is unavailable on payday!

A business impact analysis (BIA) is the foundation of disaster recovery and business continuity planning. The outcome of the information gathered provides significant metrics, such as:

- The impact that interruptions (major and minor) will have on the organization.

- The tolerance of downtime on a system-by-system basis.

- The prioritization of critical business processes in case of such interruptions.

- Resource requirements needed to restore time-critical business processes.

The result of the business impact analysis is to provide direction and guidance to those who plan the response, recovery, and continuity efforts.

FYI: Certifying as a Disaster Recovery and Business Continuity Specialist

DRI International (DRII) was formed in 1988 as the Disaster Recovery Institute in St. Louis, MO. A group of professionals from the industry and from Washington University in St. Louis forecast the need for comprehensive education in business continuity. Alliances with academia helped shape early research and curriculum development. DRII provides basic-, entry-, and master-level industry certification that is well respected and recognized worldwide:

- Associate Business Continuity Professional (ABCP)
- Certified Functional Continuity Professional (CFCP)
- Certified Business Continuity Professional (CBCP)
- Master Business Continuity Professional (MBCP)
- Retired Business Continuity Professional (RBCP)

Certification criteria and testing information can be found at: **www.drii.org**.

IN PRACTICE: Business Continuity Assessment Policy

The goal of this policy is to require the organization to recognize the risk and impact of threats to availability of information and the information system.

The *objectives* of this policy are to:

- Require that risk assessments be conducted in regard to the availability of information and information systems.
- Assign responsibility for conducting risk assessments.
- Require that business impact analysis based upon the risk assessment be conducted annually.
- Assign responsibility for the business impact analysis.
- Define the anticipated outcome of both the risk assessment and business impact analysis process.

The *audience* is all information and information systems.

▶▶ CONTINUED ON NEXT PAGE

▶▶ CONTINUED

TABLE 11.2 Business Continuity Assessment Policy.

Section X:	[COMPANY] Information Security Policy	Effective Date:
Subsection	Business Continuity Management	Change Control #:
Policy	Business Continuity Assessment	Approved By:
Objective	In support of information security, [Company] will conduct business continuity risk assessments and business impact analyses.	
Purpose	The purpose of this policy is to ensure the [Company] recognizes risks to the availability of information and information systems and the potential impact upon the organization.	
Audience	This policy applies to all information system owners and custodians.	

Policy	• A risk assessment will be performed annually under the supervision of the information security officer to evaluate and understand:
	  • Threats to the availability of information and information systems.
	  • The likelihood of such threats.
	  • Mitigating controls to reduce the probability of a threat occurrence.
	• The risk assessment will be presented to senior management.
	• A business impact analysis will be performed annually under the supervision of the Chief Executive Officer to evaluate and understand:
	  • The impact that disruptions (major and minor) will have on the organization.
	  • Tolerance of downtime on a system-by-system basis.
	  • The prioritization of critical business processes in case of such disruptions.
	  • Establishing business objectives.	

▶▶ CONTINUED ON NEXT PAGE

11

» CONTINUED	
	• The outcome of the business impact analysis will be to provide direction and guidance to those who plan response, recovery, and continuity efforts.
Exceptions	None
Disciplinary Actions	Violation of this policy may result in disciplinary action, which may include termination for employees and temporaries; a termination of employment relations in the case of contractors or consultants; or dismissal for interns and volunteers. Additionally, individuals are subject to civil and criminal prosecution.

Disaster Strikes Without Warning

Disasters are by definition unexpected situations. However, they shouldn't be unanticipated situations. The key is to be prepared to respond. Preparation can literally make the difference between life and death. Consider the following situations:

- A surgeon may be performing surgery using computer-guided laser equipment when power is disrupted.

- A pilot may be in the process of landing when the communications systems fail.

- A researcher may be exposed to a hazardous substance and need to be monitored in a containment chamber.

In each of these situations, knowing what to do in case of an emergency is critical. Certainly, not all disasters are life-and-death situations; however, a common characteristic is the severity of impact upon the organization. The impact can be financial, reputational, or regulatory.

FYI: Heed the Warning

IT consulting and research firm Gartner estimates that two out of five enterprises that experience a physical or IT-related disaster go out of business within five years, regardless of their size. Yet despite such warnings, an April 2004 survey conducted by AT&T and the Partnership for Public Warning indicates that although about one in five firms in the 10 largest U.S. metropolitan areas have faced a disaster in the past year, only 75 percent of these firms have adopted disaster-recovery measures. For more information, go to **www.partnershipforpublicwarning.org/ppw/natlsurvey.html**.

A Plan of Action

First and foremost, organizations need to have a plan. When we say a plan, we don't mean institutional knowledge that is stored in someone's head or an informal idea of what should be done. We mean a well-organized written document that has been reviewed for accuracy and tested for success. It is the responsibility of management to support, budget, and clearly define responsibility for development, ownership, and maintenance of the plan. Executive management and/or the Board of Directors are accountable for approving the plan.

Business Continuity Plan (BCP) Components

The plan should have four components: disaster preparation, disaster response, business contingency, and business recovery. Taken as a whole, this document is known as a ***business continuity plan (BCP).*** The objective of a business continuity plan is to ensure the ongoing viability of a business; a BCP forms the backbone of any data-recovery effort an organization undertakes following a disaster.

In its *Lessons Learned from September 11, 2001,* Pricewaterhouse Coopers recommends that plans be developed based upon the following assumptions:

- Event occurs at the worst possible time

- Worst-case scenario—loss of building and systems

- Key personnel may not be available

- Not all recovery personnel may be available

- Training of new personnel may be required

- Critical third parties may be affected

- Other locations and/or business partners are similarly affected

Disaster preparation addresses what needs to be done in anticipation of a disaster. Preparation plans are a natural outcome of the risk assessment. By determining the potential threats and their likelihood, organizations can determine appropriate controls. For example, buildings in high-crime locations may employ sophisticated surveillance systems that can quickly alert appropriate authorities as well as provide evidence of the incident. Systems that are mission critical can be designed for auto fail-over redundancy. Data that is valuable can be backed up, copied, or journaled regularly and stored offsite.

Disaster response addresses what should be done immediately following a significant incident. This includes who has the authority to declare a disaster, who has the authority to contact external entities, evacuation procedures, relocation procedures, emergency communication and notification procedures, and any other procedures required to protect the health and safety of employees and the public.

Business continuity addresses alternate business processes used throughout the organization prior to full recovery. This can be turning up redundant systems such as those found at a "hot site," redirecting requests to other locations, or using manual procedures. Business continuity focuses on how the business continues to function and provide services absent normal operating conditions.

Business recovery addresses the process of recovering information systems to their original state (or a facsimile of) using a prioritized and systematic methodology. This may be as simple as restoring data or as complex as having to rebuild a data center.

FYI: NIST SP 800-34

National Institute of Standards and Technology (NIST) Publication SP 800-34 specifically addresses the development of a Disaster Recovery and Business Continuity plan. They recommend a 7-step methodology:

1. Obtaining commitment from leadership to dedicate appropriate resources to ensure the plan's success

2. Conducting a risk assessment and business impact analysis (BIA)

3. Identifying preventive controls

4. Developing recovery strategies and procedures

5. Developing operational contingency plans and procedures

6. Plan testing, training, and exercises

7. Plan maintenance

The publication can be found at **http://csrc.nist.gov/publications/nistpubs/800-34/sp800-34.pdf**.

IN PRACTICE: Business Continuity Plan Policy

Best practices dictate that every business has a Business Continuity Plan. The goal of this policy is require such a plan to be developed, approved, and maintained.

The *objectives* of this policy are to:

- Require that a business continuity strategy, plan, and procedures be developed.
- Specify the components of the plan.
- Assign ownership and responsibility for the business continuity plan.
- Require the involvement of and approval by the Board of Directors.

The *audience* is all information and information systems.

TABLE 11.3 Business Continuity Plan Policy.

Section X:	[COMPANY] Information Security Policy	Effective Date:
Subsection	Business Continuity Management	Change Control #:
Policy	Business Continuity Plan	Approved By:
Objective	In support of information security, [Company] will develop a comprehensive business continuity plan and procedures for maintaining business continuity in the case of major failures or disasters.	
Purpose	The purpose of this policy is to ensure the [Company] is prepared for business interruptions or disasters.	
Audience	This policy applies to all information system owners and custodians.	

Policy	• A business continuity strategy and plan shall be formulated and documented that is consistent with priorities and objectives that are determined through the risk assessment and business impact analysis. The plan shall address at minimum the following:
	  • Disaster Preparation
	  • Disaster Response	

▶▶ CONTINUED ON NEXT PAGE

11

▶▶ CONTINUED	
	• Contingency of Operations • Recovery of Information Systems • The owner of the plan will be the Chief Operating Officer. • The custodian of the plan will be the Information Security Officer. • The plan must be approved by the Board of Directors. The Board will be updated annually on the plan.
Exceptions	None
Disciplinary Actions	Violation of this policy may result in disciplinary action, which may include termination for employees and temporaries; a termination of employment relations in the case of contractors or consultants; or dismissal for interns and volunteers. Additionally, individuals are subject to civil and criminal prosecution.

Understanding Roles and Responsibilities

There are a myriad of roles and responsibilities in designing, approving, implementing, managing, and maintaining a business continuity plan. These roles should be predefined and documented. All participants should understand their roles and receive training where appropriate.

Defining Expectations

The Board of Directors needs to provide leadership, approve policy, and be legally accountable for the actions of the organization.

Executive management needs to provide leadership, demonstrate commitment, and devote resources to the process and project of business continuity. They are the stewards of the business continuity plan and are responsible for its development and adoption.

The business continuity team is responsible for managing a disaster and maintaining the BCP pre- and post-disaster. The team should be a cross-functional representation of the organization, including senior management, physical security, information technology, human resources, information security, and business units. The team should be led by a coordinator who is accountable for the management of the preparation, response, recovery, and continuity operations.

Operational management is responsible for defining the operational needs of their department and for creating and maintaining functional departmental contingency procedures.

The Information Technology Department needs to participate in all aspects of plan development, implementation, testing, and maintenance. Specifically, they are responsible for the recovery of information and information systems.

The Human Resources Department must be prepared to provide services to employees in case of an emergency or disaster.

The Training Department is responsible for developing and delivering business continuity training to all employees as well as implementing an awareness program.

The Internal Audit Department is charged with auditing the business continuity plan and procedures and reporting their findings to management. Their audit satisfies the best practice requirements of separation of duties and oversight.

Vendors that are referenced in the business continuity plan should understand the expectations of the organization and be contractually obligated to follow the BCP where appropriate.

Who's in Charge?

When disaster strikes, quick mobilization is essential to mitigate damages. It is imperative that there be designated leadership with the authority to act quickly. This is the primary role of the business continuity team (BCT). The BCT should be vested by management with the authority to set policy and procedure during disaster preparation, response, recovery, and maintenance periods. The BCT should represent a cross-section of the organization. The team should have an designated leader. Because this team will operate in unpredictable situations, a second-in-command person should be trained to assume the team leader position.

The responsibilities of the business continuity team include, but are not limited to:

- Assessing damage to the organization.

- Formally declaring a disaster, and activating the plan.

- Managing the response, continuity, and recovery activities.

- Providing visible leadership throughout the crisis period.

- Providing a post-disaster assessment of recovery and response efforts.

- Planning impact analysis whenever changes in systems, procedures, facilities, or organization necessitate a modification.

- Testing the plan as scheduled.

- Reviewing the plan annually with the Chief Operating Officer (COO).

11

IN PRACTICE: Business Continuity Team Policy

A business continuity plan requires leadership and management. The goal of this policy is to designate a business continuity team, outline their responsibilities and vest authority.

The *objectives* of the policy are to:

- Designate the structure of the business continuity team.
- Designate the function of the business continuity team.
- Designate the authority of the business continuity team.

The *audience* is all information and information systems.

TABLE 11.4 Business Continuity Team Policy.

Section X:	[COMPANY] Information Security Policy	Effective Date:
Subsection	Business Continuity Management	Change Control #:
Policy	Business Continuity Team	Approved By:
Objective	In support of information security, [Company] will designate and vest authority in a business continuity team.	
Purpose	The purpose of this policy is to recognize the purpose for, the roles, the responsibilities, and the authority of the business continuity team.	
Audience	This policy applies to all information system owners and custodians.	
Policy	• A business continuity team will be appointed by the Chief Operating Officer. The team will be a cross-functional representation of the organization. The team will report to the COO. • The Information Security Officer will be designated as the business continuity team leader. An alternate leader will be chosen from the team. • The business continuity team will be charged with the following responsibilities: • Assessing damage to the organization.	

▸▸ **CONTINUED ON NEXT PAGE**

> **▶▶ CONTINUED**

	• Formally declaring a disaster, and activating the plan.
	• Managing the response, continuity, and recovery activities.
	• Providing visible leadership throughout the crisis period.
	• Providing a post-disaster assessment of recovery and response efforts.
	• Planning impact analysis whenever changes in systems, procedures, facilities, or organization necessitate a modification.
	• Testing the plan as scheduled.
	• Reviewing the plan annually with the COO.
	• All employees, managers, and directors are expected to abide by the requirements of the disaster recovery plan and the authority of the disaster recovery team.
Exceptions	None
Disciplinary Actions	Violation of this policy may result in disciplinary action, which may include termination for employees and temporaries; a termination of employment relations in the case of contractors or consultants; or dismissal for interns and volunteers. Additionally, individuals are subject to civil and criminal prosecution.

Preparing for Disaster

Disaster preparation requires that specific key elements be predefined. These elements include:

- Establishing an organizational structure to respond to an emergency.

- Designating an emergency command center.

- Preparing notification procedures.

- Designating alternate operations sites.

- Investing in redundant infrastructure or alternate sites for data processing.

- Developing and implementing procedures to support response, recovery, and continuity activities.

11

Organizational Structure

The organizational structure and/or chain of command may change during an emergency or disaster. A process needs to be outlined for an orderly transition of power if the situation warrants. The succession of executive leadership should be codified by the Board of Directors and clearly understood by all parties involved. While the business continuity team assumes the authority for the response, continuity, and recovery effort, all employees and business partners are expected to assume duties that may be outside of the normal course of work. This expectation should be stated in all job descriptions, individual and union contracts, and contractor scope of work.

Command Center Location

The purpose of a command center is to have a designated location where the business continuity team reports in case of an emergency or disaster. The command center is initially used to direct operations, and then may be used as a meeting center until normal business operations resume. Both a primary and an alternate command center should be pre-stocked with the BCP manuals, tables, chairs, whiteboards, and phones so that the center can be immediately operational. Team members should have applicable keys and access codes for the location. The process of setting up the control center will begin as soon as the first team member arrives. While it is essential to designate and prepare this space, the area need not be dedicated to this purpose. A conference room, a training room, or even a large office can easily and quickly be transformed.

Notification of Personnel

A disaster may occur with little or no warning. Natural disasters such as a hurricane or ice storm are sometimes predicted in advance. It is more common, however, that there is no notice of an impending disaster. Notification procedures should be documented in the plan for both types of situation. The procedures should describe the methods used to notify recovery personnel during business and nonbusiness hours.

Notification procedures should be documented clearly in the contingency plan. A common notification method is a call tree. This technique involves assigning notification duties to specific individuals, who in turn are responsible for notifying other recovery personnel. The call tree should account for primary and alternate contact methods and should discuss procedures to be followed if an individual cannot be contacted.

Relocation of Operations

In cases of natural, environmental, or physical disaster, relocation of critical business functions may be necessary. Relocation strategies need to consider both delivery and operational business functions. *Delivery functions* provide service or product to the customer. An example would be the teller line at a bank or a customer call center. *Operational business functions* provide the core infrastructure of the organization. They include accounting, marketing, human resources, office services, security, and information technology.

It is not practical to consider relocating all staff. That would require redundant offices. However, the critical functions and staff required to continue an acceptable level of operations in the wake of a disaster *do* need to be considered. The relocation plan must consider staffing levels, space considerations, utility and environmental needs, transportation, and logistics.

Alternate Data Center Sites

Alternate data center sites provide facilities for continued information processing activity. As shown in Table 11.5, there are five schools of thought regarding alternate data center facilities: Hot Site, Warm Site, Cold Site, Mobile Site, and Mirrored Site. Organizations need to evaluate the options available to them and invest appropriately.

TABLE 11.5 Alternate data center facilities.

Site Type	Description
Hot Site	A hot site is a fully operational location which has been configured with redundant hardware, software, and communications capability. Data has been streamed to the hot site on a real-time or near-time basis.
Warm Site	Warm sites have been configured to support operations including communications capabilities, peripheral devices, power, and HVAC. "Spare" computers may be located at warm sites which then need to be configured in the event of a disaster. Data will need to be restored.
Cold Site	A cold site is an available alternate location that has power, HVAC, and secure access.
Mobile Site	Mobile sites are self-contained units. The units generally arrive equipped with the required hardware, software and peripherals. Data needs to be restored.

11

Responding to a Disaster

What happens in those initial moments following a disaster has both an immediate impact as well as a significant ripple effect. Disaster response can either be chaotic or orderly. The difference between these scenarios is established procedures and responsibilities. Think back to elementary school days. Hopefully, you never experienced a fire at your school. But if you had, chances are that everyone would have evacuated the building safely. Why? Teachers and staff had specific assignments. Evacuation routes were mapped out. Students were taught not to panic, to line up single file, to follow a leader, and to gather at a specific location. All of these procedures and roles were reinforced through regularly scheduled fire drills.

There are four stages of disaster response, as shown in Figure 11.1.

The primary goals of the response phase are to limit human injury, limit damage to the organization, make an initial assessment of the damage, and determine the appropriate activity.

Detection

The detection of an event that could result in a disaster is the responsibility of whoever first discovers or receives information about the situation. In all cases, safety of employees and customers is first priority.

Notification

Whoever detects an event that could or has resulted in a disaster should immediately notify a member of the business continuity team (BCT). Notification can be made in person, by telephone, by fax, by e-mail, or by any other practical method as long as it is confirmed that the business continuity team member has received notification.

Declaration

Once notified, team members evaluate the situation and, if warranted, activate the plan. The contacted team members should notify other team members. The team members will notify management. Managers are then responsible for notifying their staff. Managers are responsible for keeping an updated employee list.

FIGURE 11.1 Four stages of disaster response.

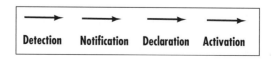

Detection   Notification   Declaration   Activation

Activation

Activation of the business continuity plan is the responsibility of the BCT team leader; if the team leader is not available, the alternate team leader will activate the plan. If both are unavailable, then responsibility falls to the first available team member. At this point, decisions are made regarding use of the command center, relocation of personnel and operations, as well as recovery site. The business continuity team should be the authoritative body to activate the plan, set policy, and establish procedures during the disaster and recovery period.

The very process of plan activation opens the door for a host of non-operational business concerns. How these concerns are going to be addressed and who is responsible should be decided pre-disaster and incorporated into the business continuity plan.

Public Safety Communication between the organization and police, fire, and other emergency organizations is critical in any emergency that impacts the safety of employees, customers, or the general public. For widespread disasters, communication may need to be established with federal agencies such as the Federal Emergency Management Agency (FEMA).

Employee Relations Employees must be kept informed of developments and advised of bulletins and news reporting speculation or misinformation. Logistical issues such as should employees remain at work or report to work needs to be communicated. Transportation may need to be arranged. Safety and security of personnel and their families may need to be considered.

Media Relations To prevent miscommunication and misinformation, press releases, statements, or comments from the organization should be made only through a designated communications liaison. Employees should be instructed that all news media requests and questions must be referred to the designated spokesperson without comment (on or off the record).

Customer Relations Customers must be kept informed of what is happening in a disaster. They are interested and concerned about their relationship with the organization and the organization's ability to service their needs.

Crime Sadly, looting and vandalism during a disaster is a fact of life. Response responsibilities include invoking enhanced protection measures for personnel and property.

11

Planning for Contingencies

The goal of contingency plans is to continue to provide services to customers, comply with regulatory requirements, and continue internal operations during a period when information systems and/or a normal operating environment is not available. Contingency operations may be implemented either at the original site or at an alternate location. It is not realistic to assume that all services and operations can continue. Critical services and operations should have been identified during the risk assessment process.

Business Contingency Procedures

Similar to recovery procedures, *business contingency procedures* need to be task based and detail the specific steps necessary to carry out a required operation. These procedures are different than standard operating procedures (SOP). Standard operating procedures assume normal operating conditions. Business contingency procedures assume that the opposite conditions exist and that alternate methods of operation are required. Consider the following scenarios.

Scenario A Physical access to facilities at a maximum security prison is regulated by a biometric fingerprint access control system. The access control system is managed and monitored by an information system. The back-end information system becomes unavailable due to power loss. The business contingency procedure would address an alternate method to lock and unlock doors. This may be a physical key or perhaps an access code. In either case, knowing where the key is or what the code is would be essential to operations. The related contingency procedure would be to switch over to a generator until power is restored.

Scenario B A bank offers its customers the option of telephone banking services. Due to a fire, the telebanking phone system is not operational. The best-case contingency procedure would be to fail-over to a redundant system. Unfortunately, most organizations are not replete with redundant systems. Realistic contingency procedures would involve rerouting telebanking calls to Customer Service and ensuring that the Customer Service Representatives (CSR) could service the customers or at the very least provide information about when the telebanking system would be available.

Scenario C A federal agency is forced to vacate its premises due to a biochemical threat. The agency receives and processes unemployment claims. Its most critical task is producing unemployment checks based upon the claims. Unemployed individuals depend upon receiving these payments in a timely manner. Business contingency procedures address relocation of personnel and equipment, claimant notification, and alternate methods to accept and process claims as well as to print and distribute checks. Procedures may include notifying recipients by phone that payments are delayed, estimating payments based upon the previous week's claims, and/or coordinating with another agency for processing and postal services.

Business Contingency Documentation

Business contingency documentation should follow the same form as standard operating procedures. As with standard operating procedures, *business contingency operating procedures (BCOPs)* are instructions that should be understandable to everyone who needs to use them. They should be written as simply as possible. It is best to use short, direct sentences so that the reader can quickly understand and, if necessary, memorize the steps in the procedure. In Chapter 8, we introduced four formats for writing procedure documentation; simple step, hierarchical, graphic, and flowchart. These same formats are recommended for writing business contingency operating procedures.

Recovering from Disaster

In the recovery phase, the organization begins the process of restoring a normal level of services and capabilities. While the other phases have involved a cross-section of the organization, responsibility for recovery of information systems is generally the domain of the Information Technology department. Recovery activities can range from immediate fail-over to redundant systems to the significantly longer process of procuring equipment, restoring data, and potentially rebuilding facilities. Regardless of the strategy employed, it is critical that procedures have been documented and tested.

Developing recovery plans and procedures can be a daunting task. A successful approach is to break the plan down into categories such as mainframe, network, communications, infrastructure, and facilities. Having a documented inventory, easily accessible copies of software, tested data backups, and up-to-date vendor lists make the recovery process significantly easier.

Recovery Strategies

It is fairly common for each category to have its own recovery strategy. Strategies vary based upon cost, complexity, priority, and resource availability. For example, very few organizations can afford a "spare" mainframe, but it is likely they will have a redundant router. The criticality

TABLE 11.6 Recovery categories.

Category	Description
Mainframe	Mainframe recovery is specific to the services of a mainframe computer. Mainframes are high-performance computers made for high-volume, large-storage, processor-intensive computing. They are typically used by large businesses for core processing functions and for scientific purposes. A mainframe can usually execute many programs simultaneously at a high speed.
Network	Network recovery includes those technology systems that provide network infrastructure services, such as authentication (login), e-mail, printing, antivirus protection, and Web browsing.
Communications	Communications recovery encompasses internal and external transmission systems including Local Area Network (LAN), Wide Area Network (WAN), data lines (T1, Frame Relay, ATM), and Internet connectivity. Included in this category are connectivity devices such as switches, routers, and firewalls.
Infrastructure	Infrastructure recovery encompasses those systems providing a general operating environment including HVAC, electrical, and phone systems.
Facilities	Facilities recovery addresses the need to either rebuild, renovate, or relocate the physical plant.

assigned in the business impact analysis provides the framework for choosing the appropriate strategy.

Procedures

During an emergency is not the time to figure out how to recover or restore a system, nor is it the time to determine inventory or search for vendor contacts. All of these items need to be addressed beforehand and documented in step-by-step procedures. The procedures should assume that the person doing the recovery is not intimately familiar with the information system or component. The procedures should explain what needs to be done, where it needs to be done, and how it needs to be done so that any reasonably intelligent person can follow the steps outlined and accomplish the task. The key to disaster recovery is the ability to respond using predefined tested methodology.

IN PRACTICE: E-mail System Recovery

This is a sample of a recovery procedure for an e-mail system. This document is concise and provides direction for the recovery personnel. Additional documentation that may be required for the recovery effort is specified and the location noted.

TABLE 11.7 Sample recovery procedure.

PREPARATION	
Action	Completed
Preconfigured Server stored off-site	–
Daily backups of the information store	–

INFORMATION SYSTEMS	
Action	Completed
Notify all locations and dept managers by phone/fax that e-mail services are down	–
Advise BCP Lead of plan, progress, and any schedule revisions	–
Retrieve spare ABCMAIL server from off-site storage	–
If necessary, upgrade service packs and patches to equal level of failed server	–
Restore information store (mailboxes and public folders) from tape backup according to the Microsoft Exchange recovery instructions. Restore instructions are located in the Microsoft Exchange Procedures Manual	–
If greater than 30 days since last ghost image, machine account password will be out of synch. Follow procedures outlined in Microsoft Knowledge Base article 216393. Instructions are located in the Microsoft Exchange Procedures Manual	–
Test e-mail availability—identify that most recent messages are present	–
Notify the BCP Lead that the system is available and of the date/time of the restored data	–
Notify Users that system is available for use	–
Ensure that replacement system is included in tape backup rotation	–
Change Control Notes:	

11

Recovery Manual

A recovery manual is a comprehensive document that incorporates recovery procedures on a system- or device-specific basis. Recovery procedures should be a logical progression of steps. Procedures may reference other documents. A well-organized recovery manual includes a table of contents and, if possible, an index.

Testing and Maintaining the Plan

It would be hard to understate the importance of testing response, recovery, and continuity plans and procedures. Proactive testing approaches are essential. Until tested, plans and procedures are purely theoretical. The objective of a testing program is to ensure that plans and procedures are accurate, relevant, and operable under adverse conditions. As important as demonstrating success is uncovering inadequacies. The worst time to find out that your plans were incomplete, outdated, or just plain wrong is in the midst of a disaster.

Testing Methods

There are five standard testing techniques. The extent and complexity of testing will depend upon the criticality of the function. The more essential the function, the more rigorous the testing program should be. Testing should be conducted on a scheduled basis and no less than annually.

Preliminary Review Plans and procedures are distributed to each functional area for review. The anticipated outcome is the validation that all critical processes, personnel, and responsibilities have been identified.

Structured Walkthrough Representatives from each functional area meet to walkthrough the plan and procedures to verify accuracy and completeness. A structured walkthrough may also be used as a training exercise to clarify and highlight critical elements. This can be done for response, recovery, and continuity plans and procedures.

Tabletop Simulation Tabletop simulations focus on testing a specific scenario. Based upon a defined disaster scenario, participants practice the steps required for response, recovery, and continuity. Only the materials and data available in a real disaster are used in the tabletop simulation. The anticipated outcome is to identify strengths and weakness in a nonthreatening environment.

Parallel (Functional) Testing Parallel testing is an operational test of a specific system or activity. In regard to recovery operations, redundant or backup systems are brought online and processing capability compared to real operational output. In regard to continuity procedures, manual or alternate processes are initiated. Parallel testing validates plans and procedures and provides the experience required to respond in an actual situation. Business operations are not disturbed during parallel testing.

Full-scale Testing Full-scale testing is the most comprehensive type of test. Normal operations are suspended. Recovery and continuity plans and procedures are implemented. The business operates under disaster conditions. Full-scale testing can be expensive and risky. It is, however, the most accurate test of plans and procedures.

Maintaining the Plan

Business environments are dynamic. For example, the organization may upgrade phone systems, acquire additional locations, adopt new software, or change service priorities. This is why the business continuity plan needs to be revisited on a scheduled basis to ensure that its components accurately reflect the needs of the organization. Revisiting the BCP goes hand in hand with reviewing the risk assessment and business impact analysis. The BCP also should be considered whenever a change driver is introduced.

Responsibility for maintaining the plan should be assigned to a specific role. Generally, this responsibility is considered a function of the Information Security Officer. Organizations that do not have an ISO should assign responsibility to a senior level operations manager. An all too common mistake is to expect the IT department to take ownership. Certainly, the IT staff is a vital part of the process. However, the organization needs to perceive business continuity as a functional plan of action and not as a technological quick fix.

11

Agreements with Vendors

Business continuity plans often depend upon vendors to provide services, equipment, facilities, and personnel. This reliance must be supported by vendor service level agreements. *Service level agreements (SLAs)* generally specify how quickly a vendor must respond, the type and quantity of replacement equipment guaranteed to be available, personnel and facility availability, and the status of the organization in the event of a major disaster involving multiple vendor clients. SLAs should be reviewed annually.

FYI: What the Regulators Are Looking For

The best way to know what to expect from an audit is to be privy to audit work papers. Fortunately, one of the best set of work papers is public domain. The Federal Financial Institutions Examination Council (FFIEC) is a formal interagency body empowered to prescribe uniform principles, standards, and report forms for the federal examination of financial institutions by the Board of Governors of the Federal Reserve System (FRB), the Federal Deposit Insurance Corporation (FDIC), the National Credit Union Administration (NCUA), the Office of the Comptroller of the Currency (OCC), and the Office of Thrift Supervision (OTS) and to make recommendations to promote uniformity in the supervision of financial institutions.

The FFIEC develops and publishes guides and audit work papers for use by field examiners in financial institution regulatory agencies. These resources are found in the *FFIEC Information Technology Examination Handbook InfoBase*. The Handbook is available to the public and can be download from the FFIEC Web site at **www.ffiec.gov**.

Auditing the Plan

Regulated industries and sectors such as healthcare and financial services are required to have business continuity plans. Organizations subject to a SAS 70 review or SEC compliance are expected to have business continuity plans. Regulators and auditors will examine the BCP for relevancy, management approval, completeness, accuracy, and organization. You can anticipate they will ask the following questions:

- Is the plan written?

- Has management approved the plan?

- How often is the risk assessment and business impact analysis reviewed? By whom?

- How often is the plan reviewed? By whom?

- Are all policies and procedures documented?

- Where is the documentation stored?

- Who is on the BCP team?

- What training have they had?

- What training has the user community had?

- How has the plan been tested? Is there a written testing plan?

- How often is the plan tested? Are the results documented?

- If third parties are involved, what is the process for testing/verifying their procedures?

- Who is responsible for maintaining the plan?

IN PRACTICE: Business Continuity Plan Testing and Maintenance Policy

A business continuity plan requires testing and maintenance on a scheduled basis. The goal of this policy is to designate a testing and maintenance criteria and responsibility.

The *objectives* of the policy are to:

- Assign BCP plan testing responsibility and criteria.
- Assign BCP plan review and update responsibility and criteria.
- Assign BCP plan audit responsibility and authority.

The *audience* is all information and information systems.

TABLE 11.8 Business Continuity Plan Testing and Maintenance Policy.

Section X:	[COMPANY] Information Security Policy	Effective Date:
Subsection	Business Continuity Management	Change Control #:
Policy	Business Continuity Team	Approved By:
Objective	In support of Information Security, [Company] will test, maintain, and audit the Business Continuity Plan.	
Purpose	The purpose of this policy is to assure the relevancy, accuracy, and completeness of the Business Continuity Plan.	
Audience	This policy applies to all information system owners and custodians.	

▸▸ CONTINUED ON NEXT PAGE

11

» CONTINUED	

Policy	• The Business Continuity Team lead is responsible for ensuring that each element in the BCP be tested annually.
	  • Preliminary review
	  • Structured walkthrough
	  • Tabletop simulation
	  • Parallel testing
	  • Full-scale testing
	• The Chief Operating Officer is responsible for conducting an annual review of the BCP.
	• The COO will delegate responsibility for keeping the plan up-to-date.
	• The plan will be audited annually by the internal audit department. Finding will be presented directly to the Chief Executive Officer.

Exceptions	None
Disciplinary Actions	Violation of this policy may result in disciplinary action, which may include termination for employees and temporaries; a termination of employment relations in the case of contractors or consultants; or dismissal for interns and volunteers. Additionally, individuals are subject to civil and criminal prosecution.

Summary

Normal business operations can be disrupted at a moment's notice. Organizations must be prepared for disasters, emergencies, and other crises. Not investing the time and effort required to face disruptions is negligent and may lead to the failure of the organization. It is the responsibility of executive management to ensure that threats are evaluated, impact to business processes recognized, and resources allocated.

An up-to-date, tested, and audited business continuity plan and procedures should be a priority for all organizations. Studies have proven that a significant proportion of organizations that suffer a disaster never fully recover. Business continuity plans address four stages of a disruption: disaster preparation, disaster response, business contingency, and business recovery. The business continuity team is charged with implementing the plan.

We have learned valuable lessons from the events of September 11, 2001. The importance of planning and preparation and the need for organizational training has become evident. Business continuity plans do more than protect business assets; in the long run, they protect employees and their families, investors, business partners, and the community. Business continuity plans are, in essence, a civic duty.

Test Your Skills

MULTIPLE CHOICE QUESTIONS

1. The primary objective of business continuity planning is:

   A. assurance

   B. availability

   C. accounting

   D. authentication

2. A disaster is best described as a(n):

   A. planned activity

   B. isolated incident

   C. significant disruption of normal business functions

   D. change in management structure

3. Flood, fire, and wind are examples of which type of threat?

   A. malicious act

   B. environmental

   C. logistical

   D. technical

4. Fraud, blackmail, sabotage, and terrorism are examples of which type of threat?

   A. environmental

   B. logistical

   C. malicious act

   D. natural

11

5. The process of determining the impact of a disruption is known as a:
   A. risk assessment
   B. business continuity plan
   C. business impact analysis
   D. disaster recovery procedure

6. The process of determining threats that can disrupt operations is known as a:
   A. risk assessment
   B. business continuity plan
   C. business impact analysis
   D. disaster recovery procedure

7. Which of these is NOT a business continuity plan component?
   A. procurement
   B. preparation
   C. response
   D. contingency

8. Who should assume command of operations in the event of a disaster?
   A. the FBI
   B. the business continuity team
   C. the Chairman of the Board
   D. the Information Security Officer

9. Final approval of the business continuity plan should be given by:
   A. the business continuity team
   B. the Information Security Officer
   C. the Director of Information Technology
   D. the Board of Directors or executive management

10. The business continuity team is tasked with all of the following activities EXCEPT:
    A. testing the plan
    B. activating the plan
    C. providing visible leadership
    D. auditing the plan

11. Which type of alternate data processing facility is fully equipped with all resources required to maintain operations?

   A. Hot Site
    B. Warm Site
   C. Cold Site
   D. Off Site

12. Which type of alternate data processing facility does not have equipment but does have power and HVAC?

   A. Hot Site
   B. Warm Site
   C. Cold Site
   D. Off Site

13. Which type of alternate data processing facility has peripheral equipment, power, HVAC, and communication capability?

   A. Hot Site
   B. Warm Site
   C. Cold Site
   D. Off Site

14. The four stages of disaster response are:

   A. detection-notification-declaration-activation
   B. detection-declaration-notification-activation
   C. notification-detection-declaration-activation
   D. detection-notification-activation-declaration

15. The objective of a contingency plan is to be able to:

   A. become fully operational
   B. recover systems
   C. notify authorities
   D. continue to provide services

16. Responsibility for recovery of information systems is generally assigned to:

    A. the business continuity team
   B. the Information Security Officer
   C. the Information Technology Department
   D. the Compliance Officer

17. The anticipated outcome of this type of testing is to identify strengths and weakness in a nonthreatening environment.
    A. structured walkthrough
    B. tabletop simulation
    C. parallel or functional
    D. full-scale

18. This testing validates plans and procedures and provides the experience required to respond in an actual situation without disrupting operations.
    A. structured walkthrough
    B. tabletop simulation
    C. parallel or functional
    D. full-scale

19. The anticipated outcome of this test is the validation that all critical process, personnel, and responsibilities have been identified.
    A. structured walkthrough
    B. tabletop simulation
    C. preliminary review
    D. full-scale

20. The purpose of an audit is to:
    A. verify completeness
    B. verify management approval and understanding
    C. verify depth of procedures
    D. all of the above

EXERCISES

Exercise 11.1: Risk Assessment

1. Make a list of at least six threats to the continuing operation of your school. Explain the threat source and the probability of occurrence.

2. Match each threat with a control that would mitigate or lessen the potential risk.

Exercise 11.2: Impact Analysis

1. Assuming you currently have a bank account, find out the following about your bank:

- Location of the operations center
- Number of branches
- ATM locations
- Internet banking site URL
- Telephone banking phone number
- Customer service phone number

2. Listed below are various disruptions in service. Rank from 1-5 (1 is the lowest, 5 is the highest) the impact on you, the customer. Consider each event independently.

   ATM system unavailable, branches open

   Closest local branch closed, others open

   Internet banking unavailable, branches open

   Core processing system unavailable, deposits accepted, withdrawals less than $100, other account information unavailable

   Communications capabilities between branches disrupted, tellers work in off-line mode.

3. Now rank the preceding list as a member of the bank's executive management. Do your rankings change? Why or why not? How should the business continuity planners reconcile the differences in the perception of impact?

Exercise 11.3: Alternative Processing Sites—What's Available?

1. Research local options for:
   a. Hot Site Data Center
   b. Warm Site Data Center
   c. Cold Site Data Center

2. Research regional and national options for Hot Sites.

3. Create a matrix comparing and contrasting the options.

Exercise 11.4: Continuity and Recovery Procedures

1. Your personal computer fails. Write continuity procedures so that you can continue to do your assigned schoolwork.

2. Your personal computer fails. Write recovery procedures to restore the system and data to its pre-failure state.

Exercise 11.5: Auditing

1. You have been asked to audit the business continuity plan and procedures of a Web hosting company. You begin by interviewing the CEO, the Information Security Officer, and the Director of IT. Develop a list of questions to use on each of the interviews.

2. Go online and see if you can find any "canned" questionnaires. Compare what you find to the list you have developed.

PROJECTS

Project 11.1: Early Stage BCP Development

1. You have been tasked with developing a business continuity plan for your school. Begin by making a list of all of the tasks that are required to complete this assignment.

2. You must first begin with a risk assessment and business impact analysis. Write a draft memo to the president of the university explaining these procedures. Include your recommendations as to who you should interview as a part of this process as well as who should make the impact decisions. (*Note:* Do not send this memo.)

3. Decide who should be invited to join the business continuity team. Compose a draft e-mail that invites individuals to serve on this team and explains their responsibilities (*Note:* Do not e-mail this draft.)

4. Find out if your school has a business continuity team (it may be known as a disaster recovery team) and who the members are. Request an interview with one member. Discuss how this individual perceives his/her roles and responsibilities. Write a brief summary of the interview and compare it to your e-mail in Step 3.

Project 11.2: Reviewing a BCP

1. Obtain a copy of your school's business continuity plan (it may be known as a disaster response plan). If you cannot locate a copy, use the Internet to locate one from another school or organization.

2. Break the plan down into specific elements: preparation, response, contingency, and recovery. Does the plan include all four elements? If not, what is missing?

3. Identify roles and responsibilities referenced in the plan.

4. Identify testing and review processes referenced in the plan.

5. Critique the plan in terms of clarity and ease of use.

Project 11.3: BCP Testing

1. Obtain a copy of your school's business continuity plan (it may be known as a disaster response plan). If you cannot locate a copy, use the Internet to locate one from another school or organization.

2. Select a specific operational area to design testing for. Write a summary of the contingency and recovery procedures.

3. Based upon the information in the plan, create an outline for each of the following test scenarios:

   • Preliminary review
   • Structured walkthrough
   • Tabletop simulation
   • Parallel (functional) testing
   • Full-scale testing

In your outline, include who should be involved in the test, where the test should take place, a description of the test, how long the test should take, and the impact to the organization.

Case Study

Commerzbank 9-11-2001 (Case Study adapted by permission of CNT [provider of storage solutions] success story)

The tragic events of September 11, 2001, rippled outward from ground zero at the World Trade Center to affect millions of individuals and organizations around the globe. One of the first to feel the impact was Commerzbank, located just across the West Side Highway from the Twin Towers. Like other businesses in the area, the bank evacuated all personnel from its World Financial Center facility following the attack. But unlike some of the other affected companies, Commerzbank had a powerful backup system already in place, and so was able to continue business virtually without interruption.

▶▶ CONTINUED ON NEXT PAGE

▶▶ CONTINUED

About Commerzbank

Founded in 1870, Commerzbank opened its New York branch in 1971. Commerzbank AG is involved, through a family of subsidiaries, in a broad range of financial activities including commercial and investment banking, export financing, and stock brokerage, collectively employing over 30,000 individuals worldwide. In Europe, banking subsidiaries engage in direct banking, mortgage banking, real estate, finance leasing, and consumer finance. Commerzbank North America is a wholesale bank serving hundreds of major clients, many of them Fortune 500 companies. Specialties include corporate banking, syndication, and real estate and public financing. The New York branch was the first to be established in the U.S. by a German banking firm and now manages information-processing operations for the bank's New York, Atlanta, Los Angeles, and Chicago branches.

When Disaster Struck

On September 11, 2001, the bank's backup plan was built around a secondary site located 30 miles away in Rye, New York. By sheerest coincidence, the installation of the backup system had just been completed, and the first full-blown test of communications between the Manhattan and Rye locations took place three days earlier on September 8. A simulated disaster fail-over scenario was tested on September 9 and 10, in which the entire Manhattan database was transferred to Rye. The next day, the real disaster struck.

Flashback

The project had begun a year earlier. The Manhattan facility consisted of two separate data systems: a HP/Compaq HSG80 running VMS and an EMC Symmetrix running SRDF. At that time, all backups were being done entirely onsite. Recognizing the risk of keeping primary and backup data at the same location, management established the remote site at Rye, where they duplicated both the HP/Compaq and EMC systems.

At each site, the EMC system was connected via ESCON to a pair of nine-slot CNT channel extenders. Data from the EMC Symmetrix in Manhattan was transmitted to the corresponding system in Rye over two T3 lines and an OC-3. Meanwhile, the two HP/Compaq systems communicated using routers and IP

▶▶ CONTINUED ON NEXT PAGE

⏵⏵ **CONTINUED**

over a shared T3 line, part of the existing corporate backbone. That line carried a variety of traffic including corporate e-mail. Data backups on the HP/Compaq systems were performed at night. Because of the amount of competing daily traffic on the same network, a full backup of data on the HP/Compaq system took an entire week, with each new replication beginning as the previous one was completed. The two-site system, as configured, met its original goal of providing off-site backup, but manager Kazi Zahid recognized two remaining issues. The first issue was the risk to current data, in the event of a primary system loss, posed by the one-week replication cycle. The second was the growing cost of communication facilities. The shared T3 was already operating near capacity, and the cost of a second facility would be about $4,000 per month. But 9/11 came before such issues could be addressed.

Within minutes of the attack on the Twin Towers, incoming communication links from the Federal Reserve and New York Clearing House were rerouted to the backup site with the throw of a switch, and a skeleton staff was making its way toward Rye to keep the system in operation. Despite transportation snarls, 16 staffers made it to Rye that day. Within a few days, fully two-thirds of the staff was working out of that facility, while the remaining third were relocated to a mid-town Manhattan facility for the eight months it took to refit the lower Manhattan location.

After the Crisis

When the downtown site reopened in May of 2002 and staff returned to that facility, Rye ceased to be an active production facility and returned to its role as a testing, training, and development facility and remote data storage site.

Questions

1. It was more than luck that Commerzbank recovered as well as it did. Analyze the case study and develop a comprehensive list of what Commerzbank did right. Include all four phases in your analysis.

2. What should Commerzbank be doing to maintain this level of continuity?

3. What can other organizations learn from this experience?

Part Three

Regulatory Compliance

Part Three, Regulatory Compliance, focuses on the practical application of policies and procedures to meet or exceed federal regulations and industry best practices.

Over the past five years, Congress has enacted a number of significant regulations designed to safeguard the privacy of confidential and/or sensitive information. Chapter 12 examines the impact of the Gramm-Leach-Bliley Act (GLBA) on financial institutions. Chapter 13 examines the impact of the Security Rule of the Health Insurance Portability and Accountability Act on the medical community. The goal of both of these chapters is to create an information security program that meets regulatory standards and honors the public trust. Chapter 14 examines the impact of three pieces of legislation: the Federal Information Security Management Act (FISMA), the Family Educational Rights and Privacy Act (FERPA) and the Sarbanes-Oxley Act (SOX).

The last chapter of this book is devoted to small business security. Chapter 15 focuses on developing, adopting, implementing, and maintaining useful and realistic policies, procedures, and practices for the small businesses environment.

- **Chapter 12:** Regulatory Compliance for Financial Institutions
- **Chapter 13:** Regulatory Compliance for the Health Care Sector
- **Chapter 14:** Information Security Regulatory Compliance for Critical Infrastructure
- **Chapter 15:** Security Policies and Practices for Small Businesses

Chapter 12

Regulatory Compliance for Financial Institutions

Chapter Objectives

After reading this chapter and completing the exercises, you will be able to do the following:

- Know information security regulations for financial institutions.
- Identify financial sector regulatory agencies.
- Understand the components of a GLBA-compliant information security program.
- Implement a GLBA-complaint information security program.
- Respond to the ever-increasing threat of identity theft.

Introduction

It is a common misperception that a financial institution's most significant asset is money. In reality, its most significant asset is *information* about money as well as transactions and customers. Protection of information assets is necessary to establish and maintain trust between the financial institution and its customers. On a broad scale, the financial industry has a primary role in protecting the nation's financial services infrastructure. More specifically, institutions have a responsibility to protect the privacy of individual consumers from harm, including fraud and identity theft.

In this chapter, we will examine, from a policy perspective, the regulations applicable to the financial sector. We will focus on Title 5 Section 501(b) of the Gramm-Leach-Bliley Act (GLBA), from which the Interagency Guidelines Establishing Information Security Standards and the FTC Safeguards Act were established. Compliance with these regulations is mandatory. Banks and other financial institutions are audited on a scheduled basis for compliance. Noncompliance has significant penalties, including being forced to cease operations. As we examine the various regulations, we will also discuss how federal examiners assess compliance. We will conclude the chapter with a look at the most significant financial security issue of our time—identity theft—and the new regulations that address this ever-growing problem.

What Is the Gramm-Leach-Bliley Act?

Depending on your age, you might remember a time before the Internet, before e-mail, and even before the personal computer. In that "ancient" time, banks served primarily as places where people kept their money. Imagine that! Anyone old enough to remember the Great Depression of the 1930s might remember the Glass-Steagall Act of 1932, which prohibited national and state banks from affiliating with securities companies. This act was passed in response to the massive failures of financial institutions during that profound event in American history.

Similar to the Glass-Steagall Act, the Bank Holding Company Act of 1956 prohibited banks from controlling a nonbank company. This act was amended by Congress in 1982 to further forbid banks from conducting general insurance underwriting or agency activities.

On November 11th, 1999, the GLBA was signed into law by President Bill Clinton, allowing banks to engage in a wide array of financial services. Also known as the Financial Modernization Act of 1999, the GLBA effectively repealed the restrictions placed on banks during the six preceding decades. The act sought to "modernize" financial services by ending regulations that prevented the merger of banks, stock brokerage companies, and insurance companies. Prior to the GLBA, the insurance company that maintained your health records was by law unrelated to the bank that mortgaged your house and the brokerage house that traded your stocks. Once merged, however, these companies would have the ability to consolidate, analyze, and sell the personal details of their customers' lives. In theory, financial institutions would now have access to an astonishing amount of private personal information.

The GLBA also allowed information that many would consider private—including bank balances and account numbers—to be bought and sold by banks, credit card companies, and other financial institutions. Because of the potential for misuse of information, Title 5 of the GLBA specifically addresses protecting both the privacy and the security of financial information. The Financial Privacy Rule governs the collection and disclosure of customers' personal financial information by financial institutions. Section 501(b) requires all financial institutions to implement and maintain safeguards to protect customer information known as ***nonpublic*** *personal information (NPI).* NPI includes (but is not limited to) names, addresses, and phone numbers when linked to bank and credit card account numbers, income and credit histories, and social security numbers.

To Whom Does the GLBA Pertain?

The GLBA applies to financial institutions (banks) that collect information from their own customers, as well as to financial institutions—such as credit reporting agencies—that receive customer information. The GLBA also applies to companies that provide a variety of financial products and services to consumers. There "nontraditional" services include:

- Automobile dealers
- Check-cashing businesses
- Consumer reporting agencies
- Courier services
- Credit card companies
- Credit counselors
- Data processors
- Debt collectors
- Educational institutions that provide financial aid
- Financial planners
- Insurance companies
- Mortgage brokers
- Mortgage lenders
- Printers that produce checks and related documents that require Magnetic Ink Character Recognition (MICR) encoding
- Property appraisers
- Real estate agents
- Retail stores that issue credit cards
- Securities firms

This is a very interesting list. Unlike banks and other traditional financial institutions, a number of the listed businesses would be considered a "small business" or a not-for-profit institution such as a private school. Indeed, many are family owned. It has been our experience that many have no idea that there is a federal regulation that pertains to them!

12

Who Enforces GLBA?

The GLBA gives authority to eight federal agencies and the states to administer and enforce the Financial Privacy Rule and Section 501(b). The agency tasked with enforcing the regulations, as well as the type and severity of the penalties, depends upon the type of financial institution or financial services organization (see Table 12.1).

Section 501(b) requires the agencies shown in Table 12.1 to establish appropriate standards for the financial institutions subject to their respective jurisdictions relating to administrative, technical, and physical safeguards for customer records and information. In response, the agencies (with the exception of the FTC) published *12 CFR, Part 30, et al. Interagency Guidelines Establishing Standards for Safeguarding Customer Information Final Rule* in the Federal Register on February 1, 2001. The effective date of the regulation was July 1, 2001.

As noted earlier, the FTC was tasked with regulating "nontraditional" financial services in respect to privacy and security. On May 23, 2002, the *FTC 16 CFR Part 314 Standards for Safeguarding Customer Information; Final Rule* was published in the Federal Register. The effective date of the regulation was May 23, 2003. The Safeguard Act is not as stringent as the rules applied to federally insured institutions. The FTC does not

TABLE 12.1 GLBA enforcement agencies.

GLBA Enforcement Agency	Financial Institutions
Board of Governors of the Federal Reserve System	Bank holding companies; member banks of the Federal Reserve System
Commodity Futures Trading Commission	Commodities brokers
Department of the Treasury, Office of the Comptroller of the Currency (OCC)	National banks; federal branches of foreign banks
Department of the Treasury, Office of Thrift Supervision (OTS)	Savings associations insured by the FDIC
Federal Deposit Insurance Corporations (FDIC)	Banks they insure, not including Federal Reserve System members
Securities and Exchange Commission (SEC)	Securities brokers and dealers; investment companies
National Credit Union Administration	Federally insured credit unions
Federal Trade Commission (FTC)	Institutions not covered by the other agencies

conduct regulatory compliance audits. When the FTC has "reason to believe" that the law has been or is being violated, and it appears to the FTC that a proceeding is in the public interest, the agency issues a complaint. The complaint is not a finding or ruling that the respondents have actually violated the law. Such action marks the beginning of a proceeding in which the allegations will be ruled upon after a formal hearing.

FYI: What Is the Federal Register?

Published by the Office of the Federal Register, National Archives and Records Administration (NARA), the Federal Register is the official daily publication for rules, proposed rules, and notices of federal agencies and organizations, as well as executive orders and other presidential documents. It is updated daily by 6 a.m. and is published Monday through Friday, except on federal holidays. The official home page of the Federal Register is **www.archives.gov/federal_register/**.

FFIEC to the Rescue

The Federal Financial Institutions Examination Council (FFIEC) is a formal interagency body empowered to prescribe uniform principles, standards, and report forms for the federal examination of financial institutions by the Board of Governors of the Federal Reserve System (FRB), the Federal Deposit Insurance Corporation (FDIC), the National Credit Union Administration (NCUA), the Office of the Comptroller of the Currency (OCC), and the Office of Thrift Supervision (OTS) and to make recommendations to promote uniformity in the supervision of financial institutions.

The FFIEC publishes the FFIEC InfoBase Handbook. The InfoBase concept was developed by the Task Force on Examiner Education to provide field examiners in financial institution regulatory agencies with a quick source of introductory training and basic information. It is used as the *de facto* guide to information technology and information security examination. The InfoBase incorporates the following topics: Audit, Business Continuity Planning, Development and Acquisition, E-Banking, FedLine, Information Security, Management, Operations, Outsourcing Technology Services, Retail Payment Systems, Supervision of Technology Service Providers, and Wholesale Payment Systems. Resources include examiner handbooks, audit workpapers, presentations, and resource pointers. For anyone tasked with interpreting and implementing the Interagency Guidelines, the InfoBase is a must-read. The InfoBase can be accessed at **www.ffiec.gov**.

12

TABLE 12.2 GLBA definitions.

Term	Definition
Board of directors	Managing officials.
Customer	Consumer who has established a continuing relationship with an institution.
Customer information	Any record containing nonpublic personal information about a customer, whether in paper, electronic, or other form, that is maintained by or on behalf of the bank.
Customer information system	Any methods used to access, collect, store, use, transmit, protect, or dispose of customer information.
Service provider	Any person or entity that maintains, processes, or otherwise is permitted access to customer information through its provision of services directly to the bank.

Understanding the GLBA Security Regulations

To understand the scope and mandate of the information security regulations, you will need to be familiar with the terminology. For the purposes of the guidelines, the definitions shown in Table 12.2 apply.

What Are Interagency Guidelines?

Financial institutions depend upon information and information systems to conduct business. It is this very dependence that makes them vulnerable. The agencies that regulate federally insured financial institution were changed with developing rules to protect this information. This section of the chapter focuses on those rules as published in the *Interagency Guidelines Establishing Standards for Safeguarding Customer Information*. To distinguish these rules from the FTC rules, we will refer to them as the *Interagency Guidelines*. The FTC rules will be referred to as the *Safeguards Act*.

The Interagency Guidelines require every covered institution to implement a comprehensive written information security program that includes *administrative, technical,* and *physical* safeguards appropriate to the size and complexity of the bank and the nature and scope of its activities (see Table 12.3).

TABLE 12.3 Information security safeguards.

Administrative Safeguards	Security policies, procedures, management, and training designed and implemented with the intent of establishing and maintaining a secure environment.
Physical Safeguards	Security controls designed to protect data systems and physical facilities from natural threats and/or man-made intrusions.
Technical Safeguards	Security measures that specify the use of technology to secure the confidentiality, integrity, and availability of information.

Development and Implementation of an Information Security Program

At a minimum, the criteria for designing a GLBA-compliant information security program should include:

- Ensuring the confidentiality of customer information.

- Protecting against any anticipated threats or hazards to the integrity of such information.

- Protecting against unauthorized access to or use of such information that could result in substantial harm or inconvenience to the customers.

- Protecting against accidental or intentional loss.

- Establishing procedures for the safeguarding of information assets, systems, and networks vital to the continued operation of the bank.

- Providing customers and management with accurate and timely information.

The objectives of the information security program are to:

- Ensure the security and confidentiality of customer information.

- Protect against any anticipated threats or hazards to the security or integrity of such information.

- Protect against unauthorized access to or use of such information that could result in substantial harm or inconvenience to any customer.

12

The requirements of the information security program include:

- Involving the Board of Directors.

- Assessing risk.

- Managing and controlling risk.

- Adjusting the program.

- Reporting to the Board.

It is up to each institution to develop a program that meets these objectives and incorporates these requirements commensurate with the size and complexity of the bank and the nature and scope of its activities. ISO 17799 standard provides an excellent framework to develop a GLBA-compliant information security program.

Involving the Board

The Interagency Guidelines require that the Board of Directors or an appropriate committee of the Board approve the bank's written information security program. The Board is also tasked with overseeing the development, implementation, and maintenance of the information security program, including assigning specific responsibility for its implementation and reviewing reports from management. As corporate officials, the Board of Directors has a fiduciary and legal responsibility. For example, financial institutions that do not comply with the GLBA are subject to civil penalties of $100,000 *per violation.* Officers and directors of that institution can be held personally liable as well, with penalties of $10,000 *per violation.*

Board members are generally chosen for their experience, business acumen, and standing in the community. It can be assumed that they understand business goals, processes, and inherent risks. Even experienced professionals, however, do not always have an in-depth natural understanding of information security issues. Institutions are expected to provide their Boards with educational opportunities to become and remain proficient in the area. Recognizing that this is a specialized body of knowledge, the Interagency Guidelines include the provision for delegation.

Delegating Information Security Tasks

Information security crosses many boundaries and involves multiple domains. Financial institutions that successfully implement an information security program have adopted a cross-functional multidisciplinary approach, as shown in Figure 12.1.

Examples of delegation include:

- Assigning information security management oversight to a *Senior Vice President.*

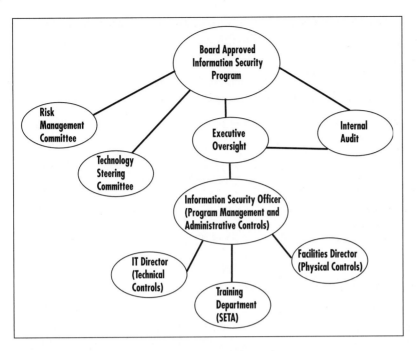

FIGURE 12.1 Security program delegation.

- Assigning implementation, management, and maintenance of an information security program, including administrative controls, to the *Information Security Officer.*

- Assigning implementation and maintenance of technical controls to the *Director of Information Technology.*

- Assigning implementation and maintenance of physical controls to the *Facilities Manager.*

- Assigning design and delivery of information security training and awareness programs to the *Training Department.*

- Assigning verification of controls to the *Internal Audit Department.*

- Assigning risk evaluation to the *Risk Management Committee.*

- Assigning the evaluation of technology initiatives responsibility to the *Technology Steering Committee.*

Assessing Risk

A risk management program is a critical component of an information security program. Risk management decisions are based upon a thorough risk analysis. To this end, banks are expected to identify and evaluate threats to the organization, risks, and mitigating controls. The Interagency Guidelines state that each bank shall do the following:

- Identify reasonably foreseeable internal and external threats that could result in unauthorized disclosure, misuse, alteration, or destruction of customer information or customer information systems.

- Assess the likelihood and potential damage of these threats, taking into consideration the sensitivity of customer information.

- Assess the sufficiency of policies, procedures, customer information systems, and other arrangements in place to control risks.

Information and Information Systems Inventory

The natural starting point of a risk assessment is an information and information systems inventory. The scope of this inventory includes detailed documentation as well as system characterization. You may recall from our discussion of asset classification in Chapter 5 that *system characterization* articulates the understanding of the system, including the boundaries of the system being assessed, the system's hardware and software, and the information that is stored, processed, and transmitted. A key part of system characterization is the ranking of information and information system components according to their protection level and importance to the institution's operations. This process is known as a *criticality analysis*. Criticality analysis process was fully discussed in Chapter 5.

Identifying and Assessing Threats

In accordance with GLBA, financial institutions must reasonably anticipate threats and possible attacks against information and systems that may affect the institution's condition and operations or may cause data disclosures that could result in substantial harm or inconvenience to customers based upon the system criticality and information sensitivity. *Threats* are defined as potential for violation of security, which exists when there is a circumstance, capability, action, or event that could breach security and cause harm. *Threat assessment* is the identification of types of threats that an organization might be exposed to. *Threat analysis* is the systematic rating of threats based upon associated risk and probability. *Threat risk* refers to the potential level of impact and is based upon institutional, industry, and technology knowledge. *Threat probability* refers to the likelihood of this threat materializing in a given timeframe, absent appropriate mitigating controls.

The result of a threat assessment and analysis is based upon numerous factors, including the size and type of the institution, services offered, geographic location, experience of personnel, infrastructure design, operating systems, vulnerability of applications, and cultural attitudes and norms. Certain threats to information are common to financial institutions. The threats listed in Table 12.4 are generally considered to have the potential for significant impact to financial institutions with a high probability of occurrence absent mitigating controls.

TABLE 12.4 Common threats to financial institutions.

Threat	Motivation	Explanation
Malware, Trojan	Destruction of information, monetary gain, unauthorized data alteration	Malicious software programs that have the potential to alter or destroying data, collect data, replace programs, or transmit data; they can render a system inoperable
Scanning, Browsing Unauthorized Access	Challenge, ego, rebellion	Hackers who are looking to exploit vulnerabilities in computers, operating systems, applications, and networks
Vendor Connectivity	Nonmalicious intent, malicious intent	Administrative access into critical systems generally for the purpose of providing support
Web Identity Theft	Destruction of information, illegal information disclosure, monetary gain, unauthorized data alteration	Site spoofing or misdirection
I-Banking Fraud	Fraud, illegal information disclosure, monetary gain, unauthorized data alteration	Unauthorized access to I-Banking
Improper Handling of Information	Curiosity, revenge, unintentional errors and omissions	Information not handled in accordance with its sensitivity level
Shoulder Surfing / Physical Browsing	Curiosity	Shoulder surfing is when an unauthorized individual views information on a screen/printer that an authorized individual has accessed; browsing is the ability of an unauthorized party to casually view private information
Dumpster Diving	Curiosity, revenge, challenge	Access to paper records in the trash, recycling bin, or shredding bins
Loss of Mobile Equipment (Laptop, PDA) control	Accidental, challenge, profit	Mobile equipment that may contain NPI that is lost, stolen, misplaced, or left in an unprotected area

12

Mitigating Controls

Controls must be in place to mitigate the risks that the identified threats pose to the confidentiality, integrity, and availability of the systems that process, store, and/or transmit customer or organizational information. The level of control needs to be based upon the severity and probability of a threat. GLBA requires that institutions assess the sufficiency of controls.

An efficient way to accomplish this task is to match each threat to its mitigating controls and then evaluate the depth and breadth of the controls. This assessment involves the following steps:

1. Prioritize information systems based upon the results of the criticality analysis. Classify the systems as Tier I, Tier II, etc. The idea here is that all systems are not expected to be protected equally. The systems determined to be the most critical operationally will need significant protection, while those at the other end of the scale may require minimal protection.

2. Prioritize the identified threats to information systems based upon the results of the threat analysis. Similar to Step 1, classify the threats into tiers or levels. The idea here is that not all threats are equally dangerous. The less dangerous the threat, the less protection required. It is important to remember that we are not working with infinite resources. The need for security must be balanced with the cost of providing the protection.

3. Start by matching up the most critical systems and the highest priority threats. For each threat, list the mitigating controls. Then evaluate the depth of defense. Make sure that each control has procedural documentation.

4. Design a testing process and schedule for each control. Assign testing and oversight responsibility. Table 12.5 illustrates this step.

Managing Risk

For purposes of managing risk, the Interagency Guidelines require that financial institutions design their information security programs to control the identified risks, commensurate with the sensitivity of the information as well as the complexity and scope of their activities. Each bank must consider whether the following security measures are appropriate and, if so, adopt those measures the bank concludes are applicable:

■ Access controls on customer information systems, including controls to authenticate and permit access only to authorized individuals and controls to prevent employees from providing customer information to unauthorized individuals who may fraudulently seek to obtain this information.

TABLE 12.5 Mitigating controls testing matrix.

Threat	Risk Level	#	Mitigating Control	Test Procedure	Test Frequency
Malware	10	1	Automatic distribution of antivirus software	Checklist / Audit	Daily
		2	Network wide port scanning	Summary Report	Weekly
		3	Limited administrative access	Checklist / Audit	Monthly
		4	Audit log review and alerts	Report Review	Daily
		5	Data backup	Checklist / Audit	Monthly
		6	User download restrictions	Group Policy Audit	Semiannually
		7	Employee training	Test at Completion of Training Program	Annually
		8	Incident response procedures	IR Simulation Testing	Quarterly
Unauthorized Access	9	1	Patch management procedures	NSS Report	Monthly
		2	Network wide port scanning	Summary Report	Monthly
		3	Limited open ports at the firewall	Report of Changes	Real time
		4	Access controls required for all systems	Review of ACL	Annually
		5	Strong password policies	Review of Group Policies	Annually and On-demand
		6	Logging and auditing of unsuccessful login attempts	Report Review	Weekly; report to be located on shared directory

12

- Access restrictions at physical locations containing customer information, such as buildings, computer facilities, and records storage facilities to permit access only to authorized individuals.

- Encryption of electronic customer information, including while in transit or in storage on networks or systems to which unauthorized individuals may have access.

- Procedures designed to ensure that customer information system modifications are consistent with the bank's information security program.

- Dual control procedures, segregation of duties, and employee background checks for employees with responsibilities for or access to customer information.

- Monitoring systems and procedures to detect actual and attempted attacks on or intrusions into customer information systems.

- Response programs that specify actions to be taken when the bank suspects or detects that unauthorized individuals have gained access to customer information systems, including appropriate reports to regulatory and law enforcement agencies.

- Measures to protect against destruction, loss, or damage of customer information due to potential environmental hazards, such as fire and water damage or technological failures.

Financial institutions are required to regularly test the key controls, systems, and procedures of the information security program. The frequency and nature of such tests should be determined by the bank's risk assessment. Tests should be conducted or reviewed by independent third parties or staff independent of those that develop or maintain the security programs.

Using the ISO Framework for Achieving Risk Management Objectives

The GLBA security program objectives can be mapped to the ISO security domains. Organizations that adopt the ISO 17799 standard will have an excellent framework for compliance activities (see Table 12.6).

Logical and Administrative Access Controls

The goal of logical and administrative access control is to provide access only to authorized individuals whose identity is established and authenticated. Activities should be limited to the minimum required for business purpose based upon "need to know" and "least privilege" concepts. Access control invokes three activities: identification, authentication, and authorization. *Identification* is ascertaining who the person or process is. *Authentication* is the verification of identity. *Authorization* is the process of granting access. The Interagency Guidelines focus on access controls in relation to access rights administration, authentication, network access, operating system access, application access, and remote access policies and procedures.

TABLE 12.6 Correlating security programs to the ISO.

Security Program Component	Relevant ISO Sections
Logical and Administrative Access: 　User Access Management 　Authentication 　Network Access 　Operating System Access 　Application Access 　Remote Access	Section 6 Personnel Security Section 9 Access Control Section 8 Operations Security
Physical Security	Section 7 Physical Security
Data Security	Section 8 Operations Security Section 10 Systems Development
Malicious Code	Section 8 Operations Security
Systems Development, Acquisition, and Maintenance	Section 10 Systems Development
Personnel Security	Section 6 Personnel Security
Electronic and Paper Based Media Handling	Section 5 Asset Classification Section 8 Operations Security
Logging and Data Collection	Section 8 Operations Security Section 9 Access Control
Service Provider Oversight	Section 3 Organizational Security Section 8 Operations Security
Intrusion Detection and Response	Section 8 Operations Security Section 9 Access Control
Business Continuity Considerations	Section 11 Business Continuity

12

Access Rights Administration Financial institutions must have an effective process to administer access rights. Access rights administration applies to employees, directors, vendors, contractors, and customers. All information system users should be provided with an initial information security orientation and ongoing training as appropriate.

FFIEC-recommended access rights administration procedures include:

- Having a formal documented process in place to enroll, authorize, authenticate, and monitor user accounts and activities.

- Assigning users and system resources only the access required to perform their required functions.

- Updating access rights based upon personnel or system changes.

- Periodically reviewing users' access rights.

- Designing appropriate confidentiality and acceptable user policies or affirmation agreements.

Authentication *Authentication* is the verification of identity by a system based upon the presentation of unique credentials to that system. Authentication may be single factor (one credential) or multifactor (two or more types of credentials). The type and complexity of authentication is directly related to the criticality and sensitivity of the information as well as the environmental access risks. Environmental access risks include location of the user and the method used to connect (e.g., wireless, VPN, Web-based).

FFIEC-recommended authentication procedures include:

- Selecting authentication mechanisms based on the risk associated with the particular application or services.

- Considering whether multifactor authentication is appropriate for each application, taking into account that multifactor authentication is increasingly necessary for many forms of electronic banking and electronic payment activities.

- Encrypting the transmission and storage of authenticator (e.g., passwords, PINs, digital certificates, and biometric templates).

Network Access Computer networks often extend connectivity far beyond the financial institution and its data center. Networks provide system access and connectivity between business units, affiliates, third-party service providers, business partners, customers, and the public. This increased connectivity requires additional controls to segregate and restrict access between various groups and information users.

FFIEC-recommended network access procedures include:

- Group network servers, applications, data, and users into security domains (e.g., untrusted external networks, external service providers, or various internal user systems).

- Establish appropriate access requirements within and between each security domain.

- Implement appropriate technological controls to meet those access requirements consistently.

Operating System Access Computers, be they personal, midrange, or mainframe, depend upon the operating system to function. Operating systems serve as a computer's command and control center. Having administrative access to an operating system is akin to having the keys to the kingdom. Common operating systems used in the financial sector include Microsoft Windows, IBM OS/400 and AIX, Linux, and Sun Solaris. Operating systems must be secured from unauthorized access, misuse of privilege, exploitation of inherent vulnerabilities, and excessive administrative control.

FFIEC-recommended operating system access procedures include:

- Securing access to system utilities.

- Restricting and monitoring privileged access.

- Logging and monitoring user or program access to sensitive resources and alerting on security events.

- Updating the operating systems with security patches.

- Securing the devices that can access the operating system through physical and logical means.

Application Access Mission-critical applications like core banking applications require additional security and access controls. Users and processes should be allowed access based upon the principle of least privilege. Administrative access should be logged and subjected to oversight. Vendor access should be restricted and managed appropriately.

FFIEC-recommended application access control procedures include:

- Using authentication and authorization controls appropriately robust for the risk of the application.

- Monitoring access rights to ensure they are the minimum required for the user's current business needs.

- Using time-of-day limitations on access as appropriate.

- Logging access and security events.

- Using software that enables rapid analysis of user activities.

Remote Access Remote access includes Internet and dial-in capabilities. Remote access systems must be restricted and strictly controlled. The upside of remote access is the ability to extend the functionality of the information system. The downside of remote access is the increased risk of attack.

FFIEC-recommended remote access control procedures include:

- Disabling remote communications at the operating system level if no business need exists.

12

- Tightly controlling access through management approvals and subsequent audits.

- Implementing robust controls over configuration to disallow potential malicious use.

- Logging and monitoring remote access.

- Securing remote access devices.

- Using strong authentication and encryption to secure communications.

Physical Security

Physical security includes protection from physical access, damage, theft, and destruction. Not all areas require the same degree of protection. Conceptually, the facility and the equipment can be divided into zones. The zones are classified based upon criticality and sensitivity of information and information systems contained within and then secured accordingly. For financial institutions, zones might include the operations center, the data center, the vault, branches, customer service centers, and remote access locations.

FFIEC-recommended physical security procedures include:

- Implementing appropriate preventative and detective controls in each zone to protect against the risks of physical penetration by malicious or unauthorized people.

- Implementing appropriate preventative and detective controls in each zone to protect against the risks of damage from environmental contaminants.

- Implementing appropriate preventative and detective controls in each zone to protect against the risks of electronic penetration through active or passive electronic emissions.

Data Security

Encryption techniques (symmetric, asymmetric, and cryptographic hash) can be used to protect the confidentiality of information as well as provide proof of authenticity and nonrepudiation. Encryption techniques are used when an additional layer of security is required. Encryption techniques are incorporated into various communication protocols such as transaction layer security (TLS), wireless transaction layer security (WTLS), secure shell (SSH), and Internet Protocol Security (IPSec). Virtual private network security (VPN) is provided by authentication and authorization for the connection and the user, as well as encryption of the traffic. Encryption can also be used to secure e-mail, FTP, and telnet sessions.

FFIEC-recommended data security procedures include:

- Ensuring that encryption implementations have sufficient strength to protect the information from disclosure until such time as disclosure poses no material risk.

- Verifying that encryption implementations include effective key management practices.

- Ensuring that encryption implementations appropriately protect the encrypted communication's endpoints.

Malicious Code

Malicious code or malware is defined as any program (or part thereof) that acts in an unexpected, potentially damaging manner. Malicious code includes viruses, worms, Trojans, backdoors, and logic bombs. Malware writers are now creating blended threats combining types of malicious code. Malicious code is insidious and can attack servers, client devices (desktops, laptops, handhelds), and communication devices. While malicious code can be injected into programs at the development stage, more often it is transmitted as mobile code. E-mail, Instant Messaging, peer-to-peer applications, and Web-based active content are often the means to distribution. Malware has the ability to affect confidentiality, integrity, and availability.

FFIEC-recommended malicious code control procedures include:

- Using antivirus products with real-time protection on clients and servers.

- Using an appropriate blocking strategy on the network perimeter.

- Filtering input to applications.

- Creating, implementing, and training staff in appropriate computing policies and practices.

Systems Development, Acquisition, and Maintenance

Best practices in system development, acquisition, and maintenance dictate that security controls are incorporated into software prior to development and implementation. Financial institutions must ensure that any custom software that they develop or purchase has been tested for a secure implementation. Particular attention should be paid to commercial off-the-shelf (COTS) software. Often, COTS applications default to an insecure state upon implementation and require hardening. In all cases, a comprehensive patch management program is required to protect against exploits of discovered vulnerabilities.

FFIEC-recommended systems development, acquisition, and maintenance procedures include:

12

- Defining security requirements before developing or acquiring new systems.

- Incorporating widely recognized standards in developing security requirements.

- Incorporating appropriate security controls, audit trails, and logs for data entry and data processing.

- Implementing an effective change control process.

- Hardening systems before deployment.

- Establishing an effective patch process for new security vulnerabilities.

- Overseeing vendors to protect the integrity and confidentiality of application source code.

Personnel Security

Internal users pose an inherent danger because they are granted logical and physical access to information and information systems. Users may exploit their access for malicious criminal activities, such as corporate espionage, fraud, and embezzlement. They may engage in misbehavior due to job dissatisfaction or unsatisfied curiosity. Conversely, nonmalicious activity such as accidental deletion, data alteration, and loss of equipment may cause unintentional harm to the institution. Screening, training, and awareness programs, contractual agreements, and oversight all mitigate personnel risks.

FFIEC-recommended personnel security procedures include:

- Performing appropriate background checks and screening of new employees.

- Obtaining agreements covering confidentiality, nondisclosure, and authorized use.

- Using job descriptions, employment agreements, and training to increase accountability for security.

- Providing training to support awareness and policy compliance.

Electronic and Paper-Based Media Handling

Financial institutions store sensitive and confidential data on various media, including hard drives, CD/DVD, tape, optical and portable devices, and paper. Protection of the data requires protection of the media from theft, destruction, loss, unauthorized access, alternation, and publication. Financial institutions must address five components of media security: handling, storage, transit, reuse, and disposal (including recycling).

FFIEC-recommended electronic and paper-based media handling procedures include:

- Establishing policies for handling and storing information.

- Ensuring safe and secure disposal of sensitive media.

- Securing media in transit or transmission to third parties.

Logging and Data Collection

Logs can effectively trace user and system activity. Information gathered from logs can be used proactively to assess an organization's security posture, detect potential incidents, predict resource utilization, and verify equipment health. Logs can also be used for forensic purposes in incident response and analysis.

FFIEC-recommended logging and data collection procedures include:

- Identifying the system components that warrant logging.

- Determining the level of data logged for each component.

- Establishing policies for securely handling and analyzing log files.

Service Provider Oversight

Financial institutions commonly outsource aspects of their operations, such as core banking, item processing, help desk and technical services, Internet banking, ATM, Web hosting, and customer call centers. However, outsourcing doesn't change the fact that the institution owns and must protect the data. The Interagency Guidelines require financial institutions to ensure that service providers have implemented security controls in accordance with GLBA requirements.

FFIEC-recommended service provider oversight procedures include:

- Using appropriate due diligence in service provider research and selection.

- Implementing contractual assurances regarding security responsibilities, controls, and reporting.

- Requiring nondisclosure agreements regarding the institution's systems and data.

- Providing a third-party review of the service provider's security though appropriate audits and tests.

- Coordinating incident response policies and contractual notification requirements.

Intrusion Detection and Response

Financial institutions are an attractive target for intruders. Even with the best controls in place, the question remains—when and how will an attack happen? Financial institutions must have in place the capability to detect,

12

react, and respond to an intrusion. The earlier an intrusion is detected, the greater the possibility of mitigating the damage.

FFIEC-recommended intrusion detection and response procedures include:

- Preparing for an intrusion, including analysis of data flows, decisions on the nature and scope of monitoring, consideration of legal factors, appropriate policies governing detection and response, and the formation and equipping of response teams.

- Applying detection implementation, including the proper use of technology.

- Responding correctly to an intrusion, including the containment and restoration of systems and appropriate reporting.

Business Continuity Considerations

Business continuity plans generally include activating alternate operational and data processing sites, primary usage of redundant equipment, turning up alternative lines of communication, and significant involvement of third parties. Depending upon the event, all or some of the elements of the security environment may change. Business continuity plans should incorporate security controls commensurate with normal operating conditions.

FFIEC-recommended business continuity security procedures include:

- Identifying personnel with key security roles during a continuity plan implementation, and training personnel in those roles.

- Determining security needs for back-up sites and alternate communication networks.

Training, Training, and More Training!

The Interagency Guidelines require institutions to train staff to implement their information security programs. This is widely interpreted as embodying the NIST SETA model of security education, training, and awareness. You may recall this model from Chapter 6. The goal of education is to explain *why,* and the anticipated outcome is insight and understanding. The goal of training is to explain *how,* and the anticipated outcome is knowledge and skill. Lastly, the goal of awareness is to explain *what,* and the anticipated outcome is information and awareness. The impact of education is long-term, the impact of training is immediate, and the impact of awareness is short-term.

Testing the Controls

Controls are meaningful only if they work. All controls need to be tested, with priority given to high-risk critical systems. Segregation of duties applies to security testing. Whoever is assigned to test the controls should be independent of those responsible for the design, installation, maintenance, and operation of the tested system. There are three standard types of diagnostic tests: penetration tests, audits, and assessments.

Penetration Tests A *penetration test* (or *pen test*) subjects a system or device to real-world attacks. The goal of a pen test is to identify the extent to which a system can be compromised before the attacked is identified and responded to. Penetration tests can be conducted in one of two ways: black-box (with no prior knowledge of the infrastructure to be tested) or white-box (with complete knowledge of the infrastructure to be tested). Each approach has its supporters. Regardless of the approach taken, however, a pen test typically involves a comprehensive analysis of publicly available information about the target (footprinting), a network enumeration phase where target hosts are identified and analyzed, and an analysis of the behavior of security devices such as screening routers and firewalls. Vulnerabilities within the target hosts are then identified and verified and the implications are assessed.

Audits *Auditing* compares current practices against a set of standards, which can be either internal or external, such as those used by regulatory examiners. Internal standards are codified in policy. Hence, the importance of only committing to policy what is doable and realistic.

Assessments An *assessment* is a study to locate security vulnerabilities and identify corrective actions. An assessment differs from a pen test as the tester has full knowledge of and full access to the systems being tested. An assessment differs from an audit as it does not use a predefined set of standards but rather invokes best practices and up-to-date information and security knowledge. Assessments focus on a process and how the process can be improved. Take, for example, the integrity issue of patch management. While an assessment may report which particular patches are missing, it is more likely to report on how often patches are applied, by whom, and under what circumstances.

Adjusting the Program, Reporting to the Board, and Implementing the Standards

The last three sections of the Interagency Guidelines address the need for the information security program to be dynamic, the importance of Board involvement, and the effective date of compliance.

12

Adjusting the Program

A static security program provides a false sense of security. The pace of technological and economic change is staggering. Monitoring the effectiveness of the security program is essential to maintain a secure environment. Effective monitoring includes both technical and nontechnical evaluation. The Interagency Guidelines require each institution to monitor, evaluate, and adjust the information security program in light of any relevant changes in technology, the sensitivity of customer information, internal and external threats to information, and the bank's own changing business arrangements, such as mergers and acquisitions, alliances and joint ventures, outsourcing arrangements, and changes to customer information systems.

Reporting to the Board

The Interagency Guidelines require each institution to report to the Board of Directors or designated committee at least annually. This report should describe the overall status of the information security program and the bank's compliance with the Interagency Guidelines. The report needs to address risk assessment, risk management and control decisions, service provider arrangements, resulting of testing, security breaches or violations as well as management responses, and recommendations for changes to the security program.

Effective Date of Compliance

All banks must implement an information security program pursuant to the Interagency Guidelines effective July 1, 2001. The examining agencies will issues additional guidance as applicable.

What's Different About the FTC Safeguards Act?

There are four main differences between the Interagency Guidelines and the FTC *Standards for Safeguarding Customer Information,* also known as the Safeguards Act. First, the Safeguards Act applies to organizations or *individuals* that are significantly engaged in providing financial products or services to consumers, including check-cashing businesses, data processors, mortgage brokers, nonbank lenders, personal property or real estate appraisers, and retailers that issue credit cards to consumers. Second, the Safeguards Act is not as comprehensive as the Interagency Guidelines. Third, organizations subject to the Safeguards Act are not audited for compliance unless a compliant is filed. Lastly, the effective date of the Safeguards Act was May 23, 2003.

Objectives

As described in the GLBA, the objectives of the Safeguards Act are to:

- Ensure the security and confidentiality of customer records and information.

- Protect against any anticipated threats or hazards to the security and integrity of such records.

- Protect against unauthorized access to or use of such records or information that could result in substantial harm or inconvenience to any customer.

It is expected that each organization will develop, implement, and maintain an information security program that incorporates administrative, physical, and technical controls designed to meet these objectives. The plan must be written. The depth and complexity of the plan is related to the size and complexity of the organization, the nature and scope of the organization's activities, and the sensitivity of customer information.

Elements

The FTC Safeguards Act defines the minimum elements that must be addressed in the information security program.

1. Designate an employee or employees to coordinate your information security program.

2. Identify reasonably foreseeable internal and external risks to the security, confidentiality, and integrity of customer information that could result in the unauthorized disclosure, misuse, alteration, destruction, or other compromise of such information, and assess the sufficiency of any safeguards in place to control these risks. At a minimum, such a risk assessment should include consideration of risks in each relevant area of operations, including:

   a. Employee training and management.

   b. Information systems, including network and software design, as well as information processing, storage, transmission, and disposal.

   c. Detecting, preventing, and responding to attacks, intrusions, or other systems failures.

3. Design and implement information safeguards to control the risks you identify through risk assessment, and regularly test or otherwise monitor the effectiveness of the safeguards' key controls, systems, and procedures.

12

4. Oversee service providers by:

    a. Taking reasonable steps to select and retain service providers that are capable of maintaining appropriate safeguards for the customer information at issue.

    b. Requiring your service providers by contract to implement and maintain such safeguards.

5. Evaluate and adjust your information security program in light of the results of the testing and monitoring required by paragraph (3) of this section; any material changes to your operations or business arrangements; or any other circumstances that you know or have reason to know may have a material impact on your information security program.

FYI: FTC Enforces GLBA's Safeguards Act Against Mortgage Companies

The Federal Trade Commission charged two mortgage companies with violating the agency's GLBA Safeguards Act by not having reasonable protections for customers' sensitive personal and financial information. In a complaint filed against Nationwide Mortgage Group, Inc. (Nationwide) and its president John D. Eubank, the FTC alleged that the Fairfax, Virginia-based mortgage broker failed to implement safeguards to protect its customers' names, social security numbers, credit histories, bank account numbers, income tax returns, and other sensitive financial information. Sunbelt Lending Services, Inc. (Sunbelt), a subsidiary of Cendant Mortgage Corporation with headquarters in Clearwater, Florida, has agreed to settle similar FTC charges. These are the FTC's first cases enforcing the Safeguards Act.

According to the FTC's complaints, both companies failed to comply with the Act's basic requirements, including that they assess the risks to sensitive customer information and implement safeguards to control these risks. In addition, Nationwide failed to train its employees on information security issues; oversee its loan officers' handling of customer information; and monitor its computer network for vulnerabilities. Sunbelt also failed to oversee the security practices of its service providers and of its loan officers working from remote locations throughout the state of Florida.

For more information: **http://www.ftc.gov/opa/2004/11/ns.htm**.

Identity Theft and Regulatory Compliance

Identity theft is one of the most significant issues of our times. *Identity theft* occurs when someone possesses or uses your name, address, social security number (SSN), bank or credit card account number, or other identifying information without your knowledge with the intent to commit fraud or other crimes. A 2003 FTC survey showed that over a one-year period, nearly 10 million people—or 4.6 percent of the adult population—had discovered that they were victims of some form of identity theft. According to the 2003 Identify Theft Resource Center (ITRC) report, victims now spend an average of 600 hours recovering from this crime. The Federal General Accounting Office (GOA) study on identity theft (GAO-02-363, issued March 2002) included costs to federal agencies. The executive office for U.S. Attorneys estimated cost of prosecuting a white-collar crime case was $11,443. The Secret Service estimates the average cost per financial crime investigation is $15,000. The FBI estimates the average cost per financial crime investigation is $20,000.

Responding to Identity Theft

In response to this problem, the regulatory agencies responsible for the United States banking sector have issued in early 2005 Supplement A– Interagency Guidance on Response Programs for Unauthorized Access to Customer Information and Customer Notice. We are going to refer to this supplement as "The Guidance."

The Guidance interprets section 501(b) of the GLBA and the Interagency Guidelines and describes response programs, including customer notification procedures, that a financial institution should develop and implement to address unauthorized access to or use of customer information that could result in substantial harm or inconvenience to a customer.

Additional Security Controls The Guidance enumerates a number of security measures that each financial institution must consider and adopt, if appropriate, to control risks stemming from reasonably foreseeable internal and external threats to the institution's customer information.

- Access controls on customer information systems, including controls to authenticate and permit access only to authorized individuals and controls to prevent employees from providing customer information to unauthorized individuals who may fraudulently seek to obtain this information.

- Background checks for employees with responsibilities for access to customer information.

- Response programs that specify actions to be taken when the financial institution suspects or detects that unauthorized individuals

12

have gained access to customer information systems, including appropriate reports to regulatory and law enforcement agencies.

Response Program The Guidance stresses that every financial institution is instructed to develop and implement a risk-based response program to address incidents of unauthorized access to customer information. The response program should be a key part of an institution's information security program. The program should be appropriate to the size and complexity of the institution and the nature and scope of its activities.

At a minimum, The Guidance emphasizes that an institution's response program should contain procedures for the following:

- Assessing the nature and scope of an incident, and identifying what customer information systems and types of customer information have been accessed or misused.

- Notifying its primary federal regulator as soon as possible when the institution becomes aware of an incident involving unauthorized access to or use of *sensitive* customer information.

- Consistent with the agencies' Suspicious Activity Report (SAR) regulations, notifying appropriate law enforcement authorities, in addition to filing a timely SAR in situations involving federal criminal violations requiring immediate attention, such as when a reportable violation is ongoing.

- Taking appropriate steps to contain and control the incident to prevent further unauthorized access to or use of customer information, for example, by monitoring, freezing, or closing affected accounts, while preserving records and other evidence.

- Notifying customers when warranted.

For purposes of this Guidance, *sensitive customer information* means a customer's name, address, or telephone number, in conjunction with the customer's social security number, driver's license number, account number, credit or debit card number, or a personal identification number or password that would permit access to the customer's account. *Sensitive customer information* also includes any combination of components of customer information that would allow someone to log onto or access the customer's account, such as user name and password or password and account number.

Notification The Guidance specifically outlines notification procedures. Where an incident of unauthorized access to customer information involves customer information systems maintained by an institution's service providers, it is the responsibility of the financial institution to notify the institution's customers and regulator. Per the Guidance, financial institutions have an affirmative duty to protect their customers' information against unauthorized access or use. Notifying customers of a security incident involving the unauthorized access or use of the customer's information in accordance with the standard set forth is a key part of that duty.

Timely notification of customers is important to manage an institution's reputation risk. Effective notice also may reduce an institution's legal risk, assist in maintaining good customer relations, and enable the institution's customers to take steps to protect themselves against the consequences of identity theft. When customer notification is warranted, an institution may not forgo notifying its customers of an incident because the institution believes that it may be potentially embarrassed or inconvenienced by doing so.

The FTC and Identity Theft

The Federal Trade Commission is making identity theft a priority. The FTC manages the Identity Theft Data Clearinghouse, which is the federal government's portal for tracking identity theft complaints. The FTC also maintains the Consumer Sentinel database, which collects information about consumer fraud and identity theft from over 150 other organizations and makes it available to law enforcement partners across the nation and throughout the world. Between January and December 2004, over 635,000 consumer fraud and identity theft complaints were logged in the database. Consumers reported losses from fraud of more than $547 million. Launched in 1997, the Sentinel database now includes over two million complaints.

FYI: Help for Victims of Identity Theft

The FTC has established the Identity Theft Toll-Free Hotline and the ID Theft Web site (**www.consumer.gov/idtheft**) to give identity theft victims a central place in the federal government to report their problems and receive helpful information.

12

Summary

Financial institutions must protect the information with which they are entrusted. In support of this goal, Congress passed legislation requiring financial institutions to implement, maintain, and monitor an information security program. The Gramm-Leach-Bliley Act requires that appropriate standards be developed and assigns this task to eight federal agencies. The seven agencies that monitor federally insured banks collaborated and published the *Interagency Guidelines Establishing Standards for Safeguarding Customer Information*. The FTC was charged with overseeing organizations that provide "nontraditional" financial services such as insurance, financial aid, and credit and published the *Standards for Safeguarding Customer Information*.

The intent of both regulations is to ensure the confidentiality, integrity, and availability of nonpublic personal information. The regulations outline the goals and objectives of the required information security program. It is up to each institution to implement a comprehensive written information security program that includes *administrative, technical,* and *physical* safeguards appropriate to the size and complexity of the bank and the nature and scope of its activities.

Test Your Skills

MULTIPLE CHOICE QUESTIONS

1. The most significant information security regulation for the financial sector is:

   A. Sarbanes-Oxley

   B. HIPAA

   C. Gramm-Leach-Bliley

   D. FERPA

2. The Financial Modernization Act of 1999:

   A. deregulated bank services

   B. mandated use of computers

   C. required banks to merge

   D. prohibited banks from controlling a nonbanking company

3. The Financial Privacy Rule governs all of the following activities EXCEPT:

   A. collection of personal financial information

   B. disclosure of personal financial information

   C. sharing of personal financial information inside an organization

   D. sharing of personal financial information between organizations

4. Which information set would NOT be considered NPI?

   A. name, address, social security number

   B. name, address

   C. name, checking account number

   D. name, social security number

5. The GLBA pertains directly to all of the following organizations EXCEPT:

   A. universities

   B. insurance companies

   C. courier services

   D. cleaning services

6. The Safeguards Act was developed by the:

   A. Federal Reserve System (FRS)

   B. Securities and Exchange Commission (SEC)

   C. Federal Trade Commission (FTC)

   D. Federal Deposit Insurance Company (FDIC)

7. Which of the following statements is NOT true?

   A. The Safeguards Act applies to all federally insured institutions.

   B. Compliance with the Safeguards Act is not proactively audited.

   C. The Interagency Guidelines are more stringent than the Safeguards Act.

   D. Enforcement of the Safeguards Act begins with a complaint.

8. The Interagency Guidelines require a written security program that includes all of the following EXCEPT:

   A. legal safeguards

   B. physical safeguards

   C. technical safeguards

   D. administrative safeguards

12

9. Financial institutions can be fined up to how much per violation?

   A. $100

   B. $1,000

   C. $10,000

   D. $100,000

10. Circumstances, capabilities, actions, or events that could cause harm are known as:

    A. risks

    B. threats

    C. variables

    D. vulnerabilities

11. A threat assessment is a(n):

    A. identification of types of threats an organization might be exposed to

    B. systematic rating of threats based upon level of risk and probability

    C. potential level of impact

    D. likelihood of a threat materializing

12. A threat analysis is a(n):

    A. identification of types of threats an organization might be exposed to

    B. systematic rating of threats based upon level of risk and probability

    C. potential level of impact

    D. likelihood of a threat materializing

13. A threat probability is a(n):

    A. identification of types of threats an organization might be exposed to

    B. systematic rating of threats based upon level of risk and probability

    C. potential level of impact

    D. likelihood of a threat materializing

14. This test subjects a system or device to real-world attacks.

    A. audit

    B. penetration test

    C. assessment

    D. interview

15. This test compares current practices against a set of standards.

    A. audit

    B. penetration test

    C. assessment

    D. interview

16. This test locates security vulnerabilities and identifies corrective actions.

    A. audit

    B. penetration test

    C. assessment

    D. interview

17. This type of attack occurs when someone possesses or uses your name, address, social security number, bank or credit card account number, or other identifying information without your knowledge with the intent to commit fraud or other crimes.

    A. Denial of Service attack

    B. hijacking

    C. identity theft

    D. man-in-the-middle attack

18. In a situation involving unauthorized access to NPI, banks are expected to notify customers:

    A. immediately

    B. when warranted

    C. never

    D. only after notifying law enforcement

19. Interagency Guidelines recommend background checks:

    A. for all vendors

    B. for the Board of Directors and executive management

    C. for all employees

    D. for employees with responsibilities for access to customer information

20. What is the effective date for compliance with the Interagency Guidelines?

    A. 2003

    B. 2004

    C. 2005

    D. 2006

12

EXERCISES

Exercise 12.1: Identifying Types of Institutions

1. Refer back to Table 12.1. Review the types of institutions.

2. For each agency listed, locate a local financial institution subject to its regulatory oversight.

3. Prepare a list of financial institutions and their regulators.

Exercise 12.2: The FTC

1. Visit the FTC Web site at **www.ftc.gov**.

2. Prepare a summary of FTC activities in regard to information security.

3. Prepare a summary of FTC information security resources for business.

Exercise 12.3: The Federal Register

1. Locate and print a copy of either the Interagency Guidelines or the Safeguards Act.

2. Find and highlight the actual regulations.

3. Prepare a brief explaining the purpose of the balance of the document.

Exercise 12.4: Prioritizing Threats

1. Review Table 12.4.

2. Choose a bank in your area. Based upon the bank's size, location, stability, and history, prioritize the threats listed in Table 12.4. Be prepared to defend your answers.

Exercise 12.5: Mitigating Controls

1. Refer back to Table 12.5. Choose one of the threats.

2. You have been tasked with explaining the mitigating controls to the Board of Directors. The members of the Board are not technologically savvy. Write a summary of each mitigating control.

PROJECTS

Project 12.1: Designing an Information Security Program

1. You have been tasked with writing a summary of the requirements of a GLBA-compliant information security program for the Board of Directors. The report will also be shared with the federal examiners. An outline of the report has already been developed.

   200X Information Security Program for ABC Bank of Anytown, U.S.A.

   A. Introduction to the Information Security Program

   B. Objectives of the Information Security Program

   C. Scope of the Information Security Program

   D. Oversight and Delivery of the Information Security Program

   E. Information Security Program Overview

   F. Identification and Classification of Information Systems

   G. Information Security Risk and Vulnerability Assessment

   H. Management and Control of Information Security Risk

2. Using the outline as your guide, you will complete the report. Begin with describing your institution (you may choose any size or type of bank).

3. Continue with sections B-H. Your report should not exceed five pages.

Project 12.2: Should Educational Institutions Be Subject to the GLBA?

1. Read the American Council on Education's (ACE) petition to the FTC regarding exemption from the GLBA. It is written by Stanley O. Ikenberry and can be found at **www.acenet.edu/washington/ legalupdate/2000/03march/graham_privacy_rule.html**.

2. Prepare a response explaining why the NPI collected, processed, stored, and transmitted at educational institutions should be subject to the Safeguards Act.

3. Discuss your response with a member of the faculty or staff at your school. Document their opinion.

12

Project 12.3: GLBA Compliant Policies

1. Policies need to be developed to support the implementation of an information security program. Based upon the program objectives as outlined in the Interagency Guidelines, create a list of required policies.

2. Match the policies to the ISO Security Domains.

3. Write one policy per domain.

▶▶ Case Study

High-profile cases involving banks selling consumer information with adverse consequences for customers occurred in the late 1990s. These cases fueled support for Title V of the GLBA.

In November 1997, Charter Pacific Bank of Agoura Hills, California, sold millions of credit card numbers to an adult Web site company, which then proceeded to bill customers for access to Internet porn sites and other services they did not request. Some of the customers billed did not even own a computer. The Web site company had set up numerous merchant accounts under different names to avoid detection. In September 2000, the FTC announced that it had won a $37.5 million judgment against the Web site company. While the bank maintained that it did not do anything wrong, it has since then stopped selling credit card numbers to merchants.

In 1998, NationsBank (later merged with Bank of America) was fined millions for securities law violations because it shared customer information with its affiliate subsidiary, Nations Securities. The subsidiary then convinced low-risk customers to buy high-risk investments. Many NationsBank customers suffered large losses, including senior citizens who lost most of their life savings.

1. In each of these situations, what did the bank do that was wrong?

2. What was the implication of each bank's actions?

3. Could these situations have occurred post-GLBA?

4. What should banks do to reduce the risk of identity theft?

Chapter | 13

Regulatory Compliance for the Healthcare Sector

Chapter Objectives

After reading this chapter and completing the exercises, you will be able to do the following:

- Understand the security regulations required of the healthcare sector by the HIPAA Security Rule.
- Write HIPAA-compliant policies and procedures.
- Execute the HIPAA implementation specifications.
- Conduct a compliance audit.
- Relate the ISO 17799 security framework to HIPAA security compliance.

Introduction

Congress enacted the Health Insurance Portability and Accountability Act of 1996 (HIPAA, Public Law 104-191) to simplify and standardize healthcare administrative processes. The overall purpose of the act is to enable better access to health insurance, reduce fraud and abuse, and lower the overall cost of healthcare in the United States. The HIPAA statue is composed of five titles, including healthcare insurance coverage and healthcare finance. Title II includes the HIPAA administrative simplification requirements, which address how electronic healthcare transactions are transmitted and stored. The provisions of HIPAA mandate the Department of Health and Human Services (HHS) to develop and publish rules to implement the HIPAA administrative simplification requirements. HHS published five rules: Code Set, Transaction Identifiers, Electronic Data Interchange (EDI), Privacy, and Security.

On August 20, 2003, the Department of Health and Human Services published the HIPAA Security Rule. The intent of the rule is to establish a minimum standard for the security of electronic health information known as electronic protected health information (ePHI). This rule is applicable to any entity that stores or transmits ePHI, including healthcare providers, health plans, and healthcare clearing houses. Organizations that the rule applies to are referred to as covered entities.

In this chapter, we will examine the components of the Security Rule. We will discuss the policies, procedures, and practices that entities need to implement to be considered compliant with HIPAA regulations. Compliance is important not just because it is the law. Compliance is a civic duty. Compliance is good business practice and honors the trust that patients put in their providers.

Understanding the Security Rule

The HIPAA Security Rule specifically focuses on safeguarding electronic protected health information (ePHI). ePHI is information that is classified as ***individually identifiable health information (IIHI) and stored, processed, or transmitted digitally or electronically.*** IIHI is information that reasonably can be used to identify an individual person. The standards and implementation specifications apply to both public and private sector entities that process, store, or transmit ePHI.

FYI: The Security Rule

The Final Rule adopting HIPAA standards for the security of electronic health information was published in the Federal Register on February 20, 2003. A PDF version of the Final Rule can be downloaded from **www.cms.hhs.gov/hipaa/hipaa2/regulations/security/03-3877.pdf**.

Additional information regarding the Security Rule including FAQ, education materials, planning guides, and a glossary of terms can be found at the Center for Medicare and Medicaid Services (CMM) Web site: **www.cms.hhs.gov/hipaa/hipaa2/**.

The National Institute of Standards and Technology (NIST) has published Special Publication 800-66: An Introductory Resource Guide for Implementing the Health Insurance Portability and Accountability Act (HIPAA) Security Rule. The publication can be downloaded from the NIST Web site: **csrc.nist.gov/publications/nistpubs/800-66/SP800-66.pdf**.

TABLE 13.1 Covered entities.

Covered Entity Category	Covered Entity Description
Healthcare Provider	Any provider of medical or other health services, or supplies.
	Note: In order to be considered a covered entity, the provider must electronically process, store, or transmit any personally identifiable health information.
Health Plan	Any individual or group plan that provides or pays the cost of medical care.
Healthcare Clearinghouse	A public or private entity that processes another entity's healthcare transactions.
Medicare Prescription Drug Card Sponsor	A non-governmental entity that offers an endorsed discount drug program under the Medicare Modernization Act. This fourth category of "covered entity" will remain in effect until the drug card program ends in 2006.

HIPAA Goals and Objectives

The main goal of the HIPAA Security Rule is to protect the confidentiality, integrity, and availability of all electronic protected health information that a covered entity creates, receives, maintains, or transmits. In Chapter 3, we discussed the CIA Triad and defined these elements as follows:

■ *Confidentiality* is the protection of information from unauthorized people, resources, and processes.

■ *Integrity* is the protection of information or processes from intentional or accidental unauthorized modification.

■ *Availability* is the assurance that systems and information are accessible by authorized users when needed.

HIPAA Key Principles

The framers of the regulations were realists. They understood that these regulations were going to apply to organizations of various sizes and types throughout the country. They were careful not to mandate specific actions. As a matter of fact, many in the healthcare sector have criticized the Department of Health and Human Services for being too vague and not

13

providing enough guidance. The rule says that a covered entity may use any security measures that allow it to reasonably and appropriately implement the standards and implementation specification, taking into account:

- The size, complexity, and capabilities of the covered entity.

- The covered entity's technical infrastructure, hardware, and software capabilities.

- The costs of security measures.

- The probability of potential risks.

The standards were meant to be scalable, meaning that they can be applied to a single-physician practice or to an HMO with thousands of employees. The standards are technology neutral and vendor nonspecific. Covered entities are expected to choose the appropriate technology and controls for its unique environment. This does not need to be an overwhelming or expensive process. The bottom line is that if covered entities subscribe to security best practices and principles, they will easily achieve compliance.

Penalties for Noncompliance

The final Security Rule became effective April 21, 2003. Covered entities are expected to be in compliance by April 21, 2005. Small health plans have until April 21, 2006. Small health plans are defined as those with annual receipts of $5 million or less. It is important to note that compliance is not a one-time occurrence. Covered entities must *achieve* and *maintain* compliance. Covered entities that do not comply with the Security Rule are subject to a number of penalties. Civil penalties are $100 per violation, up to $25,000 per year for each requirement violated. Criminal penalties range from $50,000 in fines and one year in prison to up to $250,000 in fines and ten years in jail. The Center for Medicare and Medicaid Services (CMS) has been assigned responsibility for enforcement and related actions.

Of grave concern to the medical community is that noncompliance may be used in liability cases. Attorneys may choose to sue on behalf of clients who believe their rights have been violated.

Security Rule Organization

The Security Rule is organized into five categories: administrative safeguards, physical safeguards, technical safeguards, organizational requirements, and documentation requirements. Within these three categories are standards and implementation specifications. In this context, a **standard** defines what a covered entity must do; **implementation specifications** describe how it must be done. While the rule does not provide a detailed roadmap, the order in which the standards are presented provides guidance for implementation.

Administrative Safeguards *Administrative safeguards* are defined in the Security Rule as the "administrative actions, policies, and procedures used to manage the selection, development, implementation, and maintenance of security measures to protect electronic protected health information and to manage the conduct of the covered entity's workforce in relation to the protection of that information." The administrative safeguards make up more than half of the Security Rule. They are the documented policies and procedures for managing day-to-day operations, the conduct and access of workforce members to ePHI, and the selection, development, and use of security controls.

Physical Safeguards *Physical safeguards* are defined as the "physical measures, policies, and procedures to protect a covered entities' electronic information systems and related buildings and equipment, from natural and environmental hazards, and unauthorized intrusion." The physical safeguards are a set of requirements meant to protect ePHI from unauthorized physical access.

Technical Safeguards *Technical safeguards* are defined as "the technology and the policy and procedures for its use that protect electronic protected health information and control access to it." The technical safeguards focus on using technology to control access to ePHI.

Organizational Requirements *Organizational requirements* include standards for business associate contracts and other arrangements, including memoranda of understanding between a covered entity and a business associate when both entities are government organizations; and requirements for group health plans.

Policies and Procedures and Documentation Requirements *Documentation requirements* include the adoption of reasonable and appropriate policies and procedures to comply with the standards, implementation specifications, and other requirements of the Security Rule; maintenance of written (which may be electronic) documentation and/or records that includes policies, procedures, actions, activities, or assessments required by the Security Rule; and retention, availability, and update requirements related to the documentation. Covered entities must maintain all documentation for a period of six years from the date of creation or the date it was last in effect.

Implementation Specifications

Many of the standards contain implementation specifications. An implementation specification is a more detailed description of the method or approach covered entities can use to meet a particular standard.

13

Implementation specifications are either *required* or *addressable*. Where there are no implementation specifications identified in the Security Rule for a particular standard, such as for the "Assigned Security Responsibility" and "Evaluation" standards, compliance with the standard itself is required.

- A *required* implementation specification is similar to a standard, in that a covered entity must comply with it.

- For *addressable* implementation specifications, covered entities must perform an assessment to determine whether the implementation specification is a reasonable and appropriate safeguard for implementation in the covered entity's environment.

Administrative Safeguards

The first nine standards are categorized as administrative safeguards. There are a total of 23 implementation specifications, 12 of which are required and 11 of which are addressable.

The Security Management Process §164.308(a)(1)(i)

The very first standard sets the stage for everything that follows. The requirement is that each organization will have a formal security management process in place to address a full range of security issues. Security management includes the following mandatory implementation features:

- Conducting a risk analysis.

- Implementing a risk management program.

- Developing and implementing a sanction policy.

- Developing and deploying an information system activity review.

Conducting a Risk Assessment (Required) The regulation begins with specifying that organizations assess potential vulnerabilities and risks to the confidentiality, integrity, and confidentiality of ePHI. What is implied is that the covered entity has identified relevant information systems and classified the information. Therefore, the first step in the risk assessment phase is to identify types of ePHI. For most covered entities, ePHI-type information includes data found in billing, medical records, digital records, transcription, correspondence, and clinical studies. After identifying the type of information, the information systems that are used to process, store, and transmit the information must be documented. Lastly, the supporting infrastructure must be recognized.

Once all relevant systems have been identified, then the process of risk assessment can commence. The depth and scope of the risk assessment should be consistent with the type and size of the entity. The goal of the risk

TABLE 13.2 HIPAA administrative safeguards and ISO 17799.

Standard	Objective	Relevant ISO Section
Security management process	Implementation of policies and procedures to prevent, detect, contain, and correct security violations.	Section 3 Security Policy Section 4 Organizational Security Section 5 Asset Classification Section 6 Personnel Security Section 7 Physical Security Section 8 Operations Security Section 9 Access Control Section 10 Systems Development Section 11 Business Continuity Section 12 Compliance
Assigned security responsibility	Designation of a security officer.	Section 4 Organizational Security
Workforce security	Policies, procedures, and processes that ensure only properly authorized workforce members have access to ePHI.	Section 5 Asset Classification Section 6 Personnel Security Section 7 Physical Security Section 9 Access Control
Information access management	Policies, procedures, and processes for authorizing, establishing, and modifying access to ePHI.	Section 5 Asset Classification Section 6 Personnel Security Section 7 Physical Security Section 9 Access Control
Security awareness and training	Security awareness and training program for all users who access ePHI.	Section 6 Personnel Security Section 8 Operations Security Section 9 Access Control
Security incident procedures	Policies, procedures, and processes for reporting, responding to, and managing security incidents.	Section 4 Organizational Security Section 6 Personnel Security Section 8 Operations Security

13

▶▶ CONTINUED ON NEXT PAGE

Contingency plan	Policies, procedures, and processes for responding to a disaster or emergency that damages information systems containing ePHI.	Section 5 Asset Classification Section 8 Operations Security Section 11 Business Continuity
Evaluation	Ongoing compliance review.	Section 4 Organizational Security Section 12 Compliance
Business associate contracts and other arrangements	Contractual obligations that ensure the business associates will appropriately safeguard ePHI.	Section 4 Organizational Security

assessment is to identify the threats to the confidentiality, integrity, and availability of ePHI. The threat assessment should focus on the network infrastructure, security processes, personnel activities, third parties, and contingency planning.

The network infrastructure includes servers, workstations, devices, transmission lines, operating systems, and applications. Security processes include security administration, monitoring, incident response, patch management, and malware protection. Personnel activates include password management, acceptable use and defined access roles and responsibilities, and access controls.

Third parties include vendor oversight and business partner practices. Contingency planning relates to continuity planning. In short, the risk assessment process is a review of the organization's security posture. It is worth mentioning that a risk assessment is a formal process and that the findings and determinations must be recorded in a written document.

Implementing a Risk Management Program (Required) A risk management program consists of actions taken to document and mitigate the risks identified in the risk analysis to a reasonable and appropriate level. The determination of "reasonable and appropriate" is left to the discretion of the covered entity. Factors to be considered are the size of the entity, the level of risk, the cost of mitigating controls, and the complexity of implementation and maintenance. At a minimum, a risk management program includes documentation of security implementation decisions, a mechanism for remaining current on threats and vulnerabilities, a process for periodic risk assessments, and procedures for ongoing management of security-related activities.

Developing and Implementing a Sanction Policy (Required) Covered entities must implement sanction policies for security violations in regard to ePHI. Specially, covered entities must have a written policy that clearly states the ramifications for not complying with the Security Rules as determined by the organization. Implied in this requirement is a formal process to recognize and report security violations. The policy needs to apply all employees, contractors, and vendors. Sanctions might range from a reprimand to termination. Again, this is left to the discretion of the organization.

It is also implied that all employees have not only been made aware of the sanction policy but have been trained and understand what is expected of them in regard to security behavior. Appropriate to this requirement is a signed employee affirmation agreement.

Developing an Information System Activity Review (Required) The expectation here is that the covered entity has a mechanism in place to review information system activity and that these reports are reviewed regularly. System activity includes network, application, personnel, and administrative activities. Before a review can be implemented, three basic questions must be addressed:

- First, what system activity is going to be monitored? The short answer: audit logs, access reports, and security incident tracking reports are the most common methods of tracking system activity.

- Second, how is this going to be accomplished? Generally, using built-in or third-party monitoring/audit tools for operating systems, applications and devices, as well as incident reporting logs.

- Third, who is going to be responsible for the overall process and results? This is usually assigned to the security officer. Realistically, the security officer may not have the technical skills to interpret the reports, in which case it needs to be a combination of information technology staff (either internal or outsource) and the security officer.

Assigned Security Responsibility §164.308(a)(2)

The requirement is to appoint a security official who is responsible for the development and implementation of the policies and procedures required for the entity. This standard serves as the sole implementation specification.

The Security Rule specifically states that the covered entity must designate an individual as the security officer. The security officer is responsible for overseeing the development of policies and procedures, management and supervision of the use of security measures to protect data, and oversight of personnel access to data. A formal job description should be developed that accurately reflects the assigned security duties and

13

responsibilities. This role should be communicated to the entire organization, including contractors and vendors.

It is important to select a person who can assess effective security and who can serve as a point of contact for security policy, implementation, and monitoring. It should be pointed out that responsibility for compliance does not rest solely with the security officer. Management is still accountable for the actions of the covered entity. The entire organization is expected to engage in compliance-related activities. The goal is to create a culture of security and compliance.

Workforce Security §164.308(a)(3)

This regulation focuses on the relationship between people and ePHI. The purpose of this standard is to ensure that there are appropriate policies, procedures, and safeguards in place in regard to access to ePHI by the entire workforce. The term *workforce* is purposely used instead of *personnel*. Personnel are generally those on an organization's payroll. Workforce includes anyone who does work at or for the organization. In addition to employees and principals, this includes vendors, business partners, and contractors such as maintenance workers. There are three implementation specifications for this standard:

- Implementing procedures for authorization/supervision.

- Establishing a workforce clearance procedure.

- Establishing termination procedures.

All three implementation specifications are addressable.

Implementing Procedures for Authorization and/Supervision (Addressable) Covered entities must implement procedures for the authorization and/or supervision of workforce members who work with ePHI or in locations where it might be accessed. Implied in this specification is that the organization has defined roles and responsibilities for all job functions. In other words, who should have permission to access to ePHI in the normal course of doing their job? Permission to access ePHI should be clearly stated in written job descriptions. This is the first instance of an addressable implementation specification. Larger covered entities would be expected to document workforce access, including type of permission (view, alter, retrieve, store), at what times, under what circumstances, and for what purposes. A small medical practice may specify that all internal staff need access to ePHI as a normal part of their job. In this case, detailed documentation for employees would not be required.

What about workforce personnel who do not need access to ePHI in regard to delivery of patient care but may be at sites where ePHI is located? Examples would include building maintenance workers, cleaners, and computer technicians. In these situations, the covered entity needs to have a policy for authorizing the access as well as a policy on supervision. An example of authorization/supervision would be requiring the contractor to be preauthorized to work at the facility. Upon arrival, the contractor would be required to show identification, sign in, and be escorted to the work area. Upon completion, the contractor would need to be escorted out of the area and sign out.

Establishing a Workforce Clearance Procedure (Addressable)

The goal of this specification is that organizations establish criteria and procedures for hiring and assigning tasks. In other words, ensuring that workers have the necessary knowledge, skills, and abilities to fulfill particular roles and that these requirements are a part of the hiring process. The implied activity here is that all roles in the organizations have been clearly identified and documented. As a part of this process, covered entities need to determine the type of screening required for the position. This can range from verification of employment and educational references to criminal and credit checks. It was not the intent of Congress to mandate background checks, but rather to require reasonable and appropriate screening prior to access to ePHI.

Establishing Termination Procedures (Addressable)

When an employee's or contractor's role in the organization changes or their employment ends, the organization must ensure that their access to ePHI is terminated. Compliance with this specification includes having a standard set of procedures that should be followed to recover access control devices (ID badges, keys, tokens), recover equipment (laptops, PDAs, pagers), and deactivate computer access accounts. Implementation generally involves coordination between the Human Resources (HR) department and the Information Technology (IT) department. As a check to this process, HR should send a periodic list to IT of all terminated employees. Conversely, IT should send HR a list of all employees who have not logged in during a specified amount of time. The security officer should be copied on this correspondence.

Information Access Management §164.308(a)(4)

The goal of the Information Access Management standard is to require that covered entities have formal policies and procedures for granting access to ePHI. You may be thinking, haven't we already done this? Let's review what has been required in the preceding standards. First, we determined what roles, jobs, or positions have permission to work with or around ePHI. Then we set criteria hiring and termination criteria and procedures for those who have access to ePHI. In this section, we are determining the procedures for actually authorizing and establishing access to ePHI. There are three implementation specifications in this section:

- Isolating healthcare clearinghouse functions.

- Implementing policies and procedures to authorize access.

- Implementing policies and procedures to establish access.

There is one required specification and two addressable specifications.

Implementing Policies and Procedures for Authorizing Access (Addressable) Once an organization has decided what roles need access and who will be filling the roles, the next step is to decide how access will be granted to ePHI. In this section, we are approaching the question from a policy perspective. Later on we will revisit this question from a technology perspective. The first decision is at what level or levels will access be granted. Options include hardware level, the operating system level, application level, or transaction level. Many organizations will choose a hybrid approach. The second decision is the defined basis for granting access. Options here include *identity-based access* (by name), *role-based access* (by job), or *group-based access* (by function). Larger organizations may gravitate toward role-based access as the job may be very well defined. Smaller entities will tend to use identity-based or group-based access as one person may be tasked with multiple roles.

Implementing Policies and Procedures for Access Establishment and Modification (Addressable) Assuming the organization has made its decisions on access authorization, the next step is to develop policies and procedures to establish, document, review, and modify a user's right of access to a workstation, transaction, program, or process. In other words, how do we know who has been granted access? What is expected is that each user's rights can be clearly identified. To do so, each user must have a unique identification. There must be documentation as to the roles or groups the user is assigned to. There needs to be a process to audit access control lists and access activity. Lastly, there needs to be a process in place to communicate any change in status, role, or responsibility that would impact access to ePHI.

Security Awareness and Training §164.308(a)(5)

Users are the first line of defense against attack, intrusion, and error. To be effective, they must be trained and then reminded of the imminent dangers. This regulation requires that the organization implement a security awareness and training program on specific topics. Implied in this standard is that the organization provides training on the overall security program, policies, and procedures. The type of training provided is up to the organization. The goal is to provide training that is appropriate for the audience. The training program should be documented and there should be a mechanism for evaluating the effectiveness of the training. Web-based training has become increasingly popular for ease of administration, management, and 7x24 delivery. In designing and implementing a training program, the entity needs to address immediate compliance requirements, training programs for new users as they begin employment, periodic retraining, and ongoing awareness programs. There are four implementation specifications for this standard:

- Establishing a security awareness program.
- Providing training on malicious software.
- Providing training on login monitoring procedures.
- Providing training on password management.

All of these specifications are addressable.

Establishing a Security Awareness Campaign (Addressable) A security awareness program is designed to reminder users of potential threats and their part in mitigating the risk to the organization. According to NIST, the purpose of awareness presentations is simply to focus attention on security. Awareness presentations are intended to allow individuals to recognize IT security concerns and respond accordingly. Security awareness should be an ongoing campaign. Suggested delivery methods include posters, screen savers, trinkets, booklets, videos, e-mail, and flyers. The campaign should be extended to anyone who interacts with the covered entities' ePHI. This includes employees, contractors, and business partners. As we have discussed in other chapters, this type of program is by no means specific to the healthcare sector. Security awareness programs are an essential component of maintaining a secure environment. Even the most security conscious federal agency has posters prominently displayed as you walk through a locked door reminding you to check that no one else entered with you and to verify that the door clicked shut behind you!

13

Providing Training on Malicious Software (Addressable) Users need to be trained in proper procedures for guarding against, detecting, and reporting malicious software. By malicious software (or malware), we are referring to viruses, worms, Trojans, and spyware. Training topics should include how to keep computer systems updated with the latest version of antivirus software, how to recognize malware, how to respond to suspicious system behaviors, and how to report suspicious incidents.

Providing Training on Login Monitoring Procedures (Addressable) Users need to be trained in procedures for monitoring login attempts and reporting discrepancies. While it is not expected that users will monitor event logs and audit trails, they are expected to be on the lookout for suspicious behavior. An example would be noticing that someone else had unexpectedly logged in at their workstation or finding their password credential no longer valid.

Providing Training on Password Management (Addressable) Users need to be trained how to create, change, and safeguard passwords. Password selection needs to be in accordance with the organization's policy. It is assumed that, wherever possible, covered entities will adopt strong password policies. According to the NSA Gold Standard, strong passwords include at least 8 characters, use mixed case letters, and incorporate numbers and/or symbols. Users need to know how to change their password if they suspect it has been compromised. Most importantly, users need to understand how to safeguard their password. This includes not writing it down, not sharing it, and not choosing obvious words or phrases.

Security Incident Procedures §164.308(a)(6)

In Chapter 6, we defined a security incident as any adverse event whereby some aspect of an information system or information itself is threatened: loss of data confidentiality, disruption of data integrity, disruption or denial of service. This regulation addresses both reporting of and responding to security incidents. Implied in the standard is that the information users and custodians have had the appropriate training as well as the recognition that outside expertise may be required. There is one implementation specification, and it is required.

Security incident reporting is the foundation of a successful response and recovery process. A security incident reporting program has three components: training users to recognize suspicious incidents, implementing an easy and nonintimidating reporting system, and having staff follow through with investigations and report back their finding to the user. Covered entities are required to have documented procedures in place to support a security incident reporting program.

Incident response procedures address who, how to, and within what time frame an incident report should be responded to. Procedures should include an escalation path based upon the criticality and severity of the incident. This should include when to contact law enforcement and forensics experts as well as when it is appropriate to contact patients regarding a security breach. All incidents should be documented. This information should then be incorporated into the ongoing risk management process.

Contingency Plans §164.308(a)(7)

The contingency plan requirement would have been more aptly named business continuity plan. In Chapter 11, we discussed the four components of a BCP: disaster preparation, disaster response, business continuity, and business recovery. This regulation is closely tied to those components. The objective of the regulation is to establish (and implement as needed) policies and procedures for responding to an emergency or other occurrence (for example, vandalism, system failure, and natural disaster) that damages systems that contain ePHI. What is not stated but implied in the standard is the need for a business continuity/crisis management team that is responsible for the activation and management of the plan. There are five implementation specifications for this standard:

- Conducting an application and data criticality analysis.

- Establishing and implementing a data backup plan.

- Establishing and implementing a disaster recovery plan.

- Establishing an emergency mode operation plan.

- Testing and revising procedures.

   Three specifications are required, two are addressable.

Conducting an Application and Data Criticality Analysis (Addressable)

The purpose of this analysis is to assess the relative criticality of specific applications and data in terms of providing patient care. The goal is to identify activities and materials involving ePHI that are critical to business operations. For example, access to electronic medical records would be critical to providing care. On the other hand, claims processing, while important to the financial health of the entity, does not in the short term affect patient care. This analysis varies from a standard criticality analysis as we are not assessing the sensitivity of the information. It is implied that all ePHI is sensitive and needs to be protected. This analysis focuses on continuity of operations and tolerance of disruptions. As part of this analysis, attention should be paid to preventative controls that can mitigate the risk or impact of downtime.

Establishing and Implementing a Data Backup Plan (Required)

The standard requires that covered entities establish and implement procedures to create and maintain retrievable exact copies of ePHI. This means that all ePHI needs to be backed up on a scheduled basis. The implementation mechanism is left up to the organization. However, the procedures to back up (and restore) the data must be documented and the responsibility to run and verify the backup must be assigned. In addition to verification that the backup job ran successfully, test restores should be conducted regularly.

13

Testing both verifies the media and provides a training opportunity in a low-stress situation. There are few situations more nerve-wracking than that of learning how to restore data in a crisis situation. Backup media should not remain on-site. It should be securely transported off-site. The location where it is stored needs to be secured in accordance with the organization's security policy.

Establishing and Implementing a Disaster Recovery Plan (Required) This implementation specification specifically requires that covered entities be able to restore any data that has been lost. The initial interpretation is the ability simply to restore data. In actuality, the process is much more complex. Organizations must consider worst-case scenarios. What if the building was not accessible? What if equipment was destroyed? What if the communications infrastructure was unavailable? What if trained personnel were unavailable? A disaster recovery plan should be developed that addresses the recovery of critical infrastructure, including information systems and communications (phone, data, and Internet) as well as restoration of data.

Establishing an Emergency Mode Operations Plan (Required) An emergency mode operation is defined as those business processes that must occur to provide availability and protect the security of ePHI during and immediately after a crisis. In Chapter 11, we referred to this as *contingency operations*. In this context, the goal of a emergency mode operations plan is to continue to provide services to patients and to protect patient information from harm during a period when information systems and/or a normal operating environment is not available. Emergency mode operations may be implemented at either the original site or at an alternate location. Critical services and operations should have been identified in the applications and data criticality analysis. An example of continuing to provide service would be the ability to access patient records even if the facility was inaccessible. An example of protecting data would be disconnecting the organization from the Internet if the firewall was no longer functional.

Testing and Revising Procedures (Addressable) As discussed in Chapter 11, plans and procedures are purely theoretical until they are tested. The objective of a testing program is to ensure that plans and procedures are accurate, relevant, and operable under adverse conditions. As important as demonstrating success is uncovering inadequacies. This implementation specification raises important questions. Organizations are required to assess how the plans will be tested, who will do the testing, how often the testing will occur, who will review the testing results, and how the test results will be analyzed.

Evaluation §184.308(a)(8)

All covered entities are required to comply with the HIPAA Security Rule. The evaluation standard focuses on developing criteria and metrics for reviewing all standards and implementation specifications for compliance. This standard serves as the sole implementation specification.

All covered entities need to evaluate their compliance status. This is an ongoing process and should occur both on a scheduled basis and whenever change drivers warrant reassessment. The evaluation can be conducted internally if the organization has staff appropriately trained for the task. Optionally, third parties can be hired to conduct the assessment and report their findings. Prior to contracting with a third party, the vendor should be required to document credentials and experience with HIPAA compliance. The evaluation should review all three categories of requirements—administrative, physical, and technical. The desired outcome of the evaluation is acknowledgement of compliance activities and recommendations for improvement.

There is not a formal certification or accreditation process for HIPAA compliance. There is no organization or person who can put an "official" stamp of approval on the compliance program. The process is one of self-certification. It is left to the organization to determine if its security program and compliance activities are acceptable. If challenged, the organization will need to provide thorough documentation to support its decisions.

Business Associate Contracts and Other Arrangements §164.308(b)(1)

Covered entities share ePHI for a variety of reasons. The Security Rule states that a covered entity may permit a business associate to create, receive, maintain, or transmit electronic protected health information on a covered entity's behalf only if the covered entity obtains satisfactory assurances that the business associate will appropriately safeguard the information. This standard does not apply with respect to:

- The transmission of ePHI by a covered entity to a healthcare provider concerning the treatment of an individual.

- The transmission of ePHI by a group health plan or an HMO or health insurance issuer on behalf of a group plan to a plan sponsor.

- The transmission of ePHI from or to other agencies providing services when the covered entity is a health plan that is a government program providing public benefits.

The standard does apply to any third parties that provide the following services: claim processing or billing, transcription, data analysis, quality assurance, practice management, application support, hardware maintenance,

13

and administrative services. The criteria is that the third party may be processing, storing, transmitting, or otherwise accessing ePHI with the exception of the organizations noted above. This standard serves as the sole implementation specification.

The implementation specification requires covered entities to document the satisfactory assurances required through a written contract or other arrangement with the business associate that meets the applicable requirements. In order to be in compliance with the Privacy Rule, most organizations already have business associate agreements in place. This implementation specification is a natural extension of that agreement. This agreement should be modified or amended to include contractual language stating the business associate's responsibility to safeguard the confidentiality, integrity, and/or availability of ePHI.

Implied in this standard is that the covered entity will establish criteria and procedures for measuring contract performance. Procedures may range from clear lines of communication to on-site security reviews. Of particular importance is a process for reporting security incidents relative to the relationship. If the criteria aren't being met, then a process needs to be in place for terminating the contract. Conditions that would warrant termination should be included in the business associate agreement as well as in performance contracts.

Physical Safeguards

The next four standards are categorized as physical safeguards. There are a total of ten implementation specifications, four of which are required and six of which are addressable. The objective is to protect ePHI from unauthorized physical access.

Facility Access Controls §164.310(a)(1)

Facility is defined as the physical premises and the interior and exterior of a building. Facility access controls are policies and procedures to limit physical access to ePHI information systems and the facility or facilities in which they are housed, while ensuring that properly authorized access is allowed. There are four implementation specifications for this standard:

- Creating a facility security plan.

- Implementing access control and validation procedures.

- Keeping maintenance records.

- Establishing contingency operations.

All four implementation specifications are addressable.

Creating a Facility Security Plan (Addressable) The organization needs to have a plan to secure the premises and the equipment within from

TABLE 13.3 HIPAA physical safeguards and ISO 17799.

Standard	Objective	Relevant ISO Domain
Facility access controls	Physical access controls to protect systems/media that process, store, and transmit from unauthorized access while ensuring that properly authorized access is allowed.	Section 7 Physical Security Section 9 Access Control
Workstation use	Appropriate use of workstations and the characteristics of the physical environment of workstations that can access ePHI.	Section 7 Physical Security Section 9 Access Control
Workstation security	Physical safeguard for all workstations that access ePHI.	Section 7 Physical Security Section 9 Access Control
Device and media controls	Physical safeguards for device and media reuse, disposal, and removal.	Section 5 Asset Classification Section 7 Physical Security Section 9 Access Control

unauthorized physical access, tampering, and theft. The most basic control that comes to mind are door locks. Implied in this specification is the need to conduct a risk analysis to identify vulnerable areas. The risk analysis would focus on the building perimeter, interior, and computer room/data centers. Areas that would be examined include entry points such as doors, windows, loading docks, vents, roof, basement, fences, and gates. Based upon the outcome of the risk assessment, the facility security plan may include controls such as surveillance monitoring, environmental equipment monitoring, environmental controls (air conditioning, smoke detection, and fire suppression), and entrance/exit controls (locks, security guards, access badges).

Implementing Access Control and Validation Procedures (Addressable) The goal of this specification is to implement procedures that provide facility access to authorized personnel and visitors and exclude unauthorized persons. Facility access controls are generally based upon their role or function. This applies to employees, contractors, and visitors. As this is an addressable specification, covered entities should assess each of the following and make decisions appropriate to their structure.

- Procedures for visitor access such as required identification, sign-in/sign-out log, and/or escort.

- Procedures for access to restricted areas such as a computer room, data center, or wiring closet.

- Procedures for facility access during nonworking hours.

- Procedures for facility access during an emergency.

Keeping Maintenance Records (Addressable) Organizations are expected to document repairs and modifications to the physical components of a facility that relate to security such as walls, doors, and locks. This information may be used for risk management decisions and/or security incident investigations. Organizations that lease space should require the owner to provide such documentation. Consider this example: In January 2005, a clinic located in leased space experienced a theft of laptops. There was no sign of forced entry. The breach occurred within one month of new door locks being installed at the clinic. Upon investigation, the police found that the landlord had installed new master locks. Unbeknownst to the clinic, copies of the master key were given to multiple personnel employed by the landlord. The roommate of a building worker was found to have the laptops.

Establishing Contingency Operations (Addressable) This implementation specification supports the overall contingency plan. An organization needs to establish procedures to ensure authorized physical access in case of emergency. Generally, these procedures are manual overrides of automated systems. The access control system for a computer room may have been designed to use a swipe card or biometric identification. If the facility were to lose power, these controls would be useless. Assuming that entry into the computer room is required, a contingency or alternate plan would be necessary.

Workstation Use §164.310(b)

The workstation use specification calls for the proper use of workstations that contain or have access to ePHI. These safeguards are generally outlined in an acceptable use policy or employee affirmation agreement. This standard serves as the sole implementation specification.

The implementation specification requires that policies and procedures be implemented specific to a type of or class of workstation based upon function, location, or access to ePHI. Implied in the specification is that an inventory of workstations that process, store, transmit, or access ePHI has been done and that a risk assessment has been conducted. You can't secure what you don't know you have from unknown threats. Of particular concern are workstations that are either located outside of the facility or taken off-site (laptops). Covered entity workstations might be located at other facilities or at employee or contractor homes. Additional precautions must be taken to secure these systems from unauthorized access. Laptops are particularly vulnerable to theft. Additional controls such as locks and/or encryption devices may be warranted.

Workstation Security §164.310(b)

The workstation security specification applies to all workstations that access ePHI. The objective is to restrict workstation access to authorized users. This differs from the previous specification. Workstation use is based upon specific class, type, or use of the workstation and the unique needs associated with the workstation. Workstation security is global. This standard serves as the sole implementation specification.

All workstations should be secure from unauthorized access. Physical safeguards and other security measures should be implemented to minimize the possibility of access to ePHI through workstations. If possible, workstations should be located in restricted areas. In situations where that is not possible, such as exam rooms, workstations should be physically secured (locked) and password-protected with an automatic screen saver. Shoulder surfing is of particular concern here. Shoulder surfing in its most basic form is when a passer-by can view information on another person's computer screen by looking at the monitor. In recent years, more sophisticated forms of shoulder surfing have emerged, including using a video or picture phone to capture images. Workstations located in semi-public areas such as reception desks need to be positioned away from the viewing public. If that is not possible, they should be encased in privacy screens.

Device and Media Controls §164.310(d)(1)

Media and devices that contain ePHI can be portable, may be reused, and ultimately will be discarded. This standard recognizes that fact and requires policies and procedures that govern the receipt and removal of hardware and electronic media that contain ePHI into and out of a facility as well as within a facility. Examples of devices and media include hard drives, diskettes, CDs, tapes, PDAs, iPODs, and USB storage devices. There are four implementation procedures for this standard:

- Implementing disposal policies and procedures.
- Implementing reuse policies and procedures.

13

- Maintaining accountability for hardware and electronic media.
- Developing data backup and storage procedures.

Two specifications are addressable and two are required.

Implementing Disposal Policies and Procedures (Required)

Covered entities are required to implement policies and procedures to address the final disposition of ePHI and/or the hardware or electronic media on which it is stored. This means that there needs to be a process to destroy data. Options might include using software to permanently wipe the data or using a physical mechanism such as shredding or crushing to literally destroy the media or device.

Implementing Reuse Policies and Procedures (Required)

It is not uncommon for media to be reused. Examples are backup tapes, portable storage devices, and even the old-fashioned diskette. Often overlooked are hard drives in workstations that are being recycled either within or outside of the organization. Don't assume that because a policy states that ePHI isn't stored on a local workstation that the drive doesn't need to be cleaned. ePHI is found in the most unexpected of places. The implementation specification requires that organizations implement procedures and designate responsibility for removal of ePHI before the media is made available for reuse.

Maintaining Accountability for Hardware and Electronic Media (Addressable)

The objective of this implementation specification is to be able to account at all times for the whereabouts of ePHI. Implied is that all systems and media that house ePHI have been identified and inventoried. The goal is to ensure that ePHI is not inadvertently released or shared with any unauthorized party. This is easy to understand if you envision a paper medical record (chart). Before the record is allowed to leave the premise, it must be verified that the request came from an authorized party. The removal of the chart is logged and a record kept of the removal. The logs are reviewed periodically to ensure that the chart has been returned. This specification requires the same type of procedures for information stored in electronic form.

Developing Data Backup and Storage Procedures (Addressable)

This specification suggests that before moving or relocating any equipment that contains ePHI a backup copy of the data should be created. The objective is to ensure that in case of damage or loss an exact, retrievable copy of the information is available. Concurrent with this action is the implied requirement that the backup media will be stored in a secure location separate from the original media.

Technical Safeguards

The next five standards are categorized as technical safeguards. There are a total of nine implementation specifications, four of which are required and five of which are addressable. The objective is to use technical control to protect ePHI from unauthorized access.

TABLE 13.4 HIPAA technical standards and ISO 17799.

Standard	Objective	Relevant ISO Domain
Access control	Implementation of access controls for information systems that contain ePHI to allow access only to authorized persons or processes.	Section 9 Access Control
Audit controls	Mechanisms to record and examine activity in information systems that contain or use ePHI.	Section 8 Operations Security Section 9 Access Control
Integrity controls	Technical controls that protect ePHI from improper modification or destruction.	Section 8 Operations Security Section 10 Systems Development
Person or entity authentication	Technical controls that verify the identification of persons or processes seeking access to ePHI.	Section 9 Access Control
Transmission security	Preventing unauthorized access to ePHI that is being transmitted over an electronic communications network.	Section 7 Physical Security Section 8 Operations Security Section 10 Systems Development

13

Access Control §164.312(a)(1)

The intent of the access control standard is to utilize technical controls to allow access to ePHI to only those users and processes that have been specifically authorized for access, and to deny access to all other users and processes. Implied in this standard are the fundamental security concepts of deny-all, least privilege, and need-to-know. The access control standard has four implementation specifications:

- Requiring unique user identification.

- Establishing emergency access procedures.

- Implementing automatic logoff procedures.

- Encrypting and decrypting information at rest.

Two specifications are required and two are addressable.

Requiring Unique User Identification (Required) Each user and process that accesses ePHI must be assigned a unique identifier. This can be a name and/or number. The naming convention is at the discretion of the organization. The purpose is to ensure that system activity can be traced to a specific user or process.

Establishing Emergency Access Procedures (Required) Organizations must identify a method of supporting continuity of operations should normal access procedures be disabled or unavailable due to system problems. Generally, this would be an Administrator or Super User account that has been assigned override privileges and cannot be locked out.

Implementing Automatic Logoff Procedures (Addressable) Covered entities need to implement electronic procedures that terminate a session after a predetermined time of inactivity. The assumption here is that users may leave their workstations unattended, during which time any information their accounts have permission to access is vulnerable to unauthorized disclosure. Although the implementation standard incorporates the term "logoff," other mechanisms are acceptable. Examples of other controls include password-protected screen savers, workstation lock function, or disconnection of a session. Based upon the risk analysis, it is up to the organization to determine both the "predetermined time of inactivity" as well as the method of termination.

Encrypting and Decrypting Information at Rest (Addressable) The decision to encrypt data at "rest" (as opposed to in transmission) is based upon the level of risk. Generally, encryption of stored data is considered appropriate when it is likely to be exposed to unauthorized users or processes. Examples would include ePHI stored on portable devices such as laptops or ePHI accessible through Internet-based applications. Encryption adds an additional layer of protection over and above assigned access permissions.

Audit Controls §164.312(b)

The audit control standard requires implementation of hardware, software, and/or procedural mechanisms that record and examine activity in information systems that contain ePHI. This standard is closely tied to the administrative standards requiring information system review and security management. This standard serves as the sole implementation specification.

Organizations must have the means available to monitor system activity. Audit controls can be automatic, manual, or a combination of both. For example, system logs may run continuously in the background while audit of a specific user activity may need to be manually initiated as the need arises.

Numerous monitoring tools are available. Most operating systems and applications have at least a minimum level of auditing as part of the feature set. The market is replete with third-party options. Relevant security events to monitor include:

- All failed logons.
- Users who failed to log on due to an invalid username or an incorrect password.
- All account lockouts for a time period.
- Initial daily logon time for each user over a time period.
- Which computers users log into.
- Possible security log tampering for a time period.
- Failed object access events (e.g., to secured files).
- Modifications to user accounts.
- Modifications to software.
- Attempts to use privileges that have not been authorized.
- High security events of the past day, week, or month.
- Modification or deletion of logs or system activity reports.

Integrity Controls §164.312(c)(1)

Earlier in this chapter, we defined *integrity* as the protection of information or processes from intentional or accidental unauthorized modification. The standard requires organizations to implement technical controls that protect ePHI from improper alteration or destruction. This standard serves as the sole implementation specification.

This implementation specification is addressable. The key to implementation is identifying the likely sources that could jeopardize information integrity. Common threats to integrity include operating system and application vulnerabilities, malicious software, Internet/intranet hackers, and file alteration. Controls to address these threats include:

- Patch management procedures.

- Antivirus software and scanning.

- Antispyware software and scanning.

- Internal port scanning for instances of unauthorized utilities and software.

- File integrity checkers.

- Database integrity utilities.

- E-mail filtering of potentially dangerous attachments.

- Border devices such as firewalls and intrusion-detection devices (IDS).

Person or Entity Authentication §164.312(d)

Authentication is defined as the process of identifying an individual, usually based on a username and password. Authentication is different from authorization, which is the process of giving individuals access based on their identity. Authentication merely ensures that the individual is who he or she claims to be, but says nothing about the individual's access rights. The person or entity authentication standard requires verification that a person or process seeking access to ePHI is the one claimed. An entity can be a process or a service. This standard serves as the sole implementation specification.

The access control standard requires unique user identification. Authentication controls require verification of the unique user identification. There are two commonly used authentication approaches, single factor and multi-factor.

- Single Factor:
  - Something a person knows, such as a password or PIN.
  - Something a person has or is in possession of, such as a token or smartcard.
  - Something a person is—biometric identification.
- Multi-factor:
  - Combination of two or more of the above factors.

It is up to the covered entity to decide the appropriate approach. In all cases, users should receive training on how to protect their authentication.

Transmission Security §164.312(e)(1)

The transmission security standard states that covered entities must implement technical security measures to guard against unauthorized access to ePHI that is being transmitted over an electronic communications network. Implied in this standard is that organizations identify scenarios that may result in modification of the ePHI by unauthorized sources during transmission. Based upon the assumption that the facility is secure, the focus is on external transmission. There are two implementation specifications:

- Implementing integrity controls.

- Implementing encryption.

    Both specifications are addressable.

Implementing Integrity Controls (Addressable) Covered entities are required to assess the need for controls to ensure that ePHI has not been altered or modified during transmission. External communications include FTP, e-mail, WAN connections, or Web access. If organizations choose to use these mechanisms to transmit ePHI, then they must implement appropriate controls. Examples of integrity controls include point-to-point networks, virtual private networks (VPN), and application layer protocols such as SSL, SSH, and HTTPS.

Implementing Encryption (Addressable) The implementation specification requires that covered entities implement a mechanism to encrypt ePHI whenever deemed appropriate. Implied is that areas at high risk of transmission interception, such as wireless and external e-mail, have been identified. The current issues are the cost of secure encryption mechanisms as well as lack of interoperability. Given the lack of industry standards and the immaturity of the technology, many organizations have chosen not to allow high-risk ePHI transmission. This is the one area of the Security Rule most likely to change as the security industry matures.

Organization Requirements

The next two standards are categorized as organizational requirements. There are a total of ten implementation specifications, all of which are required.

Business Associates Contracts §164.314(a)(1)

Contracts between a covered entity and its business associates must meet the specific requirements in regard to ensuring the confidentiality, integrity, and availability of ePHI. A covered entity will be considered not in

TABLE 13.5 HIPAA organizational requirements and ISO 17799.

Standard	Objective	Relevant ISO Domain
Business associate's contracts	Define the security requirements of business associate's cause for termination of contracts and exceptions to the rule.	Section 4 Organizational Security
Group health plans	Define the security requirements of group health plans.	None

compliance with the law if the covered entity knew of a pattern of an activity or practice of a business associate that constituted a material breach or violation of the business associate's obligations unless the covered entity took reasonable steps to cure the breach or end the violation. If such steps are unsuccessful, the covered entity must either terminate the contract or arrangement, if feasible. If not feasible, the problem must be reported to the HSS Secretary.

This standard has six implementation specifications:

- Contract must provide that business associates adequately protect ePHI.

- Contract must provide that business associates' agents adequately protect ePHI.

- Contract must provide that business associates will report security incidents.

- Contract will provide that business associates must comply or risk termination.

- Contract will provide for government entity exceptions.

- Contract covers certain other arrangements for covered entities and business associates.

All six implementation specifications are required.

Business Associates Must Adequately Protect ePHI (Required)

Contracts between covered entities and business associates must provide that business associates will implement administrative, physical, and technical safeguards that reasonably and appropriately protect the confidentiality, integrity, and availability of ePHI that the business associate creates, receives, maintains, or transmits on behalf of the covered entity.

The contract should clearly state the type of ePHI that the business associate creates, receives, maintains, or transmits.

Business Associates' Agents Must Adequately Protect ePHI (Required) Contracts between covered entities and business associates must provide that any agent, including a subcontractor, to whom the business associate provides such information, agrees to implement reasonable and appropriate safeguards to protect it. The key here is to communicate with the business associate to identify if the business associate subcontracts any work related to the covered entity.

Business Associates Must Report Security Incidents (Required) Contracts between covered entities and business associates must provide that business associates will report to the covered entity any security incident of which it becomes aware. A procedure needs to be in place for business associates to report such incidents.

Business Associates Must Comply or Risk Contract Termination (Required) A written agreement must be established with the business associate that establishes the circumstances under which a violation of agreements relating to the security of ePHI constitutes a material breach of the contract. The contract must be terminated if the covered entity learns that the business associate has violated the contract or materially breached it and it is not possible to take reasonable steps to cure the breach or end the violation. If contact termination is not feasible, the problem must be reported to the Secretary of HHS.

Government Entity Exceptions (Required) If both parties are government entities, then the business associate will issue a Memorandum of Understanding (MOU) in lieu of a contract.

Statutory Obligation (Required) Exceptions can be made for business associates that are required by law to perform a function or activity on behalf of a covered entity.

Standard Requirements for Group Health Plans §164.314(b)(1)

This section addresses amending group health plan documents to incorporate provisions that the plan sponsor and any agents of the sponsor implement administrative, technical, and physical safeguards that will reasonably and appropriately protect the confidentiality, integrity, and availability of ePHI that it creates, receives, maintains, or transmits on behalf of the group health plan. This section is limited in scope and is applicable only to group health plan sponsors.

13

TABLE 13.6 HIPAA policy and procedure requirements and ISO 17799.

Standard	Objective	Relevant ISO Domain
Policies and procedures	Implement reasonable and appropriate policies and procedures to comply with the Security Rule.	Section 3 Security Policy
Documentation	Maintain all documentation in written or electronic form.	Section 3 Security Policy

Policies and Procedures

The last two standards are categorized as policy and procedure requirements. There are a total of four implementation specifications, all of which are required.

Policies and Procedures §164.316(a)

Covered entities are required to implement reasonable and appropriate policies and procedures to comply with the standards, implementation specifications, or other requirements of the Security Rule. This standard serves as the sole implementation specification.

Covered entities are required to implement reasonable and appropriate policies pursuant to the Security Rule and implementation specifications. Organizations must periodically evaluate written policies to verify that:

- Policies and procedures are sufficient to address the standards and implementation specifications.

- Policies and procedures accurately reflect the actual activities and practices of the covered entity, its staff, its systems, and its business associates.

Documentation §164.316(b)(1)

The documentation standard requires that all policies, procedures, actions, activities, and assessments related to the Security Rule be maintained in written or electronic form. There are three implementation specifications:

- Retaining documentation.

- Making documentation available.

■ Updating documentation.

All three specifications are required.

Retaining Documentation (Required) Covered entities are required to retain all documentation related to the Security Rule for a period of six years from the date of creation or the date it was last in effect, whichever is later. This requirement is consistent with similar retention requirements in the privacy rule.

Making Documentation Available (Required) Documentation must be easily accessible to all persons responsible for implementing the procedures to which the documentation pertains. This would include security professionals, systems administrators, human resources, contracts, facilities, legal, compliance, and training.

Updating Documentations (Required) Documentation needs to be reviewed periodically and updated as needed in response to operational, personnel, facility, or environmental changes affecting the security of ePHI. Particular attention should be paid to version control.

Summary

The original intent of the HIPAA regulations was to simplify and standardize the healthcare administrative processes. Administrative simplification called for the transition from paper records and transactions to electronic records and transactions. The Security Rule was designed to ensure that the electronic information, known as electronic protected health information or ePHI, was safeguarded from breaches of confidentiality, integrity, and availability.

The final Security Rule was adopted in 2003 with a 2005 implementation date. At the time of its adoption, there were few other security regulations. Most healthcare providers viewed it as yet another unfunded government mandate. Since adoption, the need to protect ePHI has become self-evident. It is interesting to note these regulations mirror what we now consider security best practices. The ISO 17799 framework corresponds to both the intent and implementation specifications of the HIPAA regulations. The healthcare industry is rapidly assuming a leadership position in the implementation of information security controls. Both providers and patients benefit. Providers are protecting valuable information and information assets. Patients have peace of mind knowing that their trust is being honored.

13

Test Your Skills

MULTIPLE CHOICE QUESTIONS

1. The HIPAA Security Rule is not applicable to which of the following?

    A. dentists

    B. medical billing companies

    C. pharmaceutical sales organizations

    D. clinical research labs

2. ePHI stands for:

    A. electronic personal health information

    B. electronic private health information.

    C. electronic public health information.

    D. electronic protected health information

3. Which of the following statements is NOT true?

    A. HIPAA is technology neutral.

    B. HIPAA is vendor nonspecific.

    C. HIPAA requires a firewall.

    D. HIPAA is scalable.

4. Which federal agency is responsible for the Security Rule?

    A. Department of Health and Human Services

    B. Department of Energy

    C. Department of Commerce

    D. Department of Education

5. By this date, all entities will need to comply with the Security Rule.

    A. 2003

    B. 2004

    C. 2005

    D. 2006

6. Which of these is NOT a Security Rule category?

    A. documentation

    B. compliance

    C. physical

    D. technical

7. Which of these statements is true?

    A. All implementation specifications are required.

    B. All implementation specifications are optional.

    C. Implementation specifications are either required or addressable.

    D. Addressable specifications can be ignored.

8. Which best defines a business associate?

    A. a person or organization that creates, stores, processes, or transmit data on behalf of the covered entity

    B. a healthcare provider with whom patient information is shared in the course of treatment

    C. an employee who creates, stores, processes, or transmit data on behalf of the covered entity

    D. a person or organization that provides any service to the covered entity

9. Which of following is NOT a security management implementation specification?

    A. conduct a risk analysis

    B. implement a risk management program

    C. retain documents for six years

    D. conduct an information system activity review

10. The role of a security officer:

    A. is optional

    B. can be a committee

    C. is accountable by law for compliance

    D. must be a designated individual

11. Which would be considered an optional topic for end-user security training?

    A. malware protection

    B. the role of the security officer

    C. the cost of implementing HIPAA

    D. the reasons for security safeguards

13

12. What is the primary role of end-users involved in a security incident?
    A. reporting
    B. response
    C. recovery
    D. removal

13. User accounts need to be:
    A. role-based
    B. shared
    C. unique
    D. secret

14. Maintenance records need to be kept for:
    A. painting the facility
    B. plowing the parking lot
    C. installing cubicles
    D. repairing locks

15. When users leave their workstations for a break, they should:
    A. do nothing
    B. lock the workstation
    C. log out
    D. turn off the monitor

16. Which of the following is NOT an example of an integrity control?
    A. patch management
    B. malware protection
    C. port scanning
    D. portable storage

17. Transmitting ePHI in e-mail is not recommended because:
    A. e-mail is clear text
    B. e-mail can be forwarded
    C. both A and B
    D. neither A nor B

18. Documentation must be retained for:

    A. two years

    B. four years

    C. six years

    D. ten years

19. All documentation related to the Security Rule must be:

    A. stored in both paper and electronic form

    B. stored in either paper or electronic form

    C. stored off-site

    D. stored only in electronic form

20. If a business associate does not comply with the Security Rule, then the covered entity has an obligation to:

    A. inform the business associate and try to rectify the problem

    B. sue the business associate

    C. avoid the issue

    D. immediately report the problem to the Government

EXERCISES

Exercise 13.1: Health Insurance Portability and Accounting Act of 1996

1. HIPAA is more than the Security Rule. Research the act and write a brief explanation of each of the titles.

2. Include in your report the compliance deadlines for each regulation.

Exercise 13.2: HIPAA and ISO 17799

1. Explain the relationship between HIPAA and the ISO 17799 framework.

2. Choose one standard and map out in detail the relationship between HIPAA standards and implementation specifications and the security domains.

Exercise 13.3: Key Factors for Compliance

Compliance requires time, effort, and resources. Address each of the following factors for success and explain why it is important.

1. Obtain and maintain senior management support

13

2. Conduct and maintain inventory of ePHI

3. Be aware of political and cultural issues raised by HIPAA

4. Determine what is reasonable and appropriate

5. Document everything

Exercise 13.4: HIPAA and SETA (Security Education Training and Awareness)

1. Senior leadership needs to be educated on HIPAA requirements. Research and recommend a program.

2. Your security officer and network engineer both need to be trained on HIPAA. The security officer will be working on the administrative standards, and the network engineer on the physical and technical standards. Research and recommend training.

3. Your users all need to be trained on login monitoring, password management, malware, and incident reporting. Research and recommend a program.

Exercise 13.5: Documentation Retention and Availability

1. All HIPAA-related documentation must be retained for a minimum of six years. This includes policies, procedures, contracts, and network documentation. Assuming you will revise the documentation, devise a standard version control procedure.

2. Recommend a way to store the documentation.

3. Recommend an secure, efficient, and cost-effective way to make the documentation available to appropriate personnel.

PROJECTS

Project 13.1: Creating an HIPAA Security Program Manual Outline

1. You have been tasked with designing an HIPAA security program manual. You may choose to write a manual for any one of the following covered entities:

   • A 100-bed hospital in a metropolitan location.

   • A consortium of three nursing homes. The nursing homes share administrative and clinical staff. They are all connected to the same network.

- A multi-specialty medical practice consisting of 29 physicians.

Based upon your choice, create an organizational chart and a network diagram.

2. Your second step is to write an introduction explaining what the HIPAA Security Rule is and why compliance is required.

3. The third step is to design a table of contents. The TOC should correspond to the regulations but should also include the policies and procedures required for each implementation specification.

4. The fourth step is to create a task list. For each policy and procedure listed in the table of contents, assign development to a specific role in the organization (e.g., human resources, building maintenance).

Project 13.2: Designing Administrative Policies

1. Based upon the outline in Project 13.1, you are going to develop policies. Refer back to the ISO policies in this book as appropriate.

2. Write a policy for each of the nine administrative standards. Be sure to reference the regulation number. Include a section in each policy that references associated procedures.

- Security management process
- Assigned security responsibility
- Workforce security
- Information access management
- Security awareness and training
- Security incident procedures
- Contingency plan
- Evaluation
- Business associate contracts and other arrangements

Project 13.3: Addressable Implementation Specification

1. Based upon the covered entity chosen in Project 1, review each of the addressable implementation specifications.

2. Respond to each addressable implementation standard, noting its applicability to your type of entity.

3. If the specification is not applicable, explain why.

13

▶▶ Case **Study**

(Examples Adopted from NIST SP800-66 draft)

Mary Bronner, the head of a small (10 employees) healthcare service provider organization, has been reviewing HIPAA standards and realizes that she must formally assign a person to be responsible for HIPAA implementation. Currently no one on staff has the expertise in security needed to do the job. The organization has two choices: (1) train an existing employee or (2) hire a new resource. From a cost perspective, Ms. Bronner would prefer to train existing staff. The organization has three IT specialists on staff who currently support the small local area network (LAN) installed one year ago. Ms. Bronner believes that it would not be difficult to train a resource from this operation to coordinate HIPAA security implementation. She has also asked the training manager to identify recommended sources so that a comprehensive training strategy can be developed. The new function will also be discussed at the weekly staff meeting.

1. Do you agree with Ms. Bronner's decision?

2. Place yourself in the role of the training manager. Recommend a strategy.

   A large urban health organization hires a consultant to design its HIPAA security program. The consultant reviews job descriptions and interviews the Chief Technology Officer, the Privacy Officer, the Chief Information Officer, and the Executive Officer. The consultant notes that security responsibilities are currently assigned to an "IT Security Committee," not a specific individual identified by name, title, or both as required by the HIPAA Security Rule. The consultant recommends that either (1) a specific member of the IT Security Committee be designated as the organization's security officer responsible for the overall HIPAA security program, including HIPAA implementation, or that (2) a new position be created and a new employee be hired to fill it.

3. Who would you recommend for the position? Why?

4. Write a job description for the new position. In addition to describing the duties, include title, position in the organizational structure, compensation, experience, and education required.

Chapter | 14

Information Security Regulatory Compliance for Critical Infrastructure

Chapter Objectives

After reading this chapter and completing the exercises, you will be able to do the following:

- Articulate the need for information security at a national level.
- Understand the intent and objectives of the Federal Information Security Management Act (FISMA).
- Relate the privacy requirements of the Family Educational Rights and Privacy Act (FERPA) to information security elements.
- Relate the integrity requirements of the Sarbanes-Oxley Act (SOX) to information security elements.
- Develop an information security program that encompasses multiple regulations and requirements.

Introduction

As defined in the *National Strategy to Secure Cyberspace,* our nation's critical infrastructure is composed of public and private institutions in the sectors of agriculture, food, water, public health, emergency services, government, defense industrial base, information and telecommunications, energy, transportation, banking and finance, chemicals and hazardous materials, and postal and shipping. These sectors rely on technology and connectivity. The strategy defines the healthy functioning of cyberspace as essential to our economy and our national security. Our ever-increasing dependence on information systems is closely aligned with the need to consider and secure the confidentiality, integrity, and availability of the systems and the information assets contained within.

In the best of all worlds, individual organizations within each sector would take the initiative to secure and protect their information systems. They would recognize their role as stewards of their information systems as well as their responsibility in regard to systems they connect to. The reality is that security isn't always viewed this way. In a worst-case scenario, security is viewed as costly, cumbersome, and burdensome. Even when security is valued, however, it is still often seen as intrusive, overwhelming, and confusing.

Information security regulations have been developed to address the potential for abuses of the confidentiality, integrity, and availability of systems that our economy and our citizens depend upon. In the two previous chapters, we studied the current regulations for banking and finance (GLBA) and health care (HIPAA). In this chapter, we are going to look at three regulations: the Federal Information Security Management Act (FISMA), the Federal Educational Rights and Privacy Act (FERPA), and Sarbanes-Oxley (SOX). FISMA affects all federal agencies and is related to a majority of the identified critical sectors. FERPA is specific to educational institutions and focuses on protecting student information. SOX focuses on corporate governance, financial disclosures, and integrity of financial information. We will conclude the chapter by relating the various requirements to the ISO 17799 framework.

E-Government Is Becoming a Reality

In the fall of 2001, the Office of Management and Budget (OMB) and federal agencies identified 24 e-government initiatives. The 24 are divided among four key portfolios: government to citizen, government to business, government to government, and internal efficiency and effectiveness. Since then, designated agencies have been designing and implementing programs to support these initiatives. The benefit of e-government is efficiency, cost savings, and increased responsiveness. The added responsibility is to ensure the confidentiality, integrity, and availability of the information and information systems used to provide these services to citizens, businesses, and governmental agencies. For more information on these initiatives visit **www.whitehouse.gov/omb/egov/c-presidential.html**.

Security at a National Level

Concurrent with the development of the e-government initiatives, e-government legislation was introduced to the Senate by Sen. Joseph

Lieberman (S.803) on May 1, 2001, and to the House of Representatives by Rep. Jim Turner (H.R. 2458) on July 7, 2001. The stated goal of the legislation was to enhance the management and promotion of electronic government services and processes by establishing a Federal Chief Information Officer within the Office of Management and Budget, and by establishing a broad framework of measures that require using Internet-based information technology to enhance citizen access to government information and services, and for other purposes.

S.803 and H.R.2458 became the E-Government Act (Public Law 107-347) and was passed by the 107th Congress and signed into law in December 2002. Title III of the E-Government Act recognized the importance of information security. Title III, entitled the Federal Information Security Management Act (FISMA), requires every federal agency, and any organization whose information systems possess or use federal information, to develop, document, and implement an agencywide risk-based information security program. The information security program is subject to mandatory periodic testing. It is important to stress that all organizations such as contractors, grantees, state and local governments, and industry partners that operate, use, or simply have access to federal information systems must comply with FISMA.

Elements Required for Compliance

FISMA focuses on the confidentiality, integrity, and availability of information and information systems as well as assurance and accountability. *Assurance* refers to the processes, policies, and controls used to develop confidence that security measures are working as intended. Assurance activities include auditing, monitoring, testing, and reporting. *Accountability* refers to assigning responsibility for compliance. To meet the accountability objective, FISMA establishes the Chief Information Officer (CIO) of each federal agency as the focal point for information security.

FISMA charged three government agencies with related responsibilities. The National Institute of Standards and Technology (NIST) has been tasked with developing technical security standards and guidelines for unclassified federal systems. The Office of Management and Budget (OMB) has been tasked with developing and overseeing implementation of government-wide policies, principles, guidance, and standards for the federal government's IT security program. The U. S. House Committee on Government Reform has been charged with oversight in a variety of subject areas in its jurisdiction, including federal systems security. The House Committee is responsible for issuing the Federal Computer Security Report Card.

14

FYI: FISMA 2004 Report to Congress

In FY 2004, federal agencies spent $4.2 billion securing the government's total information technology investment of approximately $59 billion, or about 7 percent of the total information technology portfolio. The complete report issued by the Office of Management and Budget can be found at **www.whitehouse.gov/omb/inforeg/2004_fisma_report.pdf**.

NIST to the Rescue

FISMA outlines objectives, elements, and mandatory requirements. What the legislation does not do is provide guidance. That's where The National Institute of Standards and Technology (NIST) comes in. NIST was enlisted to support FISMA by developing publications that provide guidance and best security practices to government agencies. NIST is a nonregulatory federal agency within the U.S. Commerce Department's Technology Administration. Over the years, NIST has published a number of publications that provide computer security guidance for federal agencies. NIST publications are an invaluable resource to the private sector as well as the public sector. It would behoove every practitioner of information security to become familiar with NIST publications and guidance.

FISMA required NIST to develop a series of official publications relating to information system security standards and guidelines that provide the following:

- Standards to be used by federal agencies to categorize all information and information systems collected or maintained by or on behalf of each agency based on the objectives of providing appropriate levels of information security according to a range of risk levels.

- Guidelines recommending the types of information and information systems to be included in each category.

- Minimum information security requirements (e.g., management, operational, and technical controls) for information and information systems in each such category.

NIST Publications to Address FISMA

NIST has published the specific standards and guidelines mandated by FISMA. All of these publications are public domain and can be downloaded at no charge from NIST at **http://csrc.nist.gov/publications**. NIST publications are issued as Special Publications (SP), NISTIRs (Internal Reports), and ITL Bulletins. The Special Publications series include the Spec. Pub. 500 series (Information Technology) and the Spec. Pub. 800 series (Computer Security). Computer security-related Federal Information Processing Standards (FIPS) are also available.

The FISMA Implementation Project

As mandated by FISMA, NIST is actively engaged in developing resources to be used in support of FISMA compliance. NIST has undertaken a three-phase approach.

- The first phase of the FISMA Implementation Project focused on the development of security standards and guidelines required by the legislation.

- The second phase of the FISMA Implementation Project is slated for 2006 and is to focus on the development of a program for accrediting public and private sector organizations to conduct security certification services for federal agencies.

- The third phase of the FISMA Implementation Project, also planned for 2006, will focus on the development of a program for validating commercial off-the-shelf (COTS) and government off-the-shelf (GOTS) security tools.

The NIST FISMA Implementation Project report can be read online at **http://csrc.nist.gov/sec-cert/ca-proj-phases.html**.

The Future of FISMA

In his March 2004 testimony before the House Committee on Government Reform, Robert F. Dacey, GOA Director of Information Security Issues, stressed the importance of FISMA compliance. He emphasized that continued adherence to FISMA regulations will lead to achieving sustainable results. He praised the work of NIST in exceeding its mandate by developing guidance on incident handling, building an information security awareness program, developing certification and accreditation standards, and focusing on risk management. The future of FISMA is that every federal agency will be expected to comply and that independent audit results will be reported annually to the Congress, the White House, and the American people.

Protecting the Privacy of Student Records

14

Educational institutions are subject to a myriad of information security federal regulations. Schools that offer financial aid and/or financial counseling are subject to the Gramm-Leach-Bliley Act (GLBA), schools that offer heathcare services may be subject to the Health Insurance Portability and

Accountability Act (HIPAA), and schools that receive funds from the Department of Education are subject to the Family Educational Rights and Privacy Act (FERPA).

The Family Educational Rights and Privacy Act (FERPA) is a federal law that protects the privacy of student education records. The law applies to all schools that receive funds under an applicable program from the Federal Department of Education. FERPA was signed into law in 1974 and has been amended nine times. The most recent amendment, "FERPA Final Regulations Relating to Electronic Consent and Signature, 34 CFR Part 99," was published in the Federal Register on April 21, 2004.

The intent of this regulation is protecting privacy (confidentiality). The implementation element to assuring confidentiality is security. It is interesting to consider the impact over time of this regulation on the practice of information security. When first adopted, records were either paper- or mainframe-based. Security controls were primarily administrative- or policy-based. More than thirty years later, the controls required for assuring the privacy of student records span all of the security domains.

What Is the Objective of FERPA?

Students have a right to know about the purpose, content, and location of information kept as a part of their educational records. They also have a right to expect that information in their educational records will be kept confidential unless they give permission to the school to disclose it. Implied in this statement is that the information will be available upon request.

FERPA gives students the following rights regarding educational records:

- The right to access educational records kept by the school.

- The right to demand educational records be disclosed only with student consent.

- The right to amend educational records.

- The right to file complaints against the school for disclosing educational records in violation of FERPA.

What Is an Educational Record?

Any record that contains personally identifiable information that is directly related to the student is an educational record under FERPA. Educational records may include written documents, computer media, microfilm and microfiche, film or photographs. Faculty notes, data compilation, and administrative records kept exclusively by the author of the records that are not accessible or revealed to anyone else are not considered educational records.

Types of Educational Records

There are two types of educational records as defined under FERPA. Each type has different disclosure protections. Therefore, it is essential to have a classification system that clearly identifies the type of information.

Directory Information Schools may disclose, without consent, directory information such as a student's name, address, telephone number, date and place of birth, honors and awards, and dates of attendance. Students and parents must be given an opportunity to inform the school that they do not want this information to be disclosed.

Nondirectory Information Nondirectory information is any educational record not considered directory information. Nondirectory information must not be released to anyone, including parents of the student, without the prior written consent of the student. Faculty and staff can access nondirectory information only if they have a legitimate academic need to do so (need-to-know). Nondirectory information may include Social Security numbers, student identification number, race, ethnicity and/or nationality, gender, transcripts, and grade reports.

Exceptions to the Rule Generally, schools must have written permission from the parent or eligible student to release any information from a student's education record. However, FERPA allows schools to disclose those records, without consent, to certain parties or under the specific conditions (34 CFR § 99.31).

What Does FERPA Have to Do with Information Security?

Everything! Stated in the regulations are the requirements that the confidentiality of student records be protected and that the information be available upon request. Implied in the regulation is that the integrity of the information be verifiable. Assuming that the records are processed, stored, and transmitted digitally, we must implement confidentiality, integrity, and availability controls and safeguards to comply with the regulations.

To protect student information, we must first identify where and how the information is processed, stored, and transmitted. We have to classify the information appropriately, identify the threats to the data, analyze the risks, and implement mitigating controls. We need a mechanism to identify appropriate access and ways to control, manage, and monitor access. We need physical controls that protect the systems that host the data. We need secure methods of data disposal as well as secure retention. We need the data to be protected in transmission from interception or eavesdropping. We need a process to report and respond to violations of confidentially. We

14

need information system users to understand when and how this information can be accessed and shared. In other words, this seemingly simple regulation requires a complete information security program supported by policies, plans, and procedures.

FYI: FERPA Policy

For more information on FERPA, visit the Department of Education Web site at **www.ed.gov**. Colleges and universities commonly post their FERPA policies on their own Web sites.

It All Started with a Corporate Scandal

The U.S. Public Company Accounting Reform and Investor Protection Act of 2002 (the Sarbanes-Oxley Act) is not about technology. As a response to the corporate financial scandals of the late 1990s, such as WorldCom and Enron, Sarbanes-Oxley (SOX) is about improving transparency and accountability in business processes and corporate accounting. It regulates processes and business practices. Companies subject to the SOX Act are required to document and evaluate processes, leading to senior management certification and auditor attestation that effective controls are in place. These controls implicitly extend to information security. It is interesting to note that SOX places heavy emphasis on protecting the integrity and availability of financial data.

- Section 404: Requires companies to identify the control framework used by management to evaluate effectiveness of internal controls, and requires the senior leadership team to attest to effectiveness in year-end financial report(s).

- Section 302: Requires the senior leadership team to attest to the accuracy of company's quarterly and annual reports, certify that these reports reflect the company's financial position, note weaknesses in controls exposed by audit, and describe how controls are integrated into the company's operations.

Compliance with Section 404 originally became effective on June 15, 2004, for all SEC reporting companies with a market capitalization in excess of $75 million. This was later extended to November 15, 2004. For all other companies that file periodic reports with the SEC, the compliance deadline was April 15, 2005.

What Does SOX Have to Do with Information Security?

The days of green ledger paper are long gone. Information systems are used to process, store, and transmit financial information. The internal controls referenced in the regulation extend beyond accounting controls and encompass information security controls. Compliance with Section 404 requires companies to establish an infrastructure to protect and preserve records and data from destruction, loss, unauthorized alteration, or other misuse. This infrastructure must ensure there is no room for unauthorized alteration of records vital to maintaining the integrity of the business processes. Information security in regard to SOX compliance follows a familiar pattern:

- Mapping the information systems that process, store, and transmit financial data.

- Identifying risks related to these information systems.

- Designing and implementing controls designed to mitigate the identified risks and monitoring them for continued effectiveness.

- Documenting and testing application and general information security controls.

- Ensuring that application controls apply to specific business processes and transactions and are application specific.

- Ensuring that general controls apply to all information systems, support services, and personnel.

- Ensuring that information security controls are updated and changed, as necessary, to correspond with changes in internal control or financial reporting processes.

- Monitoring information security controls for effective operation over time.

Adopting a Control Framework

SOX requires companies to identify the control framework used by management to evaluate the effectiveness of internal controls. A control is defined by the IT Governance Institute as "the policies, procedures, practices and organizational structures designed to provide reasonable assurance that business objectives will be achieved and that undesired events will be prevented or detected and corrected. A control objective is a statement of the desired result or purpose to be achieved by implementing control procedures." A control framework is a model or collection of controls that covers all internal controls expected in an organization. The two generally accepted control frameworks are defined and published by COSO and CobiT®.

14

FYI: COSO and CobiT®

COSO is a private sector organization comprising the Institute of Internal Auditors (IIA), the American Accounting Association (AAA), the American Institute of Certified Public Accountants (AICPA), Financial Executives International (FEI), and the Institute of Management Accountants (IMA). The COSO framework focuses on five areas: control environment, risk assessment, control activities, information and communication, and monitoring. For more information, go to **www.coso.org**.

The IT Governance Institute was formed by the Information Systems Audit and Control Association (ISACA) in 1998 to advance the understanding and adoption of IT Governance principles. CobiT® 3rd edition is published by the IT Governance Institute. CobiT® was first released by the Information Systems Audit and Control Foundation (ISACF) in 1996. For more information, go to: **www.isaca.org**.

Relevancy of ISO 17799:2000

Chapters 12, 13, and 14 have focused on an alphabet soup of government regulations:

- The Gramm-Leach-Bliley Act (GLBA)

- The Health Insurance Portability and Accountability Act (HIPAA)

- The Federal Information Security Management Act (FISMA)

- The Federal Educational Rights and Privacy Act (FERPA)

- The Sarbanes-Oxley Act (SOX)

All of these major pieces of legislation have common elements, which are addressed in the ISO 17799 security domains. Organizations choosing to design their information security programs based upon the ISO 17799 framework will have naturally incorporated a substantial number of requirements. Organizations subject to SOX will need to supplement their security programs with a generally accepted internal controls framework such as COSO or CobiT®.

ISO 17799 Security Domain Recap

The field of information security is very broad. The ten domains referenced in the ISO 17799:2000 are indicative of the breadth and depth of knowledge necessary to secure information assets and information systems. Table 14.1 reviews the focus of each domain. The section numbers refer to the numbering scheme used by the ISO. Sections 1 and 2 are introductory sections.

TABLE 14.1 ISO 17799 security domains recap.

ISO Section	Recap
Section 3: Security Policy	Security Policy focuses on management support and commitment codified in an information Security Policy document.
Section 4: Organizational Security	Organizational Security focuses on the need for a comprehensive information security infrastructure to support the development, implementation, and maintenance of a secure environment. Specifically addressed are the roles and responsibilities of management, security officers, information system users (privileged and nonprivileged), contracted third parties, business partners, and government agencies, including regulatory and public safety.
Section 5: Asset Classification	Asset Classification focuses on defining and protecting organizational assets. This domain addresses inventory, ownership, custodianship, classification, labeling, and handling.
Section 6: Personnel Security	Personnel Security focuses on the human side of security. This domain addresses the information system lifecycle from recruitment to post-termination.
Section 7: Physical and Environmental Security	Physical and Environmental Security focuses on securing and protecting the premises, equipment, and media. This domain addresses environmental issues, perimeter security, access control, equipment sitting, media reuse and disposal, and workspace security.

▸▸ CONTINUED ON NEXT PAGE

14

▶▶ CONTINUED

Section 8: Communications and Operations Management	Communications and Operations Management focuses on the organization's ability to securely operate day-to-day. This domain addresses operational procedures, change control, incident management, malicious code, network management, and information exchange.
Section 9: Access Control	Access Control focuses on controlling access to information assets. This domain addresses access criteria and requirements, user management and responsibilities, network-host-application level access control, access monitoring, and remote computing.
Section 10: Systems Development and Maintenance	Systems Development and Maintenance focuses on appropriate application level and operating system controls. This domain addresses system security requirements, application security requirements (both custom and COTS), cryptography, and system integrity.
Section 11: Business Continuity Management	Business Continuity Management focuses on an organization's ability to respond, react to, and recover from interruptions to normal operating conditions. This domain addresses business continuity planning, testing, and maintenance.
Section 12: Compliance	Compliance focuses on the organization's ability to remain in compliance with regulatory, statutory, and contractual security requirements. This domain focuses the mechanism to audit and verify compliance.

Summary

We live in a remarkable age of digital technology. Information that was once written on a solitary piece of paper is now accessible worldwide. The ability to deliver goods and services has been transformed. Coupled with this transformation are new responsibilities. As a civic duty, every organization, public and private, that processes, stores, or transmits information electronically is obligated to secure the information and information systems. Our national security, our economy, and our sense of well-being demand this.

The federal government has recognized that this important task is often overlooked. To rectify this situation, the government has codified the requirements and adopted sector-specific legislation. In the last two chapters, we examined the impact of GLBA and HIPAA. In this chapter, we examined FISMA, FERPA, and SOX. Federal agencies, as well as all organizations that access federal information, are subject to FISMA. To support compliance activities, the National Institute of Standards and Technology (NIST) has and continues to publish guidance on a variety of topics. Educational institutions that receive funding from the Department of Education are subject to FERPA. Lastly, publicly traded SEC registered companies must comply with section 404 of SOX. It is widely anticipated that the government will broaden its scope and eventually require information security compliance of all critical infrastructure sectors.

Test Your Skills

MULTIPLE CHOICE QUESTIONS

1. Federal agencies must comply with this legislation:
   A. FEPRA
   B. SOX
   C. GLBA
   D. FISMA

2. This regulation requires the privacy of student educational records:
   A. FISMA
   B. FERPA
   C. GLBA
   D. HIPAA

3. This regulation was a response to corporate financial scandals:
   A. GLBA
   B. FERPA
   C. SOX
   D. FISMA

14

4. This regulation requires compliance by private sector companies if they access federal government information systems:

    A. FISMA

    B. FERPA

    C. SOX

    D. GLBA

5. According to FISMA, accountability is best achieved by:

    A. conducting a risk assessment

    B. documenting policy and procedures

    C. providing training

    D. designating a Chief Information Security Officer

6. This federal agency has been charged with developing technical security standards for unclassified federal systems:

    A. DOE

    B. NIST

    C. NSA

    D. OMB

7. This federal agency has been charged with developing and overseeing implementation of government wide policy for the IT security program:

    A. DOE

    B. NIST

    C. NSA

    D. OMB

8. Oversight for the federal nonclassified government information security program belongs to:

    A. the OMB

    B. the White House

    C. the House Committee on Government Reform

    D. the federal CISO

9. FERPA was originally signed into law in:

    A. 1966

    B. 1974

    C. 1982

    D. 1999

10. The overarching intent of FERPA is protecting the:
    - A. integrity of educational records
    - B. validity of educational records
    - C. confidentiality of educational records
    - D. availability of educational records

11. For an educational record to be subject to FERPA, it must:
    - A. contain personally identifiable student information
    - B. request to be covered by the student
    - C. include transcripts
    - D. have been created after 1999

12. SOX is primarily focused on:
    - A. production reporting
    - B. financial reporting
    - C. marketing and sales records
    - D. personnel records

13. The common denominator of all SOX-regulated companies is:
    - A. they are included in the Fortune 100
    - B. they have revenues over $100 million
    - C. they are SEC registered and publicly traded
    - D. they are suspected of financial mismanagement

14. SOX section 404 is primarily concerned with:
    - A. internal controls
    - B. external controls
    - C. business partner relationships
    - D. government reporting

15. This controls framework is developed by and endorsed by a consortium of public accounting firms:
    - A. ISO 17799
    - B. COSO
    - C. CobiT®
    - D. SOSO

16. This controls framework is published by the IT Governance Institute:

    A. ISO 17799

    B. COSO

    C. CobiT®

    D. SOSO

17. Universities that provide healthcare services are subject to this regulation:

    A. GLBA

    B. SOX

    C. FERPA

    D. HIPAA

18. Universities that provide financial aid are subject to this regulation:

    A. GLBA

    B. SOX

    C. FERPA

    D. FISMA

19. Universities that are awarded grants and directly access federal information systems are subject to this regulation:

    A. GLBA

    B. SOX

    C. FERPA

    D. FISMA

20. Which of these is NOT considered a critical infrastructure sector?

    A. government

    B. defense

    C. commerce

    D. farming

EXERCISES

Exercise 14.1: National Strategy to Secure Cyberspace

1. Download and read the Summary of the National Strategy to Secure Cyberspace. It can be found at **www.whitehouse.gov/pcipb/**.

2. Summarize the intent of the strategy.

3. Comment on the following question: Should government be involved with recommending or requiring information security programs for nongovernmental institutions?

Exercise 14.2: Identifying the Regulations

1. Create a table that lists each of the federal regulations discussed in Chapters 12, 13, and 14.

2. For each regulation, specify the following:
   - Applicable sector
   - Intent of regulation
   - Federal agency assigned oversight and/or enforcement responsibility

Exercise 14.3: Higher Education Compliance

1. Is your school subject to FERPA? Explain your answer.

2. Is your school subject to HIPAA? Explain your answer.

3. Is your school subject to GLBA? Explain your answer.

4. Is your school subject to FISMA? Explain your answer.

Exercise 14.4: CSO vs. CFO

1. Research and define the position of a Chief Security Officer.

2. Research and define the position of a Chief Financial Officer.

3. Which regulation(s) discussed in this chapter involves both roles and why?

Exercise 14.5: FERPA Permissions

1. FERPA regulations state that schools may disclose directory information without a student's permission. However, students must be given an opportunity to remove their information from the directory. This is referred to as being able to "opt-out." Do you agree with this rule, or do you believe that explicit "opt-in" permission should need to be granted instead? Write a brief essay explaining your position.

14

2. FERPA regulations state that faculty notes kept exclusively by the author are not considered education records. Assume that a faculty member saved her notes in a shared folder on the university network. Other departmental faculty members regularly access this shared folder. In your opinion, does this change the classification of the data? Write a brief essay explaining your answer.

PROJECTS

Project 14.1: FISMA and Federal Agencies

1. All federal agencies are required to comply with FISMA regulations. Choose one of the following agencies:

   - Department of Energy (DOE)
   - Department of Defense (DOD)
   - Department of Justice (DOJ)
   - Department of Transportation (DOT)

   Write a brief summary outlining the mission of the agency.

2. Research and report on the agency's compliance with FISMA.

3. Locate a copy of the latest "Federal Computer Security Report Card." What grade was the agency awarded?

Project 14.2: Spending Money on Information Security

1. One of the major complaints regarding information security regulations is that they place an unfair burden on organizations as they are costly unfunded mandates. Do you think that it is fair for governments to require private organizations to comply with regulations that will cost them money?

2. How much do U.S. corporations spend on information security annually? What is the estimated cost of implementing SOX? How much does the U.S. government spend on information security annually? What are the predicted spending trends? In your opinion, is this amount of money justified?

Project 14.3: Internal Control Framework

1. CobiT® is a widely adopted information technology internal controls framework. CoBiT® is distributed by ISACA. Access ISACA's Web site at **www.isaca.org**. What is the purpose of ISACA?

2. What is the relationship between internal audit and information security compliance?

3. Portions of CobiT® are available to download on a complimentary basis. Download and read the Executive Summary. What is meant by "Plan - Do - Check - Correct"? How does this philosophy integrate with an information security program?

Case Study

The fictional University of Freedom was founded in 1890. The university offers undergraduate, graduate, and medical degrees. The medical college operates three healthcare clinics offering services to both the university and the communities in which they are located. The medical school is also involved in federally funded research projects. The university has a substantial endowment and awards over one million dollars in financial aid annually. The University Compliance Officer has determined that the university is subject only to HIPAA and FERPA. There is some disagreement among the administration as to the validity of this claim. The Compliance Officer has formally charged the Director of Information Technology with ensuring HIPAA security compliance and the Registrar with FERPA compliance. Neither the IT Director nor the Registrar is comfortable with their respective assignments. The university President wants one central authority and one set of policies to cover all compliance-related requirements.

Questions:

1. Do you agree with the Compliance Officer's determination regarding regulations?

2. Are the official appointments made by the Compliance Officer appropriate?

3. Will one set of information security policies suffice?

4. Who would you recommend be given ownership of information security compliance?

14

Chapter 15

Security Policies and Practices for Small Businesses

Chapter Objectives

After reading this chapter and completing the exercises, you will be able to do the following:

- Relate to the unique security needs of small businesses.
- Define the type of policies appropriate for small businesses.
- Author security policies for small businesses.
- Develop security procedures for small businesses.
- Implement security best practices for small business.

Introduction

Small business owners are busy people. They often wear many hats and work long hours. They expend their time and energy on building and running a company. They rarely, if ever, concentrate on building and running a "secure" company. They are not purposely negligent. They acknowledge basic security measures such as the need for firewalls and virus protection, but in general they simply do not believe that they have much to worry about. "After all," they reason, "who would want to target my business when there are so many bigger targets out there." While it is true that small businesses are not directly attacked as often as larger ones, there are three flaws with this reasoning. First, small businesses often end up as part of larger attacks, such as mass worm outbreaks or efforts to harvest credit card numbers. Second, because security is becoming tighter than ever at larger companies, small business networks look increasingly tempting to attackers. And finally, this assumes that all attacks come from the outside. The fact remains that a significant number of small businesses that experience an attack never fully recover and eventually go out of business.

This chapter focuses on the small business environment. We do not expect the vast majority of small business even to consider adopting the ISO 17799 framework. However, small businesses do need to adopt policies and procedures that are reasonable in scope, cost effective, and meaningful. Small businesses are the lifeblood of the international economy. They foster innovation and develop young talent. They bring diverse groups of people together. They provide the means to live a dream. For these reasons, the information resources they depend upon to function must be protected from harm.

What Is a Small Business?

There are a variety of official opinions on what defines a small business. The United States Small Business Administration (SBA) defines a small business as one that is independently owned and operated, is not dominant in its field of operation, and employs fewer than 500 people. The United States General Accounting Office (GAO) classifies a small business as one with less than $6.5 million in annual revenue. The Australian Bureau of Statistics defines a small business as one that has fewer than 20 employees and is independently owned and operated, closely controlled by the owner/managers who contribute most, if not all, of the operating capital. The principal decision making rests with the owner/managers. Regardless of these definitions, that fact remains that most small businesses are exactly that-small. Despite their size, however, they are very important. Consider the following facts.

Small businesses . . .

■ Total approximately 23 million in the United States.

■ Represent 99.7 percent of all employer firms.

■ Employ half of all private sector employees.

■ Pay 44.3 percent of the total U.S. private payroll.

■ Generate 60 to 80 percent of net new jobs annually.

■ Create more than 50 percent of nonfarm, private gross domestic product (GDP).

■ Employ 39 percent of high-tech workers (such as scientists, engineers, and computer workers).

(Sources: U.S. Bureau of the Census; Advocacy-funded research by Joel Popkin and Company [Research Summary #211]; U.S. Department of

Labor, Bureau of Labor Statistics, Current Population Survey; U.S. Department of Commerce, International Trade Administration).

A significant number of small businesses depend on information systems for a variety of financial, management, marketing, and production purposes. They rely on e-mail for communication. They access resources via the Internet. While they couldn't image functioning without these systems, they devote limited resources to the management and maintenance of information systems. Generally, they do not have in-house technology departments or Information Security Officers. When they engage outside expertise, it is often because there is a problem or something "broke." What may not be readily apparent to most small businesses is the depth of dependency on information systems and the overall impact of a breach of confidentiality, integrity, and/or availability. Small businesses are not immune from computer crime. The bottom line is that the businesses that will thrive and prosper over time will be the ones that have learned to be proactive in protecting these vital resources.

What Should a Small Business Do?

Every small business should have a security policy. The security policy defines an organization's approach to security. Policies do not need to be overly complicated. As a matter of fact, the more straightforward the better. The policy needs to reflect the culture of the organization and deliver a message of commitment. Most importantly, small businesses must be willing to enforce the policy.

Small businesses need to teach their employees about security. We have found that once employees understand why security matters and what their responsibilities are, they willingly become the first line of defense against intrusion. Written policies are not only teaching tools but they demonstrate how serious the business is. As a condition of employment, employees should be required to sign a statement of compliance. They also need to be aware of the consequences of violation. An inexpensive security awareness campaign can reap huge benefits for a small business. The outcome of continued communications is that good security practices become a part of everyday operations.

Additional Considerations

Some small businesses are subject to government regulations, insurance policy requirements, and/or other special agreements that require additional considerations and precautions.

Federal Regulations Government regulations may require that specific types of information be secured. For example, health care providers are regulated by the Health Insurance Portability and Accountability Act (HIPAA), which guards against the misuse of personally identifiable health

15

information and limits the sharing of that information. Specifically, health care providers must guard patient information against unauthorized access, alteration, deletion, and transmission. Similarly, a host of small firms such as real estate brokers, mortgage brokers, and investment advisers are subject to the Gramm-Leach-Bliley Act, which requires businesses to protect personally identifiable financial information.

Insurance Policies Insurance policies, especially business liability policies, may require specific steps for ensuring the security of data on your computers. Some policies even go so far as to dictate the equipment and procedures that must be in place.

Special Agreements Special agreements include contracts such as terms of service agreements, which often cover the privacy guarantees businesses provide to their clients, and nondisclosure agreements, which prevent you from sharing confidential information collected from clients.

What Policies Should a Small Business Have?

Table 15.1 shows the basic policies that every small business should have.

You will notice that two difference syntaxes in Table 15.1. *Expected behavior* specifies how we expect users to act on a daily basis. A basic tenet is that policies should not be so vague as to be open to interpretation. In reality, we often ask users to use their judgment in applying a policy. This is necessary because of the how dynamic business environments are. *Rules for* or *rules relating to* specify a specific course of action for a defined situation. Expected behavior policies are often referred to as end-user policies, while *rules-based* policies are considered operational polices.

How Should the Policies Be Presented?

Policies always need to be presented positively. A starting point is with the title of the document. The title should reflect the attitude of the organization and its goals. A successful way to introduce end-user policies is to incorporate them into a master "Employee Information Security Affirmation Agreement" document. This title speaks more clearly to the essence of what we want of our employees. We want them to affirm their role in the information security program, not feel a victim of yet another policy. After providing training, we ask them to sign a document that affirms their agreement with end-user policies. Particularly in a small business, employee buy-in is a critical success factor.

Why Have a Confidentiality Policy?

To state the obvious, company information belongs to the company. It is up to the business to make sure that the information is protected from unauthorized or inappropriate disclosure. To do so, they may use technical

TABLE 15.1 Recommended small business policies.

Policy	Objective
Confidentiality Policy	Expected behavior in regard to the use of company information
Acceptable Use Policy	Expected behavior in regard to the use of company information resources
Internet Use Policy	Expected behavior in regard to the use of the Internet and Internet access
E-mail Use Policy	Expected behavior in regard to the use of e-mail and e-mail systems
Incident Reporting and Response Policy	Expected behavior in regard to reporting to and responding to an incident
Password Management Policy	Rules relating to how user-level and system-level passwords are created, managed, and changed
Information Protection Policy	Rules relating to the processing, storage, and transmission of sensitive information
Virus Protection Policy	Requirements for the use of anti-malware software as well as rules for reporting and containing malware infections
Remote Access Policy	Rules for remotely connecting to the internal network
Change Control Policy	Rules relating to the implementation of a potential significant change to an information system
Data Backup and Recovery Policy	Rules for the creation, management, and maintenance of redundant copies of data

controls like login authentication or access control lists, physical controls like locks and alarms, or administrative controls such as a confidentiality policy or agreement.

Make It Legal

A confidentiality policy or agreement is a legal document. We are going to refer to it as an *agreement* because employees must agree to and sign it, otherwise there is minimal legal standing. The primary goal of the agreement is to obtain injunctive relief in case of a violation of or breach of confidentiality. In other words, it is a way to go to court and stop the offending action. A confidentiality policy may be a standalone document or part of an employee affirmation agreement. Either is fine as long as the document is signed by the employee.

15

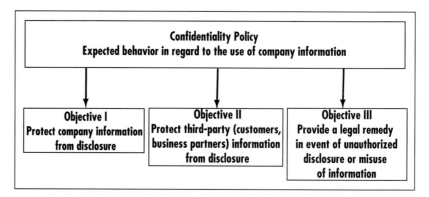

FIGURE 15.1 Confidentiality policy overview.

Not One, not Two, but Five

As we discussed in Chapter 6, confidentiality agreements perform several functions:

- They specify the types of information that can and cannot be disclosed without explicit permission.

- They provide a legal remedy in case of disclosure.

- They protect patent rights.

- They define how information is to be handled and for what length of time.

- They explain what happens to information when there is no longer a "need to know" such as when employment is terminated or a contract ends.

Structure of the Agreement

By agreeing to the confidentiality policy, the employee recognizes and acknowledges the confidential nature of certain information and promises not to disclose it. The policy should include the following sections:

- Recognition of the company's right to nondisclosure of information.

- Acknowledgement of the obligations of confidentiality.

- Agreement not to improperly use the information.

- Understanding that all company information must be returned at the termination of employment.

Protect the Agreement

Confidentiality agreements should be a mandatory condition of employment for all users. An agreement should be signed at time of hire and then annually. A copy should be given to the employee or contractor. The signed original should be securely stored. In the best of all worlds, this agreement is never used. If the situation arises, however, it can be used not only to protect the company but also the company's clients and business partners.

What Is Acceptable Behavior?

An acceptable use policy can appear to an unsuspecting user as a very harsh document. It is difficult, if not impossible, to develop a comprehensive list of all of acceptable behaviors. Contrary to its name, acceptable use polices generally highlight unacceptable behavior, namely what you should not do. It is recommended to enlist the help of a cross-section of the audience in the drafting of the actual document. After the policy is adopted, this group can be a powerful ally. In essence, they will become your security champions. We also suggest including the reasons why the policies were created and adopted as a part of the security training. This goes a long way towards "softening the blow" and insuring good will and companywide acceptance.

Ownership

The first item that should appear in an acceptable use policy is that all the equipment and information employees utilize or have access to in the course of their employment belongs to the company. The network infrastructure, the connectivity to the Internet, the desktop computer on their desk, and every bit of information contained therein are company property, and all represent a financial investment by the company made with the intent of providing employees with a productivity tool. Users should have no expectation of privacy when using company resources. This includes saved files, e-mails, and voicemail.

Employees often don't realize this and use company resources for personal use, such as participating in online auctions (eBay) or downloading music. Beyond the loss of productivity incurred by the company comes the fact that every time an employee surfs the Web, he is potentially putting the

FIGURE 15.2 Acceptable use policy overview.

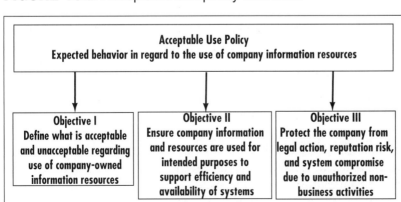

Acceptable Use Policy
Expected behavior in regard to the use of company information resources

| **Objective I** Define what is acceptable and unacceptable regarding use of company-owned information resources | **Objective II** Ensure company information and resources are used for intended purposes to support efficiency and availability of systems | **Objective III** Protect the company from legal action, reputation risk, and system compromise due to unauthorized non-business activities |

15

network and the organization at risk. Worms, virus infections, social engineering, and hoax messages can all result from surfing to the "wrong" site and even the "right" site if it has been compromised. The company may be held liable for any illegal activities that occur while using its resources. An all-too-familiar illegal activity is copyright violations that stem from software and music piracy.

IN PRACTICE: Business-Centric Use of Bandwidth?

A small accounting firm just spent close to $20,000 upgrading its network, including new computers and the latest operating system. The firm was just around the corner from tax season and wanted to get the upgrade done with plenty of time for everyone to get used to the new software and equipment. The firm's owner called her IT consultant in a less than pleasant mood to complain about how slow everything was since the costly upgrade. This was puzzling to the consultant, who was certain that he had tested all systems thoroughly before signing off on the job.

Upon a visit to the site, the consultant found out quite quickly what the true issue really was. Employees had decided that they really enjoyed listening to streaming audio broadcasts all day long. Many had developed an affinity for the "Weatherbug" application, which streams local weather information to end-users. Because all employees were doing it, they choked the bandwidth that the company was paying for to access the Internet. The company was actually considering purchasing a line with more bandwidth—at an extra cost!

The consultant helped management realize that the existing traffic was not "legitimate" business traffic. He noted that it would cost the firm less to buy portable radios for all employees to use at their desks, rather than to lease a more expensive line to the Internet! But because the company did not have an acceptable use policy, and because these employees did not understand that they were putting a strain on the performance of their network link by continually streaming music from multiple workstations, employees were costing the company a fair amount of money.

Once the streaming applications were removed, the firm realized the dramatic increase in speeds due to the upgrade and had its most productive tax season ever. Even the mild animosity directed toward the IT consultant by the staff for taking away their "fun" went away.

Hardware and Software

It is not acceptable for users to install any hardware on their company-provided computer without prior written approval of management or owners. There are multiple reasons for this restriction. It requires expertise to install hardware on a personal computer—not just to turn the screws, but to know what hardware is compatible with any particular computer and its operating system (OS). If you install the wrong hardware and hardware device driver, you may corrupt the operating system beyond a "quick fix" and even to the point of reinstallation of the OS to correct the problem. Reinstalling an OS can take anywhere from 20 minutes to several hours—all lost productivity and a threat to one major security principal you know as availability.

Likewise, attaching an unauthorized wireless access point or gateway is a major breach in security. By default, wireless networks are wide open and available. Wireless access points are susceptible to "war-driving," which is the act of driving around and detecting open networks. Anyone with a laptop computer, an inexpensive wireless network card, freely downloaded software, and an antenna made from something as simple as a potato chip could hack into a wireless network. Most wireless networks are completely unsecured. Indeed, many manufacturers of wireless devices leave encryption turned off by default. War-driving is more than a geek prank. Some intruders seek to access files and damage systems.

Similarly, it is not acceptable for users to install new software on company-owned computers without prior authorization. Not only is there the risk of introducing a virus or a worm—or even a Trojan backdoor remote access tool—there is also the risk of installing software that is not compatible with the current configuration. This can result in a computer crash, which means loss of productivity and, potentially, a loss of data.

Yet another reason to prohibit the installation of unapproved software is copyright violation. The organization cannot concern itself with whether or not a piece of nonapproved software has been legally acquired. If during an audit, illegal copies of software titles are found on an organization's information resources, it is the organization that pays the penalty.

Misuse of Resources

Other activities prohibited by policy should include the following:

- Using company resources to conduct personal business of any kind.

- Using company resources to harass, offend, or threaten another individual.

- Using company resources to access, create, record, store, transmit, distribute, image, modify, print, download, or display inappropriate or unprofessional materials.

- Using company resources to engage in any illegal activity.

15

Internet Use—Where to Draw the Line?

This policy can be a tough act to balance. On the one hand, a company does not want to be perceived by employees as a tyrant by denying all non-business-related Internet access. On the other hand, it must be understood that Internet access is granted at the company's expense for employees to conduct business—not to surf for hours in search of stock quotes, personal e-mail, sports scores, and other assorted news and weather updates. Users must understand that personal surfing is not considered a business activity. Noncompany use should be restricted to personal time such as breaks and lunch. In addition, some Web sites are totally inappropriate for employees to access using company equipment and bandwidth, including porno-graphic sites, piracy sites (software, music, and video), and hate-promoting sites.

Monitoring, Logging, and Blocking Internet Traffic

The Internet policy should inform employees that their use of the Internet may be monitored and logged. Logging traffic for further review is a must if the company has an official position on employees visiting inappropriate sites and the consequences that result from such behavior. Some companies actually terminate employees who visit inappropriate sites. A sound moni-toring and logging solution can become a part of a legal action for the com-pany. In other words, the company should make it as plain and clear as possible that employees using company-deployed Internet access have ab-solutely no privacy associated with their online activities. Those activities can and will be reviewed, either in real time, or after the fact, at the sole dis-cretion of the company.

FIGURE 15.3 Internet policy overview.

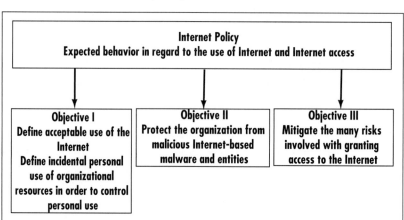

Along the same line, it is also recommended to deploy some site-blocking device such as a proxy server, a firewall, or a combination of the two that blocks outgoing Web traffic both by name and by IP. While many of these solutions come with built-in blocks for well-known inappropriate sites and keywords, they can be further configured based on the company's need.

Transmitting Data

Internet use is not just limited to Web surfing; it also includes the ability to transmit data. Transmitting data is a broad term that encompasses multiple activities, including File Transfer Protocol (FTP) activities, Instant Messaging (IM), and peer-to-peer (P2P) applications.

Instant Messaging: A Security Nightmare Instant Messaging has become a popular tool, both in the corporate and the noncorporate world. While most network security professionals recommend banning its use as a business tool, it is still widely used. Why do security professionals dislike IM? Because it was not built with security in mind—and it shows. First of all, all IM traffic is, by default, transmitted in clear text. That means that if you are exchanging confidential data over IM, anyone with a packet sniffer can read each and every line you send and receive. Then there is also the issue of not *really* knowing with whom you are interacting during an IM session. Impersonation, identity theft, and social engineering are rampant on IM. And if that were not enough, there is also the file transfer risk inherent to IM. Most of those clients come with a built-in file transfer function, which is a perfect hole in your network security through which to push viruses, Trojans, worms, and so forth under the guise of sending a user a fun cartoon or video game. In short, it is recommended that the network security policy include a clause that explicitly forbids the use of any IM software on company computers and networks.

Peer-to-Peer (P2P): Nightmare2 P2P is best known as the model used for music services like Kaazaa and formerly for Napster. It is the ability to install one single piece of software that enables a computer to become a node in a vast network of computers from which to download all sorts of files including pirated software, mp3s, and videos. Note that a machine that is a part of a P2P network not only can be used to download files from external machines, but it also becomes a machine from which files can be both uploaded and downloaded! Most P2P software titles don't bother to tell users just what it means to open a file share to the whole world!

15

Beyond the fact that these P2P networks are riddled with spyware and malware of all kinds, there is also the issue of legality—or lack thereof—tied with downloading copyrighted content without paying for a license. If such an activity takes place from a corporate network, and there is no policy against it, it can be argued that the company officially condones piracy, and is therefore liable in a court of law for all the pirated content that can be found on the company's network. In other words, complacency does not pay. Simply put, there isn't one instance when a P2P client should be allowed on a corporate network, unless it is an application built in-house and designed for a specific business purpose.

FYI: Copyright Infringement Lawsuits Brought Against Illegal File Sharers

In February of 2005, the Recording Industry of America announced its intention to sue computer users at 11 colleges and universities across the country for copyright infringement. The RIAA is suing on behalf of the major record companies. The lawsuit charges that individual users illegally distributed copyrighted music on the Internet. P2P programs such as Kazaa, eDonkey, and Grokser were used to distribute the files.

In making the announcement, RIAA president Cary Sherman commented that "It's critical to simultaneously send a strong message that the individual users of these pirate networks can be caught and face the consequences. The lawsuits are a critical deterrent. They have helped arrest the extraordinary growth of illicit p2p use."

Keeping Corporate E-mail Secure

E-mail technology has changed the way business is conducted. And because of this new "status," it has become a solution that we need to protect and secure.

When training users, it is effective to liken sending an e-mail using the company-provided solution to sending a postcard printed on company stock. It can be read by anyone and may be interpreted as the official position of the organization. Many users have never thought of it that way, and it does underscore the potentially dangerous nature of sending corporate e-mails.

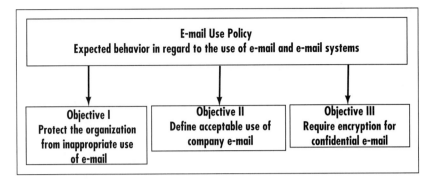

FIGURE 15.4 E-mail use policy overview.

IN PRACTICE: The Power of a Single E-mail over a Company's Future

There was a young company that was trying to make a name for itself in the corporate technical support arena. This company had landed one big client, and its fate, for better and for worse, was directly linked to its relationship with this client. One day, a disgruntled employee took it upon himself to send an e-mail to this client using his corporate e-mail account. He did not consult with management prior to sending this e-mail. Managers were unaware of his actions until they were contacted by a furious representative of their one and only client. The scalding tone and vivid language displayed in the e-mail conveyed *one low-level employee's* opinion of the relationship between this young company and its client in no uncertain terms. Unfortunately, his opinion was not a flattering one, to say the least, and because the e-mail had come with the electronic equivalent of a corporate letterhead, it had an "official" weight associated with it that did not reflect the actual situation.

The company's managers attempted to explain the e-mail, but the client decided that this act was so unprofessional that it could not count on the young company and severed the relationship. The employee was fired for cause within 24 hours. Unfortunately, he was not the only one who lost his job because of one simple e-mail and the company's lack of a written e-mail use policy and corresponding training. A couple of months later, the young company closed its doors and laid off all employees.

15

Business Use Only

Corporate e-mail is appropriate for business reasons only. Here again, the use of e-mail systems is extended by the company, at the company's expense, as a tool for employees to conduct business in the name of their company.

Corporate e-mail should never be used for personal correspondence. The mere fact that it came from a corporate network automatically can imply corporate responsibility. Imagine a situation where a person who works for a stockbroker uses her corporate e-mail to send a message to a friend advising the purchase of a certain stock. Even though the company never was involved in this e-mail—it was an unauthorized communication between two individuals over a company-owned medium—if the stock performed badly and the friend lost money, he could contend in court that since the e-mail came from the stockbroker's corporate network, he perceived the tip to be "official" and therefore the broker is at least partially responsible for the loss. Whether the suit has merit or not is beyond the point. What isn't beyond the point, however, is that the company would have to expend money and time to address the allegation.

Corporate e-mail should reflect the professionalism of the organization. Inappropriate language, threats, or attacks can and do put the organization at risk. Any personal opinions expressed that differ from company policy should be clearly delineated as such. Without such a disclaimer, options may be misrepresented. Consider the ramifications of this situation: A resident of a small Maine town was unhappy with the actions of a City Council member. Through a series of e-mails, she rather forcefully expressed her sentiment. The messages were sent from her work e-mail. The Councillor contacted the resident's boss to discuss. The resident filed charges with the police, claiming that the Councillor harassed her by contacting her workplace. The police found no grounds for the charge. One is only left to wonder what transpired between the worker and her boss.

Clear Text Communications

Employees need to realize that, unless an add-on encryption solution has been deployed, e-mail is basically clear text communication. Unless otherwise secured, confidential information should never be sent via e-mail, either to an internal or external address. Sending an e-mail without proper encryption is akin to sending a postcard in the mail. Anyone can read what is written on it as it travels along its merry way from sender to recipient.

Misuse of Resources

Anybody who's ever had an e-mail address knows the amount of junk that finds its way to the inbox. While most of it is nothing more than telemarketing brought to the e-mail medium, some of it can be malicious. The three most common forms of junk e-mail are spam, hoaxes, and chain e-mail. These e-mails consume valuable resources including processing time, storage space, bandwidth, and user productivity.

Prohibiting Spam Spam are unsolicited e-mails. As a matter of fact, the technical term for spam is UCE—Unsolicited Commercial E-mail. Certain types of spam are illegal. On December 16, 2003, President Bush signed into law the CAN-SPAM Act of 2003. The act, which took effect on January 1, 2004, imposes a series of new requirements on the use of commercial electronic mail messages. In addition, it gives federal civil and criminal enforcement authorities new tools to combat commercial e-mail that is unwanted by the recipient and/or deceptive. The act also allows state attorneys general to enforce its civil provisions, and creates a private right of action for providers of Internet access service.

No one likes receiving spam. Companies should make sure that their e-mail policies clearly state that employees may not, under any circumstances, send spam e-mails using corporate-owned e-mail solutions. Besides the legal ramifications and very negative press, the company's e-mail addresses could end up being blacklisted because of the spamming activity. This can result in embarrassment and loss of productivity.

Hoax E-mails Hoax e-mails can do as much damage as virus-infected e-mail, because they prey on people's credulity and willingness to follow directions. Directions may range from deleting files on their computers to sending money to a cancer victim. Users should be directed to not respond to or forward hoax e-mails. It is the organization's responsibility to train employees how to recognize hoaxes.

Chain E-mails Chain letters have been around for quite a while. A typical chain letter consists of a message that attempts to induce the reader to make a number of copies of the letter and then pass them on to multiple recipients. Common methods used by chain letters include emotionally manipulative stories and get-rich-quick pyramid schemes. Chain e-mails are just a new way of distributing the same. At best, they waste productivity time and bandwidth. At worst, they can carry a malicious payload, or a link to a Web site that does. Chain e-mails should never be responded to or forwarded on corporate-owned e-mail systems.

15

FYI: Well-Known Spammer Convicted

SPAM is an ever increasing problem. It is hoped that prosecution of spammers will serve as a deterrent. The first criminal spam trial in the United States concluded with the conviction of well-known spammer Jeremy Jaynes, also known as Gavin Stubberfield. Jaynes was sentenced to nine years. John Levine was an expert witness for the prosecution, and wrote a web log entry about the experience at **www.taugh.com/weblog/leesburg.html**.

Reporting and Responding to Incidents

A security incident is any situation where the confidentiality, integrity, and/or availability of the protected information or information systems are put in jeopardy. Now, as you have probably already fathomed, this is a very broad definition, one which encompasses anything from an outright hacking attack on a network to a squirrel eating all cables in the server room (don't laugh, this has happened before!).

Incidents do happen, and at the very least, the threat of an incident is always high, which means that a policy must be defined to deal with the occurrence of an incident. In case of an incident, the first reaction is a certain level of panic. One of the goals of the policy is to provide a defining framework that clearly states what needs to be done, by whom, along with who is ultimately in charge of the situation. Situations that engender panic require strong leadership and clear, precise, concise action items.

Incident Reporting

All users are responsible for recognizing unusual or suspicious activity. Examples of unusual activity include a significant slowdown of the network or having e-mails bounce back with error messages. Examples of suspicious

FIGURE 15.5 Incident reporting and response policy overview.

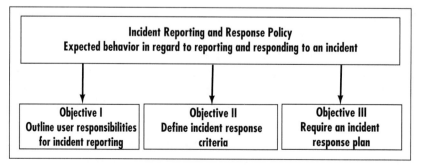

activity include the arrival of an unexpected repair person, finding papers left on a desk overnight rearranged, or a new program installed on a computer. Each of these examples may be benign or they may be the first outward sign of trouble. Users must understand not only the importance of being mindful of these activities but the importance of reporting them immediately. If we expect users to comply with this policy, we must make it easy for them to contact the appropriate individual, either by phone, e-mail, or in person.

Incident Response

Small businesses do not have the luxury of having dedicated incident response teams. Nevertheless, someone must be designated as the first contact for reporting as well as being the incident handler. The incident reporting and response policy needs to address these key questions:

- Who should be notified in case of an incident?

- How will the severity of the incident be determined?

- What should happen when an incident occurs?

FYI: InfraGard-FBI Outreach to the Private Sector

According to the Infragard Web site, "InfraGard is a partnership of businesses, the FBI, educational entities, and the National Infrastructure Protection Center. This alliance is designed to protect IT systems from hacker attacks and other intrusions by providing a network for sharing information, anonymously, about attacks and how to protect against them."

The FBI began InfraGard in an effort to protect the nation's critical information systems. InfraGard functions as a national clearinghouse of information about security intrusions, hacks, and vulnerabilities, and to offer tools to help detect, isolate, and prevent attacks.

According to Infragard, "Members are linked to each other and to the FBI by the bureau's secure 'alert network.' Companies can anonymously report incidents to all other members without fear of publicizing their vulnerability. The FBI provides encryption software to protect information exchange among members. The National Infrastructure Protection Center will use data gathered from different InfraGard chapters to compile reports on nationwide security trends. As security risk grows, the InfraGard program is becoming the FBI's front-line of defense."

For more information, see **www.infragard.net**.

15

Incident Response Plan

The incident reporting and response policy should require that an incident response plan be developed and maintained. Responsibility for this function should be assigned. A sound incident response plan should include a reasonable list of potential incidents. Each identified incident should come with a checklist that indicates who is in charge of dealing with the incident, who their backups are in case they cannot be reached, who should be notified of the incident, and what prioritized steps should be taken to deal with the situation.

Managing Passwords

One of the biggest challenges in information security is password-related policies. Why are password policies so badly received? The reason is straightforward: it's the relationship between convenience and security. How easy it would be *not* to have to remember a password to access a secure site? On the other hand, how easy would it then be for an intruder to access the same site? Passwords are designed to protect access to secure sites and information. The first rule in a password policy is that every account must have a password. The second rule is that the password is to be kept secret (this includes not writing it down)!

Password Characteristics

A small business password management policy must address the following password characteristics:

- Password Length—The longer the better. Definitely greater than seven characters. Most organizations standardize on eight characters.

- Password Complexity—Complex passwords feature three of the following four characteristics: uppercase characters, lowercase

FIGURE 15.6 Password management policy overview.

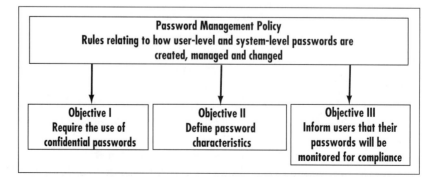

characters, numeric characters, and ASCII characters (e.g., ! @ # $ % ^ & * or ?). Complex passwords do not include the user's name. Complex passwords do not include words found in a dictionary.

- Password Age—The NSA (National Security Agency) recommends that passwords should be changed every 90 days. Administrative passwords should be changed more frequently.

- Password Reuse—The NSA (National Security Agency) recommends that password reuse of the previous 24 passwords be restricted. The goal is to prevent users from alternating between their favorite two or three passwords.

IN PRACTICE: Creating Memorable Complex Passwords

Many users complain about complex passwords because they don't know what to choose, and when they finally stumble upon a combination of characters worthy of the "complex" qualification, they can't remember them the next day. This brings two negatives to the table: users are frustrated (and more prone to spend their time complaining about the policy than embracing it) and the company's help desk costs rise because passwords need to be reset and accounts need to get unlocked. But it does not have to be this way! By offering proactive training, companies can, if not eradicate the situation entirely, at least bring it down to a reasonable level.

The first step consists of asking users to come up with a sentence, a quote, or a line from a movie or song that means something to them, but is not readily associated with them. For the sake of the example, I will take the following lines from the musical "Oklahoma":

"Oh, what a beautiful morning! Oh what a beautiful day!"

Hey, if I am going to start my day by entering a password, it may as well be something cheerful!

Now that I have my quote, I will keep only the first letter of each word. Here is what I have:

Owabm!Owabd!

Not a bad start! I already have 12 characters, upper and lowercase characters, and 2 ASCII characters.

▶▶ CONTINUED ON NEXT PAGE

15

> ▶▶ **CONTINUED**
>
> Now let's replace the two Os by zeros. This gives me the following:
>
> 0wabm!0wabd!
>
> Done. This took about 30 seconds to come up with, and it is a secure password that I can remember, because I can remember the song—or at least those two lines in the song. Mission accomplished!
>
> A side benefit of training your users to be able to create passwords that are easy to remember is that they will not be tempted to write them down. Writing a password down should be a violation of the password policy. Writing down passwords is a huge security hole. Consider this: More than 90 percent of all network penetration evolves into escalation to full admin rights! A lot of users say that "there is nothing on my computer" but fail to understand that network access is all that an experienced hacker needs.

Password Review

The password management policy should address monitoring compliance with password characteristics. Regular password audits should be conducted, as should responsibility for who conducts them. Assuming that violations will be found, the policy needs to address the consequences (which may range from training to termination) as well as who is responsible for communicating with the violator.

Protecting Information

Large organizations have the resources to weather a storm. Small businesses are extremely vulnerable to the slightest change in the business climate and are disproportionately affected by negative events. Many small businesses fail because of loss or misuse of information. Not unlike a large organization, small businesses have a responsibility to protect information. Client records, financial and accounting information, intellectual property, contact lists, e-mail correspondence, and payroll are but a few of the information assets that must be protected. The first item that must be addressed in this policy is information classification.

Is Classification Really Necessary?

Yes! This is an area where the only difference between a small and large organization literally is the size and volume. All businesses have information

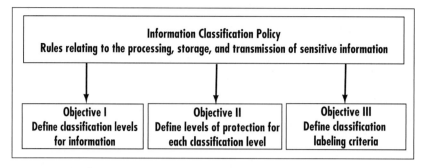

FIGURE 15.7 Information classification policy overview.

of varying degrees of sensitivity. *Information classification* is the organization of information assets according to its sensitivity to disclosure. Classification is a reflection of who should have access to the information. The natural outcome of the classification process is instructions on who can access the asset, how the asset is to be used, what security measures need to be in place, and the way the asset should ultimately be disposed of or destroyed.

Classification does not need to be complicated. Most small businesses need only three levels: confidential, restricted, and public.

Confidential *Confidential information* is meant to be kept secret and limited to only a small circle of authorized individuals. In a small business, this is often the owners or partners. The key characteristic of confidential information is that loss, corruption, or unauthorized disclosure would cause significant financial, reputational, or legal damage to the organization. Confidential information may include personnel information, business strategies, financial positions, laboratory research, or in pre-patent product schematics.

Restricted Organizations use *restricted information* internally to conduct company business. The information may relate to the organization itself or a third party. Examples include policy documents, procedure manuals, nonsensitive client or vendor information, employee lists, and organizational announcements.

Public *Public information* is specifically intended for the public at-large. Examples include published white papers, product documentation, and marketing materials.

Information Labeling

We use labels to communicate the sensitivity of information. Labels can take many forms: electronic, print, audio, visual. To protect information, classification level labels need to be as clear and universally understood as a skull and crossbones poison symbol or a traffic stop sign. In electronic form, the classification should be a part of the document name, e.g, "F11 Airplane Plan Engine Drawing—CONFIDENTIAL." On written or printed documents, the classification label should be clearly marked on the outside of the document as well as in either the document header or footer. Media, such as backup tapes, should be clearly labeled with words and, where appropriate, symbols.

Information Protection

The main objective of classification labels is to specify who should have access to each level of information as well as how the information is to be treated. Let's look at suggested criteria for each level.

This policy applies to electronic and written confidential information:

- *Access:* Documents classified as confidential are restricted to ownership unless otherwise authorized.

- *Storage:* Documents classified as confidential will be stored in separate folders with restricted access control lists. Printed information must be kept in locked cabinets.

- *Transmission:* Documents classified as confidential must be encrypted prior to external transmission.

- *Disposal:* All media that has confidential information must be destroyed prior to disposal. Printed information must be shredded.

This policy applies to electronic and written restricted information:

- *Access:* Documents classified as restricted are limited to company employees unless otherwise authorized.

- *Storage:* Documents classified as restricted will be stored in clearly identified folders with employee only access control lists. Printed information must not be stored in public areas.

- *Transmission:* Documents classified as restricted must be reviewed and authorized by management prior to external transmission.

- *Disposal:* All media that has restricted information must be destroyed prior to disposal. Printed information must be shredded.

This policy applies to electronic and written public information:

- *Access:* Documents classified as public are intended to be made available to the public at-large. Prior to release, care should be taken to ensure that the documents do not contain confidential or restricted information. All public documents should be professional in appearance and reflect well on the organization.

■ *Storage:* Documents classified as public will be stored in clearly identified folders. Care should be taken not to mix public information with restricted or confidential information. Outdated information should be removed.

■ *Transmission:* Documents classified as public must be transmitted in a professional manner. All public transmissions such as mailings, advertisements, and Web postings must be approved by management. The use of UCE /SPAM to distribute company information is expressly forbidden.

■ *Disposal:* All media that has public information should be removed when it becomes outdated. If at all possible, the media should be recycled.

IN PRACTICE: Dumpster Diving

Dumpster diving is the legal practice of rummaging through trash, whether commercial or residential, to find items of use that have been discarded. This can lead to a serious breach of security. When dumpster diving, intruders look for:

• Phone lists—Useful in social engineering attacks.

• Memos—Reveal activities inside the target organization.

• Calendars of events—Alerts the intruder as to when everyone will be elsewhere and not logged into the system. Best time to break in.

• System manuals and packing crates—Tell the intruders about new systems that might not yet be hardened.

• Printouts—Source code, customer lists, account names and numbers, network maps—a virtual treasure trove of information.

• Disks, tapes, CD-ROMs—Media with sensitive information that may not have been sanitized.

Sounds silly? Perhaps, but consider this true story of dumpster diving in Texas. By mistake, a Blockbuster employee discarded 90 pages of customer information, including credit card numbers, in a trash bin behind the store. According to police reports, thieves went "dumpster diving," probably in search of discarded movies, and found instead a wealth of store records.

15

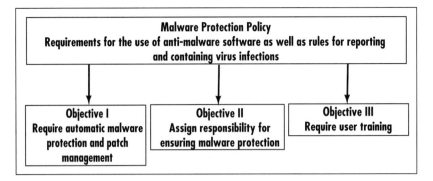

FIGURE 15.8 Malware protection policy overview.

Protecting from Malware

Viruses, worms, Trojans, and spyware are nasty and dangerous intruders. Collectively, they make up a class of software known as malware. Malware is shorthand for <u>malicious software</u>.

Viruses, Worms, Trojans, and Spyware, Oh My!

We defined this insidious class of malicious software back in Chapter 8, but this information bears repeating!

- A virus is a self-replicating program that spreads by infecting other programs. In other words, it needs a host on the target machine. An infamous example is the Melissa virus, which spread across the world attached to Microsoft Word documents sent as e-mail attachments.

- A worm is a piece of malicious code that can spread from one computer to another without requiring a host file to infect. Worms represent a greater threat than viruses and are characterized by their being designed to exploit known vulnerabilities. Infamous examples of worms are Nimda (admin in reverse), Slammer, and Code Red.

- Spyware is a relatively newer type of malware. Spyware is code that is installed on users' machines without their consent, usually via a legitimate download, or what is perceived by the user as a legitimate download. Once installed, spyware can track all Web surfing activity (and report on it to its masters), create a profile of shopping habits and preferences for a given user, hijack the browser so that the start page is redirected to another page than the one originally set up by the user, disallow access to some Internet content against the user's wishes, and so forth. Spyware is at best an invasion of users' privacy, and at worst no less than a Denial of Service attack.

- Trojan horses are potentially destructive programs that masquerade as legitimate and benign applications. For example, a user downloads what she thinks is a simple computer game. She is unaware that, although the game is fully functional, it really served as a conduit for the download of nefarious code. One of the typical activities attributed to Trojans is to open connections for an outside attacker through the use of listening ports. If a RAT (Remote Access Trojan) was downloaded, the attacker will be notified once it is installed, and will be able to take over control of the infected machine. In fact, many hackers will tell you that once they've successfully installed a RAT on a target machine, they have more actual control over that machine than the very person seated at that same machine! Examples of Trojan tools include Back Orifice and Sub-Seven, among many others.

- Key loggers are applications that run discreetly on a target machine and record each and every key entry that takes place in a session. That way, an attacker simply has to bring up that text file with all the recorded keystrokes and harvest such information as user names and passwords.

Protection Requirements

All computer systems should have antivirus protection software installed, maintained, and monitored. As an additional layer of defense, e-mail servers should have virus-scanning software to scan e-mail prior to being passed to the client. The label *antivirus software* is misleading as most antivirus software packages now protect against viruses, worms, and Trojans. Antivirus software works by scanning the contents of files to detect malicious signatures. If the software finds an instance of malware, it will delete or quarantine it. Because hundreds of instances of malware are released each month, all antivirus software must be updated regularly with the latest signature definitions so that the software can catch the latest viruses. The program should be configured to automatically download the latest definitions and programs from the Internet. Even though this can be an automatic process, it isn't "set and forget." A host of issues can arise, including being unable to connect to the vendor, a subscription lapse, or even a user uninstalling or disabling the program. The malware protection policy should assign responsibility for ensuring that the antivirus software is functioning correctly.

What About Spyware? Unfortunately, most antivirus programs do not look for spyware. Spyware has transitioned from being a nuisance to being a very real threat. According to the National Cyber Security Alliance, a staggering 91 percent of computer users have spyware on their computers

15

that can cause extremely slow performance, excessive pop-up ads, or hi-jacked home pages. In addition to antivirus software, small businesses need to require by policy antispyware software.

Don't Forget About the Users

Users must be instructed not to circumvent these controls under any circumstances. Users must also be trained in how they can minimize the threat by not playing games online, downloading software, music, screensavers or even sending warm and fuzzy greeting cards.

Recently, users who were sent greeting cards from **www.friendgreetings.com** got more than they bargained for. When they clicked on the link to access the card sent to them, an ActiveX control launched a setup program. In order to access the card, the recipient had to accept the installation and agree to the EULA (End User Licensing Agreement). The *card* they downloaded was actually a mass-mailer, which in turn e-mailed itself to all the contacts in the recipient's address book. Ironically, after this routine was completed, the users didn't even receive the one thing they were after—the card itself.

Patch Management

Worms and Trojans exploit known weaknesses in operating systems and applications. Having the latest antivirus software installed is not enough. Business must remain vigilant and continually patch their systems against discovered vulnerabilities. The last part of this policy should address patch management.

The Importance of Proactive Patch Management The importance of being proactive in patch management cannot be stressed enough. There have been several widely-publicized attacks and vulnerabilities related to Microsoft software. Many organizations with proactive security patch management in place were not affected by these attacks, because they acted on information that Microsoft made available in advance of the attack.

Table 15.2 shows several malware attacks along with the date of the attack. In each case, an Microsoft bulletin (MSRC) had previously been released that identified the vulnerability and described how to prevent future exploits of it. The last column in the table, *Days Available Before Attack,* lists the number of days that organizations had to implement the MSRC recommendations and avoid the future attack.

Being proactive does not mean being foolish or impulsive. Even though Table 15.2 demonstrates the importance of timely patch management, it is still important to evaluate the patch and test it before distribution

TABLE 15.2 Historical attack examples and related MSRC bulletins. (Source: Microsoft Corporation)

Attack Name	Date Publicly Discovered	MSRC Severity	MSRC Bulletin	MSRC Bulletin Date	Days Available Before Attack
Trojan.Kaht	May 5, 2003	Critical	MS03-007	Mar 17, 2003	49
SQL Slammer	Jan 24, 2003	Critical	MS02-039	Jul 24, 2002	184
Klez-E	Jan 17, 2002	*	MS01-020	Mar 29, 2001	294
Nimda	Sept 18, 2001	*	MS00-078	Oct 17, 2000	336
Code Red	Jul 16, 2001	*	MS01-033	Jun 18, 2001	28

if at all possible. A number of small businesses outsource this function to an IT shop. All the more reason to have a policy that specifies how often new patches should be evaluated, how they should be tested, who should make the implementation decision, and who should actually perform the implementation.

FYI: SQL Slammer Slams Systems

According to the International Computer Science Institute, at approximately 9:30 P.M. Pacific Time on Friday, January 24, 2003, SQL Slammer caused a dramatic increase in network traffic worldwide. An analysis of the SQL Slammer worm shows:

- The worm required roughly 10 minutes to spread worldwide, making it by far the fastest worm to date.
- In the early stages, the number of compromised hosts doubled in size every 8.5 seconds.
- At its peak (achieved approximately three minutes after the worm was released), it scanned the net at over 55 million Internet Protocol (IP) addresses per second.
- It infected at least 75,000 servers and probably considerably more.
- Microsoft released a patch 184 days prior to the attack.

For more information: "The Spread of the Sapphire/Slammer Worm" can be found at **www.cs.berkeley.edu/~nweaver/sapphire/**.

15

Securing Remote Access

Remote access is increasing in popularity, especially in small businesses. Why? One reason is that small businesses by definition have a relatively small number of employees. These employees may often be away from the office tending to the needs of clients or require access during traditional nonbusiness hours. A salesperson may need to access customer files, check inventory, place orders, or read e-mail. A physician may need access to patient records, digital images, or schedules. A repairman may need to access work orders. Whatever the reason, we need to make sure that the channel into the network is secure and limited to authorized users. The first issue the policy must address is who is going to be allowed remote access, under what conditions, and with whose authorization.

Extending the Internal Network

Remote users are an extension of the internal network both logically and physically. The systems they connect from must be secured in the same manner that internal systems are secured. This means that they should be up-to-date with operating system and security patches, be protected from malware and spyware, have strong password and authentication policies, be restricted from unauthorized users, and have only company-approved software and hardware devices.

Many small businesses allow employees to connect from their personal home systems. The remote access policy must address if this is allowable; if so, requirements for the home system must be specified. Expectation in regard to the security configuration must be clearly defined.

How the connection is made is another area that should be clarified in policy. The accepted standard is to use a virtual private network (VPN). The policy should specify who is responsible for installing, configuring, and maintaining the connection. The VPN connection requires an Internet

FIGURE 15.9 Remote access policy overview.

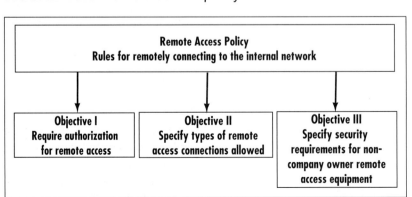

connection. Internet connections come in a variety of flavors, including dial-up, DSL, cable, and satellite. The policy should address the type of Internet connected allowed, who pays for the connection, and if the connection must be used exclusively for business purposes.

Watch Out for Wireless It is very common for home systems to be connected to a wireless network. According to In-Stat, the wireless market will grow from $1.8 billion in 2002 to $5.3 billion in 2007. North America, led by the U.S., will continue to lead in overall home networks through 2007. The total number of installed home networks will grow from 9.2 million in both the U.S. and Canada in 2002 to over 28 million by the end of 2007. An unsecured wireless network should never be allowed to connect to a company network or store any company information.

> ## FYI: Wireless HotSpots
>
> Wireless at home isn't the only worry. Wireless HotSpots are all the rage. A "hotspot" is a specific geographic location in which an access point provides public wireless broadband network services to mobile visitors through a WLAN. You can find hotspots at libraries, schools, hotels, motels, resort RV parks and campgrounds, airports, cafes, coffee shops, and restaurants. The Wi-Fi-FreeSpot™ Directory is a listing of Wi-Fi enabled locations that offer free wireless high-speed Internet access. For more information, see **www.wififreespot.com**.

Controlling Change

One aspect of IT that remains constant is that a network can remain a useful tool for a company only if it evolves hand-in-hand with that company. As users' needs grow and change, so does the network. The network is a tool that allows users not only to accomplish their professional tasks but to accomplish them in a more efficient and cost-effective way. As a flip side to that coin, users—and companies as a whole—have become more and more dependant on the "health" and availability of the network. This places network support personnel in a conundrum of sorts, in that on the one hand they are obviously concerned about keeping a network as stable as possible, while on the other hand they must apply security patches, update operating systems, and install new features and software, which potentially threatens the network stability they work so hard to achieve and maintain. *Change control* is an internal procedure by which only authorized changes are made to software, hardware, network access privileges, or business processes.

15

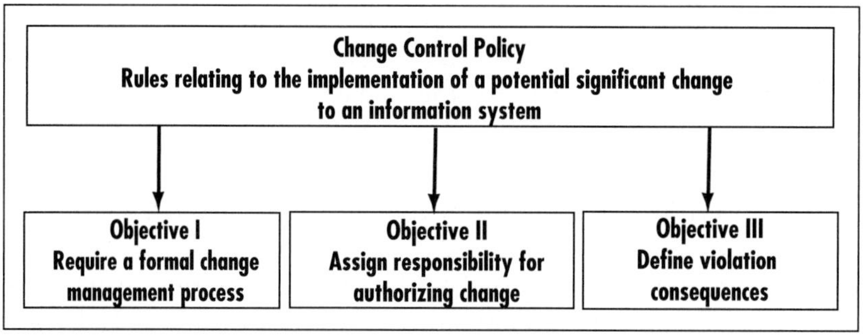

FIGURE 15.10 Change control policy overview.

Why Does a Small Business Need a Change Control Policy?

Change control is perhaps even more important for a small business than a multinational corporation. Small businesses are more likely to depend on only one or two systems to provide an array of services. If they lose access to a server that hosts a critical application, a service (e-mail), or a printer, all work could halt. The other issue to consider is that small businesses often outsource IT work. They may not always hire the same technician or even the same company to do the work. By policy, providing a standard set of change management criteria ensures that everyone is using the same process.

Change Management Process You may remember the three-phase change management process from Chapter 8: assessment, logging, and communication. These three processes should be referenced in policy.

The first phase of the change control process is a formal assessment of the existing situation, the goal of the change, and the impact of the change. Based on those three criteria, a plan can be created to map the proper course of action that will need to be followed. Someone (person or role) must be assigned responsibility for authorizing change.

Once a change has been authorized, phase two begins—logging. The following information should be documented for all changes:

- What was the system state prior to the change?
- What were the reasons that prompted the change?
- Specifically, what changes were made?
- What was the system state after the change?
- Was the change successful?

- If not, how was the system recovered?

- Date and time of the change.

- Name and contract information of the implementer.

The third phase is communication. All users impacted by the change must be notified.

Finally, the change control policy should also clearly explain the disciplinary actions that will occur if the policy is violated. A violation of the change control policy can have a disastrous impact on the stability and availability of a network, and should never be taken lightly.

Data Backup and Recovery

Information security is all about protecting data confidentiality, integrity, and availability. Data backup is a double-edged sword. While the benefits are immense, we introduce yet another media that must be secured and protected.

Business Depends upon the Ability to Access Data

If all of a company's critical information is located on a single server (true for so many small businesses) with no backup strategy in place, and that server crashes, the data may be lost forever. This can represent the end of a company. Backing up data is the act of making a copy—usually on removable media—of existing corporate data for archival and potential recovery purposes.

FIGURE 15.11 Data backup and recovery policy overview.

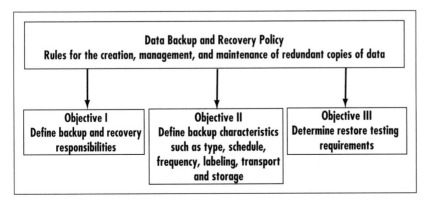

15

Types of Backups

Most backup utilities support five methods of backing up data, as shown in Table 15.3.

Storage of Backup Media

It is obvious that the same information that is deemed "confidential" that exists on the network also exists on the backup media. Therefore, it is imperative to design a storage policy that requires the same level of security for the backup media as the original media. The risk is real that the backup media, if left unattended and unsecured, could be stolen by a malicious third party. Just as real is that the media could be misplaced or discarded. Imagine needing to restore a file and having the backup media missing.

Five Cardinal Rules of Backup Media

1. Backup media should be secured from man-made and environmental damage.

2. Backup media should be stored in a different physical location than the original source.

3. Backup media should be labeled.

4. Backup media should be transported in secure containers.

5. Backup media should never be left unattended during transport.

TABLE 15.3 Five methods of data backup.

Copy backup	A *copy backup* copies all selected files but does not mark each file as having been backed up.
Daily backup	A *daily backup* copies all selected files that have been modified the day the daily backup is performed but does not mark each file as having been backed up.
Full backup	A *full backup* copies all selected files and marks each file as having been backed up.
Incremental backup	An *incremental backup* backs up only those files created or changed since the last backup and marks each file as having been backed up.
Differential backup	A *differential backup* copies files created or changed since the last full backup but does not mark each file as having been backed up.

FYI: Bank of America Confirms Lost Data Tapes

Bank of America confirmed that on January 25, 2005, a small number of computer data tapes were lost during shipment to a backup data center. The missing tapes contained U.S. federal government charge card program customer and account information.

Federal law enforcement officials were immediately contacted when the tapes were discovered missing. Bank of America worked closely with law enforcements officials to investigate the matter. The investigation found no evidence of foul play. The tapes are presumed misplaced.

"We deeply regret this unfortunate incident," said Barbara Desoer, Global Technology, Service & Fulfillment executive for Bank of America. "The privacy of customer information receives the highest priority at Bank of America, and we take our responsibilities for safeguarding it very seriously." (Source: Bank of America press release.)

Testing Restoration

The policy should include a section for test restores. The policy should begin with the requirement that restore procedures be fully documented. It should then go on to specify a test restore schedule. There are three very important reasons for testing the restoration process. The first is to ensure that the backup media and the backup device are working properly. The second is that the time to hone your restore skills is not when you are under the pressure of a disaster. The third is to make sure that the data expected to be on the tape is actually there. Test restorations provide the opportunity to practice the process in a nonstressful environment. As in all things related to security, *"An ounce of prevention is worth a pound of cure."*

Summary

In this chapter, we reviewed the types of policies recommended for the unique environment of small businesses. It is important that small businesses adopt policies and procedures that are reasonable in scope, cost effective, and meaningful. They should be drafted carefully and supported by training. Training and awareness programs are essential to positive adoption. We have illustrated that policy implementation is the basis of a secure environment.

15

It can't be stressed enough that everyone involved in a small business (including contractors) must assume responsibility for information security. They need to understand that the confidentiality, integrity, and availability of critical information cannot be assured without their active participation in maintaining a healthy, stable, and secure environment. Even though security has become a hot topic in the media, many users still don't know what viruses or worms are—let alone a remote access Trojan—and don't know that following a link to a site can bring hacking tools to the inside of the corporate network on the back stream of an apparently legitimate connection. The key to understanding is education, training, and awareness. Small businesses are the engine of our economy. Sound security policies, practices, and procedures will keep the small business engine running smoothly.

Businesses are stewards of information. Customers, patients, students, employees, and others willingly provide information to businesses upon the premise that the information will be protected. Shareholders, bankers, and entrepreneurs make significant investments upon the same principle. They have every right to believe that the stewards are committed to ensuring the confidentiality, integrity, and availability of their information and investments. Private and public sector organizations of all sizes, as well as those of us who provide advice and counsel, have a moral obligation to honor and uphold the public trust.

Test Your Skills

MULTIPLE CHOICE QUESTIONS

1. Which of the following is true about small businesses?
   A. Small businesses can fall under a federal mandate that governs how they handle protected information.
   B. Small businesses are too small to fall under any federal mandates.
   C. All small businesses are regulated by the Small Business Security Act when it comes to safeguarding protected information.
   D. All of the above are true.

2. Which of the following should be an element of a confidentiality policy?
   A. Agreement to share the information with whoever asks.
   B. Acknowledgement of the lack of obligation of confidentiality.
   C. Agreement to not improperly use the information.
   D. Understanding that company information does not have to be returned at the end of employment.

3. Companies should have an Internet use policy because:

   A. ill-informed Internet access can bring harm to the network security

   B. Internet access should be granted to employees for business reasons only

   C. both A and B

   D. neither A nor B

4. Employees should be made aware that their online activities:

   A. can never impact the company

   B. are private because they are private citizens first and foremost

   C. will never be monitored, because that is against the law

   D. can be monitored by the company

5. Which of the following fall under the "Internet use" category?

   A. Web browsing

   B. FTP

   C. Instant Messaging

   D. all of the above

6. Which of the following is an objective of a sound e-mail use policy?

   A. protecting the company from appropriate use of e-mail

   B. defining acceptable use of company e-mail

   C. forbidding encryption for confidential e-mails

   D. teaching how to spoof an e-mail "from" field

7. Personal messages:

   A. should be allowed to be sent anytime using company-provided e-mail solutions

   B. can be sent using company-provided e-mail solutions as long as they come in a ratio of 1 to 10

   C. sent using company-provided e-mail solutions can imply the company's legal responsibility

   D. all of the above

15

8. Which of the following are valid objectives of an incident reporting and response policy?
    A. define what an incident is
    B. require an incident response plan
    C. define incident response criteria
    D. all of the above

9. Which of the following can be put at risk in the case of occurrence of a security incident?
    A. data confidentiality
    B. data integrity
    C. data availability
    D. all of the above

10. When it comes to incident response, small businesses should:
    A. always have a dedicated incident response team
    B. know who should be notified in case of an incident
    C. decide what to do about the problem only at the time it occurs
    D. not worry about the severity level of the incident

11. Which of the following statements about passwords and small businesses is true?
    A. Passwords are not required for small businesses as they are not truly at risk.
    B. Passwords should never be changed.
    C. Password policy compliance should be monitored and audited.
    D. Passwords should be shared between all interchangeable employees.

12. Passwords for small businesses should be at least:
    A. 4 characters
    B. 5 characters
    C. 7 characters
    D. 8 characters

13. Complex passwords are passwords that include:
    A. uppercase characters, lowercase characters, and numbers
    B. dictionary words
    C. ASCII characters only
    D. the user's name

14. The objectives of an information protection policy include:

    A. defining classification levels for information

    B. defining levels of protection for each classification level

    C. neither A nor B

    D. both A and B

15. Small businesses:

    A. do not need an information protection policy because they are too small.

    B. should have an information protection policy only if they have been in operation for more than 10 years

    C. should classify information regardless of the size of the business

    D. should not bother classifying information because that's only a concern for medium- and big-sized businesses

16. Information labeling:

    A. is the same as information classification

    B. is a way to communicate the sensitivity of information

    C. is a way to hide the sensitivity of information.

    D. should never be a part of the document name when in electronic format

17. To protect against malware, a small business should:

    A. install antivirus software on servers and workstations

    B. install the latest Trojans and spyware on all equipment

    C. never, under any circumstances, download a file or open an e-mail attachment

    D. update the antivirus software once a month

18. Which of the following statements about remote access policies and small businesses is true?

    A. All users should have remote access to the corporate network.

    B. All users should be automatically authorized to gain remote access to the corporate network.

    C. The types of remote access connections allowed should be specified.

    D. No outside contractors should be allowed remote access to the network.

15

19. Which of the following should be included in a change management process?

    A. What was the system state prior to the change?

    B. What were the reasons that prompted the change?

    C. Was the change successful?

    D. all of the above

20. A sound backup policy should include which of the following?

    A. the name of all the employees, since everyone is responsible for backups

    B. type of backups being run and restore rights

    C. the frequency of backups, as opposed to the schedule of backups

    D. none of the above

EXERCISES

Exercise 15.1: Small Business Resources

1. Security is a challenge for small businesses. Fortunately, there are multiple resources specifically for this purpose. Each of the following organizations offers security advice to small businesses.

   • U.S. Small Business Administration found at **www.sba.gov**

   • NIST Small Business Center found at **sbc.nist.gov**

   • U.S. Federal Trade Commission found at **www.ftc.gov**

   • Internet Security Alliance found at **www.isaalliance.org**

2. Visit each site and search for resources for designing, implementing, or maintaining a secure small business environment. Document your findings.

Exercise 15.2: Defining a Contract

1. Find a legal definition of a contract.

2. Make a list of the contractual obligations that you currently have.

3. Choose one of the obligations and document the penalties for noncompliance.

4. What should the penalty be for violating a confidentiality agreement?

Exercise 15.3: Acceptable Use Do's and Don'ts

1. Create a list of at least five acceptable uses for the workstations in your computer lab.

2. Create a list of at least five nonacceptable uses for the workstations in your computer lab.

3. Locate your school's acceptable use policy and compare it to your lists. Are there any items on your lists that are not on the acceptable use policy? What would be the benefit to the school of adding the additional items?

Exercise 15.4: Instant Messaging (IM)

1. Do you use IM? If not, seek out someone who does.

2. List the reasons why you use IM.

3. List the potential security and privacy issues with IM.

4. What measures can you take to protect your account? Hint: Access the AOL Instant Messenger home page (**www.aim.com**) and search on security.

5. Do you believe the benefits outweigh the risks?

6. Would you advise a small business to use IM?

Exercise 15.5: Cost of E-mail Hoaxes

1. The costs and risks associated with hoaxes may not seem to be that high, and they aren't when you consider only one hoax on one machine. However, if you consider everyone who receives a hoax, that small cost gets multiplied into some pretty significant costs. Assume that the cost of an employee is $50 per hour. If ten recipients spend one minute each reading a hoax e-mail, what is the cost of the hoax?

2. If each of the ten recipients forwards the hoax to ten people and they all take one minute to read the e-mail, what is the cost of the hoax?

3. If each of the hundred recipients forwards the hoax to ten people and they all take one minute to read the e-mail, what is the cost of the hoax?

15

Exercise 15.6: Password Policy

Evaluate the strength (high, medium, low) of each of the following passwords. Explain your answer. Criteria should include all of the factors listed in the password management section of this chapter.

- Gogirl
- J0livesinN.J.
- Canyoukeepasecret
- *gfhr%skk##
- Pa$$word

Exercise 15.7: Backup Strategy

Which backup methodology does the statement describe?

1. Backs up all files created that day.

2. Backs up only those files created or changed since the last full or incremental backup.

3. Restoring files and folders requires that you have the last normal as well as the last of this type of backup.

4. Copies all selected files and marks each file as having been backed up.

5. Copies all selected files but does not mark each file as having been backed up.

PROJECTS

Project 15.1: Malware Protection Cost Benefit Analysis

Your small business has 15 employees. Your network has 10 desktops, 5 laptops, and 3 servers. All are Microsoft Windows-based.

1. Research and propose a centrally managed anti-malware solution. Be sure to include products that address both malware and spyware.

2. Calculate the cost of purchasing, installing, maintaining, and supporting the products annually.

3. Research how likely it is that a nonprotected computer will get a virus. Annualize the answer.

4. Estimate the cost to your business to have a computer infected. Detail your calculations.

5. Multiple the cost of an infected computer times the number of occurrences expected annually.

6. Compare this cost of infection to the cost of the control (Step 2 above). Is the control worth the investment?

Project 15.2: Remote Access

Your small business has 15 employees. Your network has 10 desktops, 5 laptops, and 3 servers. All are Microsoft Windows-based.

1. Your laptop users travel extensively. What can you do to ensure that their computers stay up-to-date with virus definitions?

2. Your laptop users often stay in hotels where they connect to the Internet. What can you do to protect the information stored on their laptops?

3. Two of your employees work from home using company workstations. They need access to company data all day long. How are you going to connect them? What can you do to protect the workstations from harm?

4. Based upon recommendations in Steps 1-3, author a remote access policy. Include in the policy how remote systems will be audited, how often they will be audited, and by whom.

Project 15.3: Writing End-User Policies

1. Of the policies discussed in this chapter, decide which are appropriate for distribution to all users. Write a brief synopsis of each.

2. Create a cover sheet for the end-user policy booklet explaining why information security and policies are important. Include the synopsis of each policy.

3. Write a one-paragraph statement that asserts the employees' commitment to honor and obey the policies. This is the statement they will be required to sign.

15

Case Study

Department Of Justice
Northern District of California
United States Attorney
11th Floor, Federal Building
450 Golden Gate Avenue, Box 36055
San Francisco, California 94102
Tel: (415) 436-7200
Fax: (415) 436-7234

Former IT Manager of Software Firm Indicted on Computer Crime Charges

The United States Attorney's Office for the Northern District of California announced that the former Information Technology Manager of Creative Explosions, Inc., a Silicon Valley software firm, was indicted today by a federal grand jury on charges that he gained unauthorized access to the computer system of his former employer, reading e-mail of the company's president and damaging the company's computer network. Creative Explosions, Inc., is based in Scotts Valley, California.

The indictment charges Roman Meydbray, 27, of San Jose, California, with two counts of unlawful access to stored communications and one count each of intentionally causing damage to a computer and unauthorized access to a computer, recklessly causing damage. An affidavit filed in support of a search warrant alleges that Mr. Meydbray deleted a domain page of Creative Explosions and made configuration changes to e-mail servers that caused e-mail to be rejected.

According to the indictment, Mr. Meydbray was employed by Creative Explosions from November 2001 to November 7, 2003, originally as Information Technology Manager and then as Network Manager. Creative Explosions is a software development company that produces and sells software programs that enable users to create high quality multimedia websites. The indictment alleges that less than two weeks after the company terminated his employment, Mr. Meydbray gained unauthorized access into Creative Explosions' computer system to change passwords on e-mail accounts, read e-mail of its president, and intentionally and recklessly cause damage.

▶▶ CONTINUED ON NEXT PAGE

> **» CONTINUED**
>
> The maximum statutory penalty for the counts of unlawful access to stored communications and causing reckless damage on a computer is five years in prison. The maximum penalty for intentionally causing damage to a computer is ten years in prison. Each offense also carries a maximum fine of $250,000 or twice the gross gain or loss whichever is greater; a three year term of supervised release; and $100 mandatory special assessment. An indictment simply contains allegations against an individual and, as with all defendants, Mr. Meydbray must be presumed innocent unless and until convicted.
>
> Mr. Meydbray is expected to make his initial appearance in February 2005 before a U.S. Magistrate Judge in San Jose, but a date has not been set yet.
>
> The prosecution is the result of an investigation by the Federal Bureau of Investigation's Cyber Crime Squad in Oakland. The investigation was overseen by the Computer Hacking and Intellectual Property (CHIP) Unit of the United States Attorney's Office for the Northern District of California. Mark L. Krotoski is the Assistant U.S. Attorney from the CHIP Unit who is prosecuting the case.
>
> A copy of this press release may be found on the U.S. Attorney's Office's Web site at **www.usdoj.gov/usao/can**. Related court documents and information may be found on the District Court Web site at **www.cand.uscourts.gov** or on **pacer.cand.uscourts.gov**.
>
> 1. Assuming that Creative Explosions has all of the policies discussed in this chapter, list which ones were violated, how, and by whom.
>
> 2. Aside from Mr. Meydbray, do you hold anyone else in the company accountable for this breach?
>
> 3. Research this case and write a synopsis of the current status.

15

Appendix A

Resources for Information Security Professionals

CERIAS: **www.cerias.purdue.edu/**

CERT: **www.cert.org/**

Dept. of Education (FERPA): **www.ed.gov**

Dept. of Health & Human Services (HIPAA): **www.hhs.gov/ocr/hipaa/**

DRI International (Disaster Recovery): **www.drii.org**

FFIEC (GLBA): **www.ffiec.gov**

Information Systems Audit and Control Association (ISACA): **www.isaca.org**

Information Systems Security Association, Inc. (ISSA): **www.issa.org**

Infragard: **www.infragard.net**

International Association for Computer Systems Security, Inc. (IACSS): **www.iacss.com/**

International CPTED Association: **www.cpted.org**

International Information Systems Security Certification Consortium (ISC2): **www.isc2.org**

International Organization for Standardization: **www.iso.org**

National Classification Management Society, Inc.: **www.classmgmt.com/**

National Security Institute: **www.nsi.org/**

NIST Computer Security Resource Center: **csrc.nist.gov/**

NSA Information Assurance: **www.nsa.gov/ia/**

SANS Institute (System Administration, Audit, Network, Security): **www.sans.org**

The Institute of Internal Auditors: **www.theiia.org**

The IT Governance Institute: **www.itgovernance.org**

Appendix B

Employee Information Security Policy Affirmation Agreement

Policy Statement

The [Company]'s intentions for publishing our new Employee Information Security Policies are not to impose restrictions that are contrary to our established culture of openness, trust, and integrity. The [Company] is committed to protecting the public, our employees, partners, and the [Company] itself from illegal or damaging actions by individuals, either knowingly or unknowingly.

The 21st century environment of connected technologies offers many opportunities to malicious or unknowing people from all over the world to anonymously attack, damage, and corrupt vital public information and to disrupt our ability to communicate effectively and accomplish the mission of our organization. Effective security is a civic responsibility and a team effort involving the participation and support of every employee and affiliate who deals with information and/or information systems. It is the responsibility of every employee and affiliate to know, understand, and adhere to these policies, procedures, standards, and guidelines and to conduct their activities accordingly.

This policy statement has been adopted to provide guidance and protection to [Company] employees and to safeguard the information resources of our customers entrusted to us.

The Chairman's Statement

Based on the International Organization for Standardization (ISO) 17799:2000 Standards for Information Security, we have endeavored to create policies that are clear, concise, and easy to understand. We have also taken into consideration the ease of use and accessibility of these documents. It is so very important that these policies do more than dictate another layer of rules and regulations that we all must follow. Our hope is that they are educational and that they speak to the most important aspects of our existence, which are the public good and our employees. I would like to thank you in advance for your support as we do our best to create a secure environment and fulfill our mission.

Sincerely,

John Doe, Chairman

1. Acceptable Use of Information Resources

These rules are in place to protect the public, our employees, and the [Company]. Inappropriate use of our information resources exposes the [Company] to risks, including virus attacks, compromise of network systems and services, and legal issues. [Company] resources are made available to employees to conduct official business. [Company] information resources are not to be used to conduct personal business, business related to outside employment, or for personal benefit. Employees are advised that there should be no expectation of privacy when using any [Company] information resources. Each employee is expected to comply with this policy. Violation of this policy may lead to progressive discipline, up to and including dismissal.

To ensure safety and security:

- Users must not share their user account(s), passwords, Personal Identification Numbers (PIN), Security Tokens (i.e., Smartcard), or similar information or devices used for identification and authorization purposes.

- Users must not attempt to access any data or programs contained on [Company] systems for which they do not have authorization or explicit consent.

- If an employee is sent, delivered, or inadvertently accesses inappropriate or prohibited material, or the material contains confidential information that the employee does not have "need-to-know" access to, or authority to receive; the employee is required to immediately secure the material from view and notify his/her supervisor.

- Users must not make unauthorized copies of copyrighted software.

- Users must not install or use nonstandard software, shareware, or freeware software, including games.

- Users must not attempt to circumvent approved antivirus software or make any changes to accepted configuration of antivirus software.

- Users must not download, install, or run security programs or utilities that reveal or exploit weaknesses in the security of a system.

- Users must report any weaknesses in [Company] computer security, any incidents of possible misuse, or violation of this agreement to their supervisor.

2. Internet Use

In addition to being an excellent resource for information, and a revolutionary way to communicate with the world, the Internet is a rapidly changing and volatile place that can accurately be referred to as "The Wild." These policies are intended to provide guidance and protection, while still making available this useful business tool to [Company] employees.

The following rules apply when using the Internet:

- All software used to access the Internet must be part of the [Company] standard software suite. This software must incorporate all vendor-provided security patches.

- Software for browsing the Internet is provided to authorized users for business and research use only, except where otherwise noted in the incidental use policy.

- Users must not download or install any software from the Internet.

- Nonbusiness-related purchases or sales made over the Internet are prohibited.

- All user activity on the Internet is subject to logging and review.

3. E-mail Use Policy

E-mail use has become the standard method of communication, used in 75 percent of all business communications. E-mail is inherently insecure, and messages can easily be intercepted and read or changed. Additionally, e-mail is the number one doorway to viruses and worms that infect and destroy valuable information. These policies are intended to offer rules of usage that will protect our information.

E-mail use is subject to the following policies:

The following activities are prohibited as they conflict with our Code of Ethics:

- Sending e-mail that is intimidating or harassing.

- Using e-mail for purposes of political lobbying or campaigning.

- Violating copyright laws by inappropriately distributing protected works.

- Posing as anyone other than oneself when sending or receiving e-mail, except when authorized to send messages for another when serving in an administrative support role.

The following activities are prohibited because they impede the functioning of network communications and the efficient operations of electronic mail systems:

- Sending or forwarding chain letters.

- Sending unsolicited messages to large groups except as required to conduct agency business.

- Sending excessively large messages.

- Sending or forwarding e-mail that is likely to contain computer viruses.

- Electronic mail users must not give the impression that they are representing, giving opinions, or otherwise making statements on behalf of [Company].

- Individuals must not send, forward, or receive confidential or sensitive [Company] information through non[Company] e-mail accounts. Examples of non[Company] e-mail accounts include, but are not limited to, Hotmail, Yahoo mail, AOL mail, and e-mail provided by other Internet Service Providers (ISPs).

- Individuals must not send, forward, receive, or store confidential or sensitive [Company] information utilizing non[Company] accredited mobile devices. Examples of mobile devices include, but are not limited to, Personal Data Assistants, two-way pagers, and cellular telephones.

- E-mail messages and Internet sites accessed are not private but are property of the [Company]. The [Company] may print and review e-mail messages and Internet sites accessed by an employee's system.

4. Incidental Use of Information Resources

As a convenience to the [Company] user community, incidental use of information resources is permitted. Only brief and occasional use is considered to be incidental.

The following restrictions on incidental use apply:

- Incidental personal use of electronic mail, Internet access, fax machines, printers, copiers, and so on, is restricted to [Company]-approved users; it does not extend to family members or other acquaintances.

- Incidental use must not result in direct costs to [Company].

- Incidental use must not interfere with the normal performance of an employee's work duties.

- Incidental use of Company information resources must not involve solicitation in any form, must not be associated with any outside business or employment activity, and must not potentially embarrass or offend the [Company], its directors, its stockholders, or its employees.

- Storage of personal e-mail messages, voice messages, files, and documents within [Company] information resources must be nominal.

- All messages, files, and documents—including personal messages, files, and documents—located on [Company] information resources are owned by [Company], may be subject to open records requests, and may be accessed in accordance with this policy.

5. Password Policy

All of the work we are doing at [Company] to secure confidential information will be ineffective if the most important aspect of information security, the daily users of our information resources, have weak passwords. Though we recognize that it is inconvenient at first, having strong passwords is the most important part of your participation. We would like to think of passwords as a "shared secret" between you and [Company] information resources.

The following policies apply to password use:

- All passwords, including initial passwords, must be constructed and implemented according to [Company]-accepted and approved standards. See Guidelines.

- User account passwords must not be divulged to anyone at any time or for any reason.

- If passwords are forgotten or disclosed or if the security of a password is in doubt, the password must be changed immediately by contacting the Help desk.

- Administrators must not circumvent the password policy for the sake of ease of use.

- Whenever possible, users must not circumvent password entry with auto logon, application remembering, embedded scripts, or hard-coded passwords in client software. Exceptions may be made for specific applications (like automated backup) with the approval of the [Company] ISO. In order for an exception to be approved, there must be a procedure to change the passwords.

- Computing devices must not be left unattended without enabling a password-protected screensaver, locking the workstation, or completely logging off of the device.

- If passwords are found or discovered on documents of any kind, the following steps must be taken:
  Take possession of the passwords and protect them.
  Report the discovery to the Help desk.
  Transfer the passwords to an authorized person as directed by the Help desk.

6. Portable Computing Policy

Laptop computers, PDAs, and other portable computing devices are a great convenience and are becoming more and more a part of doing business. They also come with many risks, including ease of theft, operation in unsecured environments, and easily intercepted wireless communications.

To protect our valuable information, users of portable computing devices must follow these rules of use:

- Only [Company]-approved portable computing devices may be used to access [Company] information resources.

- Portable computing devices must be password-protected.

- [Company] data should not be stored on portable computing devices. However, if there is no alternative to local storage, all sensitive [Company] data must be encrypted using approved encryption techniques.

- [Company] data must not be transmitted via wireless to or from a portable computing device unless approved wireless transmission protocols along with approved encryption techniques are utilized.

- All computer systems accessing [Company] resources from any external location must conform to [Company] standards for configuration and connectivity.

- Unattended portable computing devices must be physically secure. This means they must be locked in an office, locked in a desk drawer or filing cabinet, or attached to a desk or cabinet via a cable lock system.

7. Distribution

Following the appropriate posting, current employees shall receive a copy of this policy. New employees shall receive a copy of this policy upon hire.

Each employee shall sign a statement, confirming that his/her copy of this policy has been received and read. The statement (Attachment) shall be filed in the employee's personnel folder.

8. Affirmation Agreement

I certify that I have read and fully understand the [Company] information security policies set forth in this document. I understand and acknowledge my obligations and responsibilities.

I further understand that violation of these policies is subject to disciplinary action up to and including termination for employees and temporaries; a termination of employment relations in the case of contractors or consultants; or dismissal for interns and volunteers. Additionally, individuals may be subject to civil and criminal prosecution.

EMPLOYEE'S NAME:
EMPLOYEE'S ADDRESS:
ASSIGNED UNIT:
COST CENTER:

Social Security #	Employee Signature	Date
__ __		
Witnessed by Supervisor:		Date

9. Standard Definitions

Ownership of Information

All documents generated as a result of any [Company] business activity stored anywhere on or off [Company] premises; and electronic files created, sent, received, or stored on information resources owned, leased, administered, or otherwise under the custody and control of the [Company] are the property of the [Company].

Privacy

Electronic files created, sent, received, or stored on information resources owned, leased, administered, or otherwise under the custody and control of the [Company] are not to be considered private.

Information Resources

Any and all computer printouts, online display devices, magnetic storage media, and all computer-related activities involving any device capable of receiving e-mail, browsing Web sites, or otherwise capable of receiving, storing, managing, or transmitting electronic data including, but not limited to, mainframes, servers, personal computers, notebook computers, handheld computers, personal digital assistants (PDAs), pagers, distributed processing systems, telecommunication resources including cell phones and voice mail systems, network environments, telephones, fax machines, printers, and service bureaus. Additionally, it is the procedures, equipment, facilities, software, and data that are designed, built, operated, and maintained to create, collect, record, process, store, retrieve, display, and transmit information.

Incidental Use

The use of [Company] information resources for personal use must be infrequent and use only a small amount of an employee's personal time either inside or outside the regular work day. Occasional use of [Company] information resources during an employee's 15-minute break would be considered incidental. Only brief and occasional use is considered to be incidental. Solicitations of any kind are not permitted.

Portable Computing Devices

Portable computing devices include any easily portable device capable of receiving and/or transmitting data to and from IR. These include, but are not limited to, notebook computers, handheld computers, PDAs, pagers, and cell phones.

Electronic Mail (E-mail)

Any message, image, form, attachment, data, or other communication sent, received, or stored within an electronic mail system.

Internet

A global system interconnecting computers and computer networks. The computers and networks are owned separately by a host of organizations, government agencies, companies, and colleges. The Internet is the present "information superhighway."

Intranet

A private network for communications and sharing of information that, like the Internet, is based on TCP/IP, but is accessible only to authorized users within an organization. An organization's intranet is usually protected from external access by a firewall.

World Wide Web

A system of Internet hosts that support documents formatted in HTML (Hyper Text Markup Language), which contain links to other documents (hyperlinks) and to audio, video, and graphic images. Users can access the Web with special applications called browsers, such as Netscape Navigator and Microsoft Internet Explorer.

Information Security Officer

Responsible to the Director of Operations for administering the information security functions within the agency. The ISO is the agency's internal and external point of contact for all information security matters.

Glossary

A

acceptable use agreement A document that supports the security policy and clearly dictates for all employees how they are expected to use information and information systems.

accountability The process of tracing actions to their source. One of the "Five A's" of information security.

accounting The process of logging of access and usage of information or resources. One of the "Five A's" of information security.

administrative controls Information security countermeasures that rely on policies, plans, training, management, and decision making.

assurance Measurement of confidence in a control or activity. One of the "Five A's" of information security.

authentication The process of confirming an identity. One of the "Five A's" of information security.

authorization The process of granting access after proper identification and authentication. One of the "Five A's" of information security.

availability The assurance that systems and information are accessible by authorized users when needed.

B

blackouts Total loss of power.

brownouts Short periods of low voltage in utility lines. Brownouts are also called "voltage sag."

business contingency procedures Alternate methods of operation used when normal operating conditions are not available.

business continuity Covers alternate business processes used throughout the organization prior to full recovery.

business continuity plan (BCP) A plan to ensure the ongoing viability of a business. A BCP forms the backbone of any data recovery effort an organization undertakes following a disaster.

business impact analysis (BIA) The process of determining the impact a disruption has on an organization.

business recovery Covers the process of recovering information systems to their original state.

C

Challenge and Response Protocol (CHAP) An authentication method whereby the remote host that attempts to log on to the secured network is challenged both at the onset and randomly during the connection period. Because the challenge is changed every time it is sent, this is a good protection against man-in-the-middle attacks.

change control An internal procedure by which only authorized changes are made to software, hardware, network access privileges, or business processes.

change drivers Events within an organization that affect culture, procedures, activities, employee responsibilities, and relationships.

CIA triad The three tenets of information security: confidentiality, integrity, and availability.

clear text Text that has not been encrypted and is freely and clearly readable.

confidential information   Information meant to be kept secret and limited to only a small circle of authorized individuals.

confidentiality   The protection of information from unauthorized people, resources, and processes.

containment   Actions required to limit the scope and magnitude of an incident.

control objective   Anticipated outcome of implementing a specific control.

corporate culture   The shared attitudes, values, goals, and practices that characterize a company or organization.

cryptography   The process of transforming plain text into cipher text.

culture of continuity   An organizational environment in which leadership sets a tone of compliance.

D

declassification   Involves reducing the level of classification of an information item. Note that in the military, declassifying does not mean to "lower the classification level." It always means to "remove the classification level."

default deny   Access is unavailable until a rule, control list, or setting is modified to allow access.

designated incident handler   The person—or group of people—officially responsible for responding to, investigating, and overseeing a recovery and documenting the resolution of a particular incident.

digital signature   A hash of a message that uniquely identifies the sender and proves the message hasn't changed since transmission.

disaster   A disruption of normal business functions where the expected time for returning to normalcy would seriously impact the organization's ability to maintain operations.

disaster preparation   Covers what needs to be done by an organization in anticipation of a disaster.

disaster response   Covers what should be done by an organization immediately following a significant incident.

Discretionary Access Control (DAC)   Access control that is at the discretion of the data owner.

due diligence   Actions that demonstrate that an organization has made an effort to create a secure environment.

E

Electronic Protected Health Information (ePHI)   Any type of PHI that is stored, created, and transmitted electronically.

employee affirmation agreement   A document similar to an acceptable user agreement, with an added dimension of informing the user why compliance is necessary.

eradication   Focuses on eliminating a problem once it has happened, but also on eliminating the actual vulnerabilities that allowed the incident to take place.

expected behavior   How users are expected to act on a daily basis.

F

Five A's   The Five A's of information security are accountability, assurance, authentication, authorization, and accounting.

G

gap   A difference between the behavior required by a policy and the behavior that is the standard in the current culture of a company.

group-based access   Access that is granted by function.

guidelines   Similar to suggestions for the best way to accomplish a certain task. They are more dynamic than the other components of a policy and are therefore edited more often.

I

Identifiable Health Information (IHI) The individual items of data that include a patient's current, past, and future health information.

identity-based access Access that is granted by name.

identity theft Consists of gathering enough personal information about a person to impersonate him/her and to defraud the individual and/or the financial institutions through which bank accounts, credit card accounts, and loans are opened.

implementation specifications Detailed descriptions of a method or approach.

incident response plan A roadmap of incident reporting, responding, and recovery procedures.

information asset A definable piece of information that is recognized as having value to an organization.

Information custodians Individuals in charge of maintaining the infrastructure on which the actual information travels and is stored. In most company, the IT department typically will be the information custodians.

information owners Individuals responsible for protecting information.

information security policy A policy that defines how an organization plans to protect its tangible and intangible information assets.

information systems Hardware and software solutions that provide a way and a place to process, store, transmit, and communicate information.

inherent vulnerability A built-in flaw or weakness.

input validation The process of testing an interactive piece of code to see if entering false or malicious code strings instead of the expected information into the interactive application will result in a security issue.

integrity The protection of information or processes from intentional or accidental unauthorized modification.

IPSec A layer-three protocol suite used to secure the Internet Protocol (IP). It is often used in correlation with VPNs.

K

key A secret value in cryptography.

key loggers Either software or hardware solutions that keep track of each and every key tapped on a keyboard in a text file for later retrieval by a hacker.

L

least privilege A principle based on the concept of giving access only to the minimum level of resources/data needed to perform a specific task.

line noise The instance of electrical impulses carried along with standard AC current. Line noise basically creates unwanted interferences that can impair data transmission.

logic bombs A piece of malicious code that lays dormant until a certain triggering event is met. It is then unleashed on the unsuspecting network.

M

malware Malicious software, including viruses, worms, logic bombs, spyware, Trojans, key loggers, and other assorted nefarious code.

Mandatory Access Control (MAC) Access control that is based upon the relationship between the clearance level of the user and the classification level of the information or resources.

Microsoft Challenge and Response Protocol (MS CHAP) Microsoft's version of CHAP. It is considered more secure than the "regular" CHAP.

mobile computing Refers to the use of information resources outside the controlled environment of organizational facilities.

N

need-to-know Having a demonstrated and authorized reason for being granted access to information.

Nonpublic Personal Information (NPI) As defined in the GLBA, protected customer information that includes names, addresses, and phone numbers linked to bank and credit card account numbers, income and credit histories, and social security numbers.

O

offshore organizations Organizations that exist outside the country.

P

physical controls Information security countermeasures that rely on a physical solution to be implemented.

policy A set of rules combined to create a management framework that dictates how an organization will function.

policy audience That portion of an organization directly concerned by the policy. This can range from a couple of people to the entire organization. It may also refer to members of the "extended" organization, such as temporary employees and third-party consultants.

policy definitions Terms that define and clarify terminology used in the policy.

policy enforcement clause The part of the policy where sanctions for failure to comply with the policy are defined.

policy exceptions Defined exceptions to a written and implemented policy.

policy heading Contains all of the logistical information regarding a specific policy area, such as security domain section, subsection, policy number, the name of the organization and of the document, the change control documentation or number, and the signing authority.

policy objective States what the organization is striving to achieve by implementing the policy.

policy statement Focuses on the specifics or details of the policy.

policy statement of purpose The reason why a policy exists. It is designed to give specific guidance to the reader regarding achieving a policy objective.

portable storage devices (PSDs) Transportable devices for storing data.

power surge An incident characterized by an increase in the voltage that powers the electrical equipment.

procedure Provides a method by which a policy is accomplished. Procedures provide the instructions necessary to carry out a policy statement.

public data Data that can be disclosed to the public without any adverse repercussions for a company.

R

reclassification Involves changing the classification level of an information item, either up or down.

recovery The return to full operational status after an incident.

Remote Authentication Dial-In User Service (RADIUS) An open source AAA solution.

AAA stands for Authentication, Authorization, and Accounting. Using a RADIUS server is a way to decide who can log on (authentication) and what they can do once logged on (authorization), and provides a way to record a user's actions once logged on (accounting).

restricted information Business-related information that is to be used internally to conduct company business.

retention The practice of saving information for a specified period of time.

risk assessment The process by which risks are identified and the impact of those risks determined.

role-based access Access that is granted by job/position.

Role-Based Access Control (RBAC) Access control based upon the user's position or role in the company.

rules-based policies Policies that center on operational topics, as opposed to end-user-related topics.

S

secure area An area where business is conducted, and where the assets are protected from both man-made and natural harm.

security awareness An understanding of the actions required to maintain a secure environment.

security champion A vocal proponent of information security who is willing to lead by example.

security incident Any adverse event whereby confidentiality, integrity, and/or availability of an information system (or information itself) is threatened.

security posture An organization's attitude toward information security defined by its default position.

sensitive information Information restricted to those users who have a demonstrated "need to know" (also called protected or privileged information).

service level agreement An agreement between a service provider and a customer that specifically addresses availability of services.

significant roles Positions in an organization's hierarchy that are pivotal to the good functioning of the company. Significant roles include C-level management, department directors, supervisors, and managers.

single-factor authentication An authentication technique that uses only one method to verify a user's identity.

spyware Malicious code that tracks users' online activity. It can also have a more malicious payload that hijacks all browser sessions.

standard operating procedures (SOPs) Established procedures within an organization.

standards Specific minimum requirements in policies. Standards are definite and required.

statement of authority A document that prefaces a group of policies and serves as an introduction to those policies. A statement of authority explains how policies were generated.

system characterization The process of defining the relationships between the physical inventory, the information, the information system, and the organization. It helps define the importance of an information asset to the company.

systems development Code that is created from scratch to create line-of-business applications. This code can be created either in-house or by a third-party.

T

technical controls Information security countermeasures that rely on technical software or hardware to be implemented.

Terminal Access Controller Access Control System (TACACS+) A proprietary solution from Cisco, which is also licensed to other vendors such as HP. TACACS+ servers are an alternative to RADIUS servers. They are used for remote access authentication. TACACS+ is considered more reliable than RADIUS.

threat A potential danger to an asset or resource.

threat analysis The systematic rating of threats based upon associated risks and probability.

threat assessment The identification of types of threats that an organization might be exposed to.

threat probability The likelihood of a threat materializing in a given timeframe, absent appropriate mitigating controls.

threat risk The potential level of impact based upon institutional, industry, and technology knowledge.

Trojan horse A malicious program that masquerades as a functioning, legitimate, and benign application to dupe users into downloading and installing it.

two-wall challenge The two walls are defined as the lack of awareness and the "lack of awareness about the lack of awareness" exhibited by users when it comes to information security policies. In other words, not only do people not know, but they are totally unaware that they do not know, which increases the overall danger to the organization.

V

virtual private network (VPN) The use of an unsecured network such as the Internet to create an encrypted tunnel between the secure network and a remote user. When connected to the secure network via a VPN, a remote user can have up to the same level of access to data and application systems as if they were local to the secure network.

virus A piece of malicious code that requires a host file to install and replicate itself.

voltage variation Fluctuations in voltage.

W

worm A piece of malicious code that self-replicates and targets a known and identified vulnerability.

References

Chapter 1

Boran, Sean. An Overview of Corporate Information Security
WindowsSecurity.com. **http://secinf.net/policy_and_standards/An_overview_of_Corporate_Information_Security_.html** (accessed December 2004).

Centers for Medicare and Medicaid Services. **www.cms.hhs.gov/hipaa/** (accessed December 2004).

Constitution of the United States of America.

Department of Health and Human Services (HIPAA). **www.hhs.goc/ocr/hippa** (accessed November 2004).

Domb, Yoel Rabbi. Business Ethics D'var Torah. Jerusalem College of Technology. **www.besr.org/dvartorah/tezave.html** (accessed December 2004).

Federal Deposit Insurance Company (FDIC). **www.fdic.gov** (accessed November 2005).

Federal Financial Institutions Examination Council (FFIEC). **www.ffiec.gov** (accessed November 2004).

Federal Register. **www.archives.gov/federal_register** (accessed December 2004).

Federal Trade Commission. **www.ftc.gov/privacy/glbact** (accessed December 2004).

FFIEC Information Security IT Examiners Handbook, 2004.

FFIEC Management IT Examiners Handbook, 2004.

Friedman, Hershey. Biblical Foundations of Business Ethics. Action Institute for the Study of Religion and Liberty. **www.acton.org/publicat/m_and_m/2000_spring/friedman.html** (accessed December 2004).

Google. **www.google.com**. (accessed November 2004).

Gramm-Leach-Bliley Act (GLBA), Public Law 106-102, 1999.

Health Insurance Portability and Accountability Act (HIPAA), Public Law

104-191, 1996.

Information Security Policies. University of Florida. **www.it.ufl.edu/ policies/security** (accessed November 2004).

Information Security Policy Guide. State of Texas. **www.dir.state.tx.us/ security/policies/policy_guide.doc** (accessed November 2004).

Krause, Micki CISSP and Harold F. Tipton, CISSP. 2004. *Information Security Management Handbook,* Fifth Edition. Boca Raton, FL: CRC Press, Auerbach Publications.

Merriam Webster Online Dictionary. **www.mirriamwebster.com**. (accessed November 2004).

NIST SP 800-16 Information Technology Security Training Requirements, April 1998.

NIST SP 800-50 Building an Information Technology Security Awareness and Training Program, October 2003.

SANS Institute (Policies). **www.sans.org/resources/policies** (accessed December 2004).

Whitman, Michael and Herbert Mattord. 2003. *Principles of Information Security.* Boston, MA: Thompson.

Chapter 2

Adobe. **www.adobe.com**.

Boran, Sean. An Overview of Corporate Information Security Windows-Security.com. **http://secinf.net/policy_and_standards.An_overview_ of_Corporate_Information_Security.html** (accessed January 2005).

FFIEC Information Security IT Examiners Handbook, 2004.

FFIEC Operations IT Examiners Handbook, 2004.

FFIEC Management IT Examiners Handbook, 2004.

Gramm-Leach-Bliley Act (GLBA), Public Law 106-102, 1999.

Health Insurance Portability and Accountability Act (HIPAA), Public Law 104-191, 1996.

Information Security Policies. University of Florida. **www.it.ufl.edu/ policies/security** (accessed November 2004).

Information Security Policy Guide. State of Texas. **www.dir.state.tx.us/ security/policies/policy_guide.doc** (accessed November 2004).

Krause, Micki CISSP and Harold F. Tipton, CISSP. 2004. *Information Security Management Handbook,* Fifth Edition. Boca Raton, FL: CRC Press, Auerbach Publications.

NIST SP 800-14 Generally Accepted Principles and Practices for Securing

Technology Systems, September 1996.

SANS Institute (Policies). **www.sans.org/resources/policies** (accessed December 2004).

Sarbanes-Oxley Act of 2002, Public Law 107-204.

Chapter 3

FBI Alerts Public to Recent Email Scheme. United States Department of Justice, Federal Bureau of Investigation Press Release 2/22/05.

FBI Internet Crime Complaint Center. **www.ic3.gov** (accessed January 2005).

Frequently Asked Questions: International Standard ISO/IEC 17799:2000 Code of Practice for Information Security Management, November 2002. National Institute for Standards and Technology. **http://csrc. nist.gov/publications/secpubs/otherpubs/reviso-faq.pdf**.

ISO 9000 Quality Management Principles. International Organization for Standardization. **www.iso.org/iso/en/iso9000-14000/iso9000/qmp.html** (accessed December 2004).

ISO/IEC 17799:2000 Information technology - Code of practice for information security management. International Organization for Standardization.

NIST SP 800-14 Generally Accepted Principles and Practices for Securing Technology Systems, September 1996.

NIST SP 800-30 Risk Management Guide for Information Technology Systems, July 2002.

NIST SP 800-60 Guide to Mapping Types of Information and Information Systems to Security Categories, June 2004.

University of Texas Student Charged with Hacking. United States Department of Justice, US Attorney's Office, Western District Texas. **www. utexas.edu/datatheft/usao-11-03-2004.pdf**.

What is a Denial of Service Attack? *Darwin Magazine.* **www.darwinmag. com/learn/curve/column.html?ArticleID=115** (accessed January 2005).

Chapter 4

European Union Initiative eEurope 2005. EUROPA. **www.europa.eu.int/ imdex_en.html** (accessed February 2005).

FFIEC Information Security IT Examiners Handbook, 2004.

FFIEC Operations IT Examiners Handbook, 2004.

FFIEC Management IT Examiners Handbook, 2004.

Gramm-Leach-Bliley Act (GLBA), Public Law 106-102, 1999.

Health Insurance Portability and Accountability Act (HIPAA), Public Law 104-191, 1996.

ISO/IEC 17799:2000 Information technology - Code of practice for information security management. International Organization for Standardization.

The National Strategy to Secure Cyberspace. The White House. **www.whitehouse.gov/pcipb/** (accessed December 2004).

NIST SP 800-14 Generally Accepted Principles and Practices for Securing Technology Systems, September 1996.

NIST SP 800-50 Building an Information Technology Security Awareness and Training Program, October 2003.

Study Supports Controversial Offshore Numbers. Forrester Research. **http://news.com.com/2100-1022-5213391.html** (accessed February 2005).

Sarbanes-Oxley Act of 2002, Public Law 107-204.

The National Strategy to Secure Cyberspace. The White House. **www.whitehouse.gov/pcipb/** (accessed February 2005).

WebEx. **www.webex.com** (accessed February 2005).

Chapter 5

2002 Guide to the Freedom of Information Act. US Department of Justice. **www.usdoj.gov/oip/foi-act.htm** (accessed February 2005).

A Citizen's Guide On Using the Freedom of Information Act and The Privacy Act of 1974 to Request Government Records. Committee on Government Reform and Oversight. **www.tncrimlaw.com/foia_index.html** (accessed February 2005).

The Cuban Missile, 1962: The 40th Anniversary. The National Security Archive. **www.gwu.edu/~nsarchiv/nsa/cuba_mis_cri/index.htm** (accessed February 2005).

Executive Order 12958-Classified National Security Information, as Amended. National Archives. **www.archives.gov/isoo/policy_documents/executive_order_12958_amendment.html** (accessed February 2005).

The Federal Register (FR): Main Page. GPO Access. **www.gpoaccess.gov/fr** (accessed February 2005).

FFIEC Information Security IT Examiners Handbook, 2004.

FFIEC Operations IT Examiners Handbook, 2004.

FFIEC Management IT Examiners Handbook, 2004.

FirstGov. **www.firstgov.gov** (accessed February 2005).

The Freedom of Information Act (FOIA). The National Security Archive. **www.gwu.edu/~nsarchiv/nsa/foia.html** (accessed February 2005).

How to Make a FOIA Request. The National Security Archive. **www.gwu.edu/~nsaarchiv/nsa/foia/howtofoia.html** (accessed February 2005).

Information Management Inventory Guide May 2002. Department of Commerce, New South Wales Government. **www.oit.nsw.gov.au/guidelines/4.3.25a-Im-Inventoty.asp** (accessed February 2005).

ISO/IEC 17799:2000 Information technology - Code of practice for information security management. International Organization for Standardization.

NIST FIPS Standards for Security Categorization of Federal Information Systems, December 2003.

NIST SP 800-14 Generally Accepted Principles and Practices for Securing Technology Systems, September 1996.

NIST SP 800-30 Risk Management Guide for Information Technology Systems, July 2002.

NIST SP 800-47 Security Guide for Interconnecting Information Systems, August 2002.

NIST SP 800-55 Security Metric Guide for Information Technology Systems, July 2003.

NIST SP 800-60 Guide to Mapping Types of Information and Information Systems to Security Categories, June 2004.

Regulations Portal. **www.regulations.gov** (accessed February 2005).

U.S. Department of Justice (FOIA). **www.usdoj.gov/oip/foi-act.htm**.

Whitman, Michael and Herbert Mattord. 2003. *Principles of Information Security.* Boston, MA: Thompson.

Chapter 6

Americans with Disabilities Act (ADA). 42 U.S.C. 12101.

Computer Security Research Center. **http://csrc.nist.gov** (accessed December 2004).

Excite. **www.excite.com/careers_and_education** (accessed February 2005).

Fair Credit Reporting Act (FCRA). 15 U.S.C. 1681.

FFIEC Information Security IT Examiners Handbook, 2004.

FFIEC Operations IT Examiners Handbook, 2004.

FFIEC Management IT Examiners Handbook, 2004.

HotJobs. **hotjobs.yahoo.com** (accessed February 2005).

Human Resources Policy 3.7 Background Checks July 2004. University of Indiana. **www.hra.iuoui/policy_manual/policy/3-7.html** (accessed November 2004).

ISO/IEC 17799:2000 Information technology - Code of practice for information security management. International Organization for Standardization.

The Laws that Govern the Securities Industries. Securities and Exchange Commission. **www.sec.gov/about/laws.shtml** (accessed February 2005).

Monster. **www.monster.com** (accessed February 2005).

NIST SP 800-16 Information Technology Security Training Requirements, April 1998.

NIST SP 800-50 Building an Information Technology Security Awareness and Training Program, October 2003.

Pew Internet Project Data Memo. Pew Internet and American Life Project **www.pewinternet.org/pdfs/PIP_Jobhunt_Memo.pdf** (accessed February 2005).

The Riley Guide. **www.rileyguide.com** (accessed February 2005).

Rules for Conducting Employee Background Checks. JaburgWilk. **www.jaburgwilk.com/resources-article-113.html** (accessed February 2005).

Running Background Checks. NOLO. **www.nolo.com** (accessed February 2005).

Social Engineering. Gartner Group. **www.gartner.com/security** (accessed January 2005).

What is Phishing and Pharming? Anti-Phishing Working Group. **www.antiphishing.org** (accessed February 2005).

Chapter 7

Bridging the Divide: Information Security meets Physical Security. Computer World Magazine. May 28, 2003. **www.computerworld.com/securitytopics/security** (accessed February 2005).

CTPED. OneLang.com online encyclopedia. **www.onelang.com/encyclopedia/index.php/CPTED** (accessed February 2005).

FFIEC Information Security IT Examiners Handbook, 2004.

FFIEC Operations IT Examiners Handbook, 2004.

FFIEC Management IT Examiners Handbook, 2004.

ISO/IEC 17799:2000 Information technology - Code of practice for information security management. International Organization for Standardization.

Jeffery, C. Ray. 1977. *Crime Prevention Through Environmental Design,* Second Edition, Beverly Hills: Sage.

Krause, Micki CISSP and Harold F. Tipton, CISSP. 2004. *Information Security Management Handbook,* Fifth Edition. Boca Raton, FL: CRC Press, Auerbach Publications.

NIST SP 800-14 Generally Accepted Principles and Practices for Securing Technology Systems, September 1996.

Physical Security Checklist. TeCrime International. **www.tecrime.com/0secure.htm** (accessed March 2005).

Power Protection Glossary. Tripplite. **www.tripplite.com/support/glossary/index.cfm** (accessed March 2005).

Remembrance of Data Passed: A Study of Disk Sanitation. *IEEE Security and Privacy Journal,* Jan/Feb 2003 Issues.

Chapter 8

Annual Email Security Report. MessageLabs Intelligence. **www.messagelabs.com/binaries/LAB480_endofyear_v2.pdf** (accessed March 2005).

Basic Flowcharting Shapes and Symbols. SmartDraw®. **www.smartdraw.com/tutorials/flowcharts.basic.htm** (accessed March 2005).

California Security Breach Information Act SB1386.

Chaneski, Wayne. Writing Standard Operating Procedures. MMS Online. **www.mmsonline.com/articles/0498ci.html** (accessed March 2005).

Computer Security Incident Handling, Step by Step. SANS. **www.sans.org** (accessed December 2004).

Cyber Security Tip ST04-017 Protecting Portable Devices: Physical Security. US-CERT. **www.us-cert.gov/cas/tips/ST04-017.html** (accessed March 2005).

FedCIRC. **www.fedcirc.gov** (accessed December 2004).

FFIEC Information Security IT Examination Handbook, 2004.

FFIEC Operations IT Examiners Handbook, 2004.

FFIEC Management IT Examiners Handbook, 2004.

Gartner Group. **www.gartnergroup/com/security** (accessed December 2004).

ISO/IEC 17799:2000 Information technology - Code of practice for information security management. International Organization for Standardization.

Joiner Associates. 1995. *Flowcharts: Plain and Simple: Learning & Application Guides.* Madison, WI: Oriel, Inc.

Love, Byron. Operational Control Best Practices. Internosis. **www. internosis.com/pdf/Operational%20Change%20Control%20white paper.pdf**

NIST SP 800-14 Generally Accepted Principles and Practices for Securing Information Technology Systems.

NIST SP 800-45 Guidelines on Electronic Mail Security, September 2002.

NIST SP 800-61 Computer Security Incident Handling Guide, January 2004. SamSpade. **www.samspade.org**.

Science fiction novel inspires first ever Pocket PC virus SOPHOS. **www.sophos.com** (accessed February 2005).

Standard Operating Procedures: A Writing Guide. Penn State College of Agricultural Sciences. **http://pubs.cas.psu.edu/freepubs/pdfs/ud011. pdf** (accessed March 2005).

Wieringa, Douglas, Christopher Moore, and Valerie Barnes. 1998. *Procedure Writing: Principles and Practices,* Second Edition. Columbus, Ohio: Battelle Press.

Chapter 9

American Telecommuting Association. **www.knowledgetree.com/ata. html** (accessed March 2005).

Building a Secure Platform for Trustworthy Computing White Paper. Microsoft Corporation, December 2002.

FFIEC Information Security IT Examination Handbook, 2004.

FFIEC Operations IT Examiners Handbook, 2004.

FFIEC Management IT Examiners Handbook, 2004.

ISO/IEC 17799:2000 Information technology - Code of practice for information security management. International Organization for Standardization.

Introduction to RADIUS. GNU. **www.gnu.org/software/radius/radius. html** (accessed March 2005).

Lucyshyn, William and Robert Richardson. CSI/FBI Computer Crime and Security Survey. Computer Security Institute. **i.cmpnet.com/gocsi/ db_area/pdfs/fbi/FBI2004.pdf** (accessed March 2005).

MS-CHAP version 2. Microsoft Corporation. **www.microsoft.com/ windows2000/** (accessed March 2005).

NIST SP 800-14 Generally Accepted Principles and Practices for Securing Information Technology Systems, September 1996.

NIST SP 800-46 Security for Telecommuting and Broadband Communications, August 2002.

NSA Guide to Securing Microsoft Windows 2000 Group Policy: Security Configuration Tool Set.

NSA Microsoft Windows 2000 Network Architecture Guide.

NSA Guide to Securing Microsoft Windows 2000 Group Policy.

Report to Congress April 5, 2002. United State Office of Personnel Management. **www.telework.gov/IT_Report/exec.asp** (accessed March 2005).

Trustworthy Computing. Microsoft Corporation. **www.microsoft.com/security/twc/vision_frame.mspx**. (accessed January 2005).

Virtual Private Networking: Frequently Asked Questions. Microsoft Corporation. **www.microsoft.com/windowsserver2003/techinfo/overview/vpnfaq.mspx** (accessed March 2005).

Chapter 10

A Guide to Building Secure Web Applications. The Open Web Application Security Project. **http://alex.netwindows.org/owasp_guide/guide.html** (accessed March 2005).

Ethereal. **www.ethereal.com** (accessed March 2005).

FFIEC Information Security IT Examination Handbook, 2004.

FFIEC Operations IT Examiners Handbook, 2004.

FFIEC Management IT Examiners Handbook, 2004.

Howard, Michael and David LeBlanc. 2001. *Writing Secure Code.* Redmond, WA: Microsoft Press.

ISO/IEC 17799:2000 Information technology - Code of practice for information security management. International Organization for Standardization.

Menezes, Alfred J., Paul C. van Oorschot, and Scott Vanstone. 1996. *Handbook of Applied Cryptography.* Boca Raton, FL: CRC Press.

NIST SP 800-12 — An Introduction to Computer Security: The NIST Handbook, October 1995.

NIST SP 800-14 Generally Accepted Principles and Practices for Securing Information Technology Systems, September 1996.

NIST SP 800-64 Security Considerations in the Information System Development Life Cycle, October 2003 (publication original release date)(revision 1 released June 2004).

Peteet, Jeremy. Have Your Cake and Eat It Too. OWASP. **www.owasp.org/columns/jpoteet/jpoteet2.html** (accessed March 2005).

Schneier, Bruce, Nielsand Ferguson. 2003. *Practical Cryptography.* Indianapolis, IN: John Wiley & Sons.

Welcome to the ISO 17799 Project. Open Web Application Security Project (OWASP). **www.owasp.org/standards/iso17799.html** (accessed March 2005).

Chapter 11

BCP Handbook. CPM Group. **www.contingencyplanning.com/tools/ bcphandbook/** (accessed March 2005).

Building Better Backup at Commerzbank. CNT. **www.cnt.com/solutions/ bcdr/** (accessed March 2005).

Disaster Recovery Journal. **www.drj.com/** (accessed March 2005).

DRI International. **www.drii.org** (accessed March 2005).

FFIEC Information Security IT Examination Handbook, 2004.

FFIEC Operations IT Examiners Handbook, 2004.

FFIEC Management IT Examiners Handbook, 2004.

FFIEC Business Continuity Planning IT Examiners Handbook, 2003.

ISO/IEC 17799:2000 Information technology - Code of practice for information security management. International Organization for Standardization.

Krause, Micki CISSP and Harold F. Tipton CISSP. 2004. *Information Security Management Handbook,* Fifth Edition. Boca Raton, FL: CRC Press, Auerbach Publications.

Lessons Learned from September 11, 2001, Presentations to the Audit Committee of the Johns Hopkins Health System, 12/9/2001 by Price-Waterhouse Coopers.

NIST SP 800-30 Risk Management Guide for Information Technology Systems, July 2002.

NIST SP 800-34 Contingency Planning Guide for Information Technology Systems, June 2002.

NIST SP 800-61 Computer Security Incident Handling Guide, January 2004.

Public Warning, Continuity of Operations and American Business-More needs to be done to prepare for disasters. Partnership for Public Warning. **www.partnershipforpublicwarning.org/ppw/natsurvey.html** (accessed March 2005).

Schreider, Tari. *Encyclopedia of Disaster Recovery, Security & Risk Management.* Crucible Publishing Works (1998).

Chapter 12

2005 Supplement A to GLBA-Interagency Guidelines on Response Programs for Unauthorized Access to Customer Information and Customer Notice Standards.

Consumer Sentinel database. **www.consumer.gov/sentinel/trends.htm** (accessed March 2005).

Electronic Signatures in Global and National Commerce Act Public Law 106-229, 2000. (E-Sign).

Fact Sheet: Identity Theft. US Department of Treasury. **www.ustreas.gov/ offices/domestic-finance/financial-institution/cip/pdf/identity-the-fact-sheet.pdf** (accessed April 2005).

Federal Deposit Insurance Company (FDIC). **www.fdic.gov** (accessed November 2004).

Federal Financial Institutions Examination Council (FFIEC). **www.ffiec. gov** (accessed November 2004).

The Federal Register (FR): Main Page. GPO Access. **www.gpoaccess. gov/fr** (accessed December 2004).

Federal Trade Commission (GLBA). **www.ftc.gov/privacy/glbact** (accessed December 2004).

FFIEC Information Security IT Examination Handbook, 2004.

FFIEC Operations IT Examiners Handbook, 2004.

FFIEC Management IT Examiners Handbook, 2004.

FFIEC Business Continuity Planning IT Examiners Handbook, 2003.

Financial Privacy: The Gramm-Leach Bliley Act. The Federal Trade Commission (FTC). **www.ftc.gov/privacy/glbact** (accessed November 2004).

FTC Enforces Gramm-Leach-Bliley Act's Safeguards Rule Against Mortgage Companies 11/16/2002. Federal Trade Commission. **www.ftc.gov/ opa/2004/11/ns.htm** (accessed November 2004).

GLBA Information Security Program Policy No: 04.OIT.130 Rev 1.5. Georgia Institute of Technology. **www.oit.gatech.edu/inside_oit/ policies_and_plans/policies/GLBA_Information_Security_ Program_Rev1.5.cfm** (accessed November 2004).

Gramm, P., Leach, J., Bliley T. Biographical Directory of the United States Congress. **www.bioguide.congress.gov** (accessed April 2005).

Gramm-Leach-Bliley Act (GLBA), Public Law 106-102, 1999.

The Gramm-Leach-Bliley Act. Electronic Privacy Information Center. **www.epic.org/privacy/glba/** (accessed April 2005).

Gramm-Leach-Bliley Act (GLBA) Solution. Bankers Online. **www.
bankersonline.com/vendor_guru/bindview/bindview_glb.html** (accessed March 2004).

ID Theft. Federal Trade Commission. **www.consumer.gov/idtheft** (accessed November 2004).

Identity Theft: The Aftermath. Identity Theft Resource Center. **www.
idtheftcenter.org/facts.shtml** (accessed April 2005).

Information Regarding Gramm-Leach-Bliley Act of 1999. U.S. Senate
Banking, Housing and Urban Affairs Committee. **banking.senate.
gov/conf/** (accessed April 2005).

ISO/IEC 17799:2000 Information technology - Code of practice for
information security management. International Organization for
Standardization.

Chapter 13

Health Insurance Portability and Accountability Act (HIPAA), Public Law
104-191, 1996.

Health Insurance Portability and Accountability Act (HIPAA) – Administrative Simplification. Centers for Medicare and Medicaid Services.
www.cms.hhs.gov/hipaa/ (accessed December 2004).

HIPAA Security Rule Checklist. Wisconsin Medical Society. **www.
wisconsinmedicalsociety.org/physician_resources/educational/hipaa
_checklist** (accessed April 2005).

ISO/IEC 17799:2000 Information technology - Code of practice for
information security management. International Organization for
Standardization.

Medical Privacy - National Standards to Protect the Privacy of Personal
Health Information. Department of Health and Human Services
(HIPAA). **www.hhs.goc/ocr/hippa** (accessed November 2004).

NIST SP 800-14 Generally Accepted Principles and Practices for Securing
Information Technology Systems, September 1996.

NIST SP 800-61 Computer Security Incident Handling Guide, January
2004.

NIST SP 800-66 An Introductory Resource Guide for Implementing the
Health Insurance Portability and Accountability Act (HIPAA) Security
Rule, March 2000.

PricewaterhouseCoopers Interpretation of the Final Rule, April 15, 2003.
PricewaterhouseCoopers. **www.pechealth.com**.

Seattle man pleads guilty in first ever convictions for HIPAA rules violation. United States Attorney's Office, Western District of Washington.

www.usdoj.gov/usao/waw/press_room/2004/aug/gibson.htm (accessed April 2005).

Chapter 14

2004 FISMA Report. Office of Management and Budget. **www.whitehouse. gov/omb/infored/2004_fisma_report.pdf** (accessed April 2005).

24 Presidential Priority E-Gov Initiatives. Federal Enterprise Architecture Program Management Office (FEA-PMO). **feapmo.gov/resources/ 24_PPE-Gov_Init_Rev_1.pdf** (accessed April 2005).

COSO. **www.coso.org** (accessed April 2005).

Department of Education (FERPA). **www.ed.gov** (accessed April 2005).

E-GOV. **www.egov.gov** (accessed April 2005).

E-Government Act (accessed FISMA), Public Law 107-347, 2002.

Electronic Signatures in Global and National Commerce Act (E-Sign). Public Law 106-229, 2000.

Family Education Rights and Privacy Act (FERPA), 34 C.F.R. Part 99.

FirstGov. **www.firstgov.gov** (accessed February 2005).

FISMA Implementation Project. Computer Security Resource Center. **http://csrc.nist.gov/sec-cert/index.html** (accessed April 2005).

ISACA. **www.isaca.org** (accessed April 2005).

ISO/IEC 17799:2000 Information technology - Code of practice for information security management. International Organization for Standardization.

The Laws that Govern the Securities Industries. Securities and Exchange Commission. **www.sec.gov/about/laws.shtml** (accessed January 2005).

Legislative History of Major FERPA Provisions. United States Department of Education. **www.ed.gov/policy/gen/guid/fpco/ferpa/leg-history.html** (accessed April 2005).

The National Strategy to Secure Cyberspace. The White House. **www.whitehouse.gov/pcipb/** (accessed February 2005).

NIST FIPS 199 Standards for Security Categorization of Federal Information Systems, December 2003.

NIST SP 800-14 Generally Accepted Principles and Practices for Securing Information Technology Systems, September 1996.

NIST SP 800-60 Guide for Mapping Types of Information and Information Systems to Security Categories, June 2004.

NIST SP 800-61 Computer Security Incident Handling Guide, January 2004.

NIST SP 800-64 Security Considerations in the Information System Development Life Cycle, October 2003 (publication original release date) (revision 1 released June 2004).

Powering America's Future with Technology. Office of Management and Budget. **www.whitehouse.gov/omb/egov/c-presidential.html** (accessed April 2005).

Spotlight on Sarbanes-Oxley Rulemaking and Reports. Securities and Exchange Commission. **www.sec.gov/spotligh/sarbannes-oxley.htm** (accessed April 2005).

USDA Security Directive. US Department of Agriculture. **www.ocio.usda.gov/directives/index.html** (accessed April 2005).

VanDusen, William, Jr. FERPA: Basic Guidelines for Faculty and Staff, A Simple Step-by-Step Approach for Compliance. NACADA. **www.nacada.ksu.edu** (accessed April 2005).

Chapter 15

AOL Instant Messenger. **www.aim.com** (accessed March 2005).

Bank of America Confirms Lost Data Tapes. Bank of America. **www.bankofamerica.com/newsroom/press/press.cfm?PressID=press.20050225.04.htm** (accessed April 2005).

Common Sense Guide to Cyber Security for Small Businesses. Internet Security Alliance. **www.isaalliance.org** (accessed April 2005).

Copyright Infringement Lawsuits Brought Against 753 Additional Illegal File Sharers. RIAA. **www.riaa.com/news/newsletter/022805.asp** (accessed April 2005).

Fact Sheet: President Bush Signs Anti-Spam Law. The White House. **www.whitehouse.gov/news/releases/2003/12/20031216-4.html** (accessed January 2005).

Former IT Manager Of Software Firm Indicted. Department of Justice, Northern District of California. United States Attorney. **www.cand.uscourts.gov** (accessed April 2005).

Gramm-Leach-Bliley Act (GLBA). Public Law 106-102, 1999.

Health Insurance Portability and Accountability Act (HIPAA). Public Law 104-191, 1996.

Infragard. **www.infragard.net** (accessed February 2005).

ISO/IEC 17799:2000 Information technology - Code of practice for information security management. International Organization for Standardization.

Koehler, Norm CBCP, CRP. The Small And Medium Size Businesses Guide To A Successful Continuity Program. Disaster Recovery Journal. **www.drj.com/special/smallbusiness/article1-01.html**.

The National Strategy to Secure Cyberspace. The White House. **www.whitehouse.gov/pcipb/** (accessed February 2005).

NSA Guide to Securing Microsoft Windows 2000 Group Policy: Security Configuration Tool Set.

NSA Microsoft Windows 2000 Network Architecture Guide.

NSA Guide to Securing Microsoft Windows 2000 Group Policy.

Old scams pose the greatest security risk. GigaLaw. **www.gigalaw.com/newsarchives/2004_11_02_index2.html** (accessed April 2005).

Patch Management Process January 29, 2004. Microsoft Corporation. **www.microsoft.com/technet/security/topics/patchmanagement/secmod193.mspx** (accessed April 2005).

Security Guide for Small Businesses. Microsoft Corporation. **http://download.microsoft.com/download/3/a/2/3a208c3c-f355-43ce-bab4-890db267899b/Security_Guide_for_Small_Business.pdf** (accessed February 2005).

The Spread of the Sapphire/Slammer Worm. **www.cs.berkeley.edu/~nweaver/sapphire** (accessed February 2005).

Towns, Douglas. Legal Issues Involved in Monitoring Employees' Internet and E-Mail Usage. GigaLaw. **www.gigalaw.com/articles/2002-all/towns-2002-01-all.html** (accessed March 2005).

U.S. Small Business Administration. **www.sba.gov** (accessed March 2005).

Web Log of John Levine. **www.taugh.com/weblog/leeburg.html** (accessed March 2005).

Wi-Fi-FreeSpot Directory. **www.wififreespot.com** (accessed March 2005).

Index

A

Acceptable use agreement, 97, 487, 489–491. *See also* Information security affirmation agreement

Access
HIPAA requirements, 431
managing, 276–281
policies and procedures for authorizing, 436
suggested criteria for, 504
third-party, 103–105
unauthorized, 399
and use, monitoring, 298–302

Access control(s)
on customer information systems, 415
facility, 442–444
introduction, 271–272
logical and administrative, for financial institutions, 402–406
MAC, DAC, and RBAC, 75
technical, 447–449
and validation procedures, implementing, 443–444

Access Control domain, 80, 271, 474

Access control policy, 275–276

Access establishment and modification, 436

Access rights administration, 403–404

Accountability
for assets, 119
defined, 72
and FISMA, 465
See also Ownership

Accounting, defined, 72

Activation, and disaster response, 367

Address, physical and logical, 136

Addressable implementation specification, 430

Address checking, 288

Administrative safeguards, 394–395
defined, 429

HIPAA, 430–442

Agreements
acceptable use, 97, 487, 489–491
confidentiality, 39, 160, 486–489
employee, 160–163
information security affirmation, 160–162
service level, 71, 373
special, and small businesses, 486

Americans with Disabilities Act, 157

Analysis
application and data criticality, 439
BIA, 353
criticality, 139, 398
incidents, 229

Antivirus software, 507

Antivirus software architecture, 233–234

Application access, FFIEC-recommended procedures, 405

Application and data criticality analysis, 439

Application software, 135

Application software stability, 330–336

Approval, for new policy, 20

Assessments
change control, 222
to test controls, 411
See also Risk assessment

Asset classification and control, introduction, 117–118

Asset Classification and Control domain, 79, 473

Asset description, 136

Asset inventory
characteristics and attributes, 135–136
methodology, 134–135

Assets
hardware and software, 134–135
tangible and intangible, 5

See also Information assets

Assigned security responsibility, HIPAA, 431, 433–434

Assurance
defined, 72
and FISMA, 465

Attachments, security threats from, 256

Audience, policy, 39, 45

Audit controls, HIPAA, 447, 449

Auditor, internal, roles and responsibilities, 19

Audits
business continuity plan, 374–375
to test controls, 411

Authentication
defined, 72, 402
encryption and, 325–326
FFIEC-recommended procedures, 404
person or entity, 447, 450

Authorization
for access, implementing policies and procedures, 436
defined, 72, 402
implementing procedures for, 434–435
SOP documentation, 219

Authorized access, 299

Automatic logoff procedures, 448

Availability, 70–72
protected by HIPAA, 427
See also Business Continuity Management domain

Awareness training programs, 20–22, 164–167, 437

B

Background checks, 154–157
getting consent, 156
and identity theft, 415

Backup media, storing, 514

Backups
developing procedures, 446–447
establishing and implementing plan, 439–440
types of, 513–516

identity, 399, 415–417
Third-party access, 103–105
Third-party consultant, for systems security, 313–314
Threat analysis, 398
Threat assessment, 398
Threat probability, 398
Threat risk, 398
Threats
  to availability, 71
  to confidentiality, 67–68
  defined, 398
  identifying and assessing, 398
  to integrity, 69–70
  to operations, 352
  See also Vulnerability, inherent; Risk assessment
Thumbdrives, 240–242
Token, and advanced input validation, 320
Top Secret (TS) information, 122–123
Training programs
  awareness, 20–22, 164–167, 431, 436–438
  end-user security, 68
  incident reporting, 170–172
  in information security programs, 410
  investing in, 167
  NIST standards, 164–167
  security awareness, 166, 431, 436–438
  See also SETA
Transmitted information, 5, 493–494
  security, 447, 451
  suggested criteria for, 504–505
Trojan horses, 232–233, 507
Two wall challenge, defined, 21

U

U.S. Bankruptcy Code, 157
Unauthorized access, 399
Unauthorized attempts, 300

Unclassified (U) information, 123, 252
Unique identifier, 135
Unsolicited Commercial E-mail (UCE). *See* Spam
Updates, software, 331–334
Updating policy companions, difficulty of, 36
Uptime, 70–71
User access. *See* Access
User authentication for remote connections, 285–290
User identification, unique, 448
Users, roles and responsibilities, 19

V

Validation procedures, and access control, implementing, 443–444
Vendor connectivity, as threat, 399
Vendors, agreements with, 373
Virtual Private Network (VPN), 285–286, 288
Virus, 506
  defined, 232
  e-mail and, 256–257
  PDAs infected by, 292
  See also Malware
Virus protection, 68
Virus protection policy, 487, 506–509
Vulnerability, inherent, 70

W

Warm site, defined, 365
Web. *See* Internet
Web identity theft, 399
Wide area network (WAN), 288
Wireless networks, 511
Workers' compensation records, background checks and, 157
Workforce clearance proce-

dure, 435
Workforce security, HIPAA, 431, 434–435
Workstation security, 443, 445
  access to ePHI, 444–445
  designing secure areas, 186–194
  working in secure areas, 192–194
Workstation use, 443
Worms, 232, 234, 506
Writing, preplanning, 38–39